Electoral Campaigns, Media, and the New World of Digital Politics

Electoral Campaigns, Media, and the New World of Digital Politics

David Taras and Richard Davis, Editors

University of Michigan Press
Ann Arbor

Copyright © 2022 by David Taras and Richard Davis
Some rights reserved

This work is licensed under a Creative Commons Attribution-NonCommercial-NoDerivatives 4.0 International License. *Note to users:* A Creative Commons license is only valid when it is applied by the person or entity that holds rights to the licensed work. Works may contain components (e.g., photographs, illustrations, or quotations) to which the rightsholder in the work cannot apply the license. It is ultimately your responsibility to independently evaluate the copyright status of any work or component part of a work you use, in light of your intended use. To view a copy of this license, visit http://creativecommons.org/licenses/by-nc-nd/4.0/

For questions or permissions, please contact um.press.perms@umich.edu

Published in the United States of America by the
University of Michigan Press
Manufactured in the United States of America
Printed on acid-free paper
First published March 2022

A CIP catalog record for this book is available from the British Library.

Library of Congress Cataloging-in-Publication data has been applied for.

ISBN 978-0-472-07518-8 (hardcover : alk. paper)
ISBN 978-0-472-05518-0 (paper : alk. paper)
ISBN 978-0-472-90269-9 (OA)

Library of Congress Control Number: 2021951016

DOI: https://doi.org/10.3998/mpub.12013603

This open access version made available with the support of libraries participating in Knowledge Unlatched.

Contents

How Digital Media Has Changed Elections: An Introduction   1
    David Taras

Chapter 1. Owning Identity: Struggles to Align Voters during
the 2020 U.S. Presidential Election   23
    Daniel Kreiss and Shannon McGregor, University of North Carolina

Chapter 2. Trending Politics: How the Internet Has Changed
Political News Coverage   44
    *Kevin Wagner, Florida Atlantic University, and Jason Gainous,
University of Louisville*

Chapter 3. Feminism, Social Media, and Political Campaigns:
Justin Trudeau and Sadiq Khan   60
    *Kaitlyn Mendes, University of Western Ontario,
and Diretman Dikwal-Bot, De Montfort University*

Chapter 4. A Woman's Place Is in the (U.S.) House:
An Analysis of Issues Women Candidates Discussed on
Twitter in the 2016 and 2018 Congressional Elections   83
    Heather K. Evans, University of Virginia's College at Wise

Chapter 5. Two Different Worlds: The Gap between the Interests
of Voters and the Media in Canada in the 2019 Federal Election   103
    Christopher Waddell, Carleton University

Chapter 6. The Agenda-Building Power of Facebook and Twitter:
The Case of the 2018 Italian General Election   124
    *Sara Bentivegna, University of Rome–La Sapienza, and
Rita Marchetti and Anna Stanziano, University of Perugia*

vi   Contents

Chapter 7. "Many thanks for your support": Email Populism
and the People's Party of Canada   143
  Brian Budd and Tamara A. Small, University of Guelph

Chapter 8. Benjamin Netanyahu and Online Campaigning in
Israel's 2019 and 2020 Elections   163
  Michael Keren, University of Calgary

Chapter 9. Stabbed Democracy: How Social Media and
Home Videos Made a Populist President in Brazil   179
  Francisco Brandao, University of Brasilia

Chapter 10. Memes; a New Emerging Logic:
Evidence from the 2019 British General Election   200
  Rosalynd Southern, The University of Liverpool

Chapter 11. Populists and Social Media Campaigning in Ukraine:
The Election of Volodymyr Zelensky   221
  Larissa Doroshenko, Northeastern University

Chapter 12. The Changing Face of Political Campaigning in Kenya   244
  Martin Ndlela, Inland Norway University of Applied Sciences

Chapter 13. Social Media as Strategic Campaign Tool:
Austrian Political Parties Use of Social Media over Time   263
  Uta Russmann, University of Innsbruck

Chapter 14. Candidate, News Media, and Social Media Messaging
in the Early Stages of the 2020 Democratic Presidential Primary   283
  *Chris Wells, Blake Wertz, Li Zhang, and Rebecca Auger, Boston
  University*

Conclusion   307
  Richard Davis

Contributors   315

Index   321

Digital materials related to this title can be found on
the Fulcrum platform via the following citable URL:
https://doi.org/10.3998/mpub.12013603

How Digital Media Has Changed Elections

An Introduction

David Taras

The word "campaign" comes from the French word for "open country" and originated as a military term. It is meant to represent a field of battle where armies fight over which side will control territory and win the treasures of office. In this sense, contemporary election campaigns can be seen as war by other means. The side that wins is usually the side that can bring to bear the most resources and organization and can mobilize the most citizens to its cause. But as in all battles, leadership, strategy, and fortune can all play a decisive role. Today, of course, the election wars are fought on a different kind of battlefield. To a large extent the media is both the site of battle and the means by which it is fought. To win, political parties must transform themselves into media organizations. They must produce what is in effect a daily TV show in which their leaders are the stars; create different story lines each day; produce a flotilla of political ads; be able to respond almost instantly to the thrust and cut of attack and counterattack; and organize a vast moving tableau of campaign events whose real purpose is to produce the colorful visuals and quotable one-liners or catchphrases that will be irresistible to the reporters covering the campaign. The campaigns also have to be fought on social media platforms such as Facebook, Twitter, Instagram, and YouTube, each of which has different audiences and characteristics and therefore different requirements and hope that their messages go viral.

In a classic work in political science, Murray Edelman argued that political campaigns were "symbolic constructions" (Edelman 1988). Political leaders use symbolic cues—language, visual images, and behaviors—to signal voters about their identities and intentions. They focus on certain critical issues and messages while ignoring others, "assign blame and praise," and identify a common enemy. Campaigns are as much about fomenting anger and resentment and constructing the opposition as they are about discussing solutions to problems, which are often complex, weighted down with difficulties, and almost always involve painful tradeoffs.

The nature of the election terrain differs from country to country and from electoral system to electoral system. Sometimes drastically. While spending has reached almost stratospheric heights in U.S. presidential primaries and in the presidential election and sometimes in senate races as well, in Canada donors and political parties are subject to severe spending restrictions. In the race for the French and Brazilian presidencies, for instance, the two candidates that received the most votes in a first round of voting face each other in a runoff election that takes place two weeks after the first vote. This means that the eventual winner has to receive at least 50 percent of the overall vote. In other words, a majority of voters will have to have voted for them. Famously, both George W. Bush and Donald Trump became U.S. presidents despite getting fewer votes than their respective opponents, Al Gore and Hilary Clinton, because of the vagaries of an electoral college system that gives disproportionate power to smaller states. In the "first-past-the-post" system under which Canadian, Indian, and British elections are fought, small margins of victory can produce substantial majority governments. The system is designed to provide unity and deflate regional, ethnic, and linguistic tensions.

In systems based on proportional representation, such as in Austria, Italy, Germany, the Netherlands, the European Parliament, and Israel, to name a few, the inevitable result are coalition governments, with bargaining in the postelection period among potential coalition partners often taking weeks and even months to sort out. Because yesterday's election opponent may be today's coalition partner, the often intractable partisanship and bitter attacks that have increasingly characterized American politics are not as apparent in these systems.

In some countries, leaders' debates are the center pieces of the election, the moment where voters get to compare and contrast the candidates, hear them speak unfiltered by the media, and perform under stress. In some countries debates are standardized, in others they are organized in an ad hoc manner with different rules and participants pertaining each time, and in yet others there are no debates at all.

Campaigns also differ in length. In U.S. presidential campaigns, a torturous primary season, a convention period, and then the actual campaign famously extend for more than a year. There is also a silent campaign that precedes the formal campaign in which money and endorsements are secured. There is now a sophisticated literature about the "permanent campaign"; the contention is that the campaign never stops. The spectacle, the contest for power, is always being waged, is always on, all the time—although it's not clear that voters are willing to pay attention except at key moments. In the United Kingdom, campaigns are just twenty-five working days from the dissolution of Parliament to polling day. German campaigns last only six weeks. In France and Brazil, campaigning for both the first and second rounds of the presidential contest lasts for just two weeks.

Arguably, the rules under which elections are fought are designed to produce certain outcomes and not others. More often than not, they reflect and sustain the political systems that created them.

Elections as Defining Events

While elections in democratic countries can be routine events that do little more than ratify the status quo and produce the outcomes that are expected, they also allow a society to come to terms with itself, envision its future, and examine its differences and disparities. Elections can also produce dramatic and unexpected change. While elections clarify and signify the balance of power within societies, there is a school of thought that argues that election campaigns are decided by a series of fundamentals such as the health of the economy, the relative strength of the political parties, and whether leaders are trusted and inspire confidence (Sides and Vavreck 2013). If the fundamentals are in place, then the outcome of elections can usually be predicted with accuracy. Indeed, John Sides and Lynn Vavreck point out that in the United States at least most people know which party they will vote for at least a year before the election takes place (Sides and Vavreck 2013). Once having made their decision about a party or a candidate, once they have rendered a judgment, people tend to see campaign events through the lens of the choice they have already made. Undoing judgments that people have already made, are already invested in, is difficult and rare.

Some scholars preach a kind of economic determinism. They see the economy as the hinge on which elections are decided. If the economy is going well then voters are unlikely to want to throw "the bastards out" or change directions. In a poor economy, however, the public is less willing to give leaders the benefit of the doubt; there is less forgiveness for those in power.

Moreover, those who don't believe that "campaigns matter" argue that campaign events such as leaders' debates, political ads, or gaffes and miscues tend to wash away quickly and have little if any effect on the outcome. This is largely because there is a "dynamic equilibrium" in which "things are happening, sometimes vigorously or rapidly, but they produce opposing reactions, a 'dynamic equilibrium,' that is roughly the same size or magnitude and that occurs at roughly the same rates" (Sides and Vavreck 2013). Ads cancel each other out. A gaffe by one side is soon cancelled out by a gaffe made by the other. The effects of campaign debates may give one candidate a short-lived bump in the polls but the advantage tends to decay quickly. In the end, everything reverts back to the fundamentals.

The opposing position is that campaigns matter and matter a great deal. Proponents argue that the fundamentals can be overturned by a poorly run campaign, by a flawed leader who is no longer trusted, or by unexpected events that disarm and disrupt campaigns. The issues that dominate at the beginning of a campaign are rarely the ones that dominate at the end. Elections are fluid, combustible, and in more than a few instances there have been enough voters that have not made up their minds to create a last-minute swing in one direction or another. Journalists have famously made a fetish out of looking for and analyzing a campaign's "defining moments," moments in which the scene shifted, where a leader's strengths and weaknesses were most on display, and where perceptions changed. Whatever the value of the "dynamic equilibrium" as a way of looking at elections, the undisputed reality is that some moments manage to become important, are remembered, and move voters in one direction rather than another.

There is also the argument that the so-called fundamentals don't have the solidity that they once may have had as determinants of elections. Simply put, the fundamentals aren't what they used to be. Yascha Mounk, for instance, has argued that as the postwar prosperity of the 1960s and 1970s that characterized Western countries gave way to economic stagnation and devastating inequalities, as societies that were once dominated by a single racial or ethnic group have been transformed by immigration, and that as trust in institutions of almost all kinds has plummeted, democracies have "deconsolidated" (Mounk 2018). According to historian Anne Applebaum, a basic change in psychology has taken place within democracies, one that threatens the basic institutions that once sustained them (Applebaum 2020). In other words, the basic democratic fabric of Western democracies has been stretched and tattered. A new wave of identity politics swept through American politics and reached a crescendo during the 2016 U.S. presidential election with the victory of Donald Trump. A similar wave of identity politics led to the victory of the Leave side in the Brexit referendum in the United Kingdom in 2016. Emmanuel Macron overturned the party system in France by creating an entirely new party, La Republic en Marche, on his way to winning the French presidency in 2017. Jair Bolsonaro overthrew the existing party system in Brazil fighting a "kitchen table" election campaign with virtually no resources or previous name recognition. And the politics of climate change dominated the 2019 Canadian federal election with parties scrambling to catch up to public opinion.

Institutions have also been shaken by the vast changes that have taken place in the world of communications and by the emergence of social media as a preeminent means of persuasion. The election campaigns that were fought in 1994 and 2004 bear little resemblance to those of today. If we return to the analogy of elections as resembling a battlefield then its obvious that the weapons and hence the strategies that would have prevailed even a short time ago are outmoded by today's standards. Put bluntly, our argument is that the new media landscape has produced a new kind of election.

The Media Battlefield

Elections are fought through the media. The goal of every contender for power is to set the campaign agenda by shifting the public's focus to the issues that are favorable to them and away from the issues that will benefit their opponents. While the focus of this volume is on the digital campaign, it's critical to remember that television is still the preeminent media, particularly among older voters. The TV election is a vast sprawling visual caravan that never stops and never rests. In order to win the TV campaign, parties have to convince the reporters covering the campaign to replay the images and adopt the narrative that the campaigns have produced and scripted for their benefit. To this end, campaigns create pictures and backdrops that they hope the press will find irresistible; prepare edgy or memorable one-liners that can be neatly captured in seven- to ten-second sound bites; provide reporters with press releases that in effect write their stories for them; schedule events so that critics and the opposition are hard to reach or unavailable for comment; and feed, water, and charm reporters so they bond with the campaign and feel that it has become a kind of home.

As Kathleen Hall Jamieson found in her studies, campaign messaging "not only can change the standards of judgment the voters use in evaluating the candidates but also can frame voter' understanding of the contenders, their stands on issues, and their character and temperament. In short, the amount and relative weight of messaging matters" (Jamieson 2018).

The relationship that campaigns have with journalists is one of conflict and symbiosis (Grossman and Kumar 1981). Journalists come with their own priorities, story lines, and agendas and have the power to "frame" issues so that they emphasize some aspects of a story and not others and "prime" audiences about the significance that particular issues will have on the election. Some journalists see themselves as adversaries and opponents whose role is to poke holes in and tear apart the campaigns that they are covering. Almost inevitably most reporting imposes a "horse race" framework on the campaign so that every development is interpreted through the lens of whether campaigns are winning or losing, gaining or falling behind. In Harvard professor Thomas Patterson's study of the 2020 U.S. presidential election, for instance, he found that the horse race was the master narrative and central operating principle of election coverage as it had been in every election for decades. In a study of forty-three elections across the globe between 2016 and 2018, Jaques Gerstle and Alexandro Nai found that the horserace motif was preeminent in virtually every circumstance that they studied (Gerstle and Nai 2019).

Patterson also found that with the exception of CBS's coverage of Joe Biden in 2020, every other presidential contender since 1984 had received negative and often scathing and malicious coverage from reporters. It was as if candidates for the presidency had to run through a journalistic gauntlet of suspicion and abuse meant to undermine their prestige and credibility. Not surprisingly, Gerstle and Nai noted that political candidates worldwide existed within a pool of negativity generated both by the press and by their opponents. Positive stories were often ignored by reporters amid an unceasing cacophony of "rumours, controversies and trivialities" (Gerstle and Nai 2019). A poll taken during the 2019 Canadian election found that 71 percent of respondents said that what they had read or watched about the party leaders had been negative in tone. In another survey, two-thirds of those answering believed that what they had heard about the party leaders had led them to think less positively about them (Adams 2020).

Christopher Arterton has argued that almost all campaigns experience what he describes as a "press crisis," a time when journalists control the agenda and leaders are under unrelenting scrutiny and attack (Arterton 1978). Unable to get their messages out to the public, they are deprived of the oxygen needed to sustain their campaigns. Consequently many campaigns fall into a "dead zone" from which they never recover.

Yet there is also symbiosis. Journalists need what campaigns can give them. The relationship between reporters and campaigns is often the result of negotiations with access given as a reward for either favorable or unfavorable reporting. Being ostracized by a campaign carries real consequences. You can have difficulty getting stories or facts confirmed, can be denied access to candidates or campaign officials, and given the cold shoulder at news conferences or briefings. Be out of a campaign's good graces for too long and your own bosses begin to wonder why you are unable to break stories or provide the background information that other reporters are getting.

One of the few times during elections when leaders or candidates have unfiltered access to the public is during debates. The scholarly literature suggests that debates tend to have little effect on the election outcome, largely because people tend to view debates through the lens of their preconceived biases and beliefs and because effects tend to fade quickly. During the 2019 Canadian election, the effects of major events or scandals was approximately forty-eight hours, after which interest tended to fade quickly with the old patterns reasserting themselves within five to seven days (Digital Democracy Project 2020). But this is not always the case. First, debates are one of the few times that candidates step out of their protective bubbles and are exposed to direct fire from their opponents and from questioners. They are suddenly exposed in ways that they have never been before in the campaign. Debates are also the only occasion when voters can do comparison shopping seeing leaders or candidates and their opponents side by side. Moreover, audiences tend to be large, voters may be seeing candidates for the first time and may not yet have formed a judgment about them, and significant numbers of voters may be undecided and hence up for grabs. Seem nervous or uncertain, fail to grasp the moment, or bungle answers, and doubts can emerge in voter's minds. If a debate performance is reinforced by other campaign events, then it can help determine winners and losers.

Journalists can play a decisive role in the debate equation. The judgments of journalists about who won or lost can be decisive in determining voter's reactions and can even alter the initial reactions that voters may have had. Social media can also play a role. Twitter and Facebook provide users with a second window on events. Audience reactions and opinions often come flooding in as debates take place. People on social media point out mistakes, fact-check, circulate highlights, and declare winners and losers. These responses help shape perceptions about what happened in the debates including those of journalists. Once a consensus forms online it's often difficult to undo it.

Most election expenditures go to TV ad campaigns. The goal is to define your opponent before they have a chance to define themselves. While negative or "black" ads tend to be more successful because they make a deeper impression and tend to be remembered for longer by voters, going negative can be a slippery slope. If ads are seen as being untrue or nasty they can easily backfire, making the campaign that launched the ads seem desperate and dishonest. But even successful ad campaigns can have little effect. Based on a study of fifty-nine real-time randomized experiments, Coppock, Hill, and Vavreck found that even successful ads are likely to be be cancelled out by ads by opponents regardless of "context, message, sender or receiver" (Coppock, Hill, and Vavreck 2020). However devastating ads might be in hitting their targets, the effects are likely to fade quickly.

Digital Media and Political Spectacle

Our focus in this volume is on how digital media have changed election campaigning. We argue that while the effects of TV and newspaper journalism are still decisive, the election battlefield has been reshaped by digital technologies and by social media in critical ways. Where communication is still largely top-down with audiences receiving news and information from large media organizations and journalistic gatekeepers, digital media has redirected power to ordinary citizens by giving users the ability to construct their own highly individualized media echo systems. Users have become both producers and key distributors of campaign messages. People not only post their own stories and videos but they like, redact, mash-up, tweet about, meme, disrupt, and share media messages from others. Manuel Castell has described the new digital era as one of "mass self-communication" and "networked individualism" (Castell 2012). Mounk simply describes it as "one-to-many" communication (Mounk 2018).

While statistics vary from country to country, most people in most places now get a great deal of their news from social media platforms such as Facebook, Twitter, YouTube, and Instagram. The stark reality is that political messages have to be "spreadable." As Jenkins and his colleagues have put it, "If it doesn't spread, it's dead" (Jenkins, Ford, and Green 2013). Spreading those messages, having messages go viral, now depends on the impulses and whims of ordinary users that are not linked to parties or campaigns.

While scholars have touted the power and activism of audiences, there is some concern that citizens may be becoming far more passive online than was once the case. With most people now getting their news from mobile phones, some scholars are beginning to detect a more passive audience as people on the move have less time and opportunity to create, curate, spread, or comment on stories. Not only is political news lost in a torrent of other news about family, friends, pets, and celebrities, in a highly saturated and competitive attention economy more people seem to be taking the view that "If news is that important, it will find me" (Napoli 2019). They no longer have to search.

Simply put, political parties have to wage battle on many more fronts than they did even a short time ago. While they still have to produce and script a TV campaign with its compelling images, moveable sound stages, and choreographed and rehearsed sound bites, they also have to be everywhere on digital media. It's important to note that social media platforms such as Facebook, Instagram, and Twitter have different characteristics and affordances and reach different audiences, and that a single campaign message doesn't fit all platforms in the same way or with the same effectiveness. Instagram, for instance, has a younger and mostly female audience. Posts are expected to be more personal, show the candidate in everyday situations, and are filled with scenery, events, or crowds that convey campaign messages (Remillard et al. 2020). While Twitter attracts a relatively small audience compared to other social media platforms, it is a central meeting place and clearinghouse for journalists, academics, and influencers. Some scholars believe that Twitter is the new gatekeeper, a kind of "national newsroom" where opinions form and harden into place. Users tend to be more educated and more likely to vote. Facebook has a mass audience and remains the primary vehicle for expression online, particularly in Europe and Africa.

Despite the popularity of Tik Tok, Snapchat, and Instagram, YouTube is by far the most popular site for videos. Campaigns have to be constantly on guard for videos that come from ordinary users or interest groups that, because of their grassroots authentic feel, can be particularly devastating if they go viral. Campaigns must remain vigilant because attacks and crossfire can come from any direction and at any time and need be answered. Digital media have also dramatically affected the length of the news cycle. Where the news cycle was once twenty-four hours, matching the daily clock set by newspapers and conventional TV, it has now collapsed to a fraction of what it once was. News now flows all day long in a continuous stream of prompts, headlines, catch-ups, tweets, posts, and videos. The average citizen checks their smart phones approximately three times every hour and many far more than that (Alter 2017). The political pulse rate now has an instant quality. Where there was once time for well-considered responses to events and time to fact-check, rethink, canvas advisors, and devise a strategy before going public, reactions are expected to be almost immediate. Wait too long to respond to events and political leaders risk looking weak and indecisive. Needless to say, the need for speedy responses makes mistakes and miscalculations more likely. It's difficult for campaigns to set the agenda, when agendas are being imposed on them throughout the day.

The Internet has also accelerated the development of the permanent campaign. Where there was once a distinct campaign season with lulls in-between elections, we have now reached the point where in many cases campaigning never stops. Today's parties engage in near constant fundraising campaigns, continuously collect data and information on voters, maintain a daily presence on social media, and have to react to events at almost a moments notice. The Internet is now the spinal cord of any political organization. It is not only the party's public face but is also the party's backroom.

While elections are still fought largely in the mass media, data collection and the targeting of individual voters can be decisive, albeit at the margins. While in most democratic countries, privacy laws prohibit the kind of customized messaging that is widely used in the United States, an increasing number of campaigns across the globe would be able to echo former Google CEO Eric Schmidt's famous dictum, "We know where you are. We know where you've been. We can more or less know what you're thinking about" (quoted in Foer 2017). Not surprisingly, privacy advocates are horrified by the fact that political parties collect information about ordinary citizens. They believe that at the very least political parties should have to relinquish the information they have collected every few years, that "speed bumps" be put in place to limit their capacity to collect data, and that at the very least they should get permission from citizens before their data is collected.

Not everyone believes that digital politics has been successful in creating more aware and engaged citizens or in building democracy. Once marginalized and disconnected individuals and groups have found new meeting places and have been able to mobilize as never before. #Me too, #Black Lives Matter and the environmental group 350.org are examples of online activism that have helped change the culture. At the same time, extremist groups on both the right and the left have been able to enhance their political presence and reach wide audiences. The crazies now have a platform from which to spew age-old hatreds, weave conspiracy theories, and target and intimidate their enemies. Scholars now worry that existing institutions are being overwhelmed and sidelined by the torrent of grievances, causes, instant reactions, and half thought through ideas that rock the online world on a daily basis. Mounk reminds us that a surprisingly high number of younger people across the Western world have or are in the process of losing faith in democracy (Mounk 2018). Applebaum argues that we are witnessing the rise of a new authoritarian populism and with it the "twilight of democracy" (Applebaum 2020). Steven Levitsky and Daniel Ziblatt contend that social media is just one factor in causing political institutions to mutate in new and unrecognizable ways (Levitsky and Ziblatt 2018). Whatever the validity of these claims, both mainstream journalism and political parties have lost much of the trust that they once had and now find themselves viewed with increasing suspicion.

The New Election Campaign

This collection seeks to unlock the keys to campaigning in the new multimedia universe and, most critically, describe at least some of the effects that this new media world may be having on the future of democracy. Political leaders and parties must move the pieces on at least four election chessboards at the same time. They have to influence coverage in the traditional media, master the new technology of online data driven campaigning, deal with new forms of citizen engagement that can threaten and upend their campaign messages, and watch and respond to their political opponents. In order to understand this new world, contributors from a host of countries were invited to a workshop held in Provo, Utah, in late November 2019. We invited scholars who had long track records in documenting and describing political change in their countries and also sought to identify a new generation of emerging stars. The selection of countries was to some degree a product of the experts who we invited. While the United States is well represented, so are Canada and the United Kingdom. But so also are emerging democracies such as Brazil, Kenya, and Ukraine. We also wanted to capture the experiences of countries such as Israel, Italy, and Austria that either have proportional representation or have mixed systems in which proportional representation is included. This is because the need to form coalition governments that include election opponents may have conditioned how digital campaigns have to be run.

Participants were asked to describe the election campaigns that had just recently taken place in their countries, focusing in particular on the nature of online campaigning. The result, published here, is a set of chapters that capture a wide swath of national experiences and allow readers to assess the state of the art in election campaigning. While the elections described in this book took place at different times, they are for the most part the most recent available case studies. We also believe that the countries chosen for this exercise, while hardly exhaustive, provide a rich tableau of examples.

While all the chapters discuss the same themes and issues, no common framework was imposed because of the sheer diversity of the experiences, political systems, and media platforms being examined. While the destinations are similar, the journeys taken by the authors are different.

The intention is for the chapters to represent a mix of experiences. In some instances, cyber campaigns seem to have moved the election goalposts, playing a decisive role in altering the outcome of elections. In other instances, online campaigning seemed to have little effect as the traditional media continued to dominate. In still other circumstances, online campaigning seems to have been effective but only in limited ways and under certain conditions. The question at the end of the rainbow is what are the triggers, the situations, that allow social media to play a decisive role in elections and what are the conditions that create a limited or negligible role. In some senses, the chapters in this book together constitute a puzzle, with pieces sometimes fitting easily together into a wider answer and yet sometimes defying an easy fit.

The book begins with a chapter on "identity ownership" and "social sorting" in campaign strategies used during the 2020 Democratic primaries in the United States. In their study based on interviews with campaign operatives, Daniel Kreiss and Shannon C. McGregor argue that elections as well as intraparty contests in the United States are based on appeals to "megaidentity" groups and that in order to win elected office candidates have to perform their identities. They are particularly impressed by Lilliana Mason's contention that political parties in the United States have become increasingly homogeneous with few if any connections or interactions between Republicans and Democrats. The two parties exist as almost autonomous entities, as two different worlds that rarely intersect (Mason 2018).

Kreiss and McGregor argue that while social media is not the only tool that candidates use, it is vital one. This is because social media such as Facebook or Instagram focus on narrow appeals and allow candidates for office ". . . to tell a story of 'being one of' or, at the very least, 'being one with'" those that are being targeted. TV ads, for instance, tend to be a shotgun blast that even if they are intended to reach certain demographic groups don't have the same precision. Most critically, digital media allows for extensive testing. Feedback is instantaneous, a wide range of metrics can be used to analyze how campaign messages are being received, and messages can be continually tinkered with, adjusted, and reshaped as the numbers come in— and then tested again.

While Kreiss and McGregor' analysis is compelling, there are a number of important points for readers to consider. First, the hard-edged and corrosive divisions that now scar American politics may not be nearly as apparent in other societies where people are encouraged to have multiple identities and seem to have more in common with each other. Second is the question of whether election campaigns based on identity ownership exacerbate and magnify political divisions rather than heal them. In other words, does the very process of winning elections by a campaign of "identity ownership" make governing and peacemaking within societies all the more difficult?

Kevin Wagner and Jason Gainous view politicians' use of the Internet through a much different lens. Influenced by Andrew Chadwick's work on what he termed "the hybrid media system," Gainous and Wagner analyzed Twitter use by 767 major party candidates running for congressional seats during the 2018 midterm elections in the United States (Gainous and Wagner 2013). They found that close to 75 percent of tweets referred to or were linked to traditional news sources and that candidates used these stories and opinion pieces from the traditional media to legitimize and sell their own messages. Far from social media negating and erasing the power of TV and newspaper journalists, social and traditional media happily coexist, each dependent on and supporting the other.

Sometimes the nature of political cultures and the particular politics that surround issues make social media campaigns largely irrelevant. Kaitlynn Mendes and Diretnan Dikwal-Bot address this issue in their study of the feminist appeals made by Canadian Prime Minster Justin Trudeau and London Mayor Sadiq Khan during the 2015 and 2019 Canadian federal elections and the 2016 London mayor's race, respectively. What is fascinating here is the differences between networked feminism and the behavior of profeminist politicians during elections and in office. While feminists have lit up the Internet with a series of extraordinary wins, including the battles fought by #Me Too, #Not Okay, and #Slut Walk, and have achieved "unprecedented 'luminosity'" as a movement, politicians by contrast have been extremely timid in using social media to display and advertise their feminist credentials. While both Trudeau and Khan used social media to signal their feminist credentials and policies to women voters, they largely turned to the mainstream media to discuss issues that were of concern to women. Both politicians may have worried that too much profeminist advocacy on social media could have ignited a firestorm of reaction and fact-checking, not least by feminists, and it would have detracted from their main campaign messages. Where the feminist movement has seen opportunity, profeminist political leaders vying in elections have seen danger.

14 Electoral Campaigns, Media, and the New World of Digital Politics

Heather Evans takes a different tack in examining Twitter posts about "women's issues" by candidates in the 2016 and 2018 U.S. congressional elections. First, Evans found that Twitter was a particularly potent platform for "outsider" candidates, which many women were, because of its low cost and better educated and more affluent audience—an audience that was more likely to vote—and the ability that it provides for narrowcasting and targeted messaging. Although male users slightly outnumber female users, female users are more likely to search for news on the site and use it to discuss both politics and policy issues. Second, while Mendes and Dikwal-Bot found that Trudeau and Khan did not tout their feminist credentials on social media because it wasn't beneficial for them to do so, Evans discovered that women congressional candidates were considerably more likely to "speak" about women's issues than were male candidates. While Evans does not examine whether discussing women's issues correlated with winning or gaining votes, 2018 proved to be a bountiful year for electing women to Congress, and a record number were elected in 2020.

In the next chapter, Christopher Waddell, a former national editor for what is generally considered Canada's national newspaper, *The Globe and Mail*, and a former Parliamentary Bureau Chief for CBC TV, laments the effects that social media are having on how journalists cover elections. In Waddell's review of newspaper and TV coverage during the 2019 Canadian federal election, he found that there was a disturbing gap between the issues that journalists thought were important and the issues that were important to voters. Simply put, conventional media reporting, however breathless and certain of its own virtue, became increasingly detached from the public. Waddell cites a number of factors. First, the dramatic falls in revenue that had occurred because of the precipitous loss of audiences and advertising to social media meant that there were fewer journalists actually on the campaign trail and fewer instances where journalists could actually meet with and speak to voters. Confined to their newsrooms, far too many journalists turned to Facebook and Twitter as stand-ins for the campaign. What they got, however, was largely a reflection of what journalists were thinking, rather than what ordinary citizens were thinking or experiencing. As a consequence, social media was a distorted mirror that led them to misperceive the real world that was around them.

Digital media was not dominant in Italy where the continued popularity of RAI, a public broadcaster, and a vibrant private broadcasting sector that had become known for appealing to the lowest common denominator meant that most people still relied on TV for their political news. By the

2018 Italian general election, however, the Internet had made headway and was a close second as a source of political information, ahead of the print media, which had fallen to third. Nonetheless, Italy's major political figures Matteo Salvini, Luigi Di Maio, and Mateo Renzi had all built massive social media followings.

Sara Bentivegna and her colleagues argue that while digital media can play a decisive role in advertising party positions, putting candidates on display, and mobilizing followers, the true test of their effectiveness is whether they can alter the public agenda toward the issues over which leaders and their parties have "established ownership." In other words, to what extent do digital media messages influence the news agendas of the mainstream media. In an exhaustive study of news coverage and social media posts during the 2018 election, they found that both Salvini and Di Maio were able to influence the public agenda at key moments and on the issues with which they were most identified. This was not the case for Renzi, who had to react to agendas that had been set by others.

Often the key to wisdom in politics is to examine campaigns that failed. Studying what didn't happen can be as interesting as studying what did. Brian Budd and Tamara Small describe the fate of the People's Party of Canada, an authoritarian populist party led by a former Conservative Party cabinet minister, Maxime Bernier, that was erased from the election map in the 2019 federal election. In their study, Budd and Small focused on the party's use of email in the run up to and during the 2019 election, arguing that while largely ignored by scholars, email has been an effective means for party fundraising and rallying supporters. Email allows candidates and parties to bypass the media filter, is inexpensive, and unlike social media that are "public facing" has a private quality. Despite a frenetic email campaign that appealed to discontent over Canada's immigration policy and with the power of traditional elites, Bernier proved to be the wrong person, with the wrong message at the wrong time. Canada's two-party system (with two additional minor parties), the media's focus on the main contenders, a political consensus around reducing social inequalities, and Bernier's quirky reputation meant that voters barely paid attention. The conditions that allowed Bolsonaro to ride an e-populist wave in Brazil and Zelensky to crest a similar wave in Ukraine simply didn't exist in Canada in 2019. Without the right conditions, even the most focused and well-organized digital campaigns cannot succeed.

According to Michael Keren, the 2020 Israeli election is another example of the growing strength and agenda-setting power of social media. Wishing to ensure that his main rivals, the Blue and White Party and the Arab Joint List, would not come together to form a coalition government, Likud's Benjamin Netanyahu used social media to attack and delegitimize the leaders of the Joint List, depicting them as traitors and supporters of terror. While Israeli elections are still dominated by TV and newspaper coverage, social media allowed Netanyahu to conduct a relentless smear campaign based on innuendo, coded messages, and sloganeering that would not be carried by the mainstream media. He also used surrogates, including his son, to convey messages that he did not want to be directly associated with.

Keren's main concern is with the future of democracy. He argues that social media has coarsened political debate by allowing political leaders to willfully distort the truth, appeal to voters' darkest fears, and engage in hit-and-run character attacks against opponents. While scorched earth social media campaigns might help politicians win elections, the overall effect in this case was to poison the entire well of Israeli politics.

The same coexistence between social and traditional media did not take place during the 2018 Brazilian presidential election. In fact, the election of Jair Bolsonaro is arguably the most blazing example of how a once obscure politician can scale the heights of power using Facebook Live and Twitter. In his detailed study of Facebook Live and Twitter posts by the three leading candidates in the presidential election, Francisco Brandao was able to demonstrate how social media was critical in reordering Brazilian electoral politics. But the circumstances in Brazil were unique, as the old political order was crumbling. The established party system had been discredited beyond repair by the notorious "operation car wash" corruption scandal that tainted nearly all of Brazil's leading politicians. The traditional media was generally seen as monopolistic and corrupt. The economy was in shambles. Street violence had reached staggering proportions with 65,000 killings in 2017. And the impeachment campaign against former president Dilma Rousseff, which brought hundreds of thousands of Brazilians to the streets, had made social media a trusted and widely used form of communication.

With established institutions in disrepair and Bolsonaro with few resources and little access to the traditional media until he was stabbed at a rally in the middle of the campaign, which then made him a cause célèbre, the table had been set for a populist campaign driven by digital media. Bolsonaro's main weapon was Facebook Live. Often filmed in his kitchen surrounded by family members, twenty-four of the twenty-eight live videos that Bolsonaro produced reached more than a million viewers, with most reaching from four to eight million. This was a case of the medium becoming the message. The videos, which often showed his son Carlos holding the camera in the background, had a Brazilian flag duct-taped to a kitchen wall, and on one occasion had Bolsonaro appearing with clotheslines as a backdrop, came to embody his populist message and underdog status. During the 2018 Brazilian elections, at least, social media had not only arrived, it had become the dominant medium.

While digital media may have been influential and at times even a dominant medium in the 2018 Brazilian, 2018 Italian, and 2020 Israeli elections, they did not reach nearly the same apogee in the 2019 U.K. election. In an election process still dominated by television, and by the enormous reach and authority of the BBC in particular, and by a fiercely partisan and avidly read tabloid press, social media clearly played a secondary role. In Rosalyn Southern's examination of memes in the 2019 election, she found that while they had the power to disrupt, distract, and provoke, and had become part of a new "social media logic" within campaigns, they remained marginal for the vast majority of voters. Southern suggests that political campaigners in the United Kingdom are likely to become more "GIF-able," more savvy and innovative about the use of social media in the future, and that the 2019 election was part of this transition.

During the 2019 Ukrainian election, comedian and TV star Volodymyr Zelensky used multiple digital media platforms to appeal to younger voters in particular, and in a way that brought unity to a divided country. Zelensky's populist campaign won wide swaths of support in both western and southeastern Ukraine and among both Russian and Ukrainian speakers—something that had never been done before. While his success was predicated on widespread disgust with his opponent, incumbent president Petro Poroshenko, and with the corruption and stagnation that was crippling the Ukrainian economy, as well as Zelensky's singular popularity as a comedian and star of an ongoing hit TV series, it's critical to note that as a result of the 2014 Euromaidan revolution, digital media had become a way of life in Ukraine.

According to her detailed analysis of Zelensky's social media campaign, Larissa Doroshenko argued that, on one level, Zelensky's presence on social media was not populist at all, noting that he was almost never pictured with ordinary voters, in crowds, or with national symbols.But where a populist approach was most apparent was in Zelensky's online methods. He built a sizeable online army from the ground up and asked people to volunteer, download campaign materials, message friends, and most critically tell their own stories. While most campaigns fear losing control and impose a tight command structure, Zelensky's campaign was loose, decentralized, and user friendly. Zelensky's advantage may have been that he was able to benefit from a broad public consensus that had already formed. In a sense, Zelensky didn't have to create a media campaign, it created him.

The chapter dealing with Brazil and the one on Kenya add significantly to what is already a rich literature on election politics in Latin America and Africa (Bleck and Van de Walle 2018; Lupo, Oliveros, and Schiumerini 2019). What these chapters add, of course, is a focus on digital politics that is new to the literature.

While social media campaigning in Kenya resembles campaigns in Western countries in some significant ways, it differs in others. The traditional media, particularly TV and radio, still dominate the election horizon in Kenya and social media penetration is still relatively small with less than nine million users in a population of more than fifty-four million. According to Martin Ndlela, the political parties see digital media as the principal gateway to younger voters. As is the case in Europe, Facebook is by far the most used platform for campaigning, as Twitter is seen as appealing to a narrow elite audience. Instagram has not yet achieved the widespread popularity that it has in much of the West.

What's particularly noteworthy in Kenyan social media campaigns is the role played by influencers—media personalities, athletes, DJs, businesspeople, musicians, and so on. While some influencers join party campaigns out of conviction, most are paid for their services. They appear in ads, their faces are plastered on election posters, they attend party rallies, wear party colors and insignia, and perhaps most critically post on social media. In a crowded social media marketplace where voters are bombarded by posts from multiple contending parties, celebrities establish credibility and attract large audiences.

Social media use in Austrian elections have followed a similar trajectory to that of the United Kingdom. While newspapers remain the main news source and Austria's public broadcaster, the ORF, still plays a dominant role, social media use has skyrocketed. Facebook is the most popular site followed by a rising tide of Instagram use. Interestingly, Twitter has declined in popularity to the point where it has almost fallen off the map. In her study of Internet use by political parties in the 2013, 2017, and 2019 Austrian elections, Uta Russmann describes how social media has gone from being on the periphery of campaign politics to being at its center.

While Russmann's study describes a steady progression in the sophistication and importance of social media campaigns by Austrian parties between

2013 and 2019, there have been ups and downs along the way. According to Russmann, Austrian parties have had difficulty managing the torrents of messages and comments that flood into their sites. Unlike in most countries where communications between parties and online users is a one-way street because parties don't want to be sidetracked from their main messages and baited into back-alley fights and no-win debates, three of the four leading Austrian parties have tried to manage this relationship by creating teams of party supporters who tried as best they could to respond to comments and attacks. Two of the main parties employed software in the 2019 campaign to prevent swearing, invective, and anti-Semitic and racist comments from appearing on their sites.

Finally, in their study of campaigning on Twitter and Reddit during the 2019 Democratic presidential primaries, Chris Wells and his colleagues found that candidates tried to set the agenda by using the two platforms to mainly discuss their policy positions rather than making appeals based on identity, the horserace, or their images and characters. The goal was to win the battle of "association" in voters minds by tying their campaigns and those of their opponents to key issues. The authors stress that in a multi-modal media world different media can play different agenda-setting roles and target different audiences in different ways. Interestingly, their findings differ to some degree with the "identity politics" thesis about social media use that is central to Kreiss and McGregor's argument.

New Lines in the Sand

The chapters in this book raise a number of key questions about how elections are being fought, the uses of digital media, and the future of democracy. At the very least, our contributors demonstrate that there are new lines in the democratic sand. First, our authors raise questions about the relationship between traditional media and social media in election campaigns. Clearly, in quite a number of countries the traditional media still play a dominant role. This is especially the case in countries such as the United Kingdom, Italy, Austria, and Canada that have a strong public broadcasting tradition. Public broadcasters in these countries still attract sizeable audiences, are still trusted by their publics, and play vital roles in helping to set the public agenda. Added to this is that prestige newspapers such as *The New York Times* and *The Washington Post* in the United States, the tabloid press in the United Kingdom, and private broadcasters in Italy, for instance, play outsized roles in determining the shape of elections. Yet a strong mainstream media can exist side by side with effective online campaigns. As our contributors point out, mainstream reporters follow social media sometimes obsessively and can be deeply influenced by them, and as we have seen in a number of the chapters in this volume, political leaders can create online chain reactions that have altered and even upended election campaigns.

Interestingly, Wagner and Gainous point out that some campaigns incorporate reporting and commentary from the traditional media into their social media posts as a way to legitimize and reinforce their messages. In this light, digital media can be seen as hybrid media, a collage of multimedia messages that are interlaced with each other (Gainous and Wagner 2013). It's no longer easy to distinguish old and new media and there is a constant flow back and forth between the two.

But it's also important to note that there are other cases where social media campaigns pay little heed to mainstream reporting. The election of Bolsonaro in Brazil may be the most instructive. The traditional media had lost credibility with the public, and the politics of protest and the streets that had rocked Brazil in the years before the 2018 election had made social media into a primary instrument of power.

Another important strand of questions presented by our contributors is what kinds of social media campaigns make a difference in terms of election outcomes. From memes about Boris Johnson, to feminist appeals by London mayor Sadiq Khan, to the anti-immigrant tirades of Matteo Salvini in Italy, to Benjamin Netanyahu's populist Twitter attacks against the Arab Joint List, our authors evaluate which social media strategies worked and which didn't and the conditions that produced different outcomes. It's also important to consider that each of the main social media platforms that were examined has different uses, affordances, and audiences and were used differently during the election campaigns. What has emerged is a complex fabric whose many threads are not easily weaved together into a convenient or wearable conceptual garment—at least for now.

A last major question is in which cases has social media strengthened and in which ways have they damaged democracy? Of all of our authors, Michael Keren has been the most adamant in arguing that social media has cheapened and endangered democracy by lowering the level of discourse and giving extremist views a place to fester and propagate. Fear, innuendo, falsehoods, and conspiracy theories abound almost everywhere, as do the politics of self-righteousness. In addition, data collection and politics are intersecting in ways that can both enhance and endanger democracy. As mentioned earlier, venerable institutions and election systems designed for another time too often seem outmoded and unable to cope. But on the positive side, civic engagement and the ability of ordinary citizens to feel and taste politics, to become involved on their own terms and in their own ways has never been stronger. This volume has provided ample evidence of all of these new political realities.

Works Cited

Alter, Adam. 2017. *Irresistible: The Rise of Addictive Technology and the Business of Keeping Us Hooked.* New York: Penguin.

Applebaum, Anne. 2020. *Twilight of Democracy: The Seductive Lure of Authoritarianism.* Toronto: Penguin Random House Canada.

Arterton, Christopher. 1978. "The media politics of presidential campaigns." In *Race for the Presidency,* edited by James David Barber. Englewood Cliffs, NJ: Prentice-Hall.

Bleck, Jaimie, and Van de Walle. 2018. *Electoral Politics in Africa since 1990: Continuity in Change.* Cambridge, UK: Cambridge University Press.

Castells, Manuel. 2012. *Networks of Outrage and Hope.* Cambridge, UK: Polity.

Coppock, Alexander, Seth Hill, and Lynn Vavreck. 2020. "The small effects of political advertising are small regardless of context, message, sender, or receiver: Evidence from 59 real-time randomized experiments." *Science Advances* 6, no. 36.

Digital Democracy Project. 2020. *Lessons in Resilience: Canada's Digital Media Ecosystem and the 2019 Election.* Montreal: Public Policy Forum.

Edelman, Murray. 1988. *Constructing the Political Spectacle.* Chicago: University of Chicago Press.

Foer, Franklin. 2017. *The Existential Threat of Big Tech.* New York: Penguin.

Gainous, Jason, and Kevin M. Wagner. 2013. *Tweeting to Power: The Social Media Revolution in American Politics.* New York: Oxford University Press.

Gerstle, Jacques, and Alessandro Nai. 2019. "Negativity, emotionality and populist rhetoric in election campaigns worldwide and their effects on media attention and electoral success." *European Journal of Communication* 34, no. 4: 410–44.

Grossman, Michael, and Martha Kumar. 1981. *Portraying the President.* Baltimore: Johns Hopkins University Press.

Jamieson, Kathleen Hall. 2018. *Cyber-war: How Russian Hackers and Trolls Helped Elect a President.* New York: Oxford University Press.

Jenkins, Henry, Sam Ford, and Joshua Green. 2013. *Spreadable Media: Creating Value and Meaning in a Networked Culture.* New York: New York University Press.

Levitsky, Steven, and Daniel Ziblatt. 2018. *How Democracies Die.* New York: Crown Publishing.

Lupo, Noam, Virginia Oliveros, and Luis Schiumerini, eds. 2019. *Campaigns and voters in Developing Democracies: Argentina in Comparative Perspective.* Ann Arbor: University of Michigan Press.

Mason, Lilliana. 2018. *Uncivil Agreement: How Politics Became Our Identity.* Chicago: University of Chicago Press.

Mounk, Yascha. 2018. *The People Vs. Democracy.* Cambridge, MA: Harvard University Press.

Patterson, Thomas E. 2020. *A Tale of Two Elections: CBS and Fox News' Portrayal of the 2020 Presidential Campaign*. Cambridge, MA: Shorenstein Center on Media, Politics and Public Policy, John F. Kennedy School of Government, Harvard University.

Sides, John, and Lynn Vavreck. 2013. *The Gamble: Choice and Chance in the 2012 Presidential Election*. Princeton: Princeton University Press.

Sides, John, Michael Tesler, and Lynn Vavreck. 2018. *Identity Crisis: The 2016 Presidential Election and the Battle for the Meaning of America*. Princeton: Princeton University Press.

CHAPTER I

Owning Identity

Struggles to Align Voters during the
2020 U.S. Presidential Election

Daniel Kreiss, and Shannon McGregor,
University of North Carolina

Introduction

In this chapter, we focus on candidate and campaign strategic attempts at "identity ownership" (Kreiss, Lawrence, and McGregor 2020) during primary election campaigns, especially through digital and social media. To date, a robust body of literature has analyzed candidate "issue ownership" (e.g., Egan 2013), wherein politicians seek to align themselves with the issues their party is perceived by voters as having unique competency to address. Here we build on our previous work to analyze and empirically document how during primary elections candidates craft rhetoric and campaigns create communications that attempt to make some identities salient in the minds of voters, align candidates and their platforms with particular intrapartisan social identities, and craft and "extend" their own identities for electoral gain. Our argument is that through communication, and especially given the affordances of digital and social media that facilitate speaking to narrow slices of the electorate (Kreiss, Lawrence, and McGregor 2018), candidates and campaigns strive to construct and convey the identities of the groups of constituents they seek to represent, including conveying information about the policies they will pursue through the lens of appealing to these particular social groups.

23

Identity ownership occurs when voters come to associate particular parties and candidates with the social groups they claim and attempt to represent. Even more, identity ownership occurs when candidates make particular identities salient in voters' minds, and therefore politically consequential, or give rise to entirely new social identities for individuals (Egan 2019). Identities are both found as structural features of the polity—such as preexisting lines of partisan, social, and religious affiliation—but they are also made through the efforts of candidates to articulate lines of social and political division.

This chapter takes up the case of the 2020 U.S. Democratic presidential primaries and utilizes interviews with campaign staffers to document and analyze campaign attempts at intraparty identity ownership. As we demonstrate, in the course of a competitive primary process, campaigns work to identify, contact, persuade, and motivate voters to support their candidate through the lens of who they perceive these voters are on social identity terms. They often do so through leveraging new forms of data available about the electorate and digital and social media that facilitate narrowcasting to targeted voters (Bossetta 2018). While supporters of each major party in the United States sort into well-delineated social groups along the lines of such things as geography, religiosity, and race and ethnicity (Mason 2018), the primary process offers a chance to examine more differentiated, intraparty campaign strategic communications aimed at making visible and crafting lines of division *within* partisan coalitions.

Social Identity, Electoral Politics, and Party Primaries

The concept of identity ownership stems from a relatively recent body of scholarship in political science that convincingly argues for the centrality of social identity in U.S. politics. Foundational work by Green, Palmquist, and Schickler (2004) argues that over the course of an election candidates frame politics in terms of a struggle between "us" and "them," theorizing that when people reflect on their partisan attachments, they ask two questions: "What kinds of social groups come to mind when I think about Democrats, Republicans, and Independents? Which assemblage of groups (if any) best describes me?" (2004, 8). Lilianna Mason (2018) demonstrates what she calls "social sorting"—the two main parties in the United States have come to represent totally different groups of people, and citizens choose between the parties based on their social identities. In other words, Mason shows (2018, 14, 26) how these social groups are increasingly aligned, or sorted, into larger partisan categories, making parties "mega-identity" groups:

Owning Identity 25

They have become increasingly homogeneous parties, with Democrats now firmly aligned with identities such as liberal, secular, urban, low-income, Hispanic, and black. Republicans are now solidly conservative, middle-class or wealthy, rural, churchgoing, and white. These identities are increasingly aligned so that fewer identities affiliated with either party are also associated with the other side.

Though much of the electorate can be grouped into these partisan mega-identities (Mason 2018), the process of constructing and making salient particular identities in a given election cycle may lead to electoral success. For example, during the 2016 election Trump's explicit appeals made racial and ethnic identities more salient for whites and connected them to clear partisan choices (Bhambra 2018; Gest 2016; Jardina 2019), in the process bringing to the Republican fold whites who saw their racial identity as the basis for political choice (Newman et al. 2018; Perrin and Ifatunji 2020; Sides, Tesler, and Vavreck 2019).

Campaigns have long used affirmative claims of identity and communication about traditionally marginalized groups as powerful symbols to divide voters, with important implications for electoral outcomes (Hutchings and Valentino 2010; Jamieson 1992). Candidates and campaigns work to communicate who is—and who is not—part of their coalition through myriad strategies. For example, Coe and Griffin (2020) found that more than 40 percent of Trump's tweets about marginalized groups from his first year in office were negative in tone, sending powerful signals of who does not belong in power or in the country. Evidence suggests that these messages of racial or group priming (Jamieson 1992) activate people's identity attitudes, which in turn influence candidate evaluations (see Valentino and Vendenbroek 2017). While previous research suggests that implicit cues are more effective at racial priming (Mendelberg 2017), more recent evidence suggests that explicit racial cues—such as those employed by Trump's 2016 campaign—serve as powerful motivating messages about which candidates represent which groups (Jardina 2019; Hutchings and Valentino 2010).

While much work has generally treated social identities as stable items to measure via surveys, as this work suggests social groupings and divisions are constituted in and through political communication. Communication is the means for constructing, conveying, and making salient the identities of parties and candidates, and the groups of voters they seek to represent. As such, candidates seek to communicate in terms of conveying their group identities around partisan affiliation, racial and ethnic identities, genders, religious affiliations, and values and tastes, as well as to highlight differences from out-groups. What Kreiss, Lawrence, and McGregor (2020) term "identity ownership" occurs when voters perceive a candidate as a plausible "prototype" (Jackson and Hogg, 2010) for a particular group. This prototypicality is marked by the perception that a candidate fits within and represents said group's characteristics, norms, and values.

The focus of this chapter is on identity appeals during primary campaigns. Identity communication likely looks different during primaries and general elections. In the primary period, candidates compete with in-group members to build and represent party coalitions for electoral success. During general elections, candidates rely more on broad performances of partisanship while simultaneously making identity appeals across the spectrum of their parties' coalitions, designed to "get out the vote" of key groups of constituencies and competing over voters with multiple, conflicting identities (see also, Egan 2019).

Following the issue-ownership literature, we expect that voters develop preferences for candidates based on their own self-identification with social groups and perception of group norms (such as policy preferences), as well as their perceptions of others and other social groups. This suggests that those candidates who demonstrate party-consonant identities more consistently and perform their own identities and extend beyond them through surrogates in ways that accord with party coalitions and policies will likely be the most successful during a primary. Key to social identity theory—and to politics—is the concept of in-groups and out-groups. In a primary contest, candidates and voters share a mega-out-group—the opposing party—but they must still engage in intraparty identity ownership. Though Mason (2018) and others (Levendusky 2009; Abramowitz 2011; Abramowitz and McCoy 2019) convincingly argue that the majority of Americans are socially sorted into one of the two major parties, there remains variations within the multitude of social groups that make up each partisan mega-identity, as well as variation in support for the types of policy aims that the party should prioritize. In the 2020 U.S. Democratic presidential primary, for instance, this was seen clearly in the contest not only between the progressives (typified by candidates like Bernie Sanders and Elizabeth Warren) and moderates (such as Joe Biden and Amy Klobuchar) but also in the contest between a diverse slate of candidates, including the party's first openly gay candidate as well as record numbers of women and people of color who vied with white candidates, including the eventual nominee and president, Joe Biden.

Identity appeals are facilitated by digital and social media, which enable campaigns to simultaneously harness new forms of data and narrowcast channels to reach increasingly small slices of the electorate through paid and organic posts (Bossetta 2018; Kreiss, Lawrence, and McGregor 2018). While much of the twentieth century was predicated on mass mediated appeals—"air wars"—supplemented by more targeted communications through direct mail and cable television, with the advent of digitally networked and social media, practitioners now have hundreds of different channels to target the electorate and new data to leverage to figure out who to reach, how to reach them, and what to say for persuasive ends (Delli Carpini and Williams 2020). Especially through paid advertising on large social media platforms such as Facebook and Google, campaigns are increasingly able to determine who they are going to speak to and what they are going to say (Fowler 2018).

As such, digital and social media are important new venues for candidates and campaigns to engage in identity targeting and ownership attempts through both paid ads and organic posts—all of which are designed to pass through the social networks of supporters themselves (McGregor 2020; Penney 2017). That said, our aim here is to put digital and social media in context—they are not the only tools campaigns leverage in the course of an election, although they are rapidly becoming among the most important. Digital and social media have supplemented other mediums for campaign appeals—such as direct mail, television, radio, and canvassing—that continue to exist, and even thrive, in the digital era. Digital media offer unique affordances for campaigners, however, which is clear in the growing embrace of digital advertising and social media campaigning by practitioners of all stripes. This includes digital advertising that facilitates highly targeted appeals based on preexisting data, such as using the Facebook custom audiences tool, and then the matching of audiences for ads with others who share similar demographics, affinities, social networks, or interests (Kreiss 2016). It also includes organic, and often highly emotional or divisive, posts on sites such as Facebook, Instagram, Twitter, and YouTube that are designed to gain engagement from like-minded supporters and therefore greater reach through social networks and algorithmic suggestions (Wahl-Jorgensen 2019).

Through media, campaigns seek to make salient those identities within the party that their candidate can reasonably claim while at the same time working to "extend" their own identities through surrogates or communicating and demonstrating proximity to other social groups. A candidate's own biography—including their social identities and their policy histories—likely bounds the types of appeals that she can credibly make. While candidates have more latitude during general elections when partisanship holds sway—consider evangelicals' embrace of Donald Trump in the run-up to the general election in 2016 but not the primaries (Gorski 2019; Harris and Steiner 2018; Pew 2016b)—during primaries their public persona bounds the appeals they can credibly make to voters. During the 2016 Republican presidential primaries, Ted Cruz could believably perform a devout Christian persona, for example, in a way that Trump could not. We conceptualize "identity trespassing" as when performed "extensions" of a candidate's identity are perceived as inauthentic strategic attempts to invoke social identities (see Alexander 2010). In these cases, extensions of identity may backfire (Berinsky et al. 2020), particularly on social media, spaces where authenticity is prized.

Methods

To document and analyze how campaign staffers strategically target the electorate, Daniel Kreiss co-led a research group, with UNC professor Joseph Czabovsky, of ten undergraduate students to conduct interviews with campaign practitioners and, for a separate project, voters in Iowa, South Carolina, and North Carolina during the 2020 Democratic primaries. Kreiss and Czabovsky trained these ten undergraduates in qualitative interview and field observation methods. For this chapter, in April these undergraduate researchers conducted interviews with six Democratic presidential campaign staffers, representing the Bernie Sanders, Pete Buttigieg (2), Elizabeth Warren (2), and Andrew Yang campaigns. We also conducted an interview with a senior staffer for a senate campaign during the cycle (we do not divulge this campaign because of the small number of staffers working on senate races at this time and the need to preserve confidentiality). While we cannot make their names or exact roles on these campaigns public given the participation terms of this study and to enable these individuals to speak frankly, we selected these staffers because they worked in senior-level digital and communications positions and were therefore able to speak authoritatively about messaging strategy. Interviews with these presidential campaign staffers were semistructured and open-ended (see the appendix to this chapter for the interview map). They lasted approximately twenty minutes on average.

Findings

Our findings detail the attempts of practitioners to reach and sway the electorate in the context of a competitive primary campaign, where partisan in-group identity is a given and more differentiated decision-making takes place.

Campaign Targeting and Making Appeals to the Electorate

Our interviews show campaign outreach to differentiated groups in the electorate primarily happens through what Democratic campaign practitioners call "constituency organizing." "Constituency organizing" is explicit outreach to groups in the electorate that are parts of partisan coalitions. For instance, this would include targeted outreach to evangelicals for Republicans and LGBTQI+ individuals for Democrats and can occur both to individuals that are profiled and targeted as being a member of these social and identity groups through data and through existing civil society organizations that represent the interests of these groups. While this is a very old practice, it has received little attention in the political communication literature and, as such, we know little about the production of partisan and social division and polarization by campaigns more broadly.

Constituency organizing is often the purview of dedicated staffers or divisions that are responsible for appealing to these groups in the electorate. It often begins with polling that works to determine what the composition of a successful electoral coalition looks like in terms of voters and their identity groups, and then strategic consideration of how best to assemble it through messaging and outreach. As a senior senate campaign staffer during the 2020 cycle stated:

> Is it mostly women? Men? Are they Black, Latino, Asian? What exactly is our district and how much percent are these constituents in our district? So we found out that we do have obviously an influx of white individuals, older individuals, but who we were trying to focus on based off of that polling was specifically Black women too. . . . But it was just a lot of trying to figure out what appeals to Black women, what appeals to elderly individuals.

This staffer related that these messages get folded into targeted forms of outreach such as direct mail and television advertising, as well as digital advertising. All those we interviewed familiar with digital advertising related how digital ads facilitated extensive testing—where practitioners could develop multiple versions of different ads with different appeals and then test their performance with the groups they were seeking to reach out to (see also, McGregor 2020). This is an important way that digital and social media are different from earlier and other mediums. While campaigns could test the effectiveness of appeals through things like direct mail, digital media enable this work to be instantaneous (Karpf 2016). And there are many more metrics at play, such as engagement (i.e., likes, shares, click-throughs), email sign-ups, donations, volunteer commitments, voter registrations, and so on. As a staffer for Warren's campaign related, in the context of being asked about outreach strategies to constituent groups through digital ads: "we did a fair amount of testing so we would run different messages to different cohorts of the same audience, compare the performance, and then optimize towards the message that was either generating the most signups, generating the most revenue, or potentially moving voters in a more likely to consider voting first under Warren, in that direction."

These strategies also manifest themselves through field programs, where organizers go door-to-door on behalf of candidates and organize events dedicated for specific groups of voters important to an electoral coalition. Campaigns often hired these staffers because they matched the identities of those they were looking to organize—a way that candidates and their campaigns tried to "extend" their identities to encompass broader groups of people. As a 2020 Bernie Sanders presidential campaign staffer related:

> We had very intensive constituency outreach programs as a part of the organizing department. Teams of organizers who came from those constituencies were directly doing outreach in a lot of different ways, from door knocking to events to other types of volunteer outreach with everything from the African American community, to the Latino community to the Muslim community, to the LGBTQ to, every constituency. We really had a lot of strong constituency organizing.

As this staffer went on to relate, many of these groups consisted of individuals that were less frequent voters but that the campaign had profiled as being comparatively likely to support Sanders. These constituency teams were engaged in both direct voter outreach and in working through organizations that represented these voters. An important part of this process was identifying the issues that were important to these groups of voters and speaking to them—extending candidate identities through policy. And an important aspect of constituency teams was hiring staffers from the communities they were reaching out to. As this staffer continued: "We had by far the most intensive constituency outreach operation. Nobody else had as many staffers of color, staffers representing various constituencies as we did in terms of working in these communities. . . . So they were doing really aggressive messaging, the Latino community in various early states for months and months and months and months before anybody else was. And obviously not just in the Latino community, but in other communities as well, that outreach was very intensive."

Communicating Candidate Identity

Candidates during the presidential primaries saw different paths to victory and worked to connect not only the issues they would prioritize to electorally important groups but also their biographies and personal identities. For example, a senior Buttigieg staffer related how the candidate's own deeply held Christian faith became an important communications and organizing point for the campaign, especially in outreach to religious groups and, central to the candidate's strategy, as a crossover appeal to Republicans dissatisfied with the president:

> I think faith was another place where Pete was really well spoken and very outspoken about how faith informed his political views. So, we did podcasts with Sojourners, which is a progressive Christian website, talks to religion news, we did an interview with CNNs religion editor. . . . Again something that Republicans have seized on, and I'm sure you heard Pete at some point and talk along these lines, right, "God doesn't belong to a political party" is essentially what he would say. And he really took that and I think he spoke to a lot of people who are Christians or are people of faith and they just feel like Republicans had just grabbed onto that.

Another Buttigieg staffer cited that the campaign was the first to have a Faith Outreach Director, who was also part of the LGBTQ community, responsible for engaging in proactive outreach to other faith communications (such as the Jewish and Muslim communities). For example, the candidate discussed his faith on programs such as *The View* (2019), and the campaign also used its social media accounts to discuss faith and its role in the election (Buttigieg 2019). The campaign's approach to faith mirrored its director-level appointments for other coalition groups, including for Black, Latino, women, and student voters.

Like other campaigns, there were a number of constituency efforts to appeal to various social groups in the Democratic electorate. For Buttigieg, this involved deploying the candidate to forums where these social groups were represented and drawing on his biography to help make connections, as well as the biographies of the candidate's surrogates, in addition to speaking to the issues that were salient to these groups. All of these things involved forms of identity-based appeals, especially around the issues that these groups cared about and the aspects of the candidate's biography or experiences that conveyed his ability to represent them. These were about particularistic appeals designed to assemble a broad, and winning, electoral coalition. As this staffer related:

> So our campaign, our political team basically had a lot of different constituency directors. So we had a veterans outreach person. We had a faith outreach person and she was a pastor or is and basically used her network, and used her connections, and used people who reached out to the campaign to build that. Pete met with religious leaders in a lot of different cities that he would go to. We always had our outward events, our public events and stuff that people knew about. But in a lot of the cities that Pete went to, he was meeting with people behind the scenes too. And a lot of times those were religious leaders. A lot of times they were students. We would go to [redacted] and he would meet with students and faculty and talk about issues that Black students face. In Houston we would meet with Latino organizations. So a lot of that stuff was behind the scenes. They didn't necessarily see all the time.

This played out across mediums, which all the representatives of the candidates we spoke to cited. Again, campaigns leverage various mediums—from in-person appearances of the candidate to social media appeals—in highly complementary ways in the service of the ends of making identity claims. And many of these mediums facilitated narrow appeals as part of a strategic communications strategy. For example, the behind-the-scenes strategies with the leadership of various groups complemented appeals through media aimed at particular groups in the electorate, such as the targeted advertising on social media that was designed to reach and engage voters with specific constituency identities. As this senior Buttigieg staffer related:

> There was the earned media aspect of it where Pete would talk to Telemundo and Univision, he would talk to LGBT newspapers, he would call in to Black radio or do stuff with Black newspapers. And then in paid media as well. I mean, Facebook and Twitter you can just hyper target different groups. . . . And then in our advertising, our message differed from state to state when we put ads on air. Even if there's an overarching theme or message that we want to get across,

it's still going to look and feel a little different, and we're going to highlight different parts of his biography and stuff that.

Candidates and campaigns are not only appealing to existing groups within the Democratic Party's coalition; in the course of doing so they are connecting their biographies with the groups they seek to represent. And, as they do so, they further reify the identities of these groups and attempt to make them salient in the minds of voters in terms of connecting them with political choices. By appealing to voters as members of particular social and identity groups, campaigns are not only working within existing social structures, they are making them more durable and actionable for political life and choices. For example, staffers cited how candidates would draw on their biographies and narrate them in particular ways to tell a story of "being one of" or, at the very least, "being one with" those they were seeking to represent and persuade.

To take one example, a senior Yang digital campaign staffer cited how the candidate specifically "spoke to" (used in the sense of "resonated with") young men, millennials, and Generation Z members in particular. The campaign drew on these early supporters to champion the candidate, especially online (see McGregor 2020; Penney 2017). Yang's appeal to these groups was primarily through his biography and performances of his identity:

> I think most of it really relies on the candidate and their personality. The reality was that Andrew Yang was sort of a perfect person to appeal to this demographic that has mostly been left out and forgotten and I think has this hidden feeling of not living up to this American ideal that their parents lived through and many of them went to college and then didn't have jobs afterwards. . . . They were looking for someone to talk about the things that they were interested in and to champion their beliefs.

This staffer reflected others in citing that the believability and resonance of these appeals was contingent upon them being perceived as authentic. In other words, that voters saw these performances of self and narration of their identities as authentic and truly part of who the candidate *is* and the experiences that they had. This is always a performance that must be judged through the "willing suspension of disbelief" that those observing it have, or fail to if the performance fails, given that we will never truly know what a candidate's authentic self is actually like (Alexander 2010). That said, staffers seek to engineer these identity performances in explicit ways to create this believability in an authentic self, and digital media offer a crucial medium for enabling the candidate to construct and convey his authentic self. As this staffer continues:

> As a digital department, we focused on reaching that demographic where they lived mostly, which was online and social media spaces and not necessarily on television because especially at the beginning, we couldn't get airtime on television. Ad buys were very expensive. But for the most part, our messaging revolves around Andrew's personality. That demographic, young people really value authenticity and transparency and Andrew was always just the person who he was naturally, he didn't put himself up on a pedestal or have the classic politician spiel or sheen that a lot of politicians carry with them. And so whenever we could, we would just show Andrew on and off the camera as the same person.

Staffers suggested that consistency was key to successful identity performances. People are more willing to believe the performance of a candidate if it is consistent, which speaks to a candidate's authenticity. As such, this became a goal of campaigns—to convey who the candidate is and who they would represent through the lens of a consistent performance with coherent elements across many different mediums utilized in the course of a campaign. Staffers cited the importance of having a consistent message that represented an "authentic self," the thread of which would be coherent across all a candidate and campaign's messaging. As a second Buttigieg staffer related:

> On the campaign trail, Pete would say, "Future former Republicans," and part of including that was creating an environment of welcoming and inclusion, not just of race and gender and sexual orientation. So, he took the same message. He was the same person anywhere that he went. I mean, that was just strategic in itself because, A. you don't want to be caught up backtracking or flip flopping, but B. he's running to be his authentic self. And we didn't see that always from other candidates on the campaign trail who had to correct themselves.

When aspects of a candidate's biography could not speak directly to the issues of concern to particular groups, candidates took up the stories of others. This communicates identity representation. By telling someone else's story, a candidate conveys that they will acknowledge, validate, and act on someone else's experiences and represent that person—and the groups they are a part of—on the campaign and in office. In this way, candidates use the stories of others to convey their own identities and values when their own biography cannot. As this Buttigieg staffer continued:

> We had done our research, we were listening to voters and taking some of those stories and putting it into a stump speech. So for example, he would always tell the story of, there was a girl that he heard from on the campaign trail who talked about her fear of gun violence and she was just a kid and she was already thinking about that before she even went to high school. He would talk about people who he met on the trail who couldn't afford insulin, and that's how he would open up a conversation about the cost of prescription drugs.

The stories of others became entry points not only to identities a candidate could not reasonably claim but also the policies that those social groups support such as gun control and affordable access to health care, in this case.

Conclusion

The concept of identity ownership helps explain the ways particular assemblages of social groups come to be attached to and even define partisan identities over the course of many electoral cycles. This representational work is especially challenging during party primary contests when there are numerous candidates vying to represent factions within party coalitions. Our findings in this chapter show how campaigns attempt to contact and persuade various social groups during a competitive primary campaign. Where partisan in-group identity is a given, campaigns aim to differentiate their candidate through particular claims of their own identity, as well as others with which they can reasonably claim proximity, through the use of surrogates and retelling and adopting the stories of others. As we show here, a candidate can draw on her own personal identity but, as one person, can only represent so many aspects of her party's identity coalition. As such, candidates and their campaigns must then rhetorically and visually represent themselves as linked to or distinct from other social groups.

The campaign communications and candidate performances we document here reveal attempts to make particular identities salient in the minds of voters, to align candidates with particular intrapartisan identities, and to extend candidates' own identities—all toward the goal of building a coalition capable of turning out a primary victory and general election win. Any given party is shaped by the identity ownership appeals and efforts that take place during its contests for the nomination. Just as Trump's victory in the Republican primary in 2016 has come to shape and even define today's Republican Party and its coalition (Sides, Tesler, and Vavreck 2018), so too has the Democratic primary in 2020. These shifts also have implications for how the public views itself. Partisans bring aspects of their identities in line with their politics—in particular, some assume identities that align with party prototypes while at the same time discarding those that do not (Egan 2019).

As part of appealing to various identities in the electorate, campaigns drew from the actual biographies of their particular candidates. These strategies relate not only to identity ownership attempts but also to the growing personalization of politics. Whereas the news media have come to focus more on the personal identities and private lives of politicians (Holtz-Bacha, Langer, and Merkle 2014; Van Aelst, Sheafer, and Stanyer 2011), so too have politicians themselves focused their communications on their family, lifestyles, and personal tastes. This sort of self-personalizing—or intimization—(Stanyer 2013; McGregor, Lawrence, and Cardona 2017; McGregor 2018) is a rich form of communicating social identity. There are gendered differences in the way intimization is deployed—male candidates engage more in this practice, but female candidates do so in ways that highlight their caregiving roles (McGregor, Lawrence, and Cardona 2017), in ways that stoke long-held gendered stereotypes (Alexander and Andersen 1993; Banwart 2010; Banwart and McKinney 2005). Voters demand that candidates reveal more about themselves, and candidates do so, but in particularistic ways designed to make strategic identity appeals. These personalized appeals potentially cause voters to feel a sense of shared social affiliation with candidates, which can lead to increased vote intention, but there are disparities. Self-personalization "works" better for male candidates, whereas for female candidates, effects were dependent on shared partisan attributes (McGregor 2018). In short, there is reason to suspect that candidates' identity appeals are dependent not only on what they can reasonably access from their biography but also on long-standing biases among the public about who can claim political power.

Candidates' personalizing communication often takes place on social media (Metz et al. 2019), where the norms of authenticity and intimacy practically demand these types of intimate self-disclosures (boyd and Ellison 2007; Enli and Thumin 2012; Marwick and boyd 2011). Indeed, we see social media as playing a key role in identity performances, offering candidates more intimate ways to connect with often narrow groups of voters who are already supporters, have narrow social, affiliational, or interest-based identities, or seek particularistic experiences. We see these strategies, which often play out on social media, complementing other forms of broader identity performance across other mediums, which may by necessity require broader appeals to more generalized groups within the electorate (such as a television news interview watched by millions of Americans—see also Wagner and Gainous, this volume). At the same time, it is clear that candidates also use social media, both paid and organic content, to speak to narrow slices of the electorate and often make particularistic identity claims, such as around being gun owners, for abortion rights, and so on. Former President Trump's notorious "invasion" ads, presumably targeted toward those with the most negative views of immigration, are a case in point (Kaplan 2019). Trump was performing his own whiteness, and stoking white anxiety over the changing demographics of the country and shifting social, cultural, and economic power, in a way facilitated by the affordances of the social media itself.

That said, Trump has never shied from making such explicit claims to represent whites against Black and Brown others in more generalized mediums either. This is where we see social media as not so much fragmenting the electorate as reflecting the many overlapping identities of candidates and electorates and giving campaigns greater technological and performative license to appeal to and leverage them. We see social media as largely downstream from broader technological, political, and social changes that has led to the sorting of the electorate along new lines, and also note that the era of mass-mediated politics that persisted after the Cold War was a historical anomaly, but also it was hardly a time of national unity and solidaristic appeals to "Americans" as decades long struggles for civil rights and social justice attest (Hill 2004). To imagine the broadcast era as being solidaristic and digital media as bringing about divisiveness, on identity lines or any other grounds of social demarcation, is to ignore a long and complicated history of media technologies and race (McIlwain 2019).

Indeed, much of the campaign work described to us relies heavily on appeals stemming from the candidate's actual biography and identity—this bounds the appeals any given candidate can make. As our informants told us, there is an authenticity to these appeals. Authenticity is a contested concept in politics—voters and the press alike demand "authenticity" from candidate and campaign communication, which they in turn dutifully strive to perform. Authenticity—or appearing to be "righteously" driven by causes and values not votes (Serazio 2017)—is prized in politics, but is not distributed equally. Drawing from Jamieson's (1995) foundational work on female politicians' double binds, Harp, Loke, and Bachmann (2016) propose a new bind:

competence/authenticity. For example, while Hillary Clinton's "credentials are generally acknowledged, her capability as a politician is marred by questions about her authenticity as a human being to the extent that she has been caricatured as a 21-st century Lady Macbeth" (Harp, Loke, and Bachmann 2016, 203). Similar arguments were made about Elizabeth Warren. As Megan Graber wrote in *The Atlantic*: "America punished Elizabeth Warren for her competence" (Graber 2020). If white women—generally privileged as a group compared to other politically marginalized social groups—struggle to effectively communicate both the competence and authenticity required for public office, then one can imagine the charges of inauthenticity against candidates whose identity ownership attempts ring hollow given the public's image of political leadership as white and male.

Authenticity is often evoked through proximity to "real people" speaking for the candidate (Serazio 2017) or causes—a practice we detail here where campaigns brought on surrogates from various social identity groups and candidates adopted the stories of "real people" to signal their support for particular social groups and concerns that they could not reasonably claim as their own. Telling these stories to evoke identities can be seen as a form of episodic framing—especially when likened to a policy point—which elicit emotional reactions (Gross 2008). Politicians retelling the stories of others does crucial identity ownership work while at the same time evoking populist appeals that prioritize "everyday" people (Atkins and Finlayson 2012). At the same time, the use of stories to evoke advantageous social identities may in some situations be contested. Future work should examine questions such as: Who is allowed to share whose stories? What is the role of authenticity in the resharing of stories, and their credibility?

It is worth noting, as our findings on targeting suggest, that identity ownership is *not* just a product of the content of communication but also the data and campaign practices that inform those strategic communications. As more, and more fine-grained, data about people's identities have become available—such as the TV shows we watch, the restaurants we prefer, and the Facebook groups we belong to—identity ownership can almost be seen as the logical conclusion of the intersection of politics and data.

Works Cited

Abramowitz, A. I. 2011. "Expect confrontation, not compromise: The 112th House of Representatives is likely to be the most conservative and polarized House in the modern era." *PS: Political Science & Politics* 44(2): 293–95.

Abramowitz, A., and J. McCoy. 2019. "United States: Racial resentment, negative partisanship, and polarization in Trump's America." *The ANNALS of the American Academy of Political and Social Science* 681(1): 137–56.

Alexander, D., and K. Andersen. 1993. "Gender as a Factor in the Attribution of Leadership Traits." *Political Research Quarterly* 46(3): 527–45.

Alexander, J. C. 2010. *The performance of politics: Obama's victory and the democratic struggle for power.* New York: Oxford University Press.

Atkins, J., and A. Finlayson. 2013. "'. . . A 40-year-old black man made the point to me': Everyday knowledge and the performance of leadership in contemporary British politics." *Political Studies* 61(1): 161–77.

Banwart, M. C. 2010. "Gender and candidate communication: Effects of stereotypes in the 2008 election." *American Behavioral Scientist* 54(3): 265–83.

Banwart, M. C., and M. S. McKinney. 2005. "A gendered influence in campaign debates? Analysis of mixed-gender United States Senate and gubernatorial debates." *Communication Studies* 56(4): 353–73.

Berinsky, A. J., J. de Benedictis-Kessner, M. E. Goldberg, and M. F. Margolis. 2020. "The Effect of Associative Racial Cues in Elections." *Political Communication*, 1–18.

Bhambra, G. K. 2017. "Brexit, Trump, and 'methodological whiteness': On the misrecognition of race and class." *The British Journal of Sociology* 68: S214–S232.

Bossetta, M. 2018. "The digital architectures of social media: Comparing political campaigning on Facebook, Twitter, Instagram, and Snapchat in the 2016 US election." *Journalism & Mass Communication Quarterly* 95(2): 471–96.

boyd, d., and N. B. Ellison. 2007. "Social network sites: Definition, history, and scholarship." *Journal of Computer-Mediated Communication* 13(1): 210–30.

Brewer, M. B. 1991. "The social self: On being the same and different at the same time." *Personality and Social Psychology Bulletin* 17(5): 475–82.

Buttigieg, P. 2019. Tweet. December 20. https://twitter.com/petebuttigieg/status/120 8113299776299008?lang=en

Coe, K., and R. A. Griffin. 2020. "Marginalized Identity Invocation Online: The Case of President Donald Trump on Twitter." *Social Media + Society* 6(1): https://doi.org/10.1177/2056305120913979

Delli Carpini, M. X., and B. A. Williams. 2020. "Campaigns and Elections in a Changing Media Landscape." In *The Oxford Handbook of Electoral Persuasion.* New York: Oxford University Press.

Egan, P. J. 2013. *Partisan priorities: How issue ownership drives and distorts American politics.* Cambridge: Cambridge University Press.

Egan, P. J. 2019. "Identity as dependent variable: How Americans shift their identities to align with their politics." *American Journal of Political Science.* https://doi.org/10.7910/DVN/Y82RW8

Enli, G. S., and N. Thumin. 2012. "Socializing and self-representation online: Exploring facebook." *Observatorio (OBS) Journal* 6(1): 87–105.

Fowler, E. F. 2018. *Political advertising in the United States.* New York: Routledge.

Garber, M. 2020. "America Punished Elizabeth Warren for Her Competence: The country still doesn't know what to make of a woman—in politics, and beyond—who refuses to qualify her success." *The Atlantic.* March 5. https://www.theatlantic.com/culture/archive/2020/03/america-punished-elizabeth-warren-her-competence/607531/

Gest, J. 2016. *The new minority: White working class politics in an age of immigration and inequality.* New York: Oxford University Press.

Gorski, P. 2019. "Why evangelicals voted for Trump: A critical cultural sociology." In *Politics of meaning/meaning of politics*, 165–83. London: Palgrave Macmillan.

Green, D. P., B. Palmquist, and E. Schickler. 2004. *Partisan hearts and minds: Political parties and the social identities of voters*. New Haven: Yale University Press.

Gross, K. 2008. "Framing persuasive appeals: Episodic and thematic framing, emotional response, and policy opinion." *Political Psychology* 29(2): 169–92.

Harp, D., J. Loke, and I. Bachmann. 2016. "Hillary Clinton's Benghazi hearing coverage: Political competence, authenticity, and the persistence of the double bind." *Women's Studies in Communication* 39(2): 193–210.

Harris, T. M., and R. J. Steiner. 2018. "Beyond the Veil: A Critique of White Christian Rhetoric and Racism in the Age of Trump." *Journal of Communication & Religion* 41(1): 33–45.

Hill, L. E. 2004. *The deacons for defense: Armed resistance and the civil rights movement*. Chapell Hill: University of North Carolina Press.

Holtz-Bacha, C., A. I. Langer, and S. Merkle. 2014. "The personalization of politics in comparative perspective: Campaign coverage in Germany and the United Kingdom." *European Journal of Communication* 29: 153–70.

Iyengar, S., Y. Lelkes, M. Levendusky, N. Malhotra, and S. J. Westwood. 2019. "The origins and consequences of affective polarization in the United States." *Annual Review of Political Science* 22: 129–46.

Jackson, R. L., Hogg, M. A. 2010. Social identity theory. In *Encyclopedia of identity*, edited by R. L. Jackson and M. A. Hogg, 749–53. Thousand Oaks, CA: SAGE.

Jamieson, K. H. 1995. *Beyond the double bind: Women and leadership*. New York: Oxford University Press.

Jardina, A. 2019. *White identity politics*. Cambridge: Cambridge University Press.

Kaplan, T. 2019. "How the Trump Campaign Used Facebook Ads to Amplify His 'Invasion' Claim." *New York Times*, August 5.

Karpf, D. 2016. *Analytic activism: Digital listening and the new political strategy*. New York: Oxford University Press.

Kreiss, D., R. G. Lawrence, and S. C. McGregor. 2020. "Political Identity Ownership: Symbolic Contests to Represent Members of the Public." *Social Media + Society*. https://doi.org/10.1177/2056305120926495

Levendusky, M. 2009. *The partisan sort: How liberals became Democrats and conservatives became Republicans*. Chicago: University of Chicago Press.

Marwick, A. E., and D. Boyd. 2011. "I tweet honestly, I tweet passionately: Twitter users, context collapse, and the imagined audience." *New Media & Society* 13(1): 114–33.

Mason, L. 2018. *Uncivil agreement: How politics became our identity*. Chicago: University of Chicago Press.

McGregor, S. C. 2018. "Personalization, social media, and voting: Effects of candidate self-personalization on vote intention." *New Media & Society* 20(3): 1139–60.

McGregor, S. C. 2020. "'Taking the Temperature of the Room': How political campaigns use social media to understand and represent public opinion." *Public Opinion Quarterly* 84(S1): 1–21.

McGregor, S. C., R. G. Lawrence, and A. Cardona. 2017. "Personalization, gender, and social media: Gubernatorial candidates' social media strategies." *Information, Communication & Society* 20(2): 264–83.

McIlwain, C. D. 2019. *Black Software: The Internet and Racial Justice, from the AfroNet to Black Lives Matter.* New York: Oxford University Press.

Mendelberg, T. 2017. *The race card: Campaign strategy, implicit messages, and the norm of equality.* Princeton: Princeton University Press.

Metz, M., S. Kruikemeier, and S. Lecheler. 2019. "Personalization of politics on Facebook: Examining the content and effects of professional, emotional and private self-personalization." *Information, Communication & Society.* https://doi.org/10.1 080/1369118X.2019.1581244

Newman, B. J., S. Shah, and L. Collingwood. 2018. "Race, place, and building a base: Latino population growth and the nascent Trump campaign for president." *Public Opinion Quarterly* 82(1): 122–34.

Penney, J. 2017. "Social media and citizen participation in 'official' and 'unofficial' electoral promotion: A structural analysis of the 2016 Bernie Sanders digital campaign." *Journal of Communication* 67(3): 402–23.

Perrin, A. J., and M. Adesina Ifatunji. 2020. "Race, Immigration, and Support for Donald Trump: Evidence From the 2018 North Carolina Election." *Sociological Forum.* https://doi.org/10.1111/socf.12600

Serazio, M. 2017. "Branding politics: Emotion, authenticity, and the marketing culture of American political communication." *Journal of Consumer Culture* 17(2): 225–41.

Sides, J., M. Tesler, and L. Vavreck. 2019. *Identity crisis: The 2016 presidential campaign and the battle for the meaning of America.* Princeton: Princeton University Press.

Stanyer, J. 2013. *Intimate politics: Publicity, privacy and the personal lives of politicians in media saturated democracies.* Hoboken, NJ: John Wiley & Sons.

Tajfel, H., M. G. Billig, R. P. Bundy, and C. Flament. 1971. "Social categorization and intergroup behaviour." *European Journal of Social Psychology* 1(2): 149–78.

Valentino, N. and L. M. Vandenbroek. 2017. "Political Communication, Information Processing, and Social Groups." In *The Oxford Handbook of Political Communication*, edited by K. Kenski and K. H. Jamieson. New York: Oxford University Press. https://doi.org/10.1093/oxfordhb/9780199793471.013.56

Van Aelst, P., T. Sheafer, and J. Stanyer. 2011. "The personalization of mediated political communication: A review of concepts, operationalizations and key findings." *Journalism* 13(2): 203–20.

The View. 2019. "Pete Buttigieg on Gaining Popularity and Faith in Politics." March 22. https://www.youtube.com/watch?v=laSUhvHZMLI&feature=emb_title&ab _channel=TheView

Wahl-Jorgensen, K. 2019. *Emotions, media and politics.* Hoboken, NJ: John Wiley & Sons.

Webster, J. G., and T. B. Ksiazek. 2012. "The dynamics of audience fragmentation: Public attention in an age of digital media." *Journal of Communication* 62(1): 39–56.

White, K. C. 2018. *The branding of right-wing activism: The news media and the Tea Party.* New York: Oxford University Press.

Chapter Appendix: Interview Map

Script to read:

Hi, I am NAME, working on a research project on political information with the University of North Carolina at Chapel Hill. I am hoping to ask you a few questions about how the campaign crafts appeals to specific groups in the electorate. We hope that this study will contribute to our knowledge of how campaigns connect with voters and vie to represent them.

The interview will take about ten minutes. We will not ask for your name or any other identifying information. We will only identify the campaign that you work for. We hope to audio record this interview with your consent for transcription purposes only. After we complete the transcription process, we will destroy the audio file.

Do we have your consent to be interviewed?

Do we have your consent to audio record this interview?

Campaign:

Role:

Location of Interview:

Date: _____

1. Describe your role on the campaign.
2. Broadly describe what types of people are important for your campaign/candidate to appeal to.
3. Describe your campaign's strategies for reaching these people and broadly how you develop messaging/outreach strategies.
   a. Candidate speeches?
   b Candidate rallies?
   c. Campaign field operations (door-to-door contact)?
   d. Campaign television advertisements?
   e. Campaign social media posts?
   f. Campaign social media advertisements?
4. Describe how your campaign conducts its outreach in these various domains.
   a. Do you identify in advance individuals that you will contact?
      i. On what basis do you prioritize these individuals?
      ii. Can you provide examples of these types of individuals?

b. Do you identify in advance groups that you will appeal to?
   i. On what basis do you prioritize these groups?
   ii. Can you provide examples of these types of groups?
c. For these individuals and groups, how do you decide on messaging and types of appeals?

5. Broadly, how do you go about conducting interpersonal or organizational outreach to civic, religious, and other nonpolitical groups or affiliated individuals?

6. Broadly, how do you see your candidate's strategy in relation to other candidates vying for the same office?

CHAPTER 2

Trending Politics

How the Internet Has Changed Political News Coverage

Kevin Wagner, Florida Atlantic University,
and Jason Gainous, Duke Kunshan University

There is no question that the Internet is at the forefront of modern American politics. Politicians regularly announce policies, positions, and proposals through social media channels. Former President Trump used the social media platform Twitter so much that a federal court ruled that he could not block users, as his account was essentially a government outlet. "Twitter is not just an official channel of communication for the President; it is his most important channel of communication" (*Knight Institute v. Trump* 2019). Twitter, which allows users to send out short messages to potentially large numbers of followers- sometimes called microblogging - has become one of the central platforms for the dissemination of information thanks in part to its use by then President Trump. It has an estimated 275 million users, and that number is growing (Clement 2019). Not only is the Internet the source of much news, but legacy media outlets often are reflecting the discussions occurring on digital platforms. In modern American politics, the digital sphere is both a source of information and a venue for political communication. In this chapter, we examine how politicians are using social media to control and manipulate news coverage, and we consider the effect on the political process.

Online political discourse alters the political calculus in the United States by shifting who controls information, who consumes information, and how that information is distributed (Gainous and Wagner 2011). Bimber and

Davis found in seminal early work that while candidates are moving to the Internet, voters are likely to be reinforced in their positions rather than persuaded by the websites. Bimber and Davis show a remarkable foresight in anticipating the cooption of this technology by political actors (2003). In *Tweeting to Power*, we posited that online platforms exist outside the traditional media machine, allowing political actors—including parties and candidates—to shape and dictate their content (Gainous and Wagner 2014).

Below, we consider how political coverage has changed in the Internet age as a result of politicians mediating between the media and the consumer. Platforms such as Facebook and Twitter offer the opportunity for a new information flow that is no longer being structured and limited by legacy media. It allows the politician to highlight news stories and assemble information in a way that establishes a favorable narrative. The surviving legacy media, older and more static, becomes integrated in the nimbler social media structure, which can highlight or bypass extant media based on the constructed streams of content provided by politicians and political actors. As a result, modern American political news coverage is changing, and the consequence is likely altering the effect of the information on the formation of attitudes, and ultimately shifting the nature and function of the political process.

The Age of the Politician Journalist

The Internet has been moving in the direction of more user-generated content for some time, with the first iteration of the idea referred to as Web 2.0 (see Stanyer 2008). The Internet morphed from static pages to a series of platforms that allowed users to personalize news or entertainment web pages by indicating what they want to see, hear, or read (Gainous and Wagner 2011). Social media is the latest iteration of this evolution based on a user-defined experience. With the user choosing content, it has altered the relationship between political media and U.S. political actors. Social media differs from traditional media in not just speed and scope of distribution, but in the character of the interaction between the creator of the news and the consumer of the news. On a social media platform, the range of available news is the result of user choices interacting with extant networks of content that are constructed from a range of possible sources such as friends, or even political influencers. Interestingly, the engagement with the material and the nature of the interaction widens and deepens as new protocols and applications are added and expanded. Indeed, social media grows more interactive, engaging, and accessible with each iteration in a way that can crowd out other mediums (Gainous and Wagner 2014).

This opportunity is not invisible to political actors, and they have become more adept at engaging with consumers of social media. The online platforms engage with both newsmakers and the traditional media, and savvy candidates are able to leverage that interaction to increase the visibility and dissemination of their message. Indeed, media outlets are financially motivated to engage with the candidates and their social media when those candidates can drive large numbers of page views that increase media revenue (Karpf 2016). One relatively early example of this phenomena was during the 2012 Democratic National Convention. While President Obama's speech was being delivered, more than 50,000 Obama-related tweets per minute were occurring. The three-day event generated nearly 10 million tweets that were directly relevant, and countless more that were related in some way, but not easily sorted or measured (Twitter 2012). President Trump proved particularly adept at managing the hybrid environment to maximize coverage. While he still used traditional rallies, interviews, and photo opportunities, he paralleled those with social media commentary and amplification, where voters were able to participate with comments and expand the narrative (Wells et al. 2016).

The evolution of the Internet and digital platforms into an opportunity structure dominated by political actors driving messaging is, in part, a result of governance choices made in the United States. The role of the Internet and social media in the political sphere can be traced back to the liability shield given to most posted content (Kosseff 2019). As the Internet was becoming a more public and political forum, it was not clear whether online content providers were publishers. This distinction is legally significant, because publishers are responsible for their content and can be sued for harassment or libel. Since many Internet companies host posts and information they did not create, and because posts happen frequently, many platforms could not exist if they were legally responsible for anything a user posted.

Interestingly, some early legal decisions suggested that if an Internet company moderated or edited the post, they could be liable as publishers. So companies either had to let anything be posted, or nothing at all. In essence, limiting objectionable content such as profanity or creating rules limiting the scope or nature of the user-created content made an online platform a publisher. This was essentially the finding in *Stratton v. Prodigy*, where the court held that the online company Prodigy was liable for an allegedly defamatory post on its online forum because it exercised editorial control over the space through rules, board moderators, and screening software (1995). To address this, Congress in 1996 passed the Communications Decency Act, "CDA," stating in section 230, "No provider or user of an interactive computer service shall be treated as the publisher or speaker of any information provided by another information content provider." This meant that the platform could moderate their content and not be liable, which has arguably allowed the Internet to become the popular and largely unregulated forum that it is today. More simply, we treat Internet platforms like the Post Office or a newsstand. They deliver the information, but are not liable for what is said. Law Professor Jeff Kosseff popularized the importance of section 230 of the CDA through his book *The Twenty-Six Words That Created the Internet* (2019).

The CDA was at best an imperfect solution, and the law has opened online platforms to criticism for their actions or inactions. Any rules that these platforms create can be viewed by some critics as bias. Indeed, the absence of rules or the uneven enforcement of them can be seen as bias as well. As a result, some opponents of the CDA, including President Trump, have called for either a repeal or a reinterpretation of section 230, with the aim of preventing or limiting bias (Executive Order 13925 2020). How that should be done is unclear. While President Trump highlighted his concerns about section 230 in his executive order (2020), it is probably worth noting that he and other political actors from across the partisan spectrum have been among the largest beneficiaries of the provision. It is likely that companies like Twitter would have been reluctant to host provocative political posts if they could have been held liable for the content or veracity of his statements. In the absence of section 230, the Internet would likely have been a far less open forum for political coverage and discourse, as large corporations are often risk-averse.

Interestingly, the liability shield has not generated the amount of editing and moderating that some sought, and critics feared. In a statement released on Twitter, Senator Ron Wyden, one of the authors of the CDA, noted that "Section 230 does not prevent Internet companies from moderating offensive or false content" (2020). As the shield does not require neutrality to be operative, companies can be proactive in monitoring and moderating content, but largely have been restrained or inconsistent when it comes to limiting or removing content. Resultantly, there is some disappointment that the liability shield provided by section 230 did not result in Internet companies being more assertive in moderating the posts and removing objectionable content. Twitter's initial notification questioning the veracity of President Trump's tweets (2020) likely generated such a negative reaction from the president and his supporters because it was so unusual at the time. Twitter and other social media have been reluctant to moderate prominent political figures while they are in office.

Indeed, Facebook's leadership has largely declined to act in this arena despite their rules of conduct, which appear to mandate that they do so (Isaac et al. 2020). Following the 2016 election, Facebook founder and CEO Mark Zuckerberg flatly rejected the idea that false news stories about Hillary Clinton circulated through Facebook had anything to do with the result. Shortly after the election, he stated, "Personally, I think the idea that fake news on Facebook—it's a very small amount of the content—to think it influenced the election in any way is a pretty crazy idea" (quoted in Nieva 2016). Research on the election has suggested the opposite. Guess, Nyhan, and Reifler found that Facebook was a key vector of exposure to fake news during the election (2018). Indeed, even politicians at the time recognized the danger. Speaking at a Clinton campaign rally in 2016, then-President Obama warned about the dangers of false information on Facebook. "As long as it's on Facebook, and people can see it, as long as it's on social media, people start believing it" (quoted in Nieva 2016).

Facebook has backed away from the notion that it has no influence, but the company has repeatedly indicated a reluctance to limit or moderate false content provided by political actors, deferring some of those decisions to an oversight board. Despite criticism, Zuckerberg stated, "And while I certainly worry about an erosion of truth, I don't think most people want to live in a world where you can only post things that tech companies judged to be 100 percent true" (quoted in Romm 2020). In response to Facebook's refusal to remove a Trump campaign video that falsely claimed Democratic presidential candidate Joe Biden committed corrupt acts in Ukraine, Massachusetts Senator Elizabeth Warren deliberately created an inaccurate political ad posted to the social network that claimed Facebook and Zuckerberg had endorsed Trump's reelection. Facebook permitted both ads to be distributed (Wong 2019).

Indeed, the concerns about "fake news" are continually leading to new proposals and debates over the role the U.S. government or leading social media platforms should have in contesting propaganda and misinformation available online (West 2017). However, trusting either the government or the web companies themselves to determine the truthfulness of their content is at best worrisome. Despite the popularity of social media for accessing news, Americans are increasingly wary and concerned about the control these platforms exercise over the news on their sites (Shearer and Grieco 2019). The fear of both action and inaction has resulted in an online political sphere that is filled with unverified information constructed by user choices and platform algorithms and irregularly moderated by anyone. Under the liability shield, social media is an opportunity structure to reach voters, which is limited more by the creativity of the content author than by the value or veracity of the actual content. Social media sites are increasingly popular with politicians and interest groups since they are inexpensive to use, and since there is no platform liability for deceptive content, the platforms themselves are open and permissive, especially to popular accounts that draw users. It is also convenient, as the dominant platforms can reach both voters and media, and both the posting and consuming of content can be done almost anywhere there is connectivity.

Unsurprisingly, political use of social media has exploded. Members of Congress are using Twitter at almost all times, including during major national or world events and on a range of social and political topics (Clark and Evans 2020). There is already a database of millions of tweets just from members of Congress, with tens of thousands of new tweets being added every month (TweetCongress.com 2020). Online communications can exist in parallel to other mediums, meaning that politicians can comment in real time to their supporters and other media during an event. They can highlight those media sources that are favorable and disseminate them to their followers, or ignore, or perhaps denigrate, sources that show negative information or coverage. Political actors can access the audience and news providers frequently and efficiently. In the absence of substantive moderation from the social media platforms themselves, it is hard to imagine a more flexible and useful political tool. Ultimately, the politician is an active participant in not just the event, but also coverage and distribution of news about the event. The media does not simply cover the politician. Politicians cover themselves while engaging and interacting with the media with increasing degrees of sophistication and control.

With politicians driving the message, the nature of political news has changed. Prior to the digital expansion of news, journalists were forced to evaluate stories and consider not just whether they should be covered, but how that coverage should be structured. Much of the handling of politics has been grouped into three spheres: views or advocacy to which there is consensus, views that are deviant and thus not covered, and areas where there is legitimate dispute. As to the latter, journalists were to try and cover all sides fairly and comprehensively (Hallin 1994). These categories do evolve. Discussions of race or gender limitations on achievement, which were once part of media coverage of politics and society, are now no longer acceptable (see, e.g., Lewis 1939). Social media has no such moderation, and as such, allows politicians to control their message and influence the scope of political coverage. This new type of message control is evident in more recent campaigns, and especially in 2016, when then-candidate Trump referred to Twitter as having his own newspaper (Savransky 2016).

Scholars have noted that the use of social media has altered traditional campaign tactics to avoid traditional media outlets, as they often filter and interpret the campaign message. Using protocols like Facebook and Twitter allowed candidates to simply avoid traditional media and still reach and target voters (Bode et al. 2011). While Twitter messaging may seem far less substantive and influential than legacy media, recent scholarship has suggested that is not the case. One study showed that campaign messages about candidates sent via Twitter resonate just as strongly with potential voters as those sent via the traditional media (Morris 2018). Further, consumers and political actors can affect the perception of traditional news stories (Prochazka et al. 2018). Social media is not just a more flexible medium. It is an increasingly influential one that politicians concentrate on to maximize their influence (Agranoff and Tabin 2011). While the medium is in the abstract open and democratizing, the political players appear to be among the most able designers and interpreters of content. It is no surprise that they are increasingly active in engaging on this platform as a means to push their political narratives and define the news.

Sampling Political Social Media

While in theory, controlling the flow of political coverage through social media platforms seems easy, in practice, it is more complex. A good social media strategy involves working through new and existing media to reach constituents with images and messaging that they prefer. This requires to some degree a consistency of the message, made-for-media events, and soliciting and amplifying particular media outlets in order to obtain the most sympathetic coverage possible. As noted above, while social media can appear separate from the traditional media, in truth, they interact in a hybrid fashion (Chadwick 2017). Indeed, the general proposition of working through the media is still an important political skill (Wells et al. 2016).

The relationship between the political actor, traditional media, and social media is interactive. Online media provides both an opportunity structure for political actors, and a challenge to keep the eyes and attention of voters. The political actor is, in one sense, competing with traditional media as the source of information. Even on the Internet, there are often digital versions of traditional media outlets. There are also a large number of new online media outlets. There are numerous blogs, both specialized and general, web-based news services, and individual reporting. Internet-based sources ranging from blogs such as Matt Drudge's *The Drudge Report*, or online newspapers such as *The Huffington Post*, *Red State*, or *Breitbart*, are growing in number. It is a sizable environment, and the political actors must compete to some degree with it for the attention of the voter. However, effective use of online coverage requires that political actors use alternative news sources to complement and distribute coverage that is consistent with either the campaign, or the political message.

Indeed, the opportunity is there, as a majority of Americans are obtaining news through social media (Shearer and Grieco 2019). We expect sophisticated political actors to take advantage of the open forum and the established networks to cater to the needs of various subsets of voters, and to use extant networks by crafting content to appeal to those users. They can author content, or simply push existing content, through the network as a means to both shape coverage and define it. While the existing media, both Internet and traditional, are still part of this process, they are competitors or allies for control of the larger narratives, which dominate the coverage. The political actors can use the diffusion of the system to provide appealing content to the user and seize control of the narrative. The Trump campaign in 2016 was particularly effective at using social media to leverage and inexpensively increase the range and magnitude of their message (Francia 2018).

Finally, while the online forum is still a relatively new addition to the political discourse, the underlying motivations for the political actors are not. Candidates seeking to win office would devote time and resources to online versions of advertising, credit claiming, and position-taking (Mayhew 1974). We would expect candidates to be motivated in part by the desire to increase their own power (Dodd 1981), support the party (Aldrich 1995), or advocate for policy (Arnold 1990). Social media should improve the targeting and effectiveness of the messaging, but it doesn't change the underlying incentives.

We used software that interacts with Twitter's Application Programming Interface (API) to scrape all tweets from major-party U.S. congressional candidates during the 2018 midterm elections who had active campaign Twitter accounts between the end of their respective primaries and the general election. After removing inactive candidates from the data, we were left with a dataset containing 267,538 tweets from 767 different candidates for seats in both the U.S. House and Senate. We merged these data with information about candidates, including the candidate's party. We analyze these data in total elsewhere. For our purposes here, though, we selected a random sample of 100 tweets containing hyperlinks, and we went through each of these links to qualitatively assess whether candidates disproportionately posted links to stories that painted them, their party, or their positions in a positive light. We decided to keep this random selection relatively small given the difficulty involved in qualitative examination of large datasets.[1] The evidence was clear that they, indeed, try to control the flow of information to benefit themselves. Here we select a few anecdotal examples to explore how they are doing exactly this.

The pattern that emerges from this analysis suggests that candidates tweeted most often by amplifying their message through links to exisiting content, including news stories in online versions of traditional media as well as purely online platforms. The messages varied, but fell mostly into categories including campaign announcements, attack/negative campaigning, and personal characteristics about the candidates. Previous research has already established that policy-centered tweets tended to be from candidates who ran unsuccessful bids for office (Gainous and Wagner 2014). Nonetheless, the use of existing media to reinforce the message was quite clear in our data of the Twitter use. Nearly 75 percent of the tweets we reviewed used a hyperlink to additional content, much of it to political media sources that highlighted the candidates' standing (polling), positions, or personal characteristics.

We explore some examples of this use of social media below:

Example: Louis Gohmert, Republican House incumbent

Tweet: #MigrantCaravan is 'Going to Find Out We Have a Very Strong President, Not a Weak-Kneed Guy Afraid of Hurting People's Feelings' https://t.co/5u2cDyAXV1 via @cnsnews

This style of messaging is increasingly common. Congressman Louis Gohmert is leveraging a news story to reinforce his position and alignment with President Trump on the issue of immigration. This interaction between Gohmert and the Conservative News Service (CNS) is particularly reinforcing. The article linked is essentially the coverage of Gohmert's own statements. Instead of simply pushing his own message in isolation, he is linking

---

1. This random selection produced a relatively diverse sample of tweets: 77 percent Democrat (not surprising given that they tweeted much more frequently than Republicans in the full population set), 33 states, 8 percent from the Senate as opposed to the House, 68 percent from challengers (who were much more likely to tweet), 41 percent female, and 19 percent non-white.

it to the media coverage and reinforcing the message through social media. In that sense, the message gets uttered once live and then repeated by the news article and the social media reference to the article. CNS' online platform, which was linked to the Gohmert tweet, benefits as well. The tweet sends page views to CNS and encourages similar coverage since it will drive even more readership. This interplay is common and shows the increasingly symbiotic relationship between the candidate and the media. It is also illustrative of how the candidate has a far larger role in controlling the narrative.

Example: Dina Titus, Democrat House incumbent

Tweet: WOW. The #GOP's reason to object to insurance covering prenatal care? "Why should men pay for it?" Watch: #Trumpcare #ProtectOurCare https://t.co/Q55nG1Un8j

In this tweet, incumbent Congresswoman Dina Titus uses a video filmed from the floor of Congress, but instead of embedding the video directly into her email, she links to the video hosted by National Abortion and Reproductive Rights Action League (NARAL). The tweet is both position-taking and a link to potential support through a network of like-minded supporters and donors. It both amplifies her support for the pro-choice position and connects her message to a receptive audience.

Example: Andy Barr, Republican House incumbent

Tweet: Liberal Amy McGrath does not share our #KY06 values. She supports taxpayer-funded abortion at any time during a pregnancy, for any reason. She's said so herself—That's too liberal for Kentucky. Watch our new ad now! https://t.co/gMqjM6iwXt

This tweet is an attempt to leverage a political advertisement. It serves two media functions. Buying time on television is expensive, and distribution through social media is cost-effective. Second, even if the video is played on television, social media will allow the advertisement to reach at least some different consumers who may share it with others who could not otherwise see the commercial. Potential consumers of the commercial are journalists and other political actors who may have missed or dismissed a television buy. Indeed, the dissemination through social media may result in television airing the advertisement without cost. Finally, the audience that is likely to see both the television and online distribution are going to have the message reinforced.

Example: Thomas Carper, Democratic Senate incumbent

Tweet: We don't have to choose between protecting our environment and building a strong economy. We can have both, and our country's history has proven that to be true. Read my OpEd: https://t.co/MOVYb0k642 via @delawareonline

This tweet from Senator Carper references an article the senator wrote for the local paper, *The News Journal*. The link is to the online version of the op-ed he wrote concerning environmental policy. Similar to Congressman Gohmert, Carper is using the media to host his message, and then reinforcing and amplifying it through social media. The largest difference is that in this case, the media source is the online forum for the legacy newspaper. However, the underlying dynamic is similar. Both are attempting to use social media to drive messaging through portals that cover the political sphere, with the goal of directing the conversation.

Messaging Political News and the Future

In this chapter, we set out to paint a picture of the increasingly dynamic political media sphere that has developed as a result of the penetration of the Internet, and social media in particular, into the U.S. public domain. The way politics in the United States is covered is changing, as politicians and media compete to be the sources of news. Yet the political actors are still seeking to use the presumed objectivity of news outlets as a way to reinforce their message, and media outlets are increasingly dependent on the ability of policymakers with large social networks to drive viewership and consumers to their product. Part of the success of President Trump in garnering free media coverage was his ability to focus attention (Ouyang and Waterman 2020) and to drive users to complementary media websites (Karf 2016). Modern political media is involved in a cooperative competition with its own subject.

President Trump is perhaps one of the clearest examples of how this relationship swings from hostility to praise. His social media feeds are filled with compliments for the coverage he received from Fox News. When he is pleased, he will ask his followers to watch the channel and direct them to specific anchors or programs. This pattern was evident from the beginning of his presidency when he lauded positive news coverage on Twitter, stating, "A fantastic day and evening in Washington D.C. Thank you to @FoxNews and so many other news outlets for the GREAT reviews of the speech!" (Nussbaum 2017). However, he is quick to challenge any contrary coverage and regularly tries to delegitimize the media when it covers news that he finds unfavorable. In two successive tweets, he attacked the media with a now-familiar refrain, "The press is doing everything within their power to fight the magnificence of the phrase, MAKE AMERICA GREAT AGAIN!" Trump tweeted. He then added, "They can't stand the fact that this Administration has done more than virtually any other Administration in its first 2 yrs. They are truly the ENEMY OF THE PEOPLE!" (Samuels 2019).

Even Fox News was not immune from the President Trump's Twitter account when he perceived the coverage as being insufficiently laudatory. After Fox News host Neil Cavuto challenged the President's advice that Americans take hydroxychloroquine to prevent contracting COVID-19, the President responded harshly on Twitter. He wrote, "Many will disagree, but @FoxNews is doing nothing to help Republicans, and me, get re-elected on November 3rd. Sure, there are some truly GREAT people on Fox, but you also have some real 'garbage' littered all over the network, people like Dummy Juan Williams, Schumerite Chris Hahn, Richard Goodstein, Donna Brazile, Neil Cavuto, and many others." The president then added through Twitter, "They repeat the worst of the Democrat speaking points, and lies. All of the good is totally nullified, and more. Net Result = BAD! CNN & MSDNC [sic] are all in for the Do Nothing Democrats! Fox WAS Great!" (Ward 2020). These attacks were against a network that has hosted him regularly and largely treated him well. Even more revealing is Mr. Trump's underlying assumption that the network had an obligation to help Republicans, and its failure was not in failing to cover the news, but rather for being insufficiently effective at pushing stories and narratives that were supportive to him.

Part of the reason for President Trump's attack on the media is clearly strategic competition. If the news media is considered unreliable, then President Trump, or other political leaders, are the only source of truth, and there is no way to hold a politician accountable. Democracies are dependent on an informed citizenship to operate (Wagner 2010). The irony of the modern political arena is that there has never been more information available, but so many Americans are unwilling to consume it, as it is viewed as less reliable than the politician it is purporting to cover. A Harris Poll survey conducted in 2019 found that approximately one-third of Americans believe that the press is actually the enemy of the American people. The most receptive to that message are Republicans, according to the survey, as 51 percent agreed with that characterization (Bonn 2019). Further, as politicians are driving viewership, the political actors behave as if the media owe politicians deference for influencing the size of the audience. If there was a battle for control of political coverage, then for a significant number of Americans, the politicians have defeated the media. This can result in an echo chamber where only the politician is perceived as truthful.

Nonetheless, there might be a limit on the ability of political actors to define news and drive their own political coverage to the larger electorate. That power is tested by news stories that are not easily dismissed or redefined along partisan or political lines. The year 2020 saw several large challenges to President Trump's media narrative, including the COVID-19 pandemic and the protest movements that arose from the death of George Floyd at the hands of a Minnesota police officer. While measures on the immediate impact of these events were likely too early to be definitive, there was a clear indicator that President Trump was not able to control the narrative. Despite attempts to push the blame for COVID-19 onto the Chinese, the CDC, and other state officials, the measures of President Trump's handling of the pandemic were harsh. Similarly, despite President Trump's use of his Twitter account to call for a military response against the protestors, the majority of Americans were supportive of the protests (Stableford 2020). At least in the short term, when the event is widely seen as significant and broadly covered, the control of a political actor over the media message appears to be more limited.

Works Cited

Agranoff, Craig, and Herbert Tabin. 2011. *Socially Elected: How To Win Elections Using Social Media.* New York: Pendant Publishing.

Aldrich, John H. 1995. *Why Parties?* Chicago: University of Chicago Press.

Arnold, R. Douglas. 1990. *The Logic of Congressional Action.* New Haven: Yale University Press.

Bimber, Bruce A., and Richard Davis. 2003. *Campaigning Online: The Internet in U.S. Elections.* New York: Oxford University Press.

Bode, Leticia. 2012. "Facebooking It to the Polls: A Study in Online Social Networking and Political Behavior." *Journal of Information Technology & Politics* 9(4): 352–69.

Bode, Leticia, Kajsa Dalrymple, and Dhavan Shah. 2011. "Politics in 140 Characters or Less: Campaign Communication, Network Interaction, and Political Participation on Twitter." Paper presented at the 2011 annual meeting of the American Political Science Association.

Bonn, Tess. 2019. "Poll: One-third of Americans say news media is the 'enemy of the people.'" *The Hill.* July 2. https://thehill.com/hilltv/what-americas-thinking/451311-poll-a-third-of-americans-say-news-media-is-the-enemy-of-the-people

Chadwick, A. 2017. *The Hybrid Media System: Politics and Power*. New York: Oxford University Press.

Clark, J., and H. Evans. 2020. "Let's Talk about Sex: Examining the Factors Influencing Congressional Response to #MeToo on Twitter." *PS: Political Science & Politics* 53(1): 51–56. doi:10.1017/S1049096519001124.

Clement, J. 2019. "Social Media & User-Generated Content." *Statista*. https://www.statista.com/statistics/303681/twitter-users-worldwide/

Dodd, Lawrence C. 1977. "Congress and the Quest for Power." In *Congress Reconsidered*, edited by Lawrence C. Dodd and Bruce I. Oppenheimer, 269–307. Washington, DC: CQ Press.

Francia, P. L. 2018. "Free Media and Twitter in the 2016 Presidential Election: The Unconventional Campaign of Donald Trump." *Social Science Computer Review* 36(4): 440–55. https://doi.org/10.1177/0894439317730302

Gainous, Jason, and Kevin M. Wagner. 2007. "The Electronic Ballot Box: A Rational Voting Model and The Internet." *American Review of Politics* 28 (Spring and Summer): 19–35.

Gainous, Jason, and Kevin M. Wagner. 2011. *Rebooting American Politics: The Internet Revolution*. Lanham, MD: Rowman and Littlefield.

Guess, A., B. Nyhan, and J. Reifler. 2018. "Selective exposure to misinformation: Evidence from the consumption of fake news during the 2016 US presidential campaign." *European Research Council* 9(3): 4.

Hallin, D. C. 1994. *We Keep America on Top of the World: Television Journalism and the Public Sphere*. Guatemala: Routledge.

Isaac, Mike, Cecilia Kang, and Sheera Frenkel. 2020. "Zuckerberg Defends Hands-Off Approach to Trump's Posts." *New York Times*. June 2. https://www.nytimes.com/2020/06/02/technology/zuckerberg-defends-facebook-trump-posts.html

Karpf, D. 2016. "The clickbait candidate." *Chronicle of Higher Education*. June 19. http://chronicle.com/article/The-Clickbait-Candidate/236815?cid=rc_right

Knight First Amendment Inst. at Columbia Univ. v. Trump, No. 1:17-cv-5205 (S.D.N.Y.), No. 18–1691 (2d Cir.).

Kosseff, Jeff. 2019. *The Twenty-six Words that Created the Internet*. Ithaca: Cornell University Press.

Lewis, Gretchen. 1939. "So I Married a Jew." *The Atlantic*. https://www.theatlantic.com/magazine/archive/1939/01/i-married-a-jew/306262/

Mayhew, David. 1974. *Congress: The Electoral Connection*. New Haven: Yale University Press.

Morris, D. S. 2018. "Twitter Versus the Traditional Media: A Survey Experiment Comparing Public Perceptions of Campaign Messages in the 2016 U.S. Presidential Election." *Social Science Computer Review* 36(4): 456–68. https://doi.org/10.1177/0894439317721441

Nieva, Richard. 2016. "Zuckerberg: Fake news on Facebook affected election? That's 'crazy.' Facebook's CEO talks about the News Feed's role in the election and the responsibility his company has to its almost 2 billion users—most of whom are not actually dead." *CNET*. November 11. https://www.cnet.com/news/facebook-mark-zuckerberg-fake-news-affect-election-techonomy-donald-trump-crazy/

Nussbaum, Mathew. 2017. "Trump tweets praise of Fox News for inaugural coverage." *Fox News*. January 21. https://www.politico.com/story/2017/01/trump-fox-news-tweet-233963

Ouyang, Y., and R. W. Waterman. 2020. "Trump Tweets: A Desire for Attention." In *Trump, Twitter, and the American Democracy. The Evolving American Presidency.* Cham: Palgrave Macmillan.

Prochazka, F., P. Weber, and W. Schweiger. 2018. "Effects of civility and reasoning in user comments on perceived journalistic quality." *Journalism Studies.* https://doi.org/10.1080/1461670x.2016.116497

Romm, Tony. 2019. "Zuckerberg: Standing for Voice and Free Expression." *Washington Post.* October 17. https://www.washingtonpost.com/technology/2019/10/17/zuckerberg-standing-voice-free-expression/

Samuels, Brett. 2019. "Trump ramps up rhetoric on media, calls press 'the enemy of the people.'" *The Hill.* April 5. https://thehill.com/homenews/administration/437610-trump-calls-press-the-enemy-of-the-people

Savransky, R. 2016. "Trump compares Twitter to owning his own newspaper." *The Hill.* April 3. http://thehill.com/blogs/ballot-box/presidential-races/275046-trump-compares-twitter-to-owning-his-own-newspaper

Shearer, E., and Elizabeth Greico. 2019. *Americans Are Wary of the Role Social Media Sites Play in Delivering the News.* Washington, DC: Pew Research Center. https://www.journalism.org/wp-content/uploads/sites/8/2019/09/PJ_2019.09.25_Social-Media-and-News_FINAL.pdf

Stableford, Dylan. 2020. "Polls: Trump approval drops amid George Floyd protests, coronavirus." *Yahoo News.* June 8. https://news.yahoo.com/trump-polls-biden-george-floyd-coronavirus-job-approval-152747803.html

Stanyer, James. 2008. "Web 2.0 and the Transformation of News and Journalism." In *The Handbook of Internet Politics*, edited by A. Chadwick and P. N. Howard. London: Routledge.

Stratton Oakmont, Inc. v. Prodigy Services Co., 1995 WL 323710 (N.Y. Sup. Ct. 1995). https://h2o.law.harvard.edu/cases/4540/export

Trump, Donald J. @realdonaldtrump. 2020. There is NO WAY (ZERO!) that Mail-In Ballots will be anything less than substantially fraudulent. Mail boxes will be robbed, ballots will be forged & even illegally printed out & fraudulently signed. The Governor of California is sending Ballots to millions of people, anyone . . . [Tweet]. May 26. https://twitter.com/realDonaldTrump/status/1265255835124539392?s=20.

Twitter Blog. 2012. http://blog.twitter.com/2012/09/dnc2012-night-3-obamas-speech-sets.html

Wagner, Kevin M. 2010. "Rewriting the Guarantee Clause: Justifying Direct Democracy in the Constitution." *Willamette Law Review* 47: 66–79.

Ward, Myah. 2020. "Trump attacks Fox News for 'doing nothing to help Republicans, and me,' get reelected." *Politico.* May 21. https://www.politico.com/news/2020/05/21/trump-attacks-fox-news-doing-nothing-to-help-republicans-in-november-273612

Wells, Chris, Dhavan V. Shah, Jon C. Pevehouse, JungHwan Yang, Ayellet Pelled, Frederick Boehm, Josephine Lukito, Shreenita Ghosh, and Jessica L. Schmidt. 2016. "How Trump Drove Coverage to the Nomination: Hybrid Media Campaigning." *Political Communication* 33(4): 669–76. DOI: 10.1080/10584609.2016.1224416.

West, Darrell. 2017. *How to combat fake news and disinformation.* Washington, DC: Brookings Institute. https://www.brookings.edu/research/how-to-combat-fake-ne ws-and-disinformation/

Wong, Julia Carrie. 2019. "Elizabeth Warren trolls Facebook with 'false' Zuckerberg ad." *The Guardian.* October 11. https://www.theguardian.com/technology/2019 /oct/11/elizabeth-warren-facebook-zuckerberg-trump-troll

CHAPTER 3

Feminism, Social Media, and Political Campaigns

Justin Trudeau and Sadiq Khan

Kaitlynn Mendes, University of Western Ontario and
Diretman Dikwal-Bot, De Montfort University

Brexit, #MeToo, trans rights, Black Lives Matter, indigenous movements, and the rise of nationalist populism: as we write this chapter in the summer of 2020, we reflect on the rise of various high-profile campaigns and populist and social justice movements that have emerged over the past few years. As tensions rise and the public weigh in on issues such as institutional racism, homophobia, sexism, colonialism, classism, nationalism, and xenophobia, it is natural that these issues make their way into political debates and electoral campaigns. But in our increasingly digitized world, how do politicians use the media—old and new—to communicate their position on issues relating to identity politics during electoral campaigns?

While there are a range of issues we could have focused on, the global spread of #MeToo and the rise of a bourgeoning "fourth wave" feminist movement (Rivers 2017) combined with recent visibility of many self-declared feminist world leaders (Jacinda Ardern, New Zealand; Boris Johnson, United Kingdom; Theresa May, United Kingdom; Sanna Marin, Finland) makes feminism a timely choice. For example, in 2015, while on the campaign trail during the Canadian general election, Liberal leader Justin Trudeau tweeted: "I am a feminist. I'm proud to be a feminist. #UpForDebate" (@JustinTrudeau, September 22, 2015). Although this tweet was largely ignored by the mainstream media at the time, it ignited a major media event weeks later after emerging victorious from the election, sparking discussion in both mainstream and social media. Taking Trudeau as just one example, this chapter explores how and to what extent politicians use (social) media to construct their feminist identity in political campaigns. Adopting a case study approach, we explore two contemporary leaders who declared themselves feminists during political campaigns: Canadian prime minister Justin Trudeau (2015–2019; 2019–present) and London mayor Sadiq Khan (2016–present).

Throughout the research, we explore not only the extent to which these candidates harness mainstream and social media in constructing their feminist identities but the nuances in the use of each form. We ask questions such as: are there key differences in how candidates construct their feminist identities between media forms? How might the message or performance differ depending on the medium? Does the use of social media open up a dialogical relationship with candidates that may shift the campaign (or radically transform political processes)? We conclude by thinking through what analysis of identity politics reveals about the potential ways political campaigning has changed in a digital age. Drawing from a thematic analysis of 406 international mainstream news articles, both candidates' Instagram feeds, and an analysis of each candidate's tweets, we argue that for these candidates social media platforms were not the key space used to develop their feminist identities during campaigns, but were instead ancillary tools used to back up their feminist claims. The mainstream media remained the key space through which their feminist identities were constructed. We do however recognize social media's potential for communicating their feminist beliefs, values, and "wins" once in post. Furthermore, although social media provides a platform for members of the public to question or challenge candidates' feminist identities, the absence of dialogical exchange between politicians and the general public makes it more of a space to gauge public opinion than a space to truly hold them to account or transform political processes.

Representations of Feminist Identities

Since the 1970s, scholars have explored the relationship between feminism and the media, particularly the news media (see Ashley and Olson 1998; Barker-Plummer 2000; Bradley 2003; de Benedictis et al. 2019; Dean 2010; Freeman 2001; Goddu 1999; Mendes 2011, 2015; Morris 1973; Sheridan et al. 2007; van Zoonen 1992). This research was deemed important because of recognition that the news media is a key source of information on social movements (Barker-Plummer 2000; Gitlin 2003; van Zoonen 1992). Because feminism challenges structural forms of oppression around gender, race, class, and more (see Harvey 2020), feminists, most of whom were thought to be women, have historically been constructed as deviant, shrill, radical, man-hating lesbians (see Bradley 2003; Douglas 1994; Freeman 2001; Goddu 1999; Lind and Salo 2002). While other scholars have found supportive media coverage of feminism at times, they noted that this was most likely when they weren't perceived as fundamentally challenging patriarchal ideologies (see Dean 2010; Freeman 2001; Mendes 2011; van Zoonen 1992).

These findings, however, appear out-of-date in our current "fourth wave (Rivers 2017) feminist movement, in which feminism is experiencing both unprecedented "luminosity" (Gill 2017) and "popularity" (Banet-Weiser 2018) as never before seen. Indeed, in our current climate, it is not just well-known women who embrace the feminist identity but men as well. These range from celebrities such as Benedict Cumberbatch and Joseph Gordon-Levitt, to politicians such as the United Kingdom's former deputy prime minister Nick Clegg and opposition leader Ed Miliband, who posed in *ELLE* magazine's "feminism" issue wearing a "This is What a Feminist Looks Like" T-shirt. In such a context, it has become clear that feminism is not simply "having a moment" (Gill 2017, 611) but is an identity that women *and* men are increasingly adopting. In such a context it is pertinent to explore the ways feminism is addressed in political campaigns.

Feminism and Politics

Feminism has been a major cause of political transformation, especially within the last decade. This is driven by the idea that it provides a comprehensive approach to tackling inequalities (Heger and Hoffman 2019). In this regard, Filimonov and Svensson (2017) reveal that incorporating feminist ideals (e.g., intersectionality) into governance and political campaigning helps to tackle a broad range of inequalities. However, while the increasing integration of feminism into political practice is highlighted in many studies (Bashevkin 2009; Gleeson 2017; Swift 2019; von der Lippe and Varyrynen 2011), it is also noteworthy to mention others that highlight the growing resistance to left-wing ideology and the alienation of feminism from politics (Ahl et al. 2016; Briggs 2018; Norocel 2018).

Bashevkin (2009) tracks the visibility of feminism in Canadian politics. The study shows that the willingness of female politicians to voice feminist rhetoric is closely linked to changing factors of feminist and antifeminist movements as well as parliamentary factors that include changing ideology and the competitive status of their parties. Swift (2019) particularly draws attention to conservative female politicians in the United Kingdom, such as Theresa May, Amber Rudd, and Nadine Dorries, who self-identify as feminists. The study concludes that conservative feminist politicians tend to construct their personal identity through "an abstract version" of feminism, which helps them to distance themselves from feminism as well as to adopt it when "convenient" or "necessary." On the whole, the study substantiates the conception of conservative governments as more of feminism's "strategic partners" than "allies" (Evan 2016, 631).

Recent studies also capture the social context in which feminism and political practice intersect by examining social media use among politicians for feminism-related discussions. Larrondo, Morales, and Terradillos (2019) show that the era of hashtag activism has encouraged Spanish politicians to hold feminist conversations using trending feminist hashtags such as #8deMarzoHuelgaFeminista (8 March Feminist Strike) and #MasFeminis-moQUENunca (more feminism than ever). This helped to challenge sexist stereotypes, paternalism, and the gender wage gap following the feminist strike on International Working Women's day on March 8, 2018. In the same vein, Fernandez Rovira and Villegas-Simone (2019) compare feminism-related tweets between male and female politicians in Spain. Their findings show that ideological beliefs, more than gender, determine Twitter behavior regarding feminism. This challenges the conception that women in politics are inclined to support feminism and highlights the need to explore how male politicians engage with feminist rhetoric and action. As such, our study contributes to this gap in research by providing rare insight of not only ana-lyzing the political practice of male politicians in relation to feminism but focusing on those who self-identify as feminists. Exploring this relationship is important, particularly considering a previously documented alienation between the feminist label and politicians' identity in most studies (e.g., Bashevkin 2009; Filimonov and Svensson 2017; Larrondo, Morales, and Terradillos 2019). Hence by drawing attention to the construction of politi-cians' feminist identity, this study provides more insight into the context of political practice, as well as the factors that shape politicians' behavior in relation to feminism, particularly during political campaigns.

Methodology

This chapter draws from a thematic analysis of 406 mainstream news arti-cles, taken from global media coverage of the following sitting politicians who identify as feminist: Canadian prime minister Justin Trudeau and London mayor Sadiq Khan. For each politician, we collected news articles from the start of their campaign(s) and continued data collection for six months after their victory.[1] In selecting our case studies, although there were a number of high-profile, unsuccessful female candidates we could have selected, such as Hillary Clinton (candidate in the 2016 U.S. presidential election) or Jo Swinson (Liberal Democratic Party leader in the 2019 U.K. general election), we deliberately focused on men. This was largely due to the increased visibility in recent years on male feminists (such as those featured in *ELLE* magazine's "feminism" issue) and long-standing debates around if men can be feminists (see Crowe 2013; Digby 1998; White 2008). As such, we were interested in exploring the ways in which their feminist identities as *male leaders* were constructed, presented, and challenged across media forms. In opting for a case study design (Feagin, Orum, and Sjoberg 1991), we recognize other feminist male leaders we could have selected (such as Swedish prime minister Stefan Löfven), as well as many other successful (Finnish prime minister Sanna Marin) or unsuccessful feminist female candidates (Sarah Palin, United States) that are ripe for exploring. As such, we make no claims the findings are representative of all politicians, but argue this study provides a baseline for future research.

To assess the role that (social) media plays in constructing feminist identities during political campaigns, we also carried out a thematic and semiotic analysis of all tweets and Instagram posts about feminism made by the candidates during and after their campaigns. A total of 138 tweets were identified through an advanced Twitter search using the terms "feminism," "feminist," "#feminism and #feminist," "gender," and "gender equality."[2] We then conducted a thematic analysis of a selection of public responses to these tweets. These were used to provide a general flavor of how the public responded to the politician's feminist identity, record, or position. Below we begin with our finding that social media was not the key space used by our male politicians to develop their feminist identities during their respective campaigns.

---

1. Justin Trudeau was first elected as Canadian prime minister in 2015 and was reelected in September 2019. For Sadiq Khan, we focused on his 2016 mayoral campaign. In total, we collected 263 articles about Trudeau and 143 articles about Khan.

2. A search for keywords around feminism from Trudeau's Twitter account produced six tweets, and Khan produced twenty. For terms around gender equality, a search from Trudeau produced eighty-eight results, and twenty-four from Khan.

Constructing Feminist Identities during an Election

Although our sample is unable to speak more generally about what proportion of political candidates embrace or adopt a feminist identity during political campaigns, we are able to comment on when, which medium, and how our political candidates first publicly identified as feminists during their respective campaigns.

Justin Trudeau

Liberal Party leader Justin Trudeau (alongside his Liberal Democrat rival Tom Mulcair) first announced his stance as feminist midway through the 2015 federal election campaign. This took place during a speech at an "Up for Debate" event on women's issues—an event that the sitting Conservative prime minister, Steven Harper, declined to attend. As a politician known for his strategic use of social media (Lalancette and Raynauld 2019), Trudeau restated his feminist identity the following day with a tweet: "I am a feminist. I'm proud to be a feminist. #UpForDebate" (@JustinTrudeau, September 22, 2015). Although we can't be certain why Trudeau chose the Up for Debate event to "come out" as a feminist midway through the campaign, that he first declared himself a feminist at an event coordinated by women's organizations (most of which are feminist in orientation) is likely a strategic move to win the support of left-leaning progressives specifically, and women more generally.

Yet when thinking of his use of different media forms, the fact that his first feminist tweet came the day *after* his feminist coming-out speech suggests the use of social media may have been an afterthought—indicating that Trudeau's main strategy of signaling his (feminist) values was through speeches and public events covered by the mainstream media. Indeed, aside from this one tweet, there is no further evidence of his feminist stance via Instagram. Instead, days before the event, there is a photo of him paddling down the Bow River in Calgary, and enjoying time with his family at a Montreal playground days after. Although his Instagram account more generally is used to convey his values, such as the love for nature (signaling concern and appreciation for the environment) and the commitment to family (many photos of his wife and children, akin to what we might see in a family photo album), there is no further signal of his commitment to feminism or gender equality through the 2015 campaign.

It is significant to point out that while Trudeau identified as a feminist

66   Electoral Campaigns, Media, and the New World of Digital Politics

during the 2015 campaign through his Up for Debate speech and subsequent tweet, this identity did not become mainstream or widely discussed until after his electoral win the following month. It's not clear how many more times he reiterated his feminist values while on the campaign trail through speeches, but only five mainstream news articles (less than 1 percent) mentioned his feminist position during the campaign itself, all stemming from his Up for Debate speech. While we can't be sure the extent to which the mainstream media may have ignored his speeches on feminism during the campaign, we can be sure of his feminist communication via social media. Here, aside from this one tweet, he didn't mention his feminist position again during the campaign.

Yet even an examination of this tweet is worthwhile. Although to date, it has garnered 2.8k likes, 1.7k retweets, and 260 comments, the vast majority of these interactions came several months or years after it was first posted.[3] In a similar vein, the vast majority of mainstream news articles discussing his feminist identity (99 percent) were published after his victory, with headlines such as: "25 reasons why we love new Canadian Prime Minister Justin Trudeau; He's a dope-toking, kilt-wearing, boxing feminist" (Butter 2015), and "Canada's blast of fresh air" (*The Press* 2015). Similar sentiments can be found across Twitter, with some seemingly bragging about Canada's new feminist prime minister in their retweets: "the new Canadian PM :)" (@ pyz30, October 20, 2015). Although it appears as though Trudeau began to construct himself as a feminist during the election, in reality it wasn't an identity he really began to cultivate until after his electoral win.

Indeed, although Trudeau had laid the foundation for his feminist identity during the 2015 campaign, he became more visibly linked with feminism shortly after taking office, most notably when he announced Canada's first gender balanced cabinet at a press conference. This move sparked headlines such as: "Trudeau gives Canada first cabinet with equal number of men and women" (Murphy 2015). As one article noted, the move was a "symbolic gesture" and was Trudeau's "way of winking to feminists as if to say, 'I'm on your side'" (Urback 2016). While Trudeau didn't immediately post anything about the cabinet on Instagram,[4] he took to Twitter two days later, sharing a

---

3. For example, out of the 260 comments to date, only 70 were posted within one week of the original tweet. Similarly, a scan through the 91 retweets with replies, only ten were made within the first week. It is not possible to tell via Twitter when a tweet was favorited.

4. His Instagram account was established in 2013. While there are some political posts as he became leader of the Liberal Party, the majority at this time are of a more "personal" nature—photos of him with the family (trick or treating, picking pumpkins, on holiday, taking the kids to school), "aesthetic" photos of scenery or nature, or from November 2015 onwards, carrying

video of new cabinet members being sworn in with the caption: "A Cabinet that looks like Canada. Because it's 2015" (@JustinTrudeau, November 6, 2015). This tweet directly mirrors his response when asked during a press conference why he elected a gender-balanced cabinet.

His simple soundbite answer of "Because it's 2015" became a headline in itself: "Because it's 2015: Trudeau's gender-equal cabinet makes headlines around the world, social media" (Global News, November 5). His tweet, which was sent just after 5:30 p.m. that day, mirrored these news headlines, fueling further media attention. It is also evidence of Trudeau's cultivation of a "soundbite" political culture (see Deacon et al. 2006, 227) in which politicians adopt the logic of media formats and speak in "brief, pithy and memorable phrases" (Deacon et al. 2006, 227), which the media and public are likely to pick up. As we will see below, Trudeau's reliance on the mainstream media to discuss his commitment to gender equality and feminism continued throughout his first term as prime minister, and it remained evident through his second electoral campaign in 2019.

Justin Trudeau's 2019 Reelection Campaign

Trudeau's construction of feminism was substantially different in his 2019 election battle. By this point, he had become established, particularly in the mainstream media and popular culture, as a feminist leader.[5] By 2019, his feminist identity was a major point of discussion, particularly in the mainstream media, but also among the public on social media. Yet while he maintained his feminist identity in various electoral speeches, rather than visibly using the term "feminist" on social media (as he had regularly done for the first two years after his election), he switched to a language about "gender equality." From around 2018, rhetoric about gender equality becomes visible across his social media profiles, evident through text, photos, and memes. While such content predates the 2019 election campaign, there are more posts that mention "gender equality" than feminism. For example, one tweet (figure 3.1) accompanied by a photo of Trudeau at a board meeting with around a dozen, mostly white women read: "We can't lose ground on gender

---

out political duties after he was elected (meeting cabinet members or members of the public, attending Remembrance Day celebrations, and so on).

5. By this point, many news articles carried headlines such as "Justin Trudeau: I will raise my sons to be feminists" (Parker 2016), and a range of memes circulated on social media with photos of Trudeau and quotes echoing his commitment to feminism (e.g., Pinterest sites such as "5 Awesome Feminist Quotes From the Super Yummy Justin Trudeau").

Figure 3.1. Screenshot of Justin Trudeau's tweet from October 18, 2019

equality. A re-elected Liberal government will keep making it a priority and continue collaborating with women's organizations, advocates, and groups working towards equality. Always" (@JustinTrudeau, October 18, 2019).

Yet while feminism and gender equality were not particularly prevalent across his social media profiles, particularly compared to other issues such as the environment, feminism was a relatively prominent topic of discussion across mainstream news articles. A total of 138 news articles mentioned feminism during the campaign. Yet, rather than celebratory in nature, many were skeptical, with headlines like: "Women aren't buying Trudeau's feminist act" (Lilley 2019a). Indeed, in the 2019 campaign, skepticism over Trudeau's feminist record became a news story in itself, and the topic of Trudeau's feminism became a talking point in media interviews. Not only was Trudeau asked to defend his feminist record but so were others close to him, including his wife, Sophie. In one article, titled "'I kind of laugh it off': Sophie Grégoire Trudeau says PM is not a 'fake feminist'" (Gawley 2019), she went on to list a number of actions he had taken as time as prime minister that demonstrated his commitment to feminism, including appointing a gender-balanced cabinet and creating a Ministry of Women.

One advantage of speaking about feminism to the media, particularly through rallies, speeches, and moderated formats, is the limited opportunities of dialogical exchange, enabling politicians to get their points across with minimal interruption or challenges (see also Lunt 2019). Here Trudeau has the opportunity to stake his claim as a feminist leader, and aside from questions from reporters, receives little interruptions in his attempts to persuade. As a result, one might speculate that given several scandals during his tenure as PM, it may have been safer to not open up opportunities for what Dayan calls "monstration" (2009) of his feminist credentials via social media. Perhaps Trudeau avoided speaking about feminism on social media to avoid the ways the public could use it as a critical lens to hold him to account.

Yet despite this tactic, there is ample evidence of articles using a feminist analysis to interrogate his track record ("The Prime Minister of Double Standards," Di Manno 2019), or launching a series of public polls to gauge the extent to which the public believe his claims ("1 in 4 Canadian women believe Trudeau is a feminist: poll," Burman 2019; "Poll shows women don't believe Trudeau on feminist claim," Lilley 2019b). Such articles referred to a range of events during his time as leader, including firing two prominent female cabinet members and elbowing a female MP out of the way during a tussle in the Parliament. While Trudeau continued to defend his feminist stance and track record in mainstream media interviews, his social media accounts rarely mentioned feminism or women's rights, and instead focused on other issues such as the environment, multiculturalism, and economic growth (see also Lotfi 2019). We recognize that this presents an interesting contradiction and could point to how feminism tends to be prioritized by politicians only when considered convenient or necessary (Bashevkin 2009; Swift 2019). If this is the case, it raises important questions about what it means to be a feminist leader.

Sadiq Khan

While running in the 2016 London mayoral contest, Labour candidate Sadiq Khan proudly and regularly identified as a feminist in interviews, speeches, and public appearances. During his time as Labour MP, Khan was a visible supporter of progressive causes, and his Twitter feed prior to his mayoral electoral campaign is replete with messages of support for LGBT communities and issues of gender equality. Studying his social media profile, Khan has a long track record of using Twitter initially, and later Instagram (his account only began after his electoral win), to explicitly reinforce his progressive identities and views. And yet even though Khan's Twitter profile is much more visibly feminist than Trudeau's during the election campaign, we demonstrate below how it was an ancillary tool to the mainstream media for constructing his feminist identity. We consider how this may also be shaped by the U.K.'s sociopolitical landscape and the reputation and prominent role played by mainstream media in political practice.

A key message throughout Khan's electoral run was his commitment to put "gender equality at the heart of his campaign" (Gillie 2016). He regularly spoke about the need for gender equality in speeches, public events, Q&As, and by attending key events such as annual International Women's Day marches. His manifesto even outlines the need to "challenge gender inequality" and "removing barriers to women's success," along with his pledge to "make London a fairer and more tolerant city, open and accessible to all, and one in which all can live and prosper free from prejudice" (Sadiq's Manifesto 2016).

An analysis of his campaign reveals that while he promoted his manifesto priorities via social media, he put significant more effort into getting these messages into the mainstream media. While his feminist stance was not as newsworthy as Trudeau's 2019 federal campaign, it nonetheless generated a respectable forty-three news items, almost exclusively in the United Kingdom, with headlines such as "Make me mayor and I'll close gender pay gap, says Sadiq Khan" (Mason 2016). Many of these articles quoted Khan declaring himself a "proud feminist," and outlining his plans to publish London's first gender pay audit and hire more police officers on transport networks to combat sexual assault against women—a newsworthy topic at the time (see Mendes et al. 2019a).

When looking across to social media, his Twitter feed was mainly used to share mainstream news articles that discuss or confirm his feminist position and agenda. In this sense, Khan uses the mainstream media to *reinforce* his feminist credentials. For example, on March 8, 2016, International Women's Day, Khan shared a link to a *Guardian* article mentioned above, titled "Make me mayor and I'll close gender pay gap, says Sadiq Khan" (Mason 2016) (see figure 3.2). With a photo of Khan's face and *The Guardian* logo clearly visible, ensuring there is no doubt he is sharing a mainstream news story, he prefaced the tweet by writing: "Proud to be putting the fight for gender equality at the very heart of my manifesto for all Londoners. #IWD2016" (@ SadiqKhan, March 8, 2016). It is notable that his tweet included the International Women's Day hashtag, indicating his desire to connect to broader discussion and communities of those celebrating the day. Unlike Canada, where news organizations work hard to maintain a stance of neutrality and balance, the United Kingdom's print media landscape is more openly partisan (McNair 2009). Here we see evidence of Khan's strategic use of *The Guardian's* reputation—a center-left media platform to validate his progressive values.

His mainstream media strategy also feeds into his social media strategy. Conduct an interview with a mainstream news outlet, or speak at events they are likely to cover, and then tweet the resulting story. In a few cases, he

Figure 3.2. Screenshot of Sadiq Khan's Twitter account

included photos of himself at the interview or links to the news item. On March 11, 2016, for example, he took part in an interview with the feminist organization Women of the World (WOW), posting a photo of him on a black couch, with a camera to one side and a crew member to the other, crouched down and working. It's clear the photo was taken during the interview and the accompanying message read: "Good to be interviewed @WOWtweetUK on how I'll put the fight for gender equality at the heart of City Hall #WOWLDN" (@SadiqKhan March 11, 2016). So while Khan clearly uses social media to communicate his feminist views, using photos, text, and hyperlinks, it forms a secondary means of bolstering or reinforcing his feminist identity. Instead we can see through news articles that Khan gave a lot of time to establishing his feminist credentials through his engagement with the mainstream media, particularly left-leaning newspapers such as *The Guardian* and *The Independent*.

Khan's Mainstream Media Strategy

A close analysis of mainstream media coverage of Khan demonstrates the time and care he took to establish his feminist identity. Whereas Justin Trudeau credited his parents, particularly his mother, for raising him to be a feminist (Saul 2015), Khan regularly drew on his position as a father, using his two daughters to explain why he identified as a "feminist dad" (Sands and Murphy 2016). In this way, he provides personalized justification for his feminist beliefs, connecting the dots between sexism and patriarchy, and the barriers he wants to remove for his daughters. Furthermore, for those who may question how a man could identify as a feminist, scholars have noted how expressing a desire to make the world a safer place for women in their lives is an oft used strategy (see also Mendes et al. 2019b). For example, in one press interview, he spoke "indignantly" about a female journalist who was called a "totty" by an MP, noting: "It beggars belief. One of my daughters is thinking about becoming a journalist. When you have daughters it matters even more. Why should they be limited in anything because they are women?" (Sands and Murphy 2016). The use of personal stories, delivered in a one-to-one interview, is an effective strategy employed by politicians to evoke empathy, stress relatable values, and to call for urgent political action (MacDonald 2000; Vazquez 2016).

When examining news coverage of the campaign, it appears that Khan's strategy of constructing himself as a feminist was successful. The vast majority of all forty-three news articles included a description of Khan as a "feminist" or a "proud feminist"—terms that were evoked with positive connotations. Indeed, Khan not only used the feminist label to signal his values but to mark himself as "different" to his main political rival, Conservative candidate Zac Goldsmith, who said "he would never describe himself as a feminist" (Harman 2016). Indeed, Khan regularly referred to the fact he was "the only one of the two leading candidates who's a proud feminist" (Walker 2016) throughout the campaign.

Going beyond the election itself, Khan has worked hard to maintain an image as a feminist leader, continuing to speak out about gender equality after his election. He published London's first Gender Pay Audit and embarked on a high-profile campaign to tackle sexist advertising in London. These initiatives are reflected both in mainstream media articles (exactly one hundred in the first six months after his election) and social media posts. Although Khan did not have an Instagram account at the time of his 2016 election (he started it a year later), this too is filled with posts signaling his commitment to gender equality, eliminating the gender pay gap, and support for various feminist issues (tackling period poverty, LGBTQ+ rights, and more). As he faced a reelection campaign in 2021, one could argue he was "positioning himself strategically ahead of the next . . . election" (Lalancette and Raynauld 2019, 898) in defending his feminist track record and centering issues of equality and diversity in his policies.

While the previous section has demonstrated how these two self-identified politicians used mainstream and social media to construct their feminist identities, below we outline some of the key risks with making one's identity politics visible. Although embracing the feminist identity may be a technique used to signal values and secure votes from key demographics (e.g., women or progressives), it can be a risky strategy, which can lead to ridicule, negative commentary, and intense scrutiny of one's track record and future plans.

Risks of Claiming a Feminist Identity

Although the bulk of mainstream news articles during the electoral campaigns for Sadiq Khan's 2016 mayoral contest and Justin Trudeau's 2015 federal election campaign were broadly supportive of their feminist identities, this strategy at times proved risky for both candidates, particularly when feminism was evoked as a critical lens to evaluate candidates' track records. Justin Trudeau, for example, experienced public skepticism during both the 2015 and 2019 campaigns. Although the mainstream media in general responded enthusiastically to his embracing of the feminist identity, it was not the case for many members of the public. Responding in the days, weeks, and even years after his first feminist declaration via Twitter, Canadians offered many scathing comments. These ranged from questioning his commitment to feminism, probing his questionable history with women, and associating him with other high-profile men accused of sexual violence.[6]

Other responses expressed skepticism that Trudeau's embracing the term was simply an empty strategic move to win votes: "You say anything for votes!" (@clerysboy, September 22, 2015). Others played to Trudeau's "playboy" image, suggesting the move wasn't to get just any votes but to get "ladies' votes": "@JustinTrudeau Oh for goodness sake!! You say ANYthing to try and score a few more 'ladies' votes!" (@Kauwhaka, September 22, 2015). And others still suggested that his feminist declaration was a sign he was emasculated or not a "real man": "@JustinTrudeau keep your 'feminism' I'll keep my masculinity" (@jpizzle1223, March 18, 2016). Without further explanation, others proclaimed that by identifying as a feminist, they lost his vote: "@JustinTrudeau you just lost my vote with that tweet" (@AndreInOttawa, September 22, 2015).

While negative public reactions to Trudeau's feminist identity were common on Twitter, potentially more damaging was the way feminism was evoked as a critical lens in mainstream news articles. During Trudeau's 2019

---

6. This included a photo of Trudeau with former CBC radio host Jian Ghomeshi, who in 2014 sparked a major media event after allegations surfaced that he assaulted several women while on dates (see Mendes et al. 2019a for a discussion).

campaign for reelection, a significant number of articles questioned his track record as a feminist. While recognizing important moves such as appointing women to half of his cabinet, introducing "feminist" budgets that mandate gender-based analysis for all budgetary measures, publishing Canada's first Gender Statement, creating a Department for Women and Gender Equality, and putting the first Canadian woman on new banknotes, his first term as prime minister was also marked by ejecting two of his most prominent female cabinet ministers from the Liberal Party after they protested his office's interference in a corruption investigation; elbowing a female opposition MP in Parliament; allegations that he groped a reporter at a beer festival in 2000; and although not directly linked to feminism, the "brownface" scandal in which photos emerged of Trudeau's face painted brown at two separate events, thus raising broader questions about his truly "progressive" values. As such, while only five news articles focused on Trudeau's feminist position during the 2015 federal election, 138 did so for the 2019 elections, signaling the ways he was being held to account over what being a feminist leader actually means.

These critiques did not go unnoticed by the public, particularly in the 2019 election when many of these facts were reiterated in their tweets. One tweet included a political cartoon by Andy Donato in which Trudeau is gagging former minister of justice and attorney general Jody Wilson-Raybould, who, as discussed above, resigned after claims he interfered in a corruption investigation. Others noted that he "loves women, one groping incident at a time" (@DaveNestor22, September 28, 2019). These are just a few of many tweets in which members of the public used social media to challenge and question his feminist credentials.

While this pushback is at times linked with questioning the authenticity of their claims, based on track records and facts, it is at times more insidious and fueled by seeming misogyny, hate, distrust, or other forms of discrimination. For example, although Sadiq Khan's feminist proclamations were generally positively received in the mainstream and social media, we found many examples of Twitter or Instagram users questioning how he could be a feminist as a Muslim man. Here there are insinuations that the Muslim faith is one that inherently oppresses women. As one Twitter user sarcastically wrote in response to one of Khan's regular posts about closing the gender pay gap: "Not surprised, Muslims are known for treating their women equal" (@flatbiker, November 10, 2017). These xenophobic attacks are reminders that when politicians' claims about their values and identities are questioned, they are sometimes fueled by intersecting forms of oppression and discrimination. In the case of Sadiq Khan, he didn't just experience public disbelief that he could be a feminist because he was a *man* but because he was a *Muslim man.* Justin Trudeau's feminist claims were also at times questioned because he publicly stated he supported women's right to wear the niqab, supports multiculturalism, and has Muslim friends: "@JustinTrudeau and your friends at the mosque, are they feminist as well? female genital mutilation, is this one of your customs, Jethro?" (@glen_lees, September 22, 2015).

In other cases, these leaders had their masculinity questioned, with members of the public frequently confusing "feminism" with "femininity." There were various barbs about when these leaders were going to "get a sex change" ("When can we expect the sex change Sadiq" [@GreenLibDem, November 10, 2017]), suggesting they were feminists because they "don't have any balls" (@glen_lees, September 22, 2015), Others jibed, "You're feminine, not a feminist. Easy mistake" (@TADinKaty, September 29, 2019). Here this pushback often resembled discourses found among men's rights activists (see Ging 2017), which suggests deep contempt for women and feminists.

While it's clear that these male feminist politicians receive pushback that is at times racialized and gendered, further research is needed to compare these to other feminist candidates with varying identity characteristics including gender, ethnicity, religion, and sexuality. Research is also needed to assess the impact of that pushback on the candidates themselves and their election strategies. What impact do the trolling and hate-filled comments have both in candidates' willingness to speak out on these issues and how such communication is managed? To what extent do politicians or their campaign managers pay attention to online chatter—nevertheless regroup and respond? Our analysis shows almost complete lack of engagement with public responses to tweets and Instagram posts, but this doesn't mean political campaigns aren't taking note—only that different methods, measures, and levels of access are needed to confidently address them (see chapter 10).

Discussion

Our analysis demonstrates that social media discourses predominantly serve two functions: to understand public perception and responses to issues and to frame politicians' values, beliefs, and priorities across a temporal scale. Such representations, especially of politicians' personal values (in view of temporality), allow inferences to be drawn on shifts (both subtle and obvious) in the rhetorical strategy and focus of political campaigning. This enables a contextual reflection on the implication of such transformations on social movements and the attainment of justice.

76   Electoral Campaigns, Media, and the New World of Digital Politics

For instance, from "feminism" to "gender equality," Trudeau's changing rhetorical preferences reflect the contextual climate of the Canadian polity—especially in relation to the attack on his feminist credentials. His focus on the environment possibly reflects the need to align with a "less contentious social movement" that sustains his reputation as a social activist. As highlighted earlier in this chapter, the tendency to adopt and discard the feminist identity or label is not particularly gendered as female politicians have shown similar behavior (Swift 2019). On the whole, the underlying basis for such behavior indicates changing factors of feminist and antifeminist movements, changing ideology, and the competitive status of political parties.

Yet our argument throughout this chapter confirms what other scholars (Coleman and Freelon 2015; Kreiss 2015) have argued—that social media has not radically changed political campaigning. While there is increased *potential* for dialogical exchange, and greater visibility due to networked communication and the potential "virality" of content, our analysis found that politicians rely on the mainstream media to construct their feminist identities, through their coverage of public speeches, campaign rallies, public events, debates, and interviews. Social media it seemed played an ancillary role, used to back up, reinforce, and confirm feminist declarations—often offering evidence of their feminist stance by including links to mainstream news articles or other public appearances. We consider that Trudeau's and Khan's reliance on mainstream media in political campaigning points to the existing strong public broadcasting tradition in the United Kingdom and Canada. Due to the reputation of the mainstream media in these countries, candidates exemplify "issue ownership" in their use of social media by aligning with key mainstream media platforms that are known to support the values that they (or their political parties) stand for (see chapter 1). By so doing, mainstream media helps to give validity and credibility to politicians' social media campaigns (see chapter 12).

Yet, as we write this, we are acutely aware that this may change in our current circumstances. We write this chapter in an interesting and relevant time for identity politics and governance. We are now several years into the #MeToo movement that sparked global discussions about the prevalence of sexual violence and the need to tackle sexism, misogyny, and patriarchy that fuels it. Although this chapter focused on politicians' construction of feminist identities during elections, it raises relevant questions for identity politics and governance more broadly. Since 2020, the Black Lives Matter movement has been regenerated, spurred by a slew of high-profile stories of Black men (and some women) killed by the police.

We also write this chapter during the COVID-19 pandemic in which political campaigning has changed due to social distancing measures and government restrictions. Thus it is important to recognize the context in which the elections under analysis take place, and think about how COVID-19 and social distancing and lockdown measures are and will continue to impact political campaigns and their media strategies in the future. It is too early to say what the future for campaigning will hold, but we can already get a glimpse of the role both social media and identity politics played in the 2020 presidential election, as both Biden and Trump weighed in on the Black Lives Matter movement and subsequent protests, frequently through Twitter as mainstream media opportunities become limited.

Going back to the case of feminism, research shows that on the whole, the dynamics of adopting and discarding feminist rhetoric among politicians often reflects the changing ideology of feminist and antifeminist movements, parliamentary factors, and the competitive status of political parties (Bashevkin 2009; Swift 2018). Although previous studies have highlighted that feminist rhetoric is often deployed by political candidates to boost competitive status in circumstances of political disadvantage, this study has shown that such efforts are further intensified by adopting a feminist identity. This strategy is particularly useful for male politicians in a global political landscape where feminism is still largely attributed to women. As feminism continues to experience an unprecedented "luminosity" (Gill 2017) in many nations around the world, we are increasingly likely to see feminism play a major role in political campaigns, as identities that candidates embrace and as a critical lens through which their track records are evaluated. By exploring mainstream news coverage and social media accounts of two elected feminist leaders, our chapter provides the first baseline snapshot of the different ways feminism has been constructed in differing political campaigns.

While feminism was broadly viewed as a positive identity that candidates embraced as a means to signal values and boost support, our analysis demonstrates that adopting a feminist identity is not a risk-free strategy. Although we are in an age of "popular feminism" (Banet-Weiser 2018), it is clear that politicians' feminist claims are often met with skepticism, ridicule, and pushback, particularly from the public via social media. Yet while some of this public pushback does not help the feminist cause, particularly those infused with hate, we argue that the simple declaration that one is a feminist has sociocultural implications that help to destabilize preconceptions of what a "typical feminist" should look like, or who is "allowed" to be a feminist. Sadiq Khan, being a male Muslim feminist, for instance, provides the possibility for ideological, social, and political transformation across cultural and gendered lines. Yet it also opens up opportunities for multiple, intersecting forms of resistance. On the whole, the scrutiny of politicians' feminist identity on social and mainstream media platforms helps to put pressure on them to deliver on such identities. This, we optimistically suggest, has the potential to advance women's equality, as well as to substantiate the value of feminism in the polity.

Finally, we conclude this chapter by arguing that having politicians—the people who ultimately have the power to change laws, society, and culture—adopt a feminist identity is a positive step in making feminism as a political movement more accessible and accepted, but what really matters is the extent to which *they work to dismantle oppressive structures*. In other words, while exploring their feminist identities in political campaigns is important, it is more important to explore the ways they *live feminist lives* (Ahmed 2017) as politicians. This does not mean we should expect politicians to be perfect feminists—after all—living a feminist life is difficult and can be discomforting (Ahmed 2017), but it does mean we should continue to hold them to account and question the extent to which they use their power to dismantle, rather than uphold, patriarchal power (see Eltahawy 2019). Furthermore, although this study focused on politicians' use of feminism, in view of the interconnectedness of social movements and inequalities discussed above there is scope to study how politicians adopt identities in relation to sexuality, poverty, race, and the environment. On the whole, more detailed research is needed into specific scenarios under which politicians make less or more audacious claims in relation to feminism and other social movements—and the different roles that social and mainstream media play in elections.

References

Ahl, Helene, Karin Berglund, Katarina Petersson, and Malin Tillmar. 2016. "From Feminism to FemINC.ism: On the Uneasy Relationship between Feminism, Entrepreneurship and the Nordic Welfare State." *International Entrepreneurship and Management Journal* 12(2): 369–92.

Ahmed, Sara. 2017. *Living a Feminist Life*. Durham: Duke University Press.

Ashley, Laura, and Beth Olson. 1998. "Constructing Reality: Print Media Framing of the Women's Movement, 1966–1986." *Journal of Mass Communication Quarterly* 75(2): 263–77.

Banet-Weiser, Sarah. 2018. *Empowered: Popular Feminism and Popular Misogyny*. Durham: Duke University Press.

Barker-Plummer, Bernadette. 2000. "News as a Feminist Resource? A Case study of the media strategies and media representation of the National Organization for Women, 1966–1980." In *Gender, Politics and Communication*, edited by Anabel

Sreberny Mohammadi and Liesbet van Zoonen, 121–59. New York: Hampton Press.

Bartholomew, James. 2015. "Easy Virtue." *The Spectator*, April 18. https://www.spectator.co.uk/article/easy-virtue

Bashevkin, Sylvia. 2009. "Party Talk: Assessing the Feminist Rhetoric of Women Leadership Candidates in Canada." *Canadian Journal of Political Science* 42(2): 345–62.

Bienkov, Alex. 2019. "Boris Johnson called gay men 'tank-topped bumboys' and black people 'piccaninnies' with 'watermelon smiles.'" *Business Insider US*, November 22.

Boesveld, Sarah. 2015. "Leaders face credibility gap on 'new feminism.'" *Montreal Gazette*, September 22, A8.

Bradley, Patricia. 2003. *Mass Media and the Shaping of American Feminism, 1963–1975*. Jackson: University Press of Mississippi.

Briggs, Laura. 2018. *How All Politics Became Reproductive Politics: From Welfare Reform to Foreclosure to Trump*. Oakland: University of California Press.

Burman, Dilshad. 2019. "1 in 4 Canadian women believe Trudeau is a feminist: Poll." *City News*, September, 23.

Butter, Sussanah. 2015. "25 reasons why we love new Canadian Prime Minister Justin Trudeau; He's a dope-toking, kilt-wearing, boxing feminist." *London Evening Standard*, October 21, 2015.

"Canada's blast of fresh air." 2015. *The Press*, October 22.

Coleman, Stephen, and Dean Freelon. 2015. "Introduction." In *Handbook of Digital Politics*, edited by Stephen Coleman and Dean Freelon, 1–16. Cheltenham, UK: Edward Elgar Publishing.

Crowe, Jonathan. 2013. "Can Men Be Feminists?" *University of Queensland TC Beirne School of Law Research Paper* No. 13–08. http://dx.doi.org/10.2139/ssrn.2345526

Dayan, Daniel. 2009. "Sharing and showing: Television as monstration." *Annals of the American Academy of Political and Social Science* 625(1): 19–31.

Deacon, David, Dominic Wring, and Peter Golding. 2006. "Same Campaign, Differing Agendas: Analysing News Media Coverage of the 2005 General Election." *British Politics* 1: 222–56.

Dean, Jonathan. 2010. "Feminism in the papers: Contested feminisms in the British quality press." *Feminist Media Studies* 10(4): 391–407.

De Benedictis, Sara, Shani Orgad, and Catherine Rottenberg. 2019. "#MeToo, popular feminism and the news: A content analysis of UK newspaper coverage." *European Journal of Cultural Studies* 22(5–6): 718–38.

Digby, Tom. 1998. *Men Doing Feminism*. New York: Routledge.

Di Manno, Rosie. 2019. "The Prime Minister of Double Standards." *Chronicle Journal* 24 (September 2019).

Eltahawy, Mona. 2019. *The Seven Necessary Sins for Women and Girls*. Boston: Beacon Press.

Evans, Elizabeth. 2016. "Feminist Allies and Strategic Partners: Exploring the Relationship Between the Women's Movement and Political Parties." *Party Politics* 22(5): 631–40.

Fernandez-Rovira, Cristina, and Isabel Villegas-Simon. 2019. "Comparative Study of Feminist Positioning on Twitter by Spanish Politicians." *Anàlisi: Quaderns de Comunicació i Cultura* 61: 77–92.

Filimonov, Kirill, and Jakob Svensson. 2016. "(re)Articulating Feminism: A Discourse Analysis of Sweden's Feminist Initiative Election Campaign." *Nordicom Review* 37(2): 51–56.

Freeman, Barbara. 2001. *The Satellite Sex: The Media and Women's Issues in English Canada, 1966–1971*. Waterloo, Canada: Wilfred Laurier Press.

Frisk, Adam. 2015. "'Because it's 2015': Trudeau's gender-equal cabinet makes headlines around the world, social media." *Global News*, November 5. https://globalnews.ca/news/2320795/because-its-2015-trudeaus-gender-equal-cabinet-makes-headlines-around-world-social-media/

Gawley, Kelvin. 2019. "'I kind of laugh it off': Sophie Grégoire Trudeau says PM is not a 'fake feminist.'" *Burnby Now*, October 9.

Gill, Rosalind. 2017. "The affective, cultural and psychic life of postfeminism: A postfeminist sensibility 10 years on." *European Journal of Cultural Studies* 20(6): 606–26.

Gillie, Rebecca. 2016. "London Mayor election 2016: Sadiq Khan's Labour manifesto." *The Week UK*, April 28.

Ging, Debbie. 2017. "Alphas, Betas, and Incels: Theorizing the Masculinities of the Manosphere." *Men and Masculinities* 22(4): 638–57.

Gitlin, Todd. 2003. *The Whole World Is Watching: Mass Media and the Making and Unmaking of the New Left*. Berkeley: University of California Press.

Gleeson, Kate. 2017. "We Are All Feminists Now: How to Pass an Anti-Abortion Law in Australia." In *Transcending Borders: Abortion in the Past and Present*, edited by Shannon Stettner, Katrina Ackerman, Kristin Burnett, and Travis Hay, 137–54. Cham, Switzerland: Palgrave.

Goddu, Jen. 1999. "'Powerless, Public-Spirited Women,' 'Angry Feminists,' and 'The Muffin Lobby': Newspaper and Magazine Coverage of Three National Women's Groups from 1980–1995." *Canadian Journal of Communication* 24(2): 105–26.

Harman, Harriet. 2016. ">Harriet Harman: Sadiq Khan has the experience and vision to be the Mayor London needs." *London Evening Standard*, April 27.

Harvey, Alison. 2020. *Feminist Media Studies*. Cambridge: Polity Press.

Heger, Katharina, and Christian P. Hoffmann. 2019. "Feminism! What Is It Good For? The Role of Feminism and Political Self-Efficacy in Women's Online Political Participation." *Social Science Computer Review*. https://doi.org/10.1177/0894439319865909

Kreiss, Daniel. 2015. "Digital Campaigning." In *Handbook of Digital Politics*, edited by Stephen Coleman and Dean Freelon, 118–35. Cheltenham, UK: Edward Elgar Publishing.

Lalancette, Mireille, and Vincent Raynauld. 2019. "The Power of Political Image: Justin Trudeau, Instagram, and Celebrity Politics." *American Behavioral Scientist* 63(7): 888–924.

Larrondo, Ainara, Jordi Morales I-Gras, and Julien Orbegozo-Terradillos. 2019. "Feminist Hashtag Activism in Spain: Measuring the degree of online discourse on #yoditecreo, #hermanayositecreo, #cuentalo y, #noestassola." *Communication and Society* 32(4): 207–21.

Lilley, Brian. 2019a. "Women aren't buying Trudeau's feminist act." *The Sun*, September 22.

Lilley, Brian. 2019b. "Poll shows women don't believe Trudeau on feminist claim." *The Sun*, September 22.

Lind, Rebecca Ann, and Colleen Salo. 2002. "The Framing of Feminists and Feminism in News and Public Affairs Programs in U.S. Electronic Media." *Journal of Communication* 52(1): 211–27.

Lotfi, Asa. 2019. "The Winning Political Campaign of the Digital Age: Justin Trudeau's Social Media-Oriented Politics." MA thesis. Toronto: Ryerson University. https://rshare.library.ryerson.ca/articles/thesis/The_Winning_Political_Campaign_of_the_Digital_Age_Justin_Trudeau_s_Social_Media-Oriented_Politics/14656440

Lunt, Peter. 2019. "The performance of power and citizenship: David Cameron meets the people." *International Journal of Cultural Studies* 22(5): 678–90.

MacDonald, Myra. 2000. "Rethinking Personalization in Current Affairs Journalism." In *Tabloid Tales: Global Debates over Media Standards*, edited by Colin Sparks and Barbie Zelizer, 251–66. Oxford: Rowman & Littlefield.

Mason, Rowena. 2016. "Make me mayor and I'll close gender pay gap, says Sadiq Khan." *The Guardian*, March 20.

Mason, Rowena. 2019a. "Dominic Raab defends calling feminists 'obnoxious bigots.'" *The Guardian*, May 26.

Mason, Rowena. 2019b. "Eight Tory leadership candidates declare themselves feminists." *The Guardian*, May 30.

McNair, Brian. 2009. *News and Journalism in the UK.* London: Routledge.

Mendes, Kaitlynn. 2011. *Feminism in the News: Representations of the Women's Movement Since the 1960s.* Basingstoke: Palgrave.

Mendes, Kaitlynn. 2015. *SlutWalk: Feminism, Activism and Media.* Basingstoke: Palgrave.

Mendes, Kaitlynn, Jessica Ringrose, and Jessalynn Keller. 2019a. *Digital Feminist Activism: Girls and Women Fight Back Against Rape Culture.* Oxford: Oxford University Press.

Mendes, Kaitlynn, Jessalynn Keller, and Jessica Ringrose. 2019b. "Digitized narratives of sexual violence: Making sexual violence felt and known through digital disclosures." *New Media & Society* 21(6): 1290–1310.

Moore, Suzanne. 2019. "Want to be Tory leader and say you're a feminist? Show us how, exactly." *The Guardian*, May 31.

Morris, Monica B. 1973. "The public definition of a social movement: Women's liberation." *Sociology and Social Research* 57(4): 526–43.

Murphy, Jessica. 2015. "Trudeau gives Canada first cabinet with equal number of men and women." *The Guardian*, November 4.

Norocel, Ov Christian. 2018. "Anti-feminist and Truly Liberated: Conservative Performances of Gender by Women Politicians in Hungary and Romania." *Politics and Governance* 6(3): 43–54.

Oppenheim, Maya. 2019. "Where do the major parties stand on women's issues?" *The Independent*, November 10.

Parker, Ceri. 2016. "Justin Trudeau: I will raise my sons to be feminists." *World Economic Forum*, January 22.

Revell, Emma. 2019. "Jo Swinson's disingenuous cries of 'sexism' are setting back the cause of feminism." *The Telegraph*, November 22.

Rivers, Nicola. 2017. *Postfeminism(s) and the Arrival of the Fourth Wave: Turning Tides.* Basingstoke: Palgrave Macmillan.

Sadiq's Manifesto. 2016. Sadiq and London Labours 2016 Manifesto. https://labourinlondon.org.uk/sadiq/2018/02/28/sadiqs-manifesto/

Sands, Sarah, and Joe Murphy. 2016. "Sadiq Khan: My daughters have rights here—and they can wear what they like; Labour's mayoral candidate Sadiq Khan tells Sarah Sands and Joe Murphy about the importance of cultural integration, being a feminist dad, and why he's proud he wore a crown for the Queen." *London Evening Standard*, April 14.

Saul, Heather. 2015. "Justin Trudeau: The rise of the feminist and pro-choice Canadian Prime Minister who wants to legalise marijuana 'right away'; Trudeau's Liberal party won the election on Monday." *The Independent*, October 20.

Sheridan, Susan, Susan Magarey, and Sandra Lilburn. 2007. "Feminism in the news." In *Feminism in Popular Culture*, edited by Joanne Hollows and Rachel Moseley, 25–40. New York: Berg Publisher.

Swift, David. 2019. "From 'I'm not a feminist, but . . .' to 'Call me an old-fashioned feminist . . .' : Conservative women in parliament and feminism, 1979–2017." *Women's History Review* 28(2): 317–36.

Urback, Robyn. 2016. "Agnes McPhail. . . . too white?" *National Post*, March 12.

van Zoonen, Liesbet. 1992. "The Women's Movement and the media: Constructing a public identity." *European Journal of Communication* 7(4): 453–76.

Vazquez, Pablo. 2016. "Personalisation of Politics, Storytelling and Conveyed Values." *Communication and Society* 30(3): 275–91.

von der Lippe, Berit, and Tarja Väyrynen. 2011. "Co-opting Feminist Voices for the War on Terror: Laura Bush Meets Nordic Feminism." *European Journal of Women's Studies* 18(1): 19–33.

Walker, Peter. 2016. "Sadiq Khan says Tories' 'Donald Trump approach' won't work in London; Labour candidate for mayor condemns rival Zac Goldsmith and Conservatives for using 'politics of division and fear.'" *The Guardian*, April 25.

White, Aaronette M. 2008. *Ain't I a Feminist? African American Men Speak Out on Fatherhood, Friendship, Forgiveness, and Freedom.* Albany: State University of New York Press.

CHAPTER 4

A Woman's Place Is in the (U.S.) House

An Analysis of Issues Women Candidates Discussed on Twitter in the 2016 and 2018 Congressional Elections

Heather K. Evans, University of Virginia's College at Wise

In 2016, former First Lady, secretary of state, and senator Hillary Clinton became the first female major party nominee for president in the United States. Like all candidates who came before her, she faced criticism over her capability and qualifications to be the next president, but unlike those who came before her, the criticism she faced often had a gendered tilt to it (Dittmar 2016). Donald Trump, her major competitor during the general election, often mentioned her gender during debates, in campaign advertising, and on Twitter. Hashtags like #LockHerUp, #CrookedHillary, and #NotWithHer trended throughout the election cycle (Ortutay 2016). After being accused of playing the "woman card" by Trump, at the Democratic National Convention Clinton replied that if playing the "woman card" meant standing up for issues like paid family leave and affordable childcare, then "deal [her] in."

Research on the 2016 election on Twitter show that the two presidential candidates addressed very different policy issues. Clinton was significantly more likely to discuss "women's issues," like education and health care, while Trump rarely discussed women or policy issues at all (Evans, Brown, and Wimberly 2017). Not only was Clinton more likely to discuss "women's issues," she was also more likely to discuss issues overall. Other research shows that Clinton discussed more policy specific plans on Twitter, while Trump rarely discussed policy (Evans, Brown, and Wimberly 2018). While Clinton lost the 2016 election, her presidential bid is a historic moment for women, who have yet to serve as president.

Clinton's discussion of policy on Twitter is not unlike what we have seen play out on the social media platform with congressional candidates since 2012. Evans, Cordova, and Sipole (2014), for instance, have shown that female candidates for the U.S. House were more likely to send what they called "issue" tweets during the 2012 elections, and in later work, Evans and Clark (2016) showed that those female candidates were more likely to send tweets about "women's issues." Following up, Evans (2016) also showed that women were more likely to talk about all issues, "women's issues" and "men's issues."

Women, as out-party candidates, are more likely to turn to social media platforms like Twitter to campaign to increase their attention during elections. Previous research shows that those who are not in the majority are more likely to turn to new avenues to innovate, and social networks like Twitter fit the bill (Karpf 2014). Twitter is especially useful for candidates who are not currently incumbents as users are allowed to control the message, anyone can send messages in real time (bypassing traditional media gatekeepers), and the platform reaches a population that does not watch traditional television news (Wojcik and Hughes 2018; Wattenberg 2016). Younger, more affluent and educated people are more likely to use Twitter, with female users being the most prolific users who tweet about politics and engage with brands (Hillsberg 2014; Wojcik and Hughes 2018). Given these characteristics of Twitter, it should come as no surprise that women are more likely to use it and more likely to discuss issues, especially those that pertain to women as a group.

Given the growth in the number of women both running and winning congressional seats over the past two national elections in the U.S. (2016 and 2018), in this chapter, I explore whether those same earlier trends regarding policy discussion on Twitter are still present. Are female candidates for the U.S. House tweeting more about issues overall? Are women more likely to discuss "women's issues" on Twitter? Or, as some other scholars have suggested in their investigation of issues discussed by candidates in traditional television ads, were women less likely to discuss "women's issues" during the 2018 election so as not to define themselves by their gender (Parry-Giles, Farhat, Salzano, and de Saint Felix 2019)? Does the medium of Twitter still affect the ways that female candidates communicate, or are they tweeting in similar ways to their television ads?

The Electoral Context

2016 and 2018 were both record-setting years for women in politics. In 2016, the highest number of women ever ran for the U.S. Senate, at 40; 272

women ran for seats in the House of Representatives, with 167 winning their primaries, beating the prior record set in 2012 (The Center for American Women and Politics). That year, 85 women won seats in the House while 20 won seats in the Senate. Continuing that trend, during the 2018 elections, we saw a significant increase in the number of women running and subsequently serving in elected national positions. There was a 20 percent increase in the number of women elected to seats in Congress (101 representatives, 25 senators). By all means, one could argue that 2018 was truly the "Year of the Woman."

For many, the claim that an election year is the "Year of the Woman" should sound familiar. The year 1992 also received that description, as a record-breaking number of women ran and were elected to the Senate and House (four senators, twenty-four representatives). The years 2018 and 1992 had other similarities as well. Both election years came after high-profile public scandals related to sexual harassment and assault. Both were directly after very heated Supreme Court nominations (Thomas in 1992, Kavanaugh in 2018). The 2018 elections were also after the #MeToo movement went viral.

One difference between these two years is that many women may have decided to run in 2018 in large part because of the political landscape since 2016. As mentioned at the beginning of this chapter, Hillary Clinton ran as the Democratic nominee for president in 2016 and lost to Donald Trump. Her loss to Trump angered many women who saw in him a very flawed candidate. He had made derogatory comments about Megyn Kelly during the debates (she "had blood coming out of her whatever"), had called women interested in politics "nasty women" (which was mainly directed at his opponent), he had multiple sexual harassment and assault allegations against him, and his Access Hollywood tape comments about how he forces himself on women were released to the public about a month before the election.

What has also been dubbed the "pink wave," this influx in women running for seats in 2018 was also the effect of women feeling shut out of the political system. The day after Trump's inauguration, women took to the streets for the Women's March on Washington, which became the largest single-day protest in American history. Over four million people marched that day. People were marching for civil rights, LGBTQ rights, gender equality, environmental protection, affordable health care, and other issues that would face challenges under the Trump administration. While some feared that these women and their allies would turn out for the protest and then go back home and not be politically active, they did exactly the opposite. Women felt unrepresented in Congress and in other places decisions were being made: "the idea of male Representatives trying to strip health care from millions of families spurred the transformation from activist into candidate" (Alter 2018).

Gender Representation (and Twitter Style Differences)

Were women right about their underrepresentation in congress? The representation of women in Congress has notably increased over the past few decades, but women remain underrepresented as a whole (50 percent of the population is female, but only 23 percent of congressional seats are filled by women). Representation, however, is multifaceted. Women clearly lack descriptive representation, and this type of representation matters especially if they have different policy priorities than men and if those policy priorities aren't advocated for by their representatives. Research on women in politics emphasizes the important role of gender in the priorities and issue positions of women in the electorate and in public office. When it comes to the electorate, the issue position differences between men and women are well documented (Box-Steffensmeier, DeBoef, and Lin 2004; Kaufmann and Petrocik 1999). Women hold more liberal views on foreign policy and criminal justice and tend to favor government funding of health care and education and any other program aimed at helping the poor and elderly (Kaufman and Petrocik 1999; Page and Shapiro 1992).

Gender differences in the electorate have spilled over to how candidates for political office are evaluated. Female candidates tend to be more favored on issues like social welfare and education, while male candidates are viewed more favorably on foreign policy and economic issues (Alexander and Anderson 1993; Burrell 1994; Huddy and Terkildsen 1993; Lawless 2004; Sanbonmatsu 2002). Issues like education, health care, reproductive rights, and welfare have been identified by other scholars as being "women's issues," while issues about international relations and anything involving the economy are "men's issues." By women being viewed more favorably in certain areas than others, female candidates regularly face what is known as the "double bind." Female candidates may be helped by campaigning on these issues with female voters but overall may be judged by voters as only being able to address those topics and not others. This means during times when the economy is struggling, men may be evaluated as being more favorable to women simply because they are viewed as being more knowledgeable on the economy. Research in this area has shown that women are both helped and harmed at the polls by stressing these "women's issues" with different groups of voters (Herrnson, Lay, and Stokes 2003; Larson 2001; Witt, Paget and Matthews 1994).

Research on "women's issues" has shown that women tend to campaign on them when they can stand out from their competition both in traditional and social media (Dolan 1998; Larson 2001; Herrnson, Lay, and Stokes 2003; Fridkin and Kenney 2009; Evans and Clark 2016). Larson (2001), for instance, finds in her study of state legislative campaigns that female candidates are more likely than male candidates to identify "female issues" in their brochures. Other work by Herrnson, Lay, and Stokes (2003) shows that women who campaigned on "women's issues" and targeted female voters received a significant advantage at the polls in 1996 and 1998.

In terms of social media, particularly Twitter, Wagner, Gainous, and Holman (2017) state that "women face and perceive a gendered disadvantage when seeking office, which may translate into various strategic campaigning," which results in female candidates being early users of a platform like Twitter because of the capability and opportunity to shape and control the campaign dialogue. Twitter, as a media platform, has changed the way that candidates campaign in general, but it has particularly changed how outsider candidates campaign. First, unlike traditional media, Twitter can be used to send messages in real time. It is difficult for outsider candidates to gain traction in traditional news reports due to gatekeeping by both news stations and more well-known and well-financed candidates, but on Twitter anyone can start an account (it's free!) and send 280-character messages to the world. This makes the platform very attractive to lesser-known candidates. Furthermore, candidates do not have to wait to be interviewed by journalists about their positions on issues or their responses to national events, as they can send tweets about their campaigns and positions immediately.

Not only is Twitter attractive to lesser-known candidates, the platform itself can affect the ways that candidates campaign. Approximately 22 percent of U.S. adults are users of Twitter, and most are between the age of thirty-five and sixty-five (63 percent) and 56 percent are male (Lin 2019). The average Twitter user in the United States is younger, more educated, and more affluent than the average American (Wojcik and Hughes 2018). Furthermore, Democrats have a bit of an edge on the platform, with 36 percent of users reporting that they are Democrats compared to 21 percent that identify as Republicans (Wojcik and Hughes 2018). While a few more men in the United States use Twitter than women, female users of the platform are more likely to interact with brands, are more likely to check news on the site, and are Twitter's most prolific users who tweet about politics, with 61 percent of them identifying as Democrats (Hillsberg 2014; Wojcik and Hughes 2018). A large percentage of U.S. users (42 percent) are also using the platform to specifically discuss politics (Cooper 2019).

Due to these characteristics of Twitter users, and the traits of the platform itself, candidates approach the medium differently than they would other campaigning tools. Since female candidates are similar to out-party candidates given their lack of representation in Congress, they are drawn to the medium to advance their agenda and campaigns. As Evans, Cordova, and Sipole (2014) show, even early on (in the 2012 election), female candidates were more likely to have a Twitter account and tweeted more often than their male opponents. This makes sense given that out-party candidates continuously search for ways to be noticed by the public and are the first to try and be more innovative in their campaigns (Karpf 2012), so sending more tweets is one way to do so.

Given the demographic of Twitter users, we should also expect out-party candidates like women to be very strategic in how they use the platform in the topics that they tweet about. Topics that matter to a younger, more educated, and more Democratic crowd should get more attention on Twitter, which translates into how candidates who are seeking attention (and votes) use the social networking site. Evans, Cordova, and Sipole (2014) show that in 2012, the content of female candidate tweets differed from male candidate tweets. Women spent significantly more time discussing policy issues on Twitter than men. Since women make up a large majority of the prolific Twitter users who also discuss politics, we should also expect that female candidates would address issues that matter to women, which is what some work has found. Evans and Clark (2016) show that female candidates were more likely to discuss "women's issues" on Twitter in 2012. They classify a "woman's issue" as anything "that directly and disproportionally affect women as a group," feminist concerns, and crimes that affect women at a disproportionate rate (domestic violence/rape). The other more traditional "women's issues" were also included in their study, like health care, education, and welfare. Evans and Clark (2016) find that female candidates sent policy related tweets in 2012 at a significantly higher rate than their male counterparts and tweeted more about "women's issues"; and the more women that are in a race, the more policy is discussed overall. Evans (2016) further examines the 2012 U.S. House elections and seven months later. She finds that while women do tweet significantly more about "women's issues" than males do, women also tweet more about "male issues" (economy, foreign policy) both during and after elections are over.

Once women get in office, they are also more likely to focus on these issues (Osborn and Mendez 2010; Shogan 2002; Walsh 2002; Gerrity, Osborn, and Mendez 2007). When it comes to Congress specifically, women from both sides of the aisle tend to sponsor and cosponsor legislation dealing with "women's issues" more often than male representatives (Swers 2002). Even early work on the increasing number of women in the legislature revealed that when more women were added to congress, there were more bill sponsorships that dealt with "women's issues" (Vega and Firestone 1995). Female members of congress are more likely to care about, sponsor, and vote for legislation dealing with "women's issues." This means, therefore, that women being underrepresented in Congress directly relates to women being substantively underrepresented in policy.

What Were Women Talking about in 2016 and 2018?

In the rest of this chapter, I explore what candidates were talking about issue-wise on Twitter during the elections of 2016 and 2018, and whether what they discussed on Twitter differed from what they discussed on television. The research cited above is a bit dated, given the speed at which articles about social media are evolving. While other work has shown that women tweet more about issues in general, especially those pertaining to women, I explore whether those trends still hold with recent elections. Work on traditional advertising methods in 2018 has found that women were not campaigning "as women." Research from the Political Advertising Resource Center of the Rosenker Center for Political Communication and Civic Leadership at the University of Maryland shows that women who ran in 2018 sidestepped issues like equal pay and abortion access. Researchers examined fifty-two ads by twenty-five female candidates (for the House, Senate, and governor elections), and instead of finding themes related to these particular issues, they discovered that female candidates were stressing values of community and overall discontent with the government. Instead of focusing on "women's issues" in a year when "women's issues" were on everyone's mind (with #MeToo and the Brett Kavanaugh hearings), women were cautious and instead produced ads that highlighted their "toughness" (Parry-Giles, Farhat, Salzano, and de Saint Felix 2019).

Given the lack of discussing "women's issues" in female candidates' television advertisements, I may find that in my study of tweets as well, but some work has shown that the behavior of female candidates online has varied with the behavior of those candidates in other media. For instance, when it comes to negativity, female candidates tend to be just as likely as men are to produce a political television advertisement that criticizes their opponent. Online, however, female candidates are more likely to send "attack" tweets (Evans, Cordova, and Sipole 2014; Evans and Clark 2016).

As this work on negativity has found, Twitter, which is a medium where candidates speak more directly to their followers, can produce a different form of communication for candidates. Individuals who are active Twitter users and follow candidates' campaign accounts are more likely to be supporters of those campaigns (Barberá and Rivero 2015; Bode and Dalrymple 2016; Gainous and Wagner 2014; Kreiss 2016). Traditional campaign advertising may attract broader viewership than tweets, so candidates are more likely to use narrowcasting in their tweets (i.e., focusing on other, more narrow issues with their Twitter base than their traditional television advertising). On the other hand, tweets from campaign Twitter accounts are likely to be shared so that others who are not supporters of those individuals will see those tweets. For that reason, campaigns may be less likely to differ in their issue agendas when using Twitter versus traditional advertising.

Some work on the similarities between issues stressed in tweets and television advertising by those same campaigns has shown that the two issue agendas are not that different (Kang, Franklin Fowler, Franz, and Ridout 2018). Examining dozens of Senate races in 2014, Kang et al. (2018) show that issue agendas on Twitter and in advertising by the campaigns are fairly similar. Given the findings by the Rosenker Center for Political Communication and Civic Leadership at the University of Maryland, if there are no real differences between the communication styles of female candidates depending on medium, we should see that they downplay "women's issues" in 2018. On the other hand, since other work has shown that the traditional media landscape influences what campaigns tweet about (Conway, Kenski, and Wang 2015), and the media agenda was focused on "women's issues" (including #MeToo) in 2018, female candidates may have been more likely to tweet about these topics in 2018. For instance, according to data collected at the Brookings Institute during the primaries, female candidates were more likely to mention topics like abortion, education, and same-sex marriage (Podkul 2018). Since #MeToo and other issues related to gender were being discussed by traditional media, female candidates, who have more firsthand knowledge and experience with these issues, may have been more likely to tweet about these topics to garner traditional media attention.

The questions I address below are:

1. Were "women's issues" addressed on Twitter in 2016 and 2018? Given the election of Donald Trump in 2016 and the Women's March, as well as the #MeToo movement, I expect to find that "women's issues" were addressed more often in 2018.

2. Were female candidates more likely to talk about "women's issues" than male candidates?
3. Were "men's issues" addressed on Twitter in 2016 and 2018? Were "women's issues" or "men's issues" discussed more often. Which issue did everyone pay the most attention to in each election year?

Data and Methods

To examine the ways that women used Twitter during the 2016 and 2018 House elections, I compiled an original dataset of all tweets sent by all candidates for the U.S. House campaigns during the last two months of the election.[1] By collecting data across the two months prior to the election, I am (1) able to compare these results to previous data collection efforts in other studies, and (2) capture tweets that happen after the conclusion of all state primary elections. First, I collected the names, party identification, and gender of each candidate using Ballotpedia.org. Major and minor party candidates are included. I then collected each candidate's campaign Twitter account information and scraped the Twitter API using the TwittR package in R for each candidate to create a dataset of their tweets.

Following in the footsteps of Evans and Clark (2016), I then did a keyword/phrase search for statements about "women's issues." When previous scholars have examined policy issues for their gender, some scholars have included core issues that have traditionally been associated with women, like health and education, while other scholars have merged issues like equal rights and feminist issues into a broader definition of "women's issues" (Bratton 2002; Dodson and Carroll 1991; Swers 2002; Wolbrecht 2000). Like Evans and Clark (2016), I searched for issues that "directly and disproportionately affect women as a group," which include both those traditional issues like health care, welfare, education, the environment, children, and family, as well as feminist concerns that "seek to improve the social, economic, and political status of women as a group." I also include crimes that disproportionately affect women as a group, and specifically health-care

---

1. I would like to thank Bryan Gervais and Annelise Russell for their help at collecting the tweets during the 2018 congressional election. I'd also like to thank the numerous research assistants who helped gather demographic information related to these contests. In particular, I'd like to thank Mikki Woodard, Erick Rodas, and Allison Faith for their help in 2018. I'd also like to thank Miranda Estrada for her assistance in thinking about issues that should be included in the 2016 keyword list.

92 Electoral Campaigns, Media, and the New World of Digital Politics

TABLE 4.1. Gendered Issues on Twitter—Words and Phrases

Women's Issues	Men's Issues
Healthcare/Health care/ACA/Affordable Care Act/Obamacare	International relations/foreign affairs
	War
Social Security/SS/SSA/SSDC/SSDI/ Social assistance	Iraq, Afghanistan, Syria, Benghazi, Russia, China
Medicare/Medicaid	Homeland security
Welfare	9/11
Food stamps/SNAP	Dream Act/border/immigration
WIC/children/youth/kids/adolescent	Amnesty
Woman/women/female/girl	Agriculture/farm
Poverty/poor	Legalization/pot/weed/marijuana
Family/families	Liberty
Education/college/school	Guns
Abortion/pro-choice/pro-life	Business
Birth control/ Plan B/contraception/ reproductive	Economy
	Deficit, Debt
Childcare/child care/daycare	Taxes
Domestic violence/sexual assault/ domestic abuse/rape/rapist	Budget
	Spending
Sexual harassment	
Gay marriage/LGBT	
Equality/discrimination	
Glass Ceiling	
Planned Parenthood	
Bullying	
Kavanaugh (2018)	
Blasey-Ford (2018)	
#YesAllWomen	
#LoveisLove	
#MeToo (2018)	
#TimesUp (2018)	

concerns. I deleted some issues that were specific to the 2012 race from the Evans and Clark (2016) codebook and included additional keywords and phrases for the 2016 election: glass ceiling, sexual harassment, and bullying. In the 2018 data, Kavanaugh, Blasey-Ford, #MeToo, and #TimesUp were included. I also coded for "men's issues" by searching for the list of keywords and phrases that were included in Evans and Clark (2016) and Evans (2016), with some slight election year specific adjustments. A full list of the words and phrases used in my analysis is given in table 4.1.

The 2016 Election

Examining only the candidates who were actively using Twitter during the last two months of their 2016 campaigns produces a dataset of 776 candidates and 44,440 tweets for 2016, 171 female candidates and 605 male candidates. On average, candidates sent 57.3 tweets, with women tweeting 61.3 times and men sending 56 tweets.[2]

When it comes to tweeting specifically about the issues deemed "women's issues," 20 percent of the individuals running for Congress in 2016 never sent a single tweet about those topics. Women sent more tweets about "women's issues" than men (10.3 tweets to 7.1 tweets on average), which is very significant.[3] The average number of tweets sent across all candidates about women's issues was 7.8 tweets, or 14 percent of their total tweets. More than 29 percent of these candidates never discussed "men's issues," with the average number of tweets sent about these topics at 4.7 for both men and women (8.2 percent of their total tweets).

Examining the specific candidates and their tweets, I find that only two candidates tweeted one hundred times or more about topics related to "women's issues," and both of those candidates were men. Harvey Martin (Democrat, Arizona District 3) sent the most tweets about these topics at 158, and Lon Johnson (Democrat, Michigan District 1) sent 104. For "men's issues," no candidate sent more than one hundred tweets about those topics. The person who sent the most tweets was Vicki Hartzler (Missouri District 4) at ninety tweets, with Chris Cataldo (Massachusetts District 9) coming in with the second highest number of tweets about these topics at eighty-eight.

As a whole, approximately 14 percent of the tweets sent by candidates in 2016 were about "women's issues," but few of the topics included received over one tweet sent about them on average. Table 4.2 lists the issues that were discussed on average by male and female candidates. For both male and female candidates, their four most discussed "women's issues" were the same, but women out-tweeted men regarding almost each of these topics. For instance, women sent close to three times as many tweets about terms related to "women" (like girl, woman, women, female) than men did.

The only "women's issue" term included here that was tweeted about more by men than women was "health" (1.3 tweets on average compared to 1.1). When I examine the themes present in those specific tweets, I find

---

2. This difference is not statistically significant.
3. Difference of means t-test p ≤ 0.0039.

TABLE 4.2. "Women's Issues" Tweeted about Most Often

Female candidates	Male candidates
Women—2.9	Family—1.4
Family—1.8	Health—1.3
Education—1.4	Education—1.2
Health—1.1	Women—1.1

Values represent the number of tweets on average about these topics.
Female candidates sent 61.3 tweets on average and male candidates sent 56 tweets on average.

that women were more likely to discuss health care in relationship to women's health, while men were more likely to discuss the Affordable Care Act (Obamacare). For instance, Kyrsten Sinema tweeted on October 5, 2016, that "[a] woman, her family, & doctor should make decisions about her health care, not Washington politicians." These tweets were rare among tweets sent by male candidates. Out of the total number of tweets sent about "health," 57 percent of those sent by men were about the Affordable Care Act (Obamacare), while only 3 percent were about women's health, whereas 30 percent of women's tweets were about Obamacare and 10 percent were about women's health.

2018 Election

In the last two months of the election, I collected 59,886 tweets for 749 candidates who were active on Twitter, 531 male and 218 female candidates. Candidates in 2018 were more active on Twitter than candidates in 2016. The average number of tweets sent per person was 78.7, with men sending approximately 70 tweets on average while women sent 99.7 (a significant difference).[4]

When it comes to tweets about "women's issues," the data collection reveals that only 12 percent of the candidates tweeting during the last two months sent no tweets about these topics. On average, candidates sent approximately fourteen tweets about these topics, or 18 percent of their total tweets (a 4 percent increase from 2016). Women sent more tweets about these topics overall than men, with female candidates sending twenty-four tweets and male candidates sending ten tweets on average. As a proportion of their total tweets, this means that women spent approximately 24 percent

---

4. Difference of means t-test p ≤ 0.0001.

of their tweets discussing these issues, while 14 percent of men's tweets were about these topics. This difference is very significant.[5]

As table 4.3 shows, eight of the 2018 candidates sent more than one hundred tweets about "women's issues," with 75 percent of those candidates being women. The person who sent the most tweets about "women's issues" was Shawna Roberts, a Democrat who ran for the first time for the 6th District seat in Ohio against Bill Johnson (incumbent). She sent 175 tweets about these issues. Almost all the other people making the list were completely new faces for seats in Congress. The only person making the list that had served any time before 2018 was Pramila Jayapal, who had been elected in the 2016 election. Four of these candidates lost their 2018 bids, and almost all of them are Democrats (except for Bryan Leib).

When it comes to "men's issues," the data show that on average candidates sent approximately eight tweets about these topics (or 10 percent of their total tweets). This means that in 2018, like 2016, candidates tweeted more about "women's issues" than "men's issues." In this particular year, women tweet more about these topics as well. Women sent approximately nine tweets about these topics, while men sent 7.6 tweets on average. While this means that women sent a few more tweets than men did about these topics, this difference is not considered statistically significant.[6]

The candidates who sent more than one hundred tweets about these topics are also listed in table 4.3. Cathy McMorris Rodgers, Republican representative from the 5th District of Washington, sent the highest number of tweets about these issues, with 160 tweets, followed by Denny Wolff and Kevin Brady.

When I examine all of the issues defined as "women's issues" and "men's issues," I find that female and male candidates stressed different issues as their "top" issues. While both men and women sent approximately the same number of tweets on topics like business and agriculture (two of the most discussed "men's issues"), the number of tweets sent about "women's issues" comparatively are very different between the two groups. As shown in table 4.4, which displays the topics tweeted about at least an average of once over the two months before the election, women sent the most tweets about terms associated with "woman" (like woman, women, female, and girl) followed by tweets about health care, family, and education. These were the same topics women discussed in 2016, but over twice as often. Men, however, sent less than half as many tweets as women did about health care (which was

---

5. Difference of means t-test p ≤ 0.0001.
6. Difference of means t-test p = 0.1880.

TABLE 4.3. 2018 Prolific Issue Tweeters

Women's Issues	Men's Issues
Shawna Roberts (D)	Cathy McMorris Rodgers (R)
Susan Wild (D)	Denny Wolff (D)
Dwight Evans (D)	Kevin Brady (R)
Bryan Lieb (R)	
Vanessa Enoch (D)	
Mary Gay Scanlon (D)	
Pramila Jayapal (D)	
Dawn Barlow (D)	

TABLE 4.4. Topics Tweeted about at Least Once on Average

Female candidates	Male candidates
Women—5.3	Health—1.9
Health—4.4	Family—1.8
Family—3.3	Taxes—1.7
Education—2.5	Education—1.4
Taxes—2.1	Women—1.3
Children—1.9	Business—1.0
Kavanaugh—1.4	Agriculture—1.0
Business—1.0	
Agriculture—1.0	

Values represent the number of tweets on average about these topics.
Female candidates sent 99.7 tweets on average and male candidates sent 70 tweets on average.

the issue they tweeted the most about), followed by tweets about family and taxes. If anything, when we compare this list of topics to table 4.2, we see that there are very few changes for men between the two years, while women became more vocal on Twitter about both male and female issues.

Discussion and Conclusion

During the 2018 elections, many dubbed the year itself as the "Year of the Woman." We had a significant increase in the number of women running for elected offices across the country. As these results show, that increase in the number of women running in Congress made a difference in the tweets that we saw coming from candidates. There was a marked increase between 2016 and 2018 in terms of the attention paid by candidates as a whole to all issues, but the real shift is seen in the attention paid to "women's issues." In

2016, 20 percent of the candidates never mentioned even one of the topics considered here as "women's issues," whereas in 2018 only 12 percent never tweeted about them. Furthermore, the percentage of total tweets dedicated to "women's issues" increased from 14 percent to 18 percent. The attention to "men's issues" also increased from approximately 8 percent in 2016 to 10 percent in 2018.

A significant increase in issue discussion, especially when it comes to "women's issues," means that women in general had better representation in 2018. The key finding here though is that the candidates who were leading the way in talking about "women's issues" online were female candidates. Women were spending significantly more time talking about all issues on Twitter, but the real shift is seen with "women's issues." Approximately one-fourth of the tweets sent by female candidates in 2018 were about "women's issues," compared to only 14 percent of men's tweets. Furthermore, in the breakdown of the tweets themselves, I find that across the two years there isn't a real increase in the number of tweets about any of the issues discussed by men, but women became more vocal in 2018 about all issues. On Twitter then, 2018 was truly the "Year of the Woman."

Future research should parse out whether these shifts in 2018 were among all women running or were really among particular types of female candidates, like Democrats or those in competitive races. That particular year, many women ran for office in response to Trump's presidency, which meant that many of the new faces on the ballot were Democratic women, but it may be that this increase was among both Republican and Democratic women. Were all men paying attention to similar topics in 2016 and 2018? Previous work by Estrada and Evans (2019) shows that (1) partisanship mattered in 2016 (Democratic women sent more tweets about these issues than Republican women; Democratic men sent more tweets about these topics than Republican men), and (2) the group talking the most about women's issues were Democratic females, while Republican males tweeted the least about them. Almost one-third of the Republican males running in 2016 never tweeted a single word or phrase about any issue considered a "women's issue" (Estrada and Evans 2019).

The data from 2018 reveal the same patterns as the data from 2016 (see figure 4.1). When I examine the tweets by both partisanship and gender, I find that Democrats sent more than twice as many tweets about "women's issues" than Republicans.[7] Democratic women out-tweeted Republican women about these topics, but within both parties female candidates out-

---

7. Republicans sent 8.79 tweets while Democrats sent 20.44 tweets, on average.

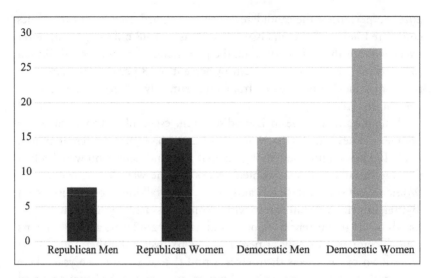

Figure 4.1. Average number of tweets about "women's issues"

tweeted their male counterparts, doubling the number of tweets sent about these policy issues. Democratic men and Republican women sent approximately the same number of tweets about "women's issues."

Future work should explore whether these findings were driven by competitiveness and determine whether men spent any more time overall talking about specific issues in 2018 than in 2016. My analysis shows that men really did not shift the amount of time given on Twitter to "women's issues" in 2018, but there were fewer Republican men who sent no tweets about these topics.[8] Women, on the other hand, sent significantly more issue specific tweets in 2018.

Furthermore, as some of the results presented here demonstrate, the ways in which these topics are discussed by candidates deserves further analysis. Male and female candidates not only discuss these topics at different rates, but the ways in which they discuss them differ as well. More than half of the tweets sent by men about "health" in 2016 were about the evaluation and changes they would propose to the Affordable Care Act, while more tweets were sent by female candidates about women's health. Future work should examine the framing around these "women's issues" by all candidates.

At the conclusion of the 2018 races, more women were elected to Con-

---

8. 18 percent of Republican men in 2018 sent no tweets about "women's issues."

gress. Future work should examine whether the increase in the number of women in Congress led to a shift in bill introductions on these topics. Previous research suggests that we should expect such a shift to happen: women tend to not only discuss these issues more often than men but they work on them in office too (Osborn and Mendez 2010; Shogan 2002; Walsh 2002; Gerrity, Osborn, and Mendez 2007). As the results show here, an increase in women running meant that overall there was a significant increase in the policy issues addressed on Twitter, especially on those issues that disproportionately affect women as a group.

These results clearly show that female candidates are using Twitter in a way that is very different than traditional campaign advertising. My results do not align with the work by Parry-Giles et al. (2019), which shows that female candidates were not campaigning "as women" on television. One reason for these differences is that traditional advertising attracts a much broader viewership than Twitter, where users are younger, more educated, more affluent, and more Democratic than the general public (Wojcik and Hughes 2018). Women also tend to be the most prolific users, who also tweet the most about politics (Wojcik and Hughes 2018). Since female candidates are using this platform in ways to reach these individuals by structuring their tweets to be attractive to these users, future work should examine whether other out-groups (like challengers in general) are more likely to tweet about these issues than discuss them in advertisements on television. Future work should also examine other forms of social media used by candidates as well, similar to the work by Mendes and Dikwal-Bot in chapter 3.

As these findings as well as previous research on candidate use of Twitter demonstrate, female candidates are affected by Twitter as a medium. Since those who follow Twitter accounts are more likely to be supporters of those campaigns than those who would be exposed to television advertisements, and female users are leading the way in terms of discussing politics on Twitter, female candidates are strategically using their tweets to reach out to those individuals. Since Twitter allows candidates to mention issues in real time, these issues discussed by female candidates also give their followers a better idea of what they think about on a day-to-day basis.

Finally, since female candidates are using this medium to talk more about "women's issues" given the characteristics of the medium itself, future work should see if their personalization of these issues affects their likeability among those who are exposed to their tweets. Personalization of messages on Twitter has been found to affect feelings of connectedness to the candidates (Kruikemeier et al. 2013) and judgments of candidates' competency and likeability (Coffe and Theiss-Morse 2016; Meeks 2017). Effects on competency and likeability, however, are not equal for men and women when using personalization in tweets (Meeks 2017); but as my results show, women as outsider candidates are using this medium to address all policy issues, at much higher rates than men. Does their personalization of these topics on Twitter help them electorally? Some work has found personalization to be associated with winning (McGregor, Lawrence, and Cardova 2014), while other work has found there to be no relationship (Meeks 2017). Given the stark differences between how male and female candidates used the platform in 2018 in terms of the volume of their messages and the issues addressed, more work is needed in this area to truly parse out the cumulative effect of these messages. One thing is for certain: Twitter as a medium is affecting the ways female candidates campaign.

Works Cited

Alexander, D., K. Andersen. 1993. "Gender as a Factor in the Attribution of Leadership Traits." *Political Research Quarterly* 46(3): 527–45.

Alter, C. 2018. "A Year Ago They Marched: Now a Record Number of Women are Running for Office." *Time.* https://time.com/5107499/record-number-of-women-are-running-for-office/

Barberá, P., and G. Rivero. 2015. "Understanding the political representativeness of Twitter users." *Social Science Computer Review* 33(6): 712–29.

Bode, L., and K. E. Dalrymple. 2016. "Politics in 140 characters or less: Campaign communication, network interaction, and political participation on Twitter." *Journal of Political Marketing* 15(4): 311–32.

Box-Steffensmeier, J. M., S. DeBoef, and T. Lin. 2004. "The dynamics of the partisan gender gap." *American Political Science Review* 98: 515–28.

Bratton, K. A. 2002. "The Effect of Legislative Diversity on Agenda Setting: Evidence from Six State Legislatures." *American Politics Research* 30: 115–42.

Burrell, B. 1994. *A woman's place is in the house: Campaigning for congress in the feminist era.* Ann Arbor: University of Michigan Press.

Center for American Women and Politics (CAWP), Eagleton Institute of Politics, Rutgers University.

Coffé, H., and E. Theiss-Morse. 2016. "The effect of political candidates' occupational background on voters' perceptions of and support for candidates." *Political Science* 68 (1): 55–77.

Conway, B.A., K. Kenski, and D. Wang. 2015. "The rise of Twitter in the political campaign: Searching for intermedia agenda-setting effects in the presidential primary." *Journal of Computer-Mediated Communication* 20(4): 363–80.

Dittmar, K. 2016. "Finding gender in election 2016: Lesson from presidential gender watch." Center for American Women and Politics.

Dodson, D. L. 1998. "Representing Women's Interests in the U.S. House of Representatives." In S. Thomas and C. Wilcox, eds., *Women and Elective Office*, 130–49. New York: Oxford University Press.

Dolan, J. 1998. "Support for women's interests in the 103rd congress: The distinct impact of congressional women." *Women & Politics* 18: 81–84.

Estrada, M. J., and H. K. Evans. 2019. "Out of the kitchen and into Congress: An analysis of how female candidates tweeted in 2016." Southern Political Science Association Meeting.

Evans, H. K. 2016. "Do women only talk about 'female issues'? Gender and issue discussion on Twitter." *Online Information Review* 40: 660–72.

Evans, H. K., K. Brown, and T. Wimberly. 2017. "Gender and Presidential Elections: How the 2016 Candidates Played the 'Woman Card' on Twitter." In Jody Baumgartner and Terri Towner, eds., *The Internet and the 2016 Presidential Campaign*. Lanham, MD: Lexington Books.

Evans, H. K., K. Brown, and T. Wimberly. 2018. "'Delete Your Account': The 2016 Presidential Race on Twitter." *Social Science Computer Review* 36(4): 500–8.

Evans, H. K., and J. H. Clark. 2016. "'You Tweet like a Girl!': How Female Candidates Campaign on Twitter." *American Politics Research* 44(2): 326–52.

Evans, H. K., V. Cordova, and S. Sipole. 2014. "Twitter style: An analysis of how house candidates used Twitter in their 2012 campaigns." *PS: Political Science and Politics* 47: 454–462.

Fridkin, K. L., and P. J. Kenney. 2009. "The role of gender stereotypes in U.S. senate campaigns." *Politics & Gender* 5: 301–24.

Gainous, J., and K. M. Wagner. 2014. *Tweeting to power: The social media revolution in American politics*. New York: Oxford University Press.

Gerrity, J., T. Osborn, and J. Mendez. 2007. "Women and representation: A different view of the district?" *Politics & Gender* 3(2): 179–200.

Herrnson, P. S., J. C. Lay, and A. K. Stokes. 2003. "Women running 'as women': Candidate gender, campaign issues, and voter-targeting strategies." *The Journal of Politics* 65: 244–55.

Hillsberg, A. 2014. "Who Rus the Social Media World? Men or Women?" Brandwatch. https://www.brandwatch.com/blog/social-media-and-women/

Huddy, L., and N. Terkildsen. 1993. "The consequences of gender stereotypes for women candidates at different levels and types of offices." *Political Research Quarterly* 46: 503–25.

Kang, T., E. F. Fowler, M. M. Franz, and T. N. Ridout. 2018. "Issue consistency? Comparing television advertising, tweets, and e-mail in the 2014 Senate campaigns." *Political Communication* 35: 32–49.

Karpf, D. 2012. *The Move-On Effect: The Unexpected Transformation of American Political Advocacy*. Oxford: Oxford University Press.

Kaufmann, K. M., and J. R. Petrocik. 1999. "The changing politics of American men: Understanding the sources of the gender gap." *American Journal of Political Science* 43: 864–87.

Kreiss, D. 2016. "Seizing the moment: The presidential campaigns' use of Twitter during the 2012 electoral cycle." *New Media & Society* 18(8): 1473–90.

Kruikemeier, S., G. V. Noort, R. Vliegenthart, and C. H. de Vreese. 2013. "Getting closer: The effects of personalized and interactive online political communication." *European Journal of Communication* 28(91): 53–66.

Larson, S. G. 2001. "Running as women? A comparison of female and male Pennsylvania assembly candidates' brochures." *Women & Politics* 22: 107–24.

Lawless, J. L. 2004. "Women, war, and winning elections: Gender stereotyping in the post September 11th era." *Political Research Quarterly* 57: 479–90.

Lin, Y. 2019. "10 Twitter Statistics Every Marketer Should Know in 2020." Oberlo. https://www.oberlo.com/blog/twitter-statistics

McGregor, S. C., R. G. Lawrence, and A. Cardona. 2016. "Personalization, gender, and social media: Gubernatorial candidates' social media strategies." *Information, Communication & Society* 20(2): 264–83.

Meeks, L. 2017. "Getting personal: Effects of Twitter personalization on candidate evaluations." *Politics & Gender* 13(1): 1–25.

Ortutay, B. 2016. "A Twitter election: A look at some memorable hashtags." Associated Press News.

Osborn, T., and J. Mendez. 2010. "Speaking as women: Women and floor speeches in the Senate." *Journal of Women, Politics & Policy* 31(1): 1–21.

Page, B. I., and R. Y. Shapiro. 1992. *The rational public: Fifty years of trends in Americans' policy preferences.* Chicago: University of Chicago Press.

Parry-Giles, S., A. H. Farhat, M. Salzano, and S. de Saint Felix. 2019. "Women who ran for Congress avoided women's issues in their campaign ads." *The Conversation.* https://theconversation.com/women-who-ran-for-congress-avoided-womens-issues-in-their-campaign-ads-109211

Podkul, A. R. 2018. "The primaries project at Brookings: Breaking out the data by party and gender." https://static.politico.com/f5/7a/74ca707840919c6a02de49f0 5ca9/brookingsgenderdata.pdf

Sanbonmatsu, K. 2002. "Gender stereotypes and vote choice." *American Journal of Political Science* 46: 20–34.

Shogan, C. 2002. "Speaking out: An analysis of Democratic and Republican woman-invoked rhetoric in the 105th Congress." *Women & Politics* 23: 129–46.

Swers, M. 2002. *The difference women make: The policy impact of women in Congress.* Chicago: University of Chicago Press.

Vega, A., and J. M. Firestone. 1995. "The Effects of Gender on Congressional Behavior and the Substantive Representation of Women." *Legislative Studies Quarterly* 20(2): 213–22.

Wagner, K. M., J. Gainous, and M. R. Holman. 2017. "I am Woman, Hear Me Tweet! Gender Differences in Twitter Use Among Congressional Candidates." *Journal of Women, Politics, and Policy* 38(4): 430–55.

Walsh, K. C. 2002. "Enlarging representation: Women bringing in marginalized perspectives to floor debate in the House of Representatives." In Cindy Simon Rosenthal, ed., *Women Transforming Congress,* 370–98. Norman: University of Oklahoma Press.

Wattenberg, M. P. 2016. *Is Voting for Young People?* New York: Routledge.

Witt, L., K. M. Paget, and G. Matthews. 1994. *Running as a woman: Gender and power in American politics.* New York: The Free Press.

Wojcik, S. and A. Hughes. 2018. "Sizing Up Twitter Users." Pew Research Center. https://www.pewresearch.org/internet/2019/04/24/sizing-up-twitter-users/

Wolbrecht, C. 2000. *The Politics of Women's Rights: Parties, Positions, and Change.* Princeton: Princeton University Press.

CHAPTER 5

Two Different Worlds

The Gap between the Interests of Voters and the Media in Canada in the 2019 Federal Election

Christopher Waddell, Carleton University

Canada's 2019 federal election will be remembered for one image—Justin Trudeau, the prime minister seeking reelection for his Liberal Party, posing in blackface.

Posted on *Time* magazine's online site in the early evening of September 18, the picture was first published in 2001 in a yearbook from a Vancouver high school, where Trudeau was a teacher and dressed as Aladdin for a school costume event.

News organizations immediately viewed the photo as a turning point in what had been a listless campaign headed to an October 21 vote. Commentators suggested the photo revealed Trudeau as a hypocrite, undermining everything he had campaigned on and his government had vocally promoted for the preceding four years, including his support for diversity, multiculturalism, inclusiveness, respect for visible minorities, and an end to racism.

The issue dominated the news cycle for days. For example, in the Factiva media database using the search terms "Trudeau and blackface" between September 18 and 25 there are seventy-nine references in the *Globe and Mail* and forty in the *National Post*, Canada's two national newspapers, plus 128 in the *Toronto Star*, twenty-five in the *New York Times*, and twelve in *The Guardian*. In the whole Factiva database for that seven-day period, there are 2,179 references to Trudeau and blackface.

For media inside and outside Canada, the photo was immediately

103

viewed as a "game changer" that would bring the election to life and cripple Trudeau's ability to win a second term. Except it didn't.

In the week following September 18, the Liberals rose three percentage points in national public opinion polls on their way to reelection, reduced to a minority government, but well ahead of any of the other parties.

In fact, the whole episode revealed the gap between what interests the media and what interests voters in an election campaign. Public opinion research and a series of events throughout the campaign, of which the most high-profile was the blackface controversy, highlighted that gulf. It existed before the campaign began and continued throughout. The breadth of the difference and the implications for the future of the media when the interests of journalists covering elections in the digital age appear increasingly alienated from the views of their audiences, are explored in this chapter.

How Canada Runs Elections

Federal elections in Canada are fairly straightforward affairs, governed by strict rules on fundraising, advertising, and spending both for parties and individual candidates in each of the Parliament's 338 constituencies. Those rules apply across the country and are set by legislation passed by the federal Parliament and administered by Elections Canada, an independent, nonpartisan agency that oversees federal elections and referendums. All Canadians vote the same way, marking an X on a paper ballot, placed in a box in polling stations. The ballots are counted at each station as soon as the polls close in the evening with the results made public immediately. Both national and individual constituency results are known and the winning party revealed usually within a couple of hours of the polls closing.

The official campaign period runs between thirty-five and fifty-one days from the day the prime minister visits the governor general to seek a dissolution of Parliament to the fixed election date, once every four years on the third Monday in October, unless in a minority Parliament where a government defeat on a confidence issue can trigger an election right away. In 2019, the campaign was forty days long with advance polls over the Thanksgiving holiday-long weekend ten days before polling day.

There are strict spending limits on political parties in the two months before the campaign officially starts, spending up to C$2 million on advertising during that period. During the actual campaign, parties can spend a maximum of C$30 million each. Individual candidates have a ceiling of between $90,000 and $130,000 depending on the number of voters in their constituency.

There are also limits on financial contributions to parties and candidates. Corporate and trade union donations are banned. Individuals can donate up to $1,600 annually to a political party and the same amount to a party's constituency association, getting income tax credits for part of their donations.

Although televised debates among the major political party leaders have been a part of most Canadian federal elections since 1966, in 2019 for the first time a nonpartisan federal Leaders' Debates Commission, rather than television networks acting as a consortium, organized two nationally televised debates (one in English and one in French) on the three main English television networks and two French-language networks. The debates were also available free of charge to online news and social media sites that wanted to show them live. The English-language audience across all media was 14.1 million and the French audience was five million in a country with 27.1 million eligible voters.

Of that total, 17.1 million voted, producing a turnout of 65.9 percent, down from the 68.5 percent recorded in 2015 when the Liberal Party under Justin Trudeau ended nine years of Conservative Party government with Stephen Harper as prime minister. While the 2015 election produced a majority Liberal government, in 2019 Justin Trudeau's majority was reduced to a minority, just as happened to his father, Pierre Trudeau, who won a Liberal majority in 1968 but slipped to a minority government four years later.

An Overview of Campaign Coverage

In fact, the 2019 campaign was a dispiriting one, described by media columnists as being about nothing. It produced a result in which all parties except the Bloc Quebecois were losers. As one columnist suggested mid-campaign, it was an election that would be won by the party leader the public disliked least. The Liberals under Trudeau took the most seats, winning 157 but falling to second in the share of the vote at 33.1 percent, behind the Conservatives 34.1 percent that translated into only 121 seats (up from ninety-nine) after a campaign during which they convinced themselves they would win. The New Democratic Party saw its seat total fall to twenty-four from forty-four and the Green Party won 6.6 percent of the vote and three seats (a gain of one) after polling around 10 percent for most of the campaign. The Bloc Quebecois was the only winner, increasing its presence in the House of Commons to thirty-two seats, all from the province of Quebec, from ten seats four years earlier.

But in analyzing media coverage what was most interesting and important was what didn't happen. Despite three years of cross-border exposure to the hyper-partisan and polarized political and media environments of the United States, none of that was replicated in Canada. More extensive analysis of public opinion about media than in many past campaigns, in part in response to concerns about the spread of misinformation and disinformation by domestic and foreign interests, found a dramatically different situation in Canada than in the United States.

The Digital Democracy Project (DDP), which produced a series of seven reports during the campaign by academics working with the Public Policy Forum, a nonpartisan Ottawa-based think tank, and the Max Bell School of Public Policy at McGill University in Montréal, was definitive in its observations:

> Our findings suggest the Canadian political information ecosystem is likely more resilient than that of other countries, in particular the U.S., due to a populace with relatively high trust in the traditional news media, relatively homogeneous media preferences with only a marginal role for hyper-partisan news, high levels of political interest and knowledge and despite online fragmentation—fairly low levels of ideological polarization overall.[1]

It was not surprising then, as Tamara Small and Brian Budd detail in chapter 7 of this book, that the People's Party of Canada, a newly established, highly ideological party with a conservative-libertarian leader and platform, attracted less than 2 percent of votes nationally, while Maxime Bernier, its leader, lost the seat he had held since 2006 as a Conservative.

The DDP conclusions came from an election monitoring project between August 1 and November 30, 2019, that collected data from a series of public opinion surveys, online media analysis, and analysis of social media content "to examine the media habits of the broader Canadian public as well as the political and journalistic class, with an eye to understanding the various relationships between media use, partisanship, political knowledge and concern over policy issues."[2]

Its reports concluded that news sources that played to partisan audiences—both left and right—had a very small role in the campaign, noting "in certain ways, Canadians appear to demonstrate important elements

---

1. Public Policy Forum, "Digital Democracy Project: Lessons in resilience: Canada's digital media ecosystem and the 2019 election," May 2020, p. 2. https://ppforum.ca/articles/lessons-in-resilience-canadas-digital-media-ecosystem-and-the-2019-election/

2. Public Policy Forum, May 2020, p. 7.

of media literacy, rating hyper-partisan or disreputable news outlets very poorly and self-reporting high levels of skepticism of stories that they see on social media."[3]

In addition, surveys conducted by the DDP found:

> Canadians trust the top media outlets at similar levels as they do friends and family, and far more than they trust the information they get from social media or political parties. Right-leaning partisans can be expected to trust the media less than left-leaning partisans, but the difference is modest. Canadians on the whole have broadly centrist and mainstream news media diets. Few Canadians are attuned to ideologically skewed media sources, even among partisans whose views align with these sources.[4]

Its surveys also found Facebook, used by 30 percent of respondents, was the most used social media platform for political content in Canada, followed by YouTube. Twitter was used less frequently as were WhatsApp and Tumbler. As one of the DDP's campaign reports stated, "this draws our attention to the fact that Twitter, and social media generally speaking, are not used by the vast majority of the public for their news about politics and public affairs."[5]

The Gap between Voters and the Media as Campaigning Began

While Canadians across the ideological spectrum generally rely on the same mainstream news sources for their political information, that doesn't mean the media and voters shared common views about the most important issues facing the country in the weeks leading to the start of the official campaign. In fact, the DDP found a significant gap between what three hundred journalists selected by the researchers from all ideological perspectives (identified as seed journalists in the chart below) and politicians on Twitter viewed as the major issues of the campaign and the issues that voters considered most important.[6]

The gulf between the strong interest of journalists in foreign affairs as

---

3. Public Policy Forum, May 2020, p. 3.

4. Public Policy Forum, May 2020, p. 12.

5. Public Policy Forum, May 2020, p. 13.

6. Public Policy Forum, "Digital Democracy Project Research memo # 1 Media, Knowledge and Misinformation," August 2019, p. 16. https://ppforum.ca/articles/ddp-research-memo-1/

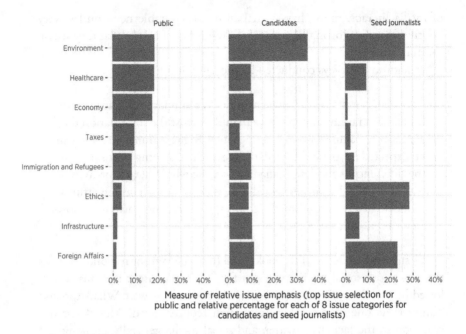

Figure 5.1. Most important issues emphasized on Twitter by the general public, candidates, and journalists—August 2019 Public Policy Forum, *Digital Democracy Project Research memo # 1 Media, Knowledge and Misinformation August 2019* p. 16—https://ppforum.ca/articles/ddp-research-memo-1/

an election issue and the minimal interest of the public in the matter is no surprise. Foreign affairs has rarely been an issue in Canadian elections. The gap on ethics was highlighted in the days before the campaign started as the federal Office of the Conflict of Interest and Ethics Commissioner released a report that concluded Justin Trudeau broke conflict of interest rules surrounding his attempt in late 2018 and early 2019 to ensure SNC-Lavalin, a global Quebec-based engineering company, could sign a deferred prosecution agreement rather than facing a trial for corruption and bribery of Libyan officials. If convicted in a court, SNC-Lavalin would be ineligible to bid on Canadian government contracts for a decade. As with the original SNC story in early 2019 about the internal Liberal government debate over seeking a deferred prosecution agreement that dominated media headlines for weeks and lead to the resignation of two cabinet ministers who disagreed with Trudeau's actions, there was major coverage of the Office of the Conflict of Interest and Ethics Commissioner's conclusions in late August. But those pre-campaign stories had little impact on voter perceptions of Trudeau or the Liberals.

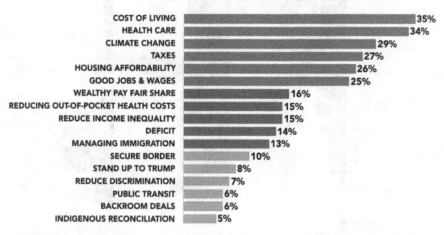

Figure 5.2. Top three issues impacting the vote

More surprising is the lack of journalists' apparent awareness of the importance of the economy in the minds of voters, even though opinion polling suggested the cost of living, taxes, and affordable housing in urban centers were major issues for voters as outlined in an Abacus Data mid-July opinion survey.[7]

There was also a gap between the public's level of interest in environmental issues and that of the media, as a Digital Democracy Project report noted:

> Media coverage of the environment is also more likely to involve climate change than other environmental issues such as single-use plastics or conservation. But while news organizations might be covering the environment, and journalists we monitored on Twitter frequently shared that coverage, there was far more disproportionate sharing of ethics-related stories, especially around the SNC-Lavalin story.[8]

Looking at the gaps in more depth, the DDP in a public opinion survey asked voters to select their most important issues in the upcoming election.

---

7. Bruce Anderson and David Coletto, "Election 2019 in a battle to define the agenda," Abacus Data, July 15, 2019. https://abacusdata.ca/election-2019-is-a-battle-to-define-the-agenda/

8. Public Policy Forum, "Digital Democracy Project Research Memo # 2 The Climate Change Conundrum," August 2019. p. 4. https://ppforum.ca/articles/ddp-research-memo-2/

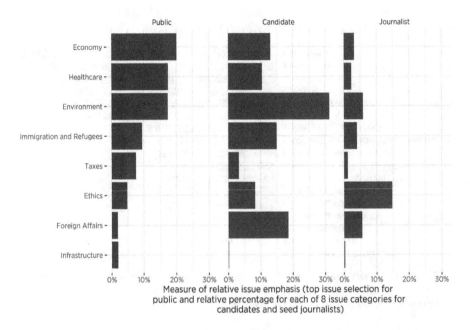

Figure 5.3. Measure of relative issue emphasis (top issue selection for public and relative percentage for each of eight issue categories for candidates and seed journalists)

It then compared that list to the top news stories shared on Twitter by all declared candidates running in the federal election and by its selected list of key journalists. Again, the gaps in perceptions between the three groups were striking, with the economy of much more importance to voters than to the media. Ethics were the flip side of that divide.[9]

As the DDP's authors observed:

> Interestingly, despite the release of the Conflict of Interest and Ethics Commissioner's report on the SNC-Lavalin scandal just two days prior to the start of the sampling period, ethics remains a bottom-tier issue of concern for surveyed Canadians—only 5% rated ethics as the most important issue. Comparatively, candidates (especially Conservative party candidates) and journalists heavily emphasized ethics-related issues on Twitter. Meanwhile both candidates and journalists underemphasized (relative to the general public), issues related to healthcare, taxes and the general economy.[10]

---

9. Public Policy Forum, August 2019, p. 7.
10. Public Policy Forum, August 2019, p. 7.

September 18 and Its Aftermath

Within a couple of hours of the publication of the blackface photo online by *Time*, Trudeau gave a hastily organized, apologetic, and contrite news scrum with the media on his campaign plane in Halifax, including admitting that in high school he had also once played singer Harry Belafonte in blackface. That night CBC television, the national public broadcaster, covered the story extensively on its main newscast at 9:00 p.m. Eastern.

As well as showing Trudeau's encounter with reporters on his campaign plane, the newscast included "man-in-the-street" interviews in Vancouver, seeking voter reaction to the picture and the story. What stood out was the lack of outrage among the people interviewed, including several members of racialized communities. Some expressed disappointment, embarrassment, thought it was dumb and juvenile, but noted that it occurred almost twenty years ago (perhaps also thinking about events in their own past). They also said the story wouldn't affect how they would vote. The public reaction was in sharp contrast to the breathless coverage on the newscast. (As a former television newscast producer, I can say with confidence that had the CBC found anyone who was outraged, that would have been featured prominently in the series of interviews.)

The *Globe and Mail* devoted seven pages to the brownface/blackface issue the next day. Talk radio hosts and media columnists and commentators regurgitated the story for days. In all the pages and hours of coverage of the issue though, there continued to be very few voices of outrage from the public to match the outrage expressed by media commentators.

As Abacus Data noted from public opinion surveys done both in the forty-eight hours after the story broke and then again a week later, "asked how they reacted to the story, 42% (42% last week) said it didn't really bother them, 38% (34% last week) said they didn't like it but felt Mr. Trudeau apologized properly and felt they could move on, and 20% (24% last week) said it truly offended them and their view of Mr. Trudeau changed for the worse."[11]

Perhaps the most interesting result was the fact that of the 24 percent who were truly offended, two-thirds of them were Conservative voters. That may be why the Liberals actually rose three percentage points to 35 percent in Abacus's national poll conducted the week after the story broke, while Conservatives fell one point to 33 percent.

Nonetheless, as Abacus noted, "Mr. Trudeau's reputation was damaged, albeit perhaps less than might have been surmised or expected. Other leaders

---

11. Bruce Anderson and David Coletto, "A better week of Trudeau's Liberals," Abacus Data, September 27. https://abacusdata.ca/a-better-week-for-trudeau-liberals/

have not gained at Mr. Trudeau's expense through this period . . . the photos and video released late last week was a shock that changed the focus and conversation of the election campaign. But so far evidence that they have fundamentally changed people's impressions or intended voting behavior is quite limited."[12] Even more surprising considering the tonnage of media coverage, in the week after the blackface story broke, the Liberals moved ahead of the Conservatives in public support for the first time since May 2019.

Digital Democracy Project researchers also looked at the public reaction to the Trudeau blackface story, comparing it with a mid-campaign story about Conservative leader Andrew Scheer who appeared to have embellished his CV, claiming he had previously been an insurance broker when in fact he just did various jobs in an insurance office for six or seven months.[13] Looking at social media responses to the two stories, DDP researchers concluded,

> In both cases, we find the peak of activity surrounding the revelations occurred for approximately 48 hours, with declining attention and very little broad-based interest five to seven days after the story broke. We find that there were similar declines in interest across political candidates, journalists and the mass public. We also find that attention to these stories was largely isolated to specific partisan-motivated communities, with fewer partisans sharing or discussing issues that hurt their preferred party.[14]

The research suggests that political content on social media consists in large part of individuals, usually like-minded, in conversations that engage and interest few outside that group. Yet much of the media appears to view social media, and Twitter in particular, as surrogates for public opinion, even though it is regularly pointed out that political discussions on Twitter rarely reach outside a circle dominated by journalists, politicians, partisans, and political junkies.

The blackface controversy wasn't the only example of media enthusiasm for digging into candidates' pasts that was met by yawns from vot-

---

12. Bruce Anderson and David Coletto, "A sensational week yet a tight race remains," Abacus Data, September 23, 2019. https://abacusdata.ca/a-sensational-week-yet-a-tight-race-remains/

13. Janyce McGregor, "Andrew Scheer's experience in the insurance industry: '6 or 7 months," CBC News, September 30, 2019. https://www.cbc.ca/news/politics/scheer-insurance-broker-monday-1.5303394

14. Public Policy Forum, "Digital Democracy Project: Lessons in resilience: Canada's digital media ecosystem and the 2019 election," May 2020, p. 104. https://ppforum.ca/articles/lessons-in-resilience-canadas-digital-media-ecosystem-and-the-2019-election/

ers. At least six candidates, standing for different parties, withdrew their nominations or had their party affiliation removed by their parties during the campaign, mostly following media revelations about the candidates' past activities or comments, sometimes years old, on social media. In the campaign's early days those media stories usually focused on past videos of Conservative candidates that were discovered and handed to journalists by Liberal Party researchers and operatives. According to Paul Adams, a journalism professor at Carleton University, this suggests that the Liberals skillfully accomplished "a sort of hack on the media, exploiting their weakness for novelty and tension. Because it was in video form, it took little or no effort to verify on the fly."[15]

The Digital Democracy Project report highlighted the gap in interest in the issue between the public and partisans, noting the campaign featured a high level of candidate resignations "because of past controversial behavior or comments coming to light. While more than 60% of partisans on both the left and right report having discussed the issue, less than half of non-partisans discussed it even once. . . . The resignation of candidates due to controversial past behavior is of far more interest to partisans and the general Twitter population than the broader Canadian public."[16]

Different Perceptions of the Leaders' Debates

The gap between how the public and the media perceive the importance and value of campaign events extended to the two nationally televised leaders' debates, one in English and one in French. They were available live on fifteen television networks, three national radio networks, and twenty-four digital platforms.

As the commission concluded in its May 2020 report on its activities:

A broad view of our evidence suggests that the debates were central to the electoral process. First, they were widely viewed by Canadians, both through traditional media and social media. Second, they served an important role in clarifying party positions. Third, those who watched the debates report greater discussion and news con-

---

15. Paul Adams, "The parties went negative and the media enabled them," Policy Options, October 23, 2019. https://policyoptions.irpp.org/magazines/october-2019/the-parties-went-neg ative-and-the-media-enabled-them/

16. Public Policy Forum, "Digital Democracy Project Research Memo # 7 The Partisan Playground," October 2019, p. 10. https://ppforum.ca/articles/ddp-research-memo-7/

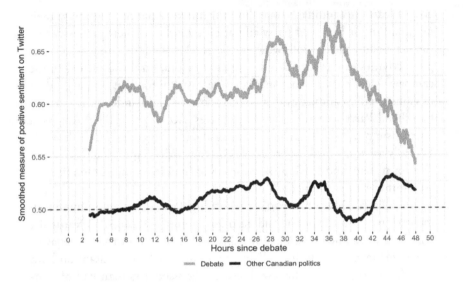

Figure 5.4. Sentiment evaluation of post-English debate-related commentary relative to that of overall discussion of Canadian politics

sumption. Fourth, we present evidence that those who watched the debates also updated their views of the parties and their leaders. On balance, the debates played an important role in increasing engagement with the issues, leaders, and choices before voters.[17]

They also revealed a gap between the generally positive view the public had of the debates and the generally negative view of the debates that dominated post-debate media coverage. Researchers commissioned by the Leaders' Debates Commission analyzed tweets from almost 4,000 Twitter accounts made up of journalists, news outlets, candidates, advocates, and the public during the two-hour debate.[18]

Their data in figure 5.4 above shows that "immediately following the English-language debate on the evening of [October] the 7th, there was overall positive sentiment [about the debate] that steadily increased until the

---

17. Leaders' Debates Commission, "Democracy matters, debates count: A report on the 2019 Leaders' debates Commission and the future of leaders debates in Canada," May 2020, p. 6.

18. See note on methodology in John R. McAndrews, Aengus Bridgman, Peter John Loewen, Daniel Rubenson, Laura B. Stephenson, and Allison Harell, "Evaluation of the 2019 Federal Leaders' Debates," Report to the Leaders' Debates Commission, January 2020, pp. 10–11. https://www.debates-debats.ca/en/report/evaluation-2019-federal-leaders-debates/

Figure 5.5. Sentiment evaluation of post-English language debate-related commentary relative to that of overall discussion of Canadian politics

morning of the 9th at which point there was a steady decrease."[19] This, the researchers concluded, seemed in response to the overwhelmingly very negative commentary about the debate format, performance of the moderators, and strict time limits placed on leaders' responses that appeared in the media the day following the debate and then seemed to trickle down to voters, turning their initially positive impressions more negative.

Researchers tested this theory by splitting the tweets of journalists and media outlets from those of the public (figure 5.5). That confirmed the gap between how the public and journalists perceived the debates. The researchers concluded:

> there are two striking findings here: 1) the sentiment of journalists is overall less positive than the mass population; and 2) the decline in positive sentiment occurred among journalists approximately 24 hours after the first debate and 12 hours before we saw a similar decline in the mass population. This suggests that the full Twitter population took sentiment cues from the journalists and the overall

---

19. McAndrews et al., "Evaluation of the 2019 Federal Leaders' Debates," January 2020, pp. 46–47.

Electoral Campaigns, Media, and the New World of Digital Politics

evaluation of the debate shifted in a negative direction well after the debate had concluded.[20]

Misinformation Missing in Action

While many issues that voters said were important to them didn't get much media coverage, news organizations spent considerable time and attention preparing to expose disinformation and misinformation in the campaign. Several national broadcast, print, and online news organizations dedicated reporters specifically to covering the issue prior to and during the campaign. For the most part the disinformation reporters had little to do throughout the election period. As the Digital Democracy Project researchers reported:

> We looked actively for disinformation—false information related to political issues disseminated with the intent to mislead the Canadian public, disrupt public democratic dialogue and potentially affect the outcome of the vote. Our finding is that disinformation did not play a major role in the 2019 Canadian election campaign. This is consistent with the findings of many other investigations by journalists, academics, government agencies and officials and the private sector. That is not to say there were no instances of disinformation, but what there was generally did not appear coordinated and had limited impact.[21]

Mind the Gap

So why was there such a gap on so many fronts between what interested the media and what interested Canadians in the campaign? This happened even after the Canadian media had watched closely and covered the multiyear debate in the United States about coverage of the 2016 presidential election and the failure of much of the U.S. media to talk to many voters outside major urban centers and understand the appeal to them of Donald Trump. Why was the media not more attuned to what interested Canadians rather than candidates, parties, and Twitter partisans in the campaign and what are

---

20. McAndrews et al., p. 47.

21. Public Policy Forum, "Digital Democracy Project: Lessons in resilience: Canada's digital media ecosystem and the 2019 election," May 2020, p. 5. https://ppforum.ca/articles/lessons-in-resilience-canadas-digital-media-ecosystem-and-the-2019-election/

the implications of their failure to see and respond to how voters perceived the campaign and its issues?

To some extent, the gulf between the interests of media and the public in campaign coverage existed well before the digital era. There has long been regular criticism of media performance after each election for too much opinion-poll-driven coverage of the horse race and who will win, at the expense of covering the issues and how the party platforms compare that likely shape voter interest and turnout.

Despite the time spent analyzing lessons from 2016 coverage in the United States, the gap in 2019 may be a sign that the Canadian media no longer have the resources or ability to provide wide-ranging campaign coverage. The cumulative impact of years of cutbacks in numbers of journalists and editors as news organizations struggled with declining revenue due to dramatic falls in advertising was finally negatively affecting the quality and breadth of the journalism being produced and the ability or perhaps the interest of the media to stay attuned to voter perceptions deeper than the latest shouting matches on Twitter or the most recent opinion poll results.

It's not that there wasn't good work done by journalists during the campaign, Adams concludes in assessing the 2019 election coverage. But, he argues, perhaps journalists took too much of their cue for what's important from politicians and parties rather than voters:

It would be wrong to say that the media alone were responsible for the negativity of this campaign. What we witnessed rather was a cycle, much of it beginning with the parties themselves, turbocharged by the media, spun through social media, then picked up again and further amplified by the politicians. This cycle could have been broken had the parties presented big ideas or divided more clearly on issues of principle or policy, but for the most part they chose not to. And there were signs of resistance in the media—reporters and columnists who worked mightily to bring us back to what mattered, or should matter: climate change, the economy, taxes and deficit, systemic racism, the scandal of the condition of Indigenous people, foreign policy even. But in the end, all their efforts to save us from this dismal election were in vain.[22]

What appears to have happened might be described as the "cable news-ization" of political coverage in Canada across newspapers, radio, television,

---

22. Adams, "The parties went negative and the media enabled them."

online, and social media channels where opinion, commentary, and outrage too frequently replaced reporting, context, and facts. There are fewer reporters and their employers no longer have the financial resources to allow them to travel as much as in the past. That's negatively changed the nature of how campaigns are covered with fewer journalists leaving their newsrooms, thereby widening the gap between the media and voters if journalists are not on the ground talking to those who will vote.

The 2019 election came after almost a decade of upheaval in the Canadian media. There have been multiyear ongoing cutbacks in all newsrooms across the country that meant fewer experienced journalists and editors assigned to campaign coverage. That hurts the quality of what's produced. News organizations suffer from the loss of context and knowledge from past campaigns that walked out the door through layoffs and buyouts of senior journalists close to retirement. The result has been more superficial coverage that lacks depth and historical context.

That shortcoming was magnified in 2019 by shrinking budgets for news coverage that constrained travel and meant more journalists were sitting in offices commenting rather than on the ground meeting voters and attending candidates' meetings. Taking the temperature on the ground of the electorate is crucial, since in a country that crosses six time zones national elections are in reality concurrent regional elections with distinct issues and usually a different collection of contending parties in each region.

The pressures facing journalists that compromise their work have also increased as they file stories daily and are asked to update them constantly while also reporting on multiple media formats—radio, television, online, Facebook, Twitter, Instagram, and other social media. That means less time for background research to provide context for stories, which translates into less substantive stories that may be quick to do (a candidate's past faux pas) or handed to them on a platter from parties. The evidence suggests this sort of coverage doesn't much interest the electorate.

Turbocharged by Twitter, too much of campaign coverage centers on media fascination with war rooms, strategy, and strategists—all staples of news channels that are continuously being monitored in all newsrooms. Media infatuation with these subjects occurs even though there is no evidence that many voters share that intrigue about insider gossip. That further widens the gap between the media and the voters in their assessments of the campaign's key moments and issues.

Devotion to the horse race by media remains as strong as ever, also stoked by tweets, with an emphasis on reporting the results of different opinion polls often on a daily basis while rarely differentiating between polls that utilize different methodologies. The result is coverage that treats as significant changes in party standings that are within a survey's margin of error if a survey has one, as online surveys do not. That problem was amplified in the 2019 election as support for the Liberals and Conservatives rarely moved outside the range of the margin of error throughout the campaign.

The media consumption habits of journalists may also be increasingly affecting what they choose to cover in campaigns. Unlike voters who are at work during the day, journalists and their editors watch cable television news channels that are on all day in their offices. They conclude three damaging things that can affect their journalistic decisions: that everyone else is also watching cable news; that what is talked about on cable news as well as the way it is talked about is important; and that this coverage reflects the reality of how voters are thinking about the candidates, their policies, and campaign events. None of these are true.

Tied to that is the belief among journalists that social media, specifically Twitter, is an accurate reflection of public opinion and reality. So the outrage that forms the basis for much of political social media interventions must reflect what issues interest voters and how they perceive the campaign and candidates. That is also not true, for as the DDP report noted, more than three-quarters of Canadians are not on Twitter.

Also in addition to watching cable news channels, a focus in most newsrooms is on Chartbeat, which provides real-time tracking of the number of people reading stories on the organization's online news site. The results are often displayed on monitors in the newsroom so everyone can see which stories that day are attracting audience attention. It is one way of determining what interests audiences but also presents the temptation for "click-bait" headlines and stories that will grab attention and drive readers to the news organization's website in the hopes of boosting audience numbers and advertising revenue. Journalists also face pressure from their editors and management to use social media as a tool to drive Chartbeat numbers promoting outrage expressed in columns that are shared on social media that elevate Chartbeat numbers. It's then a short step to choosing to assign that type of story over other more complicated stories that may take more time to report. This does not match or serve voters' interests in a campaign.

Finally, the cross-border impact of the Trump presidency and the media coverage of it in the United States has created the illusion that such a degree of political polarization must be happening in Canada as well (although the research done around the 2019 campaign demolishes that assumption). As well some in the Canadian media have decided to try to emulate the partisan divides of U.S. political journalism, although research suggests there is little appetite for that in Canada.

The cumulative impact of all this is to place a priority on opinion and commentary (as well as it being inexpensive to produce) with the knowledge that the more inflammatory and outrageous the opinion, the greater the likelihood it will get handed around on social media.

In the process, some journalists seem to have misplaced what should be their priorities by focusing on the significance of the relatively small audiences on social media compared to the many more voters who still get their news from television and mainstream media online. As a senior manager at the Canadian Broadcasting Corp., the country's public broadcaster, said in the days leading up to the election, "one of the problems is too many people here think 300 likes are more important than 300,000 viewers."[23]

As commentary and opinion replace reporting, much of the Canadian media is shifting its focus away from its traditional role of trying to tell people how to think about an issue, event, or individuals during a campaign. In the past, that was done by being on the ground, seeing things and reporting what they saw and heard as well as highlighting context, background, and first-person accounts. Reinforced by the ease of acquiring voices, content, and reaction from social media and the hoped-for rewards of driving traffic to websites, the focus for the Canadian media seems to have shifted to what to think about that issue, event, candidate, or individual from how to think about all of that.

But what if the audience isn't buying it, doesn't share the outrage and advice and doesn't agree with the way they are being told what to think, whether it is on issues in a campaign or an eighteen-year-old photo of Justin Trudeau dressed up in brownface or blackface?

The risk for the mainstream media is that under such circumstances news organizations become increasingly irrelevant to much of the public in an election campaign, if they no longer help voters sort out the consequential from the inconsequential or less consequential. After all that is the role the media traditionally proclaims for itself in arguing it is an essential pillar of democracy.

During the 2019 Canadian election campaign the gap regularly emerged between what interested Canadians and what interested political candidates and the media, with those later two often closer together in their views than the media and the public. That in itself is a cause for concern as it suggests the media in an election campaign takes more of its cues about what

---

23. Conversation with the author at CBC Toronto, October 18, 2020.

is important from the people it is covering than from the voters who will determine the election's outcome. The end result can undermine the credibility of the media if it both misinterprets the significance of what happens during a campaign and fails to anticipate or understand the outcome on election night.

But that's not the only risk. That gap comes at a time when news organizations in Canada and globally are facing an existential financial crisis due to a collapse of advertising revenue that by 2019 had been picking up speed for several years. For news organizations, failing to understand their audience's interests and concerns threatens their future. Why should audiences pay to subscribe to news online when that news does not match what interests them?

Research in Canada in recent years has shown that only 9 percent of Canadians are prepared to pay for news online, although the most recent Reuters Institute Digital News Survey released in in June 2020 reported a slight jump to 13 percent of Canadians, which may offer some encouragement to struggling news organizations.[24] Even the COVID-19 pandemic that struck months after the election did not make Canadians more receptive to paying for news. While more than half of a national survey of two thousand respondents said they were keeping up with the news on a daily basis compared to a third of respondents saying they did that in normal times, almost 80 percent of respondents agreed with the statement that "all news in general should be accessible online free of charge."[25] Asked whether "the access to free COVID-19 coverage on online news websites that normally are behind paywalls lead you to pay to subscribe to those news websites in the future?" only 8 percent said yes with a further 23 percent saying maybe. A majority, 54 percent, said no while 15 percent did not know.[26]

The economic upheaval, lockdown, and further collapse of advertising triggered by the COVID-19 pandemic has accelerated the shrinkage of the media in Canada with growing numbers of layoffs and closures.[27] That has generated more requests from news organizations for additional financial

---

24. Reuters Institute, "Digital News Study 2020," June 2020, pp. 90–91. https://reutersinstitute.politics.ox.ac.uk/sites/default/files/2020-06/DNR_2020_FINAL.pdf

25. Carleton University School of Journalism and Communication, "Carleton Researchers Find Free COVID-19 Media Coverage Leads Some to Consider Subscribing to Online News Sites," May 28, 2020. https://newsroom.carleton.ca/2020/carleton-researchers-find-free-covid-19-media-coverage-leads-some-to-consider-subscribing-to-online-news-sites/

26. Carleton University School of Journalism and Communication, May 28, 2020.

27. Steph Wechsler, "We mapped all the media impacts of COVID-19 in Canada," J-Source, April 29, 2019. https://j-source.ca/article/we-mapped-all-the-media-impacts-of-covid-19-in-canada/

aid from governments beyond a $595-million package in 2019 of wage subsidies, consumer tax credits for digital subscriptions, and tax rule changes to enhance philanthropic giving to media organizations. That comes as many Canadians don't even realize the media is in financial trouble.[28]

The 2019 election demonstrated the gap that exists between how Canadians perceive their world and how the media perceives it. That threatens further damage to news organizations that are already in crisis. Continuing financial constraints will likely force a rethinking of how future campaigns unfold and are covered in a digital era. The lack of the partisanship and polarization in Canada of both the media and where voters get their information creates an opportunity to bring the focus of campaign coverage into closer alignment to what interests voters rather than politicians and parties. A return to helping people figure out how to think about issues starting with focusing on what voters think is important, rather than telling voters what to think is important, is a crucial first step in ensuring news organizations can survive and return to playing an essential central and constructive role in democracy.

Bibliography

Adams, Paul. 2019. "The parties went negative and the media enabled them." Policy Options, October 23. https://policyoptions.irpp.org/magazines/october-2019/the-parties-went-negative-and-the-media-enabled-them/

Anderson, Bruce, and David Coletto. 2019. "Election 2019 in a battle to define the agenda." Abacus Data, July 15. https://abacusdata.ca/election-2019-is-a-battle-to-define-the-agenda/

Anderson, Bruce, and David Coletto. 2019. "A better week of Trudeau's Liberals." Abacus Data, September 27. https://abacusdata.ca/a-better-week-for-trudeau-liberals/

Anderson, Bruce, and David Coletto. 2019. "A sensational week yet a tight race remains." Abacus Data, September 23. https://abacusdata.ca/a-sensational-week-yet-a-tight-race-remains/

Carleton University School of Journalism and Communication. 2020. "Carleton Researchers Find Free COVID-19 Media Coverage Leads Some to Consider Subscribing to Online News Sites." May 28. https://newsroom.carleton.ca/2020/carleton-researchers-find-free-covid-19-media-coverage-leads-some-to-consider-subscribing-to-online-news-

Leaders' Debates Commission. 2020. "Democracy matters, debates count: A report on the 2019 Leaders' debates Commission and the future of leaders debates in Canada." May. https://debates-debats.ca/en/report/

McAndrews, John R., Aengus Bridgman, Peter John Loewen, Daniel Rubenson,

---

28. Carleton University School of Journalism and Communication, May 28, 2020.

Laurel B. Stephenson, and Allison Harell. 2020. "Evaluation of the 2019 Federal Leaders' Debates." Leaders' Debates Commission, January. https://www.debates-debats.ca/en/report/evaluation-2019-federal-leaders-debates/

McGregor, Janyce. 2019. "Andrew Scheer's experience in the insurance industry: '6 or 7 months.'" CBC News, September 30. https://www.cbc.ca/news/politics/scheer-insurance-broker-monday-1.5303394

Public Policy Forum. 2019. "Digital Democracy Project Research Memo # 1 Media, Knowledge and Misinformation." August. https://ppforum.ca/articles/ddp-research-memo-1/

Public Policy Forum. 2019. "Digital Democracy Project Research Memo # 2 The Climate Change Conundrum." August. https://ppforum.ca/articles/ddp-research-memo-2/

Public Policy Forum. 2019. "Digital Democracy Project Research Memo # 7 The Partisan Playground." October. https://ppforum.ca/articles/ddp-research-memo-7/

Public Policy Forum. 2020. "Digital Democracy Project: Lessons in resilience: Canada's digital media ecosystem and the 2019 election." May. https://ppforum.ca/articles/lessons-in-resilience-canadas-digital-media-ecosystem-and-the-2019-election/

Reuters Institute. 2020. "Digital News Study 2020." June.

Wechsler, Steph. 2019. "We mapped all the media impacts of COVID-19 in Canada." J-Source, April 29. https://j-source.ca/article/we-mapped-all-the-media-impacts-of-covid-19-in-canada/

CHAPTER 6

The Agenda-Building Power of Facebook and Twitter

The Case of the 2018 Italian General Election

Sara Bentivegna, University of Rome–La Sapienza,
Rita Marchetti and Anna Stanziano, University of Perugia

1. A Sui Generis Election Campaign

It is not unusual to see elections described as "turning points," "testing grounds," or "points of no return," whether in relation to the outcome, its significance, or the campaign climate. One description of the 2018 general election campaign in Italy has dismissed it as "the ugliest ever" (Bobba and Seddone 2018), so there is little doubt that it was a unique event.

It was unusual, first, because the electoral law denied a stable majority to either the center-right, the center-left, or the Movimento Cinque Stelle (Five-Star Movement, 5SM), thus creating expectations of ungovernability. Second, the contrast between the "old" and the "new" politics, cultivated by the media, was used as a frame to interpret both the past and future. Finally, the situation was rendered unusually problematic by the sharp conflict between the competing forces, aiming, not to achieve the impossible goal of winning an absolute majority, but to achieve more modest yet equally important objectives. Thus on the center-right there was open competition between the League's Matteo Salvini and other representatives for leadership of the coalition. To achieve this objective, Salvini attacked on all fronts, challenging both his allies and the leaders of rival coalitions. Until the elections of 2018, no one had managed to rival Berlusconi for the leadership of the center-right. On that occasion, in contrast, the challenge was taken up by Salvini from his position as leader of the League (heir to the Northern League), which in recent years had undergone a process of profound ideological change and generational turnover (Albertazzi, Giovannini, and Seddone 2018). In fact, Matteo Salvini had reinvented the League, replacing the ambition for independence for the regions of the North with a nationalist ideology (Adinolfi 2020). By the time of the election, the 5SM, which had had an antisystem profile from the start, had also undergone significant internal transformations, leading it to appoint a political leader, Luigi Di Maio, after a long period during which it was represented by several different "spokespersons" (Ceccarini and Bordignon 2016). The 5SM leader for his part aimed to make his party the largest, thereby confirming his own position of leadership (Ceccarini and Bordignon 2018). Finally, Matteo Renzi, leader of the Partito Democratico (Democratic Party, DP), was engaged in the difficult task of containing the loss of electoral consensus of his party that had begun with the referendum defeat of 2016.[1]

Against this background of no-holds-barred conflict, the sense of drama was heightened by "the events of Macerata." Macerata is a small city in central Italy where a far-right political activist—known for his racist and xenophobic views—shot at a number of people of African origin, wounding six, because he held them responsible for the killing of an eighteen-year-old girl. The incident soon became a trigger event (Boydstun 2013), opening up a number of discursive opportunities and placing the power of agenda setting in the hands of the media as often happens with unexpected external shocks (Birkland 1998). Following the shooting, the run up to the vote was marked by demonstrations against racism and fascism (expressed by threatening street graffiti and attacks on the headquarters of several political parties), requiring the party leaders to make a number of statements about the various events.

The weeks preceding the vote also saw various scandals, involving all the competing parties, including reports of the compromising pasts of some

---

1. The failure of the 2016 constitutional referendum, aimed at reforming part 2 of the Italian constitution, represented a veritable debacle for Matteo Renzi and his party. The consequences of the defeat were reflected in the outcome of the election of March 4, 2018. Having won 40.8 percent of the vote at the European elections of 2014, the DP in 2018 won only 19 percent of the vote. The unusual character of the elections of 2018 emerges clearly from the outcome, which radically changed the composition of the Italian parliament. 65.9 percent of the membership of the Chamber of Deputies had been elected for the first time, with a corresponding proportion of 64.3 percent in the case of the Senate. Against this background, the success of the 5SM and the League were striking as they obtained 32 percent and 17.4 percent of the vote respectively.

candidates, who were labelled as "unpresentable," and attempts by political representatives to gain control of waste management processes for purposes of personal gain. The intensity of the political conflict was heightened by these events, thus helping to create the climate where the campaign was described as "ugly," as mentioned above.

Despite the agenda-setting power these events gave to the news media, political actors sought to place their own preferred issues at the top of the public agenda or to take control of the issues placed there by the unfolding of events, as in the case of immigration (for Salvini) and political scandals (for Di Maio). These attempts were made during rallies, television talk shows, interviews given to the various newspapers, and, above all, through the messages posted on social media, which have now become citizens' most important source of political information (Legnante and Vaccari 2018). Political actors thus developed "complex media strategies incorporating an ever-changing menu of innovations in conjunction with traditional media management techniques" (Owen 2017, 823).

All this took place within a hybrid media ecosystem (Chadwick 2017). The product of ever increasing integration between mass media logic and networked media logic (Klinger and Svensson 2015), this has made it possible for the campaign agenda to be shaped within an information environment in which political and media actors interact with one another (Van Aelst et al. 2017). The information environment in which the 2018 campaign took place saw the culmination of the process of appropriation of social media by politicians. All were present on the various platforms and all made constant use of them—to the extent that they had a central role in the construction of communication strategies, as had already happened elsewhere (Bossetta 2018; Stier et al. 2018; Wells et al. 2016).

What were the effects on the construction of the public agenda? Did political actors use social media as an "agenda-building tool" (Seethaler and Melischek 2019)? Did the centrifugal and diversifying drives of the current stage of development of the communications media (Bennett and Pfetsch 2018; Pfetsch 2018), together with numerous breaking events, prevent the construction of a shared public agenda? Or did processes of intermedia agenda setting (McCombs 2004) serve to ensure, through ups and downs of convergence and divergence, that the contributions of news media and political actors combined to create an agenda? Finally, what role did issue ownership (Petrocik 1996) play in the competing actors' conquest of space on the agenda of the news media?

In the following sections we present data that can help answer these questions. We start by describing the characteristics of Italy's media landscape, the corpora we have used, and the methods adopted to analyze them. Illustrating the agenda overall, we aim to highlight its specific features and the points of contact between the actors involved in its construction, as well as any differences in the political actors' agenda-setting power with the respect to the news media.

2. The Media Landscape

Before discussing the methods used to analyze the public agenda during the 2018 campaign, we describe Italy's media landscape. Above all, the penetration of the Internet (92 percent) and the spread of social media usage (Newman 2019) has reached such levels as to close the gap with other European countries, and multiplied the volume of information readily available to citizens. At the same time, it is also true that, as in other countries, "getting news on social media doesn't mean that other more traditional pathways to news are ignored" (Shearer and Gottfried 2017, 17). In Italy, television continues to play a central role within the media ecosystem (Hallin and Mancini 2004), notwithstanding the changes introduced by the spread of digital technologies. The data made available by the Autorità per le garanzie nelle comunicazioni (AGCOM 2018), or the Regulatory Authority for Communication, show that television is the main source of information for 48.2 percent of respondents, followed by the Internet (26.3 percent), the press (17.1 percent), and the radio (8.4 percent). When it comes to acquiring political information, respondents rely on television (50.5 percent), the web generally (43.8 percent), the press (24.1 percent), and the radio (13.9 percent). Finally, with regard to the different combinations used by respondents to obtain information, 41.8 percent of the population use all the media; about 25 percent use three of them; 18 percent use two media; and only 11 percent use just one.

Further confirmation concerning the range of media used by Italian citizens to obtain information comes from research carried out by the Pew Internet Center (2018), which explored the use of both social media and the legacy media. The results show unequivocally that the legacy media are holding their ground in the new information environment: asked which information source they used most often, respondents mentioned RaiNews (21 percent), MediasetNews (18 percent), Google (10 percent), Facebook (6 percent), *la Repubblica* (5 percent), La 7 (4 percent), and *Corriere della Sera* (3 percent). Finally, with regard to Italians' consumption of information during the 2018 election campaign, the ITANES (2018) research confirms that television was the most important source (39.2 percent), followed by the Internet (27.9 percent), the press (15.1 percent), social media (10.4 percent), and the radio (7.4 percent). Overall, though there are predictable generational differences, the tendency of citizens to draw on multiple media sources is evident, making it necessary to explore the mechanisms through which the agenda of public debate is constructed.

In this media environment, with its wide range of choices, there exist strong connections between the agendas of the legacy media and the social media. Politicians have done their best to exploit these connections. It is no accident that the media strategies of the competing leaders were built meticulously, bringing together the social media, television, and presence on the ground, particularly in the case of Salvini (Diamanti and Pregliasco 2019). The tendency toward "media homogenization" (Boczkowski and De Santos 2007; Groshek and Clough Groshek 2013), together with the persistent use of multiple media sources by individuals, has led to a convergence of media agendas and of the latter and citizens' agendas, to the point of creating an interrelated public agenda (Bentivegna and Boccia Artieri 2020). Recent research has analyzed a broad range of news outlets during election campaigns in Italy (Bentivegna, Boccia Artieri, and Marchetti 2020)—the main prime-time news broadcasts, printed daily newspapers, news websites, online-only news, conversations on Facebook and Twitter—showing the broad convergence between Italian information sources. The issues most covered and most frequently shared by the various information sources during the 2018 election campaign arose from both specific campaign events (the events of Macerata and the cases of corruption) and parties' policy proposals (immigration, fascism, and taxes), showing that some competitors had more power to control the agenda than others. During an election campaign, leaders' statements, campaign events, and possible scandals involving parties and/or leaders push decisively in the direction of a shared media agenda. The suggestion is one that, as far as the Italian case is concerned, is based on the recognition that all political actors have invested heavily in communication via social media, which has given rise to an especially dynamic campaign (Diamanti 2018).

3. The Public Agenda between Legacy Media Social Media

In light of these considerations, the objectives of our research are to establish whether there existed a shared media agenda during the 2018 election campaign, and if so, the extent to which political actors were able to get their preferred issues on the agenda of news media and under what conditions.

In order to explore these matters, we content analyzed the media agendas and the Facebook and Twitter accounts of the main parties and leaders during the five weeks (January 31–March 4) prior to the Italian general election of 2018. The agendas compared were those of the print and news websites of three daily newspapers with national-level circulations (*Corriere della Sera*, *Il Fatto quotidiano*, and *Libero*) and of two online-only newspapers: *Fanpage* and *HuffPost*. The choice of newspapers to analyze was based on their circulation[2] and their political orientation. *Corriere della Sera*, with the largest circulation in Italy, has traditionally been a progovernment outlet and during the 2018 campaign was supportive of the governing DP. *Il Fatto quotidiano* is a newspaper that, since its foundation in 2009, has always taken an antigovernment line and over time came to support the 5SM. Finally, *Libero* is a recently established newspaper giving clear, and sometimes provocative, support to the most uncompromising elements of the center-right, such as the League. The choice of online-only newspapers (*Fanpage* and *HuffPost*) was made on the basis of their reach online (Newman 2019).

We decided to analyze traditional newspapers, news websites, and online-only news because "the news media that make up the contemporary media system is no monolithic entity" (Wells et al. 2020, 663), rather one whose varying degrees of stability and flexibility (Vonbun-Feldbauer and Matthes 2018), speed and slowness (Harder, Sevenans, and Van Aelst 2017) determine their publication cycles. Articles published by the news media[3] were selected if they contained (in their titles or texts) at least one of the keywords[4] associated with the campaign. A total of 3,499 articles published in the print editions of the newspapers were analyzed, along with 2,196 articles published on their websites and 1,212 articles appearing in the online-only news outlets (table 6.1).

We also analyzed the Facebook and Twitter accounts of the main leaders and parties: Luigi Di Maio and the 5SM (an antiestablishment party), Renzi and the DP (for the center-left), Salvini and the League (for the center-right).[5] We took into consideration the accounts of both the leaders and their

---

2. Source: The Italian Federation of Newspaper Publishers—www.fieg.it.

3. The articles taken from the media outlets were assembled using the www.volocom.it service.

4. Elezioni, Elettorale, Voto, Votato, Votare, Politiche, Berlusconi, Di Maio, Meloni, Salvini, Renzi, Grasso, Bonino, Forza Italia, FI, Movimento 5 stelle, m5s, 5 stelle, movimento cinque stelle, cinque stelle, Fratelli d'Italia, FDI, Lega, Partito democratico, PD, Liberi e uguali, LEU.

5. The Facebook posts were assembled using the Netvizz application, the Twitter posts using Twitterscraper.

TABLE 6.1. Number of Articles Analyzed by Publication

		N
Print Press	*Corriere della Sera*	1,463
	Il Fatto Quotidiano	914
	Libero	1,122
News Websites	*corriere.it*	903
	ilfattoquotidiano.it	1,293
	libero.it	1,636
Online-only news	*Fanpage*	505
	HuffPost	707
Total		8,543

parties because of the role of party accounts in reinforcing and relaunching messages posted by the leaders: a consequence of the personalization of the processes of political communication (Enli and Skogerbø 2013). The phenomenon is confirmed by the different followings of the leaders and parties on Facebook and Twitter (with Di Maio and the 5SM representing a partial exception). Di Maio, a novice political leader, had a following on Facebook that was about the same as his party's (around 1.3 million users), while on Twitter his 300,000 or so followers were far outdistanced by the 600,000 followers of the Movement. Renzi, in contrast, had a following of around 1 million on Facebook, with around 250,000 for his party, and around 3.3 million followers on Twitter, with approximately 260,000 for his party. Salvini, finally, had a following of around 2 million on Facebook as against 380,000 for the League and around 670,000 followers on Twitter as against around 29,000 for the League (table 6.2).

Posts and tweets published on the accounts of the leaders and parties were analyzed with the aim of identifying the themes around which their campaign communications strategies were built. Overall, we analyzed 3,931 tweets and 4,915 Facebook posts (see table 6.2). The data concerning the politicians' publishing activity show significant differences, with the League and Salvini having the lion's share.

The newspaper articles, Facebook posts, and tweets were analyzed using QDA Miner—a program for the qualitative analysis of texts—and its quantitative component, WordStat—a text-mining tool used for identifying the recurring themes in a text. The texts were codified using a dictionary, compiled ad hoc, which enabled us to exclude from the analysis the issues selected through the chosen keywords but unrelated to the campaign events taken into consideration.

In order to establish the extent of convergence/divergence between the

TABLE 6.2. Posts and Tweets Analyzed by Source

	Facebook		Twitter	
	N posts	Likes	N Tweets	Followers
Luigi Di Maio	431	1,376,541	118	307,637
5SM	604	1,213,624	106	602,857
Matteo Renzi	96	1,119,945	196	3,387,577
DP	230	253,483	296	258,769
Matteo Salvini	492	2,095,582	1,058	675,997
Lega*	3,062	379,162	2,159	29,046
Total	4,915		3,931	

* The limited number of posts and tweets by Lega (the League) is due to the transformation of the extsting accounts of the Northern League into the leader's more personalized accounts. For example, in December 2017, the "Lega Nord Padania" Facebook page underwent a change of name to become @legasalvinipremier.

various media, among the themes identified, we selected the top five for each actor, so that we ended up with a list of twelve themes,[6] which we subjected to a series of ad hoc analyses. First, we compared the actors' agendas by calculating the Pearson correlation coefficients. Second, time series of the frequencies of issues from all sources were examined for linear and quadratic trends. Each issue was de-trended, whether the linear or quadratic trend was statistically significant, in this way the relationship between the days could be analyzed without concerns for autocorrelation (Romer 2006). The correlations between the de-trended time series were calculated and used to evaluate the strength of relationships among the sources. In other words, we tested the relationships between the content published by political leaders and parties on Facebook and Twitter and the content of the news articles by evaluating the correlations discovered through the content analysis. Hence, the cross-lagged correlations between the de-trended time series were calculated to evaluate the strength of the relationship (i.e., predictive value) among the considered sources. To measure the power of the leaders to influence the public agenda, we evaluated the number of leads and lags. This test should not be equated with causality: such patterns over time do suggest a nonrandom relationship (Sayre et al. 2010).

6. Following the selection, some themes were excluded from the analysis because they referred exclusively to certain actors and not others. This was true of the theme of postelection alliances and scenarios, a theme that figured highly in the print media but had a much lower position on the agendas of the other actors.

4.   Actors and Themes of the Campaign

The themes appearing on the agendas of the print, digital, and online-only news media, and on those of the political leaders and parties, are reported in table 3. This provides an overview of the campaign in thematic terms. Before analyzing the relationship between themes and actors in detail, however, it is worth focusing on the agenda overall.

Besides the traditional campaign themes (employment, corruption, taxes, social welfare, immigration, Europe) the agenda features themes related to the events of Macerata—and their evolution/transformation into the issue of fascism/racism—and to political scandals. It also features the presentation of candidates for places in the cabinet of a hypothetical government led by the 5SM. The presentation took place over several days, in an attempt to keep the focus of attention on the Five Star Movement up until polling day and to emphasize its difference as compared to the other actors. Aside from these themes—which were largely the product of unforeseen events—the others mainly reflected those that citizens had indicated as being the most important: employment, immigration, security, taxes, corruption, welfare (Valbruzzi 2019).

Another feature emerging from table 6.3 is the convergence of the agendas of the news media. Looking at the individual agenda items, we see that there was a heightened degree of convergence coinciding with the unprecedented and unexpected theme of fascism/racism developed in the weeks following the events of Macerata. However, this was not the only element of convergence. Europe and the implications of its economic decisions for Italy were equally common themes, as was the 5SM's presentation of its candidate cabinet ministers, skillfully piloted day by day by the party's leaders. Thus convergence of news media agendas went beyond campaign events and scandals, revealing a high degree of convergence on the issues, the product of the campaign coverage in its entirety.

In contrast, the agendas of the political actors show significant divergence, an inevitable consequence of issue ownership and of campaign dynamics with their clashes of competing ideas. Before going into this, however, it is worth focusing on the relationship between the agendas of the news outlets and between these and the agendas of the politicians. The coefficients (table 6.4) for the correlation between the agendas of the news media confirm the findings of table 6.3, as they are all significant and especially high. These data enable us to confirm the existence of a shared agenda. The result supports the argument of Harder et al. (2017) that there is a natural and definite convergence of the agendas of news media during election cam-

The Agenda-Building Power of Facebook and Twitter

TABLE 6.3. Frequencies by Issues and Sources (January 31–March 4, 2018)

	Di Maio 5SM*	Renzi DP*	Salvini Lega*	Print Press	News Websites	Online-Only News	Total
Corruption	19.1	1.9	5.0	8.9	7.0	6.7	7.4
	(2)	(11)	(8)	(4)	(5)	(7)	(6)
Costs of politics	14.3	1.3	0.2	1.4	2.8	3.8	2.3
	(4)	(12)	(12)	(11)	(9)	(8)	(12)
Employment	4.0	5.8	5.6	5.6	6.9	7.3	6.1
	(7)	(5)	(7)	(8)	(6)	(6)	(8)
Europe and economic	7.8	15.0	8.2	19.7	16.0	12.0	14.7
constraints	(5)	(3)	(5)	(2)	(2)	(3)	(2)
Fascism/Racism	2.6	19.5	10.7	19.8	23.8	23.2	18.8
	(9)	(2)	(4)	(1)	(1)	(1)	(1)
Immigration	4.0	2.2	22.9	6.9	6.2	7.9	9.9
	(7)	(10)	(1)	(7)	(7)	(4)	(4)
Macerata Events	-	2.9	7.0	7.3	8.4	7.4	7.2
		(8)	(6)	(6)	(4)	(5)	(7)
Nominations for	15.0	4.8	3.4	15.9	15.6	21.0	13.6
Ministers 5SM	(3)	(6)	(11)	(3)	(3)	(2)	(3)
Security and crime	3.5	3.9	12.4	1.1	0.9	0.7	3.5
	(8)	(7)	(3)	(12)	(12)	(12)	(9)
Social Welfare	2.5	14.2	4.6	2.1	2.3	2.5	3.1
	(10)	(4)	(9)	(9)	(11)	(10)	(11)
Taxes	7.7	25.9	16.0	7.9	5.7	3.8	8.9
	(6)	(1)	(2)	(5)	(8)	(9)	(5)
Unpresentable	19.5	2.6	3.9	2.1	2.6	2.1	3.3
candidates	(1)	(9)	(10)	(10)	(10)	(11)	(10)
Total	100.0	100.0	100.0	100.0	100.0	100.0	100.0
	(1,702)	(1,336)	(9,657)	(14,491)	(12,910)	(6,407)	(46,503)

*Figures refer to the themes emerging from the Facebook and Twitter accounts of the leaders and the parties. Percentages represent the percent of word frequencies of overall issue emphasis in each source.

paigns. Though constantly competing for the attention of consumers, the news media continue to share a logic of "fascination with the processes of an election campaign" (Cushion and Thomas 2018) such as to produce an inevitable convergence.

As for the relationship between the agendas of the news media and those of the political actors, table 6.4 suggests convergence in some cases but not others—for example, in the case of Renzi but not Salvini and Di Maio. To interpret the result, it is necessary to consider, briefly, the question of issue ownership in the context of the 2018 campaign. Given that Salvini and the League built their campaign around very specific issues such as immigration, taxes, and security—referred to at every opportunity—divergence

TABLE 6.4. Rank Correlations of Issue Salience in All Agendas

	Di Maio 5SM	Renzi DP	Salvini Lega	Print Press	News Websites
Print Press	.187*	.544*	.313*		
News Websites	.174*	.401*	.225*	.907**	
Online-Only News	.107*	.352*	.247*	.824**	.945**

*p < 0.05; **p p < 0.001

from the agendas of the news media is to be understood as the consequence of a "targeted" investment rather than an inability to focus attention on their own issues. On the contrary, they appear to have made effective use of social media as an "agenda-building tool." Likewise, the campaign pursued by Di Maio and the 5SM was built around the theme of their difference from traditional politics. The difference was emphasized at every opportunity, through a constant focus on the issues of corruption and unpresentable candidates, occasionally in a defensive vein, especially following the events surrounding the failure of 5SM parliamentarians to adhere to its rules concerning the reimbursement of expenses. For their part, Renzi and the DP struggled to identify and focus attention on many distinctive themes, such as the public debt and Europe (Barbieri 2019), being forced, instead, to react to those highlighted by other political actors or events. The data suggest a party forced to "follow" rather than "lead" the agenda. The fact that taxes occupied the highest place seems incongruous for a reformist party and seems to be indicative of efforts to counter other political actors, specifically the center-right, by seeking to compete through confrontation rather than selective emphasis (Robertson 1976). In contrast, the attention paid to fascism/racism, in second place, would appear to be indicative of an attempt by the party to exploit events for the purposes of imposing an interpretative frame of its own. However, the attempt was less successful than had been hoped, mainly because of Renzi's indecisiveness when it came to how to react. Finally, the attention paid to Europe—occupying third place on the party's agenda—failed to produce clear overlap between the issue and the party's stance, as emerges from the data concerning the association between policy issues and political leaders revealed by the analysis of the coverage of the news media during the campaign. Hence against an average value for the presence of the issue of Europe equal to 6.8 percent, Renzi registers an association with the issue of 4.3 percent, as against 11.1 percent for Di Maio and 6.9 percent for Salvini (Roncarolo and Cremonesi 2019). In short, there is little doubt that the attention Renzi paid to issues of European policy failed to be picked up by the news media.

In conclusion, the varying degrees of convergence of the agendas of the news media and those of the political actors could be interpreted as the result of a particular communication strategy attributing to social media the function of setting the agenda (Feezell 2018) for the news media. The truth of this interpretation is examined in the following section where we consider the power of the political actors to influence the construction of the agenda.

5. Control of the Agenda: Who Leads Whom?

The partial correspondence between the agenda of the news media and that of political actors emerging from the preceding discussion must now be combined with data concerning the processes whereby the agenda is constructed, with the identification of which actors "lead" and which "follow" such processes. Considerable attention has been paid to this question—from the point of view of interaction both between social media (especially Twitter) and news media, and between specific actors (candidates, political leaders, parliamentarians) and news media (Conway et al. 2015; Groshek and Groshek 2013; Russell Neuman et al. 2014; Rogstad 2016). However, there are as yet no definitive answers.

In the case of the 2018 Italian election campaign, attempting to throw light on this issue is of particular significance given the communication strategies adopted by the competing actors. As the data presented so far have revealed, it was possible to identify two strategies being deployed during the campaign: one aimed at the selective emphasis of issues over which the political actor had established ownership, the other aimed at acquisition or confrontation with respect to issues that had come onto the public agenda. To find out the extent to which such strategies were successful—in the sense of enabling political actors to get their own issues onto the agenda of the news media—we shall attempt to answer by analyzing the cross-correlations between the historical series of the news media and those of the social media. The analysis was carried out on the first three issues for each political actor, for a total of eight issues, excluding the 5SM's presentation of ministerial candidates, which only took place during the last ten days of the campaign.

The results in table 6.5 offer numerous interesting ideas not only with regard to "who leads whom" but also with regard to the characteristics of the issues and media outlets. Before considering these matters, however, we analyze the performances of the individual political actors. The emphasis given in the tweets and Facebook posts of Di Maio and the 5SM to the issues of corruption and taxes precedes the emphasis given by the news media to these issues by two days in both cases. Salvini and the League emphasize on social media the issue of corruption two days before the news media emphasize the issue, while in the case of Europe, immigration, and security they precede the news media by one day, and by one to two days in the case of unpresentable candidates. Finally, Renzi and the DP lead the news media agenda only in the case of security (by a factor of two days), while in the case of immigration the relationship is reciprocal.

Returning to the question of who leads and who follows in the construction of the agenda, in the case of Salvini and the League the data suggest a clear "bottom-up relationship" concerning numerous issues, especially those (security and immigration) the party has always owned. The situation is less clear in the case of the other political actors. Di Maio and the 5SM, for example, show a clear bottom-up relationship with regard to corruption—an issue traditionally dear to this party—and taxes—an issue on which the party competed openly with the center-right—along with a top-down relationship with regard to unpresentable candidates, an issue closely connected to the movement's theme of political renewal. It is likely that the events related to the failures of 5SM parliamentarians in relation to reimbursements obliged it to follow rather than lead the news media given that the latter were involved in investigating the numerous cases that came to light during the campaign. Renzi and the DP, finally, found it difficult to lead the news media even with regard to the issue of fascism/racism, the one issue over which they made contradictory attempts to exercise ownership. Lastly, all the political actors referred to some issues at the same time as the news media (Lag: 0): corruption and immigration in the case of Di Maio, immigration and taxes in the case of Salvini, and immigration in the case of Renzi.

Besides issue ownership, the nature of issues and the circumstances of their occurrence, as well as the outlet's publication cycle, can explain some of the relationships identified. With regard to the nature of the issues, in the case of the fascism/racism issue there were events during the campaign marked by violence and street demonstrations. Meanwhile, the issue of unpresentable candidates was accompanied by reports of candidates under judicial investigation, the issue of corruption by appointments secretly recorded in order to report attempts to corrupt public administrators. In these cases, not surprisingly, the news media led the dance. Just as significant were the characteristics of the media outlets—such as the speed and flexibility of the news websites and the online-only news outlets—able to affect the news production cycle and therefore able to maintain a leading role in the coverage of the campaign by the news media.

The Agenda-Building Power of Facebook and Twitter 137

TABLE 6.5. Significant Cross-Correlation between News Media and Political Actors

	Di Maio—5SM	Renzi—DP	Salvini—League
Corruption			
Print Press			
News Websites	Lag 2: 0.54	Lead 5: 0.50	Lag 2: 0.39
Online-Only News	Lag 0: 0.43		
Europe and economic constraints			
Print Press			Lag 1: 0.54
News Websites		Lead 7: 0.48	Lead 3: 0.40
Online-Only News			
Fascism/Racism			
Print Press		Lead 6: 0.50	
News Websites		Lead 7: 0.56	
Online-Only News		Lead 7: 0.61	Lead 8: 0.44
Immigration			
Print Press			Lag 1: 0.48
News Websites	Lead 1: 0.38		Lag 0: 0.41
Online-Only News	Lag 0: 0.56	Lag 0: 0.62	Lead 1: 0.44
Security			
Print Press	Lead 1: 0.42	Lag 2: 0.36	Lag 1: 0.63
News Websites	Lead 1: 0.39		Lag 1: 0.52
Online-Only News	Lead 1: 0.35		Lag 1: 0.50
Taxes			
Print Press			Lag 0: 0.41
News Websites	Lag 2: 0.48		
Online-Only News			
Unpresentable candidates			
Print Press	Lead 5: 0.51		Lag 1: 0.41
News Websites	Lead 6: 0.51		Lag 2: 0.52
Online-Only News	Lead 6: 0.49		Lag 2: 0.50

Note: All cross-lagged correlations shown here are significant, $p < .05$. Leads shown indicate that news outlets predicted political leaders' and parties' emphasis a given number of days prior to the contemporary frequencies. Lags indicate that tweets and posts published by political leaders and parties predicted newspaper mentions a given number of days prior to the contemporary frequencies. Lag 0 indicates a contemporaneous relationship.

6. Social Media and Public Agenda

What were the results, in terms of communication, of "the ugliest campaign ever"? Was there a shared news media agenda? Were political actors successful—using social media as a tool for agenda-building—in directing the attention of the news media to their preferred issues?

Our data suggest, first, that election campaigns continue to be characterized by the presence of a public agenda in the sense that, notwithstanding diversification in the "marketplace of attention" (Webster 2014), the news media continue to have a common approach to the coverage of campaigns. Certainly, in the present case, a large contribution to this tendency was made by campaign incidents such as "the events of Macerata" and by political incidents as the revelations that some candidates had been under criminal investigation, etc. In short, the numerous breaking events created the conditions for a convergence of the public agenda. A further contribution was made by the media's use of strategic framing in the cases of direct confrontation between two or more actors (identified by turns as fascists and antifascists, racists and antiracists, "new" politicians and members of the "old" establishment) and in the case of political scandals. It is no accident that fascism/racism and the formation of the new 5SM government were among the top five issues on all the agendas considered. Beside this "natural" convergence, however, there was also convergence around "traditional" campaign themes such as taxes, immigration, and Europe. The mix of issues associated with breaking events, and issues more closely related to policy, was a permanent feature of the campaign and produced a news media agenda that was undoubtedly convergent as confirmed by our analysis of the correlation coefficients.

The answer to the question of the extent to which political actors were able to place their preferred issues on the public agenda by using social media is not straightforward. At first glance it seems that sometimes they were successful, other times not. Successes were clearly enjoyed by Salvini and the League, which emerged as winners of the election not only in terms of votes (rising from 4 percent to 17.4 percent) but also in terms of the public agenda, with issues such as immigration and security remaining subjects of public debate. Likewise, Di Maio and the 5SM successfully placed corruption, the costs of politics, and the contrast between the "new" and the "old politics" high on the public agenda. These issues have always been associated with the party, contributing to its identity and distinctiveness. More problematic was the situation of Renzi and the DP, with their inconsistent handling of the fascism/racism issue through their announcements of demonstrations, subsequently withdrawn, then reannounced and so on. Their attention to security slightly anticipated, and in the case of immigration coincided with, the attention paid to these issues by the news media, following a predictable attempt to attack Salvini and the League on these issues. Despite this, however, Renzi and the DP for the most part had a top-down relationship with the news media.

The alternation of "bottom-up" and "top-down" relationships indicated by the data imply different outcomes with regard to the adoption of approaches based on confrontation or selective emphasis: failure in the first case, success in the second. In both cases, however, issue ownership continues to be very important for the outcome of political actors' attempts to place their issues on the public agenda even in the context of unforeseen events, always interpretable in the light of the actor's key issues.

In conclusion, social media are used not just for self-promotion and mobilizing sympathizers but also for setting the public agenda. Whether this happens through live Facebook broadcasts, interview footage, statements released to the news media, or posts and tweets aimed at intervening in the public debate, is of secondary importance. What is important is that it happens, and that social media enable candidates and parties to adopt a communication strategy to raise awareness of their policy topics (Bossetta et al. 2020). On the other hand, our data reveal how the communicative fabric is woven day after day through the interpolation of breaking events and the constant emphasizing of certain issues, central to the definition and recognizability of the profile of the political actor.

References

Adinolfi, Goffredo. 2020. "Populism and Anti-Liberal Thought: Lega and M5S in the Italian Context." *Conhecer: Debate Entre O Público E O Privado* 10(24): 141–63. https://doi.org/10.32335/2238-0426.2020.10.24.2676

Aelst, Peter Van, Jesper Strömbäck, Toril Aalberg, Frank Esser, Claes De Vreese, Jörg Matthes, David Hopmann, Susana Salgado, Nicolas Hubé, and Agnieszka Stępińska. 2017. "Political Communication in a High-Choice Media Environment: A Challenge for Democracy?" *Annals of the International Communication Association* 41(1): 3–27.

AGCOM. 2018. "Rapporto Sul Consumo Di Informazione." https://www.agcom.it/documents/10179/9629936/Studio-Ricerca+19-02-2018/72cf58fc-77fc-44ae-b0a6-1d174ac2054f?version=1.0

Albertazzi, Daniele, Arianna Giovannini, and Antonella Seddone. 2018. "'No Regionalism Please, We Are Leghisti!' The Transformation of the Italian Lega Nord under the Leadership of Matteo Salvini." *Regional & Federal Studies* 28(5): 645–71.

Barbieri, Giovanni. 2019. "Tre Bandiere per Tre Partiti." In *Niente Di Nuovo Sul Fronte Mediale. Agenda Pubblica e Campagna Elettorale*, edited by Sara Bentivegna and Giovanni Boccia Artieri, 37–50. Milano: FrancoAngeli.

Bennett, W. Lance, and Barbara Pfetsch. 2018. "Rethinking Political Communication in a Time of Disrupted Public Spheres." *Journal of Communication* 68(2): 243–53.

Bentivegna, Sara, and Giovanni Boccia Artieri. 2020. "Rethinking Public Agenda in a Time of High-Choice Media Environment." *Media and Communication* 8(4): forthcoming.

Bentivegna, Sara, Giovanni Boccia Artieri, and Rita Marchetti. 2020. "L'agenda Pubblica Interrelata in Campagna Elettorale: Politiche 2018 Ed Europee 2019 Tra Convergenza e Divergenza Mediale." *Problemi Dell'informazione*. Forthcoming.

Birkland, Thomas A. 1998. "Focusing Events, Mobilization, and Agenda Setting." *Journal of Public Policy* 18(1): 53–74.

Bobba, Giuliano, and Antonella Seddone. 2018. "La Campagna Elettorale 2018 Tra Populismo e Polarizzazione." In *Il Vicolo Cieco. Le Elezioni Del 4 Marzo 2018*, edited by M. Valbruzzi and R. Vignati, 19–38. Bologna: Il Mulino.

Boczkowski, Pablo J, and Martin De Santos. 2007. "When More Media Equals Less News: Patterns of Content Homogenization in Argentina's Leading Print and Online Newspapers." *Political Communication* 24(2): 167–80.

Bossetta, Michael. 2018. "The Digital Architectures of Social Media: Comparing Political Campaigning on Facebook, Twitter, Instagram, and Snapchat in the 2016 US Election." *Journalism & Mass Communication Quarterly* 95(2): 471–96.

Boydstun, Amber E. 2013. *Making the News. Politics, the Media, and Agenda Setting*. Chicago: University of Chicago Press.

Ceccarini, Luigi, and Fabio Bordignon. 2016. "The Five Stars Continue to Shine: The Consolidation of Grillo's 'Movement Party' in Italy." *Contemporary Italian Politics* 8(2): 131–59.

Ceccarini, Luigi, and Fabio Bordignon. 2018. "Towards the 5 Star Party." *Contemporary Italian Politics* 10(4): 346–62.

Chadwick, Andrew. 2017. *The Hybrid Media System. Politics and Power*. Vol. 1. Oxford: Oxford University Press.

Conway, Bethany A., Kate Kenski, and Di Wang. 2015. "The Rise of Twitter in the Political Campaign: Searching for Intermedia Agenda-Setting Effects in the Presidential Primary." *Journal of Computer-Mediated Communication* 20(4): 363–80.

Cushion, Stephen, and Richard Thomas. 2018. *Reporting Elections: Rethinking the Logic of Campaign Coverage*. Cambridge: Polity Press.

Diamanti, Giovanni. 2018. "Una Campagna-Lampo Al Tempo Della Campagna Permanente." In *Una Nuova Italia*, edited by M. Cavallaro, G. Diamanti, and L. Pregliasco, 21–32. Rome: Castelvecchi.

Diamanti, Giovanni, and Lorenzo Pregliasco, eds. 2019. *Fenomeno Salvini. Chi è, Come Comunica, Perché Lo Votano*. Rome: Castelvecchi.

Enli, Gunn Sara, and Eli Skogerbø. 2013. "Personalized Campaigns in Party-Centred Politics: Twitter and Facebook as Arenas for Political Communication." *Information, Communication & Society* 16(5): 757–74.

Feezell, Jessica T. 2018. "Agenda Setting through Social Media: The Importance of Incidental News Exposure and Social Filtering in the Digital Era." *Political Research Quarterly* 71(2): 482–94.

Groshek, Jacob, and Megan Clough Groshek. 2013. "Agenda Trending: Reciprocity and the Predictive Capacity of Social Network Sites in Intermedia Agenda Setting across Issues over Time." https://doi.org/http://dx.doi.org/10.2139/ssrn.2199144

Hallin, Daniel C., and Paolo Mancini. 2004. *Comparing Media Systems: Three Models of Media and Politics*. Cambridge: Cambridge University Press.

Harder, Raymond A., Julie Sevenans, and Peter Van Aelst. 2017. "Intermedia Agenda Setting in the Social Media Age: How Traditional Players Dominate the News

Agenda in Election Times." *The International Journal of Press/Politics* 22(3): 275–93. https://doi.org/10.1177/1940161217704969

Klinger, Ulrike, and Jakob Svensson. 2015. "The Emergence of Network Media Logic in Political Communication: A Theoretical Approach." *New Media & Society* 17(8): 1241–57.

Legnante, Guido, and Cristian Vaccari. 2018. "Social Media e Campagna Elettorale." In ITANES *Vox Populi. Il Voto Ad Alta Voce Del 2018*, 63–77. Bologna: Il Mulino.

McCombs, Maxwell. 2004. *Setting the Agenda: The Mass Media and Public Opinion.* Cambridge: Polity Press.

Neuman, W. Russell, Lauren Guggenheim, S. Mo Jang, and Soo Young Bae. 2014. "The Dynamics of Public Attention: Agenda-Setting Theory Meets Big Data." *Journal of Communication* 64(2): 193–214. https://doi.org/10.1111/jcom.12088

Newman, Nic. 2019. "Reuters Institute Digital News Report." http://www.digitalnewsreport.org/

Owen, Diana. 2017. "New Media and Political Campaigns." In *The Oxford Handbook of Political Communication*, edited by Kate Kenski and Kathleen Hall Jamieson, 823–35. New York: Oxford University Press.

Petrocik, John R. 1996. "Issue Ownership in Presidential Elections, with a 1980 Case Study." *American Journal of Political Science* 4(3): 825–50.

Pfetsch, Barbara. 2018. "Dissonant and Disconnected Public Spheres as Challenge for Political Communication Research." *Javnost-The Public* 25(1–2): 59–65.

Robertson, David Bruce. 1976. *A Theory of Party Competition.* New York: John Wiley & Sons.

Rogstad, Ingrid. 2016. "Is Twitter Just Rehashing? Intermedia Agenda Setting between Twitter and Mainstream Media." *Journal of Information Technology & Politics* 13(2): 142–58. https://doi.org/10.1080/19331681.2016.1160263

Romer, Daniel. 2006. "Time Series Models." In *Capturing Campaign Dynamics, 2000 and 2004*, edited by Daniel Romer, Kate Kenski, K. Winneg, C. Adasiewicz, and K. H. Jamieson, 165–243. Philadelphia: University of Pennsylvania Press.

Roncarolo, Franca, and Cristina Cremonesi. 2019. "Journalistic Narratives and Political Communication Strategies Against the Background of a Critical Mood: The 2018 Election Campaign in the Traditional Media and Beyond." In *The Italian General Election of 2018*, edited by Luigi Ceccarini and James Newell, 191–215. Cham: Palgrave Macmillan.

Sayre, Ben, Leticia Bode, Dhavan Shah, Dave Wilcox, and Chirag Shah. 2010. "Agenda Setting in a Digital Age: Tracking Attention to California Proposition 8 in Social Media, Online News and Conventional News." *Policy & Internet* 2(2): 7–32.

Seethaler, Josef, and Gabriele Melischek. 2019. "Twitter as a Tool for Agenda Building in Election Campaigns? The Case of Austria." *Journalism* 20(8): 1087–1107.

Shearer, Elisa, and Jeffrey Gottfried. 2017. "News Use across Social Media Platforms 2017." Pew Research Center, Journalism and Media, September 5. https://www.journalism.org/2017/09/07/news-use-across-social-media-platforms-2017/pi_17-08-23_socialmediaupdate_0-02/

Stier, Sebastian, Arnim Bleier, Haiko Lietz, and Markus Strohmaier. 2018. "Election Campaigning on Social Media: Politicians, Audiences, and the Mediation of Political Communication on Facebook and Twitter." *Political Communication* 35(1): 50–74.

Valbruzzi, Marco. 2019. "Issues and Themes." In *The Italian General Election of 2018*, edited by Luigi Ceccarini and James Newell, 167–90. Cham: Palgrave Macmillan.

Vonbun-Feldbauer, Ramona, and Jörg Matthes. 2018. "Do Channels Matter? Investigating Media Characteristics in the Agenda-Building Process of an Election Campaign." *Journalism Studies* 19(16): 2359–78.

Wells, Chris, Dhavan Shah, Josephine Lukito, Ayellet Pelled, Jon C. W. Pevehouse, and JungHwan Yang. 2020. "Trump, Twitter, and News Media Responsiveness: A Media Systems Approach." *New Media & Society* 22(4): 659–82.

Wells, Chris, Dhavan V. Shah, Jon C. Pevehouse, JungHwan Yang, Ayellet Pelled, Frederick Boehm, Josephine Lukito, Shreenita Ghosh, and Jessica L. Schmidt. 2016. "How Trump Drove Coverage to the Nomination: Hybrid Media Campaigning." *Political Communication* 33(4): 669–76. https://doi.org/10.1080/1058 4609.2016.1224416

CHAPTER 7

"Many thanks for your support"

Email Populism and the People's Party of Canada

Brian Budd and Tamara A. Small, University of Guelph

In August 2018, Maxime Bernier, then a Member of Parliament (MP) for the Conservative Party of Canada, launched a Twitter diatribe against "extreme multiculturalism." In the series of five tweets, he wrote:

> extreme multiculturalism and cult of diversity will divide us into little tribes that have less and less in common, apart from their dependence on government in Ottawa. These tribes become political clienteles to be bought with taxpayers $ and special privileges.[1]

Bernier's tweets caused a political brouhaha. Multiculturalism is a no-go zone in Canadian politics. Compared to other countries, Canadians are more likely to see multiculturalism as a source of pride (Banting and Kymlicka 2010). Moreover, in a political system known for highly disciplined parties, it was a surprise for a MP to go rogue. Bernier had been a Conservative MP for more than a decade, and for much of that time served as a cabinet minister. He also ran for the leadership of the party in 2017.

Within a month of these tweets, Bernier left the Conservatives and eventually established the People's Party of Canada (PPC). The *New York Times* likened the People's Party to populist radical right-wing movements in Europe, causing a "jolt" to the Canadian landscape prided on "political decorum and multiculturalism" (Bilefsky 2019). Populism is a political ideology

---

1. https://twitter.com/MaximeBernier/status/1028801989038231552

that advocates for "the people" and the promotion of popular sovereignty against unaccountable elites and the political establishment. Scholars use the term "populist radical right" to characterize parties and leaders who combine populism with appeals to nativism, xenophobia, and authoritarianism (Mudde 2007). The PPC appears to represent an expansion of the populist, nationalist and antiestablishment sentiment sweeping the United States and Europe. This spark of populism is relevant to the study of political communication because some authors suggest a special relationship between digital technologies and populist party politics. Gerbaudo (2018, 746) describes it as an "elective affinity" where "social media savviness has in fact been a characteristic of many . . . populist movements and dark horse candidates, both on the Right and on the Left." Bernier's "extreme multiculturalism" tweets might be evidence of the affinity.

We begin by reflecting on this relationship starting with the theoretical literature and moving to a brief review of the empirical literature. Here we explore email rather than social media, which is typically studied. Email offers political actors a number of benefits for political campaigning and populist messaging. Email is woefully understudied in both the populism and digital politics literatures. We hypothesize that email will be a useful tool for engaging in populist appeals by the PPC because it allows for direct and unmediated interaction between the party and supporters. We surmise that email is conducive to populist appeals as a way to activate base supporters and draw financial support. Further, as a long-form medium, email may provide an unmediated space and creative latitude to craft populist appeals. To assess this, we conduct a content analysis of email sent by the PPC in 2019, an election year in Canada. In what follows, we provide a detailed overview of the PPC followed by our method and source of data. The results suggest that the PPC relied heavily on an antielitist populist discourse in constructing appeals to supporters. The primary focus of the PPC's email populism was on attacking partisan elites. In addition, calls for action featured prominently in email. Overall, PPC email used political messages in order to encourage supporters to assist the campaign. We conclude the analysis by suggesting some avenues for future research.

Populism and Digital Technology—A Special Relationship?

There is an ontological and epistemological debate about the nature of populism as an empirical phenomenon including conceptualizations of populism as a political logic, a political discourse, a form of political organization/

strategy, and a genre of political performance/self-presentation. Here we draw on what is often referred to as the "ideational approach" to populism. Most widely associated with the work of Cas Mudde (2004), this approach defines populism as an "ideology that considers society to be ultimately separated into two homogenous and antagonistic groups, 'the pure people' versus 'the corrupt elite,' and which argues that politics should be an expression of the volonté générale (general will) of the people" (543). As an ideology, populism is inherently "thin-centred," exhibiting a restricted ideational core attached to a limited range of political concepts and ideas (544). The ideational approach stresses that there is no uniform populist ideology but rather subtypes distinguished based on the combination of populism's core tenets (the people, the elite, and the general will) with concepts from other ideological families (Mudde and Rovira Kaltwasser 2013).

Political communication scholars have applied the ideational approach to study the relationship between populism and digital media (De Vreese et al. 2018; Gerbaudo 2018). Populism and digital technologies are assumed to share an inherent affinity for a number of reasons. First, digital technologies, especially social media, allow for populist leaders and parties to circumvent traditional media channels to engage directly with supporters (Van Kessel and Castelein 2016; Engesser et al. 2017). The ability to bypass traditional media gatekeepers is considered important for the spread of populist ideology and discourse, which tends to transgress the boundaries of normative political behavior (Moffitt 2016). Second, social media is also assumed to facilitate two-way communication between populist leaders and supporters. This bidirectionality is considered to be important for populist leaders and parties due to the people-centric and antielite nature of populist ideology (Jacobs and Spierings 2019). Finally, and perhaps most important, digital technologies have been understood as helping populists succeed at the ballot box by constructing networks of virality. The viral nature of social media has been theorized as allowing populists to reach a secondary audience of interest-bound and like-minded peer networks by circulating messages that users like, comment on, promote, and share within their own personal networks (Ernst et al. 2017).

There is a healthy body of empirical literature examining the relationship between digital technologies and populism (see chapters 9 and 11). These studies find wide-ranging interconnections between digital technologies and populist rhetoric that are difficult to characterize. There are a couple of reasons for this: first, as mentioned, as a thin-centred ideology, populism can be defined quite different. Some studies focus on left-wing populism (Waisbord and Amado 2017), while many others focus on right-wing populism (Kalsnes 2019). Even in the studies that examine right-wing populism, the elements of populism studied can differ considerably. Ernst et al. (2017) explore nine populist communication strategies. They find a range of populist communication; populist messages on the two social media ranged from as low as 5.5 percent for centrist parties to as high as 14.5 percent for right-wing parties. Mazzoleni and Bracciale (2018) explore three populist components on Facebook and Twitter by Italian party leaders in 2017. The study shows 67 percent of the posts included at least one of the three dimensions of populist ideology. In an analysis of Norway and Sweden, Kalsnes (2019) conceptualizes populist communication as of three subframes and nine frame elements and find only traces of populist messages. Next, studies also vary on the type of social media examined; some studies examine Twitter (Van Kessel and Castelein 2016; Bracciale and Martella 2017; Waisbord and Amado 2017; Maurer 2020). Facebook is also popular (Mazzoleni and Bracciale 2018; Kalsnes 2019; Tóth et al. 2019). A few study both comparatively (Ernst et al. 2017; Engesser et al. 2017). Finally, studies also vary on whether they include nonpopulist parties as part of the analysis. Maurer (2020) compared the Twitter styles of Emmanuel Macron and Marine Le Pen during the 2017 presidential runoff in France. Both candidates engaged in populist rhetoric, though Macron had fewer instances of populist messages than right-wing populist Le Pen. Overall, it is very difficult to draw broad conclusions from this research about the affinity between digital technologies and populism.

Political Email: Important Yet Understudied

Unlike studies above that explore the affinity between populism and social media, email is the object of study here. Email predates modern websites and social media by decades. Political campaigns began using email in the early 1990s. Despite its longstanding use in political campaigns, email has often been overlooked in the academic study of digital politics (Jackson 2004; Vaccari 2014). This neglect by the academic community is not related to the utility of email for political organizations. Rather it has a lot to do with the difficulty in data collection (Baldwin-Philippi 2017). Not only is it semiprivate, it is possible that political actors might narrowcast messages— that is, sending one political message to one group and a different message to another group. Unlike Twitter and more recently Facebook, studying email is complicated by the inability of a researcher to access every targeted version of an email.

Email offers political actors many benefits over social media. Email is a form of direct mail. Direct mail consists of pamphlets, brochures, fliers, or letters sent directly to citizens. Compared to other forms of campaign communication, direct mail allows for targeting of specific groups of citizens and longer messages (Benoit and Stein 2005). Political email has some advantages over paper direct mail. First, email is inexpensive. While paper mail is certainly less costly than other forms of political communication, the cost does increase with volume. With email, the cost of one email is the same as the cost of a thousand (Krueger 2006). Political actors can therefore communicate more often. Second, email focuses on base supporters (Kang et al. 2018). This is because you can only receive email if you have signed up for it. This allows political actors to speak directly to those citizens that support the message, and research assumes that those that sign up for email are more likely to be engaged in politics (Trammell and Williams 2004). Signing up for email is a form of selective exposure that allows citizens to effectively deal with the large amount of online information while at the same time avoiding information that challenges one's beliefs (Lorenzo-Dus and Blitvich 2013). Another benefit is that email allows political actors to bypass the filters of the media and the opposition (Vaccari 2014). Other digital technologies, such as websites and social media, are public facing—seen by everyone. While not completely private, email allows for a more direct and unmediated communication with supporters. We see these benefits as countering some of the unique challenges that populist parties and leaders face.

There are a few published studies on outbound political email. Andrew Paul Williams with various coauthors has published works on U.S. presidential campaigns between 2004 and 2012 (Williams 2004; Williams and Trammell 2005; Williams and Serge 2010). The conclusions across the eight years of campaigning are remarkably similar. The use of email in 2004 is described as "underwhelming" and "nothing substantive" (Williams and Trammell 2005, 94). Little had changed in email use by the 2012 campaign, where email was primarily used as a fundraising tool that offered "negligible amounts of information to the reader" (Williams and Maiorescu 2014, 181). Some parallels can be drawn between these American findings and Canada. Marland and Matthew (2017) found that many emails sent by Canadian parties included substantive information including public policy, opponents, or upcoming events. However, fundraising and calls for actions were also very important; with 63 percent of email including an ask for a donation. Thus they conclude that party email has the capacity to reshape both fundraising and information provision.

Party Politics and Digital Technology in Canada

Canada is a Westminster parliamentary democracy. The 2019 federal election, held on October 21, 2019, was for the lower chamber, the House of Commons, which is comprised of 338 members. As in the United States, members are elected using the single member plurality electoral system, where the candidate that receives more votes than any other candidate is the winner. But unlike the United States, Canada has a multiparty system. At dissolution, there were five parties with members in the House of Commons: the governing Liberal Party, Conservative Party, New Democratic Party, the Bloc Québécois, and the Green Party.

Populist parties are not new to Canadian politics (Bickerton et al. 1999). From the Progressives in the 1920s to the Reform Party in the 1990s, political parties, especially in Canada's West, have sought to promote the interests of the "common" Canadian. That said, the PPC is a curious case. Ideology is not a prominent feature of recent party politics. The "brokerage theory" suggests that instead of having distinctive ideological positions, Canadian parties appeal to an array of interest and attempt to broker a compromise between these competing interests (Brodie and Jenson 2007). The PPC is distinctively ideological; their 2019 electoral platform contains several planks common among the populist radical right including a strong opposition to immigration and multiculturalism, skepticism toward climate change, and a desire to reinvigorate democratic politics by providing a political voice to "the people" (Budd 2021). This populist radical right-wing rhetoric is often tinged with Maxime Bernier's libertarian tendencies including his rejection of supply management and corporate welfare. Bernier (2018) claimed a new party was needed because the Conservative Party was "intellectually and morally corrupt." Such an ideologically polarizing party is unusual in recent Canadian politics.

Given Canada's long history of new political parties having major electoral breakthroughs (Bickerton et al. 1999), the PPC seemed to be on the brink of change going into the federal election in October 2019. The PPC sought to occupy the right-wing space on the political spectrum. They found candidates to run in 93 percent of ridings in Canada. The PPC was able to fundraise. In the third quarter, they raised more than three-quarters of a million dollars, nearly matching the small but more established Green Party (Rabson 2019). One early poll suggested that 17 percent of Canadian voters would consider voting for the party (White 2019). The PPC received considerable attention from the traditional mass media. Despite all this, election night was a massive disappointment. The PPC received less than 2 percent of the vote, and Bernier lost his seat.[2]

Canadians on average are active and frequent users of the Internet. A 2018 survey found that, 91 percent of Canadians aged fifteen or older are active Internet users, with 94 percent of Canadians reporting they had access to some form of home Internet (Statistics Canada 2019). Canada is still home to a number of digital divides. Northern, rural, and Indigenous communities have traditionally had lower levels of Internet penetration while having access to lower quality services relative to other parts of the country (Canadian Radio-television and Telecommunications Commission 2019). Despite the increasing centrality of the Internet in the day-to-day lives of Canadians, its role in politics remains somewhat limited. Survey research has found that the use of the Internet for political purposes has been confined to a relatively small proportion of already politically engaged Canadians (Jansen et al. 2020). While elite political actors have increasingly incorporated the Internet and social media into their campaign behaviors, by and large these technologies have not ushered in a surge of political participation by Canadian citizens (Jansen et al. 2020). The emerging presence of populist politics both online and in mainstream Canadian politics represents a development that could potentially challenge this overarching trend.

Sources of Data and Method

In order to collect PPC email, one of the authors submitted their email address to the PPC's "Free Newsletter" on the party's homepage in 2018. The page indicates that nonmembers are able to sign up for the newsletter, while party members will receive the newsletter automatically. Only an email addressed is required to sign up. As mentioned, there are inherent limitations to the collection of email data. We cannot be sure that members and nonmembers are receiving the same email or same number of emails. Thomas and Sabin (2019) did find differences between email sent to members and nonmembers in their study of Conservative Party leadership candidates, though they note there was "no consistent pattern" in the distribution of email sent to one account, the other, or both (9). During the election, we used another email address to sign up for the newsletter and found the num-

---

2. The Liberal Party was returned to power with a minority government with the Conservative Party as the Official Opposition. Three other parties won seats in the House of Commons.

TABLE 7.1. PPC Email in 2019 by Campaign Period

	Dates	Number of days	Number of emails	Percentage of emails per period
Unofficial preelection	Jan 1—June 29	180	57	31.7
Official preelection	June 30—Sept 10	73	19	26.0
Election	Sept 11—Oct 21	41	12	29.3
Postelection	Oct 22—Dec 31	71	11	15.5
TOTAL		**365**	**99**	**100.0**

ber of emails during and after the election were the same for both addresses. All things being equal, we have a complete set of email sent to nonmembers. The Monday, October 21 election day was fixed by law. Canadian elections are relatively short and highly regulated for political parties, candidates, and other groups. A Canadian election can be no shorter than thirty-six days and no longer than fifty. The writ was dropped on September 11, and for the first time ever there was an official precampaign period, which is also regulated. Due to the relatively short campaign period, this analysis includes all emails sent by the PPC in 2019 (table 7.1).

We conducted a content analysis of PPC emails. Content analysis, according to Benoit (2011, 268–69), is a methodology for "measuring or quantifying dimensions of the content of messages," as it can depict and draw inferences "about the sources who produced those messages." The coding scheme includes variables from the populist literature and also research on email. We draw on a framework developed by Engesser and colleagues (2017) to analyze how populist ideology is expressed through social media. They identify five core features of populist ideology (see table 7.2 for definitions), which we apply to email.

"Please give $5 today to help us get this message out"

The main objective of this analysis is to assess the relationship or affinity between PPC email and populism. This relationship is evident. We conclude that the PPC relied heavily on an antielitist populist discourse in constructing email appeals to supporters in 2019. Roughly half (47.5 percent) of the PPC's email featured at least one of the populist appeals analyzed, and all

TABLE 7.2. Definition of Ideological Elements of Populism

Element	Definition
Emphasizing the sovereignty of the people	References to the people's will and/or the absolute sovereignty of the people.
Advocating for the people	Political appeals made by a leader or party that claim to be based on the interests or will of the people.
Attacking the elites	Attacks, accusations, or attributions of blame toward elites for the malfunctions and grievances of democracy. Elites could include political, media, supranational, and economic.
Ostracizing others	Evocations of "dangerous others" whose presence or interests threaten the safety or prosperity of the people.
Invoking the heartland	References to an imagined past or idealized conception of community comprised by and for the people.

five core components of populist ideology were found (table 7.2). Table 7.3 is an example of an email sent by the PPC in 2019 that includes populist rhetoric (ostracizing others and advocating for the people). PPC emails are highly personalized, speaking directly to the recipient throughout the email. Table 7.3 also highlights some of the common formatting traits of emails including the bolding or capitalizing of key sentences or words. The example shows that calls for action also figure prominently in email, encouraging supporters to donate, follow on social media, and share the message with others. Overall, we find that the PPC uses political messages, both populist and nonpopulist, in order to encourage supporters to assist the campaign, mainly in terms of fundraising.

Before exploring the PPC's email populism, it is worth briefly highlighting the other half of the emails. Generally, there were three main types of email in this category. First, in the lead up to the election, the PPC used email to communicate planks of their 2019 election platform. The format of these emails deviated considerably from the typical email and were essentially cut and paste sections from their platform document. While some had populist themes, other email such as "Supply Management: Making Dairy, Poultry, and Eggs More Affordable" and "Equalization: Fairness for All Provinces" were more oriented toward specific issues in Canadian politics than populism. They are also more in line with Bernier's libertarian perspective. A central component of Canadian elections is the leaders' tour, where party leaders crisscross the country going from event to event meeting with supporters and vying for media attention. Given the centrality of the leaders'

TABLE 7.3. Example of People's Party of Canada Email

From: Maxime Bernier <info@maximebernier.com>
Sent: Sunday, August 11, 2019 10:38 AM
To: Brian Budd <XXXX@XXXX.ca>
Subject: The ONLY party addressing issues Canadians want to hear about

Brian,

The **People's Party platform** **is the one Canadians have been waiting for.**
We're the ONLY party talking about issues that they want to hear about.
    Reducing immigration levels.
    Tackling the illegal refugees crisis.
    Ending official multiculturalism and preserving Canadian values and culture.
    Reducing and reforming equalization.
    Abolishing development aid to foreign countries and taking care of Canadians in
        need first.
    Phasing out supply management and lowering the price of food.
    Using the Constitution to build a pipeline.
    Lowering income taxes for all Canadians.
    Getting rid of corporate welfare.
    Respecting the Constitution and the division of power between Ottawa and the
        provinces.
    I could go on and on.
    Brian, the election campaign begins in about a month.
    Do you want all these topics to be part of the debate?
    If so, please contribute $5 today to help us get the word out.

    Many thanks for your support!

    -Max

PS: I thank you if you recently donated. You can still help us by following the PPC on
social media (see links below) and by sharing our content with your friends. Or by invit-
ing them to subscribe to our free newsletter.

Note: Underlines are hyperlink; bold and capitalization are in original.

tour, it was the focus of a second type of nonpopulist email. For instance, the PPC sent several emails about Maxime Bernier's initial exclusion and then inclusion in the official leaders' debates. This is very similar to the use of Twitter by Canadian party leaders (Small 2014). It will be discussed that fundraising and calls for action were key features of most PPC email, and there were a handful of emails for which this was the only objective. For instance, the email titled "Our candidates need you!" encouraged supporters to volunteer or get a PPC lawn or window sign.

Table 7.4 reports the types of populist appeals made in PPC email in 2019. The total does not equal 100 percent as emails can contain more than

"*Many thanks for your support*"   153

one type of appeal. Given Bernier's rhetoric about extreme multicultural-ism, it could be expected that antidiversity populist messages would char-acterize the PPC's email communication. However, this is not the case; the PPC's populist discourse was instead largely antielitist. In total, 70.2 percent of PPC email included an attack on elites while only 23.4 percent included content ostracizing others. Advocating for the people was an even more common theme in PPC email. The other two components of populist ideology—invoking the heartland and emphasizing the sovereignty of the people—appeared less frequently in the PPC's email communication and did not give way to any coherent patterns in terms of populist appeals.

Populists consider many different groups as enemies of the common peo-ple including the economic, supranational, and media elites. Elites play an important role in populist discourse as leaders and parties look to construct and base their appeals on an antagonistic division between "the people" and the political establishment (Moffitt 2016). Identifying and maligning various groups of elites as unaccountable powerholders allows populists to position themselves as the voice of popular sovereignty. Table 7.5 reports the find-ings of the groups of elites targeted by the PPC. The total does not equal 100 percent as email can feature more than one type of elite. PPC email largely focused its attacks against partisan elites (72.7 percent). They focused on highlighting the corruption and incompetence of the existing political establishment by critiquing and drawing similarities between the leaders of Canada's three major parties. Justin Trudeau and the Liberal government in particular drew heavy attention from the PPC. The Liberals were portrayed as a corrupt party catering to the whims of well-connected corporate elites and special interests. For example, in a precampaign period email, the PPC offered the following characterization of the Trudeau Liberals:

> They are liars.
> **They don't care about our future and that of our children.**
> All they care about is to spend more and buy votes with your money.
> All they care about is POWER.

Importantly, these attacks were often used as a rhetorical bridge for critiques against the Conservatives and their leader, Andrew Scheer. In requesting donations and other forms of support, the PPC portrayed the Conservative Party as part of the same corrupt political establishment as the Liberals. For example, in an election period email titled "Conservative corruption," the PPC offered the following attack:

TABLE 7.4. Populist Appeals Made in PPC Email (N = 47)

	Number of emails	Percentage of emails
Attacking the elites	33	70.2
Advocating for the people	24	51.1
Ostracizing others	11	23.4
Invoking the heartland	7	14.9
Sovereignty of the people	4	8.5

> Just like Trudeau, Andrew Scheer is ready to say and do anything to get power. He is ready to steal the election with lies and manipulations.

A similar criticism was offered in a PPC email sent in the postelection period, where the Conservatives were branded as a "corrupt, centrist party, headed by a leader with no clear convictions." These types of comparisons between the Liberals and Conservatives are indicative of the deeply partisan nature of the PPC's populism. In structuring their appeals, the PPC actively sought to frame the Conservatives as an establishment party that had become estranged from the true values and principles of conservative voters.

Also prominent in the PPC's discourse were attacks against left-wing special interests, who the PPC accused of having undue influence over government decision-making (coded as Other in table 7.5). While these left-wing special interests were rarely named, the PPC frequently accused the Liberal government and other political parties of conforming to "new linguistic, cultural and social norms pushed by the Left." In accusing the political establishment of "changing laws all the time to fit the latest left-wing fads," the PPC also criticized the "old parties" for "not trying to solve important national issues anymore." By targeting ambiguously defined left-wing groups and connecting them to unaccountable partisan elites, the PPC positioned itself as the only party strong enough to stand up and defend authentic Canadian values and national interests.

Advocating for the people was the second most common form of populist rhetoric found in PPC email (51.1 percent). Appealing to a discursively constructed "people" is considered to be perhaps the most important component of populist communication. Canovan (1981, 294) argues that virtually all forms of populism "without exception involve some kind of exaltation and appeal to 'the people.'" However, there are important variations in how different types of populists define who "the people" are. In some of their emails, the PPC offer a conception of the "people" that appears to be aligned with the xenophobic and nationalist rhetoric of other populist radical right-

TABLE 7.5. Elite Targeted in PPC Email (N = 33)

	Number of emails	Percentage of emails
Partisan	24	72.7
Other	9	27.3
Economic	7	21.2
Political	7	21.2
Supranational organization	3	9.1
Media	2	6.1

wing parties. For example, in a policy email outlining the party's plan to repeal official multiculturalism and restrict immigration, the PPC made the following appeal to nationalism:

> Official multiculturalism is based on the idea that there is no unified Canadian society and no distinct Canadian identity to integrate into, and that we are just a collection of ethnic and religious tribes living side by side. But if we want to keep our country united, and ensure social cohesion, we must focus on what unites us as Canadians, not what divides us.

However, while the PPC's messaging on immigration stressed the need to protect Canada's national culture, most of the party's emails advocating for the people tended to highlight the promotion of individual freedom and curtailing intrusive government oversight. A consistent theme across the PPC's email was a call to end "crony capitalism," curtail corporate welfare, and protect free speech. For the PPC, advocating for the interests of the people mainly took the form of scaling back government subsidies and regulations that unfairly supported large corporations. For instance, in an email criticizing preferential treatment given to a large Canadian multinational corporation, the PPC stated:

> **The role of government is NOT to protect jobs in a specific company.**
> It's to create an environment conducive to job and wealth creation that is FAIR to ALL companies.
> And one that benefits ALL Canadians.

This promotion of free market economics and self-sufficiency was used to frame many of the PPC's policy emails. On a broader level, these appeals advocating on behalf of "the people" represent an important nuance in the PPC's populist communication. Unlike other populist radical right-wing parties, the PPC based their appeals to supporters largely on traditional right-wing economic doctrines and ideologies, while incorporating appeals to nationalism and cultural preservation in a supplementary manner.

As mentioned, only around one in four PPC emails contained appeal ostracizing cultural and ethnic minorities. This is an interesting finding. Canadian media coverage of the PPC gives the impression that ostracizing others was a central pillar of the PPC's ideology (e.g., Tubbs 2019). We find this was not the case. Several of the emails sent by the PPC in both the precampaign and official campaign period focused on promoting the party's policies of reducing immigration and strengthening border security. For instance,

> Last week, an ad paid by a third party organization that supports the PPC appeared on billboards across the country.
> It said "No to Mass Immigration."
> That's a message our party agrees with.
> **We propose less immigration, better integration of immigrants in our society, and a sharper focus on Canada's economic needs.**
> But our opponents don't want to have this debate.

Ostracizing others email drew direct linkages between reduced immigration and the preservation of Canada's national culture and social stability. The linking of immigration to threats toward Canada's social and cultural stability was a defining feature of many of the PPC's precampaign and official election period email. This type of discourse also closely resembles the appeals of other populist radical right-wing parties, where threats to social identity and civic values are commonly used to justify proposed restrictions on immigration (Mudde and Rovira Kaltwasser 2013).

While there was discussions of populism (and other campaign issues), calls for action were also ever present in PPC email. Only one of the ninety-nine emails did not feature at least one type of call for action, and it ironically was an email highlighting the fact that the party had exceeded its fundraising goal. Table 7.6 breaks down calls for action. The total does not equal 100 percent as emails can contain more than one type of call for action. Almost all emails featured a fundraising appeal (91.9 percent). The amount requested varied—as low as $0.99 and as high as $1,000 (the legal contribution limit). Given that this was the first PPC campaign and was in desperate need for funds, the focus on fundraising is not surprising. About one

TABLE 7.6. Calls for Action in PPC Email (N = 99)

	Number of emails	Percentage of emails
Donate	91	91.9
Share content with others/invite others to do something	47	47.5
Engage with content	42	42.4
Attend rally/event	5	5.1
Other	4	4.0
Sign petition	3	3.0

in two emails (47.5 percent) encouraged supporters to engage with other online content—on social media, the party website, or the party platform. For instance, the email "No, the world is not on fire!" asks supporters to read a BBC article about the 2019 forest fires in Brazil in order to challenge the claims of "climate alarmists." Around one in four emails encourages supporters to share PPC emails or information with others. For instance, an email profiling Bernier's tour of western Canada included:

So many people here appreciate our message.
Our team is all fired up and ready to take on the established parties!
Brian, I wanted to share this interview with Global Calgary I did yesterday morning.
If you like it, please share it with your friends and family so they too can hear our policies.

Overall, we find a link between calls for action, especially fundraising appeals, and the political messaging of the PPC. As one email put it "Please give $5 today to help us get this message out."

Conclusion

Whereas right-wing populist parties and leaders around the world have seen electoral success, including Jair Bolsonaro (chapter 9) and Volodymyr Zelensky (chapter 11), election night was a disappointment for Maxine Bernier and the People's Party of Canada. Campaign dynamics were not in the PPC's favor in 2019. The two main parties, the Liberals and Conservatives, had been locked in a two-way race for the entire year leading up to the election. Right-wing voters, who might have given the PPC a chance, likely stayed with the Conservatives in hopes of ousting the Liberals. While at the time of writing, the PPC's election expenses were not available, it is probable that they were unable to compete financially with the Conservatives. Even if these campaign dynamics were not in place, the structure of Canadian politics presents a significant barrier to the PPC's success compared to populist parties and leaders in Europe and the United States. While xenophobic and nativist appeals were not the focus of PPC emails, popular discussion of the party tended to focus on this aspect. Despite a sizeable portion of Canadians holding hostile or conditionally supportive attitudes toward multiculturalism (Besco and Tolley 2019), scholars argue that Canada lacks many of the cultural, institutional, and electoral opportunity structures conducive to the breakthrough of populist radical right parties (Budd 2021). In terms of political culture, Koning (2019) suggests that nationalist appeals against immigration are in vain in a country where support for immigration goes hand in hand with nationalism. When parties and politicians, on occasion, take anti-immigrant stances, they are branded as racists and un-Canadian. This was the case for Bernier and PPC candidates. Canada's electoral geography presents another barrier. The concentration of immigrants and minorities in vote-rich electoral districts in Ontario, BC, and Québec leaves little incentive for most political parties to take anti-immigrant stances (Besco and Tolley 2019). Finally, illegal migration is far less an issue in Canada than in the United States and Europe. Only time will tell if these factors hold long-term, however, since Bernier claims that building the PPC is his goal in the inter-election period.

This study represents the first attempt we are aware of to document populist appeals via email. Further research of other campaigns and parties is needed to produce more generalizable insights. However, there are a few suggestive inferences we might highlight. First, while populism played a key role in the PPC's email, it appeared to be shaped less by populist radical right-wing ideology and more by immediate electoral needs. This seems to differ from other chapters in this volume that found that populist leaders in Brazil and Ukraine were able to capitalize more on digital technologies to promote their populist agendas. As a new party, the PPC focused most of its attention on attacking partisan elites, especially its direct right-wing competitor in the 2019 election, the Conservative Party. This focus on attacking other parties and leaders is likely reflective of the need for the PPC to distinguish itself and to pull support away from their electoral base. Further, while email was used to spread populist messages, it was also used largely for more typical campaign purposes, primarily fundraising. Once again, as a new political party lacking the electoral infrastructure and resources of more established parties, email was a key tool used by the PPC to secure the necessary financial resources to fund a national campaign. A worthwhile goal for future studies of email and populist communication should be to examine how populist messaging not only differs in frequency between email and other digital technologies but also in the nature of populist messages being spread. The PPC's antielite populist discourse communicated through email differs substantially from the anti-immigrant nationalist discourse communicated by Bernier in other mediums. This difference may point to strategic differences in the deployment of populist appeals across different media channels. Nonetheless, the analysis of the PPC offered here represents an important first step toward understanding the relationship between email and populist communication. It is important that scholars not disregard the role of these older digital technologies. Email continues to play an important role not only for modern campaigns but also for populist appeals.

References

Baldwin-Philippi, Jessica. 2017. "The Myths of Data-Driven Campaigning." *Political Communication* 34(4): 627–33.

Banting, Keith, and Will Kymlicka. 2010. "Canadian Multiculturalism: Global Anxieties and Local Debates." *British Journal of Canadian Studies* 23(1): 43–72.

Benoit, William L. 2011. "Content Analysis in Political Communication." In *Sourcebook for Political Communication Research: Methods, Measures, and Analytical Techniques*, edited by Erik P. Bucy and R. Lance Holbert, 268–79. New York: Taylor and Francis.

Benoit, William L., and Kevin A. Stein. 2005. "A Functional Analysis of Presidential Direct Mail Advertising." *Communication Studies* 56(3): 203–25. https://doi.org/10.1080/10510970500181181

Bernier, Maxime. 2018. "Why I Am Leaving the Conservative Party of Canada." People's Party of Canada. August 23. https://www.peoplespartyofcanada.ca/why_i_am_leaving_the_conservative_party_of_canada

Besco, Randy, and Erin Tolley. 2019. "Does Everyone Cheer? The Politics of Immigration and Multiculturalism in Canada." In *Federalism and the Welfare State in a Multicultural World*, edited by Elizabeth Goodyear-Grant, Richard Johnston, Will Kymlicka, and John Myles, 291–318. Montreal-Kingston: McGill-Queen's University Press.

Bickerton, James, Alain-G. Gagnon, and Patrick J Smith. 1999. *Ties That Bind: Parties and Voters in Canada*. Don Mills, Ontario: Oxford University Press.

Bilefsky, Dan. 2019. "A "Mad Max" Candidate Offers a Far-Right Jolt to the Canadian Election—The New York Times." *New York Times*. October 15. https://www.nytimes.com/2019/10/15/world/canada/election-bernier-far-right.html

Bracciale, Roberta, and Antonio Martella. 2017. "Define the Populist Political Communication Style: The Case of Italian Political Leaders on Twitter." *Information, Communication & Society* 20(9): 1310–29.

Brodie, Janine, and Jane Jenson. 2007. "Piercing the Smokescreen: Brokerage Parties and Class Politics." In *Canadian Parties in in Transition*, 3rd ed., edited by Alain-G. Gagnon and A. Brian Tanguay. Peterborough: Broadview Press.

Budd, Brian. 2021. "Maple-Glazed Populism: Political Opportunity Structures and Right-Wing Populist Ideology in Canada." *Journal of Canadian Studies* 55(1): 152-176.

Canadian Radio-Television and Telecommunications Commission. 2019. "Communications Monitoring Report." https://crtc.gc.ca/eng/publications/reports/policy-monitoring/2020/index.htm

Canovan, Margaret. 1981. *Populism*. New York: Harcourt Brace Jovanovich.

De Vreese, Claes H., Frank Esser, Toril Aalberg, Carsten Reinemann, and James Stanyer. 2018. "Populism as an Expression of Political Communication Content and Style: A New Perspective." *International Journal of Press/Politics* 23(4): 423–38.

Engesser, Sven, Nicole Ernst, Frank Esser, and Florin Büchel. 2017. "Populism and Social Media: How Politicians Spread a Fragmented Ideology." *Information, Communication & Society* 20(8): 1109–26. https://doi.org/10.1080/13691 18X.2016.1207697

Ernst, Nicole, Sven Engesser, Florin Büchel, Sina Blassnig, and Frank Esser. 2017. "Extreme Parties and Populism: An Analysis of Facebook and Twitter across Six Countries." *Information, Communication & Society* 20(9): 1347–64. https://doi.org /10.1080/1369118X.2017.1329333

Gerbaudo, Paolo. 2018. "Social Media and Populism: An Elective Affinity?" *Media, Culture & Society* 40(5): 745–53.

Jackson, Nigel. 2004. "Email and Political Campaigning: The Experience of MPs in Westminster." *Journal of Systemics Cybernetics and Informatics* 2(5): 1–6.

Jacobs, Kristof, and Niels Spierings. 2019. "A Populist Paradise? Examining Populists' Twitter Adoption and Use." *Information, Communication & Society* 22(12): 1681–96. https://doi.org/10.1080/1369118X.2018.1449883

Jansen, Harold J., Royce Koop, Tamara A. Small, Frédérick Bastien, and Thierry Giasson. 2020. "Democratic Citizenship: How Do Canadians Engage with Politics Online." In *Digital Politics in Canada: Promises and Perils*, edited by Tamara A. Small and Harold J. Jansen, 183–201. Toronto: University of Toronto Press.

Kalsnes, Bente. 2019. "Examining the Populist Communication Logic: Strategic Use of Social Media in Populist Political Parties in Norway and Sweden." *Central European Journal of Communication* 12(2): 187–205.

Kang, Taewoo, Erika Franklin Fowler, Michael M. Franz, and Travis N. Ridout. 2018. "Issue Consistency? Comparing Television Advertising, Tweets, and e-Mail in the 2014 Senate Campaigns." *Political Communication* 35(1): 32–49.

Koning, Edward A. 2019. *Immigration and the Politics of Welfare Exclusion: Selective Solidarity in Western Democracies*. Toronto: University of Toronto Press.

Krueger, Brian S. 2006. "A Comparison of Conventional and Internet Political Mobilization." *American Politics Research* 34(6): 759–76.

Lorenzo-Dus, Nuria, and Pilar Garcés-Conejos Blitvich. 2013. "Get Involved! Communication and Engagement in the 2008 Obama Presidential e-Campaign." In *Media Talk and Political Elections in Europe and America*, edited by Mats Ekström and Andrew Tolson, 229–51. London: Palgrave Macmillan.

"Many thanks for your support" 161

Marland, Alex, and Maria Matthews. 2017. "'Friend, Can You Chip in \$3?' Canadian Political Parties' Email Communication and Fundraising Emails." In *Permanent Campaigning in Canada*, edited by Alex Marland, Thierry Giasson, and Anna Lennox Esselment, 87–108. Vancouver: UBC Press.

Maurer, Peter. 2020. "A Marriage of Twitter and Populism in the French Campaign? The Twitter-Discourses of Challengers Macron and LePen." In *Power Shift? Political Leadership and Social Media*, edited by Davis Richard and Taras David. New York: Routledge.

Mazzoleni, Gianpietro, and Roberta Bracciale. 2018. "Socially Mediated Populism: The Communicative Strategies of Political Leaders on Facebook." *Palgrave Communications* 4(1): 1–10.

Moffitt, Benjamin. 2016. *The Global Rise of Populism: Performance, Political Style, and Representation*. Palo Alto: Stanford University Press.

Mudde, Cas. 2004. "The Populist Zeitgeist." *Government and Opposition* 39(4): 541–63.

Mudde, Cas. 2007. *Populist Radical Right Parties in Europe*. Cambridge: Cambridge University Press.

Mudde, Cas, and Cristóbal Rovira Kaltwasser. 2013. "Exclusionary vs. Inclusionary Populism: Comparing Contemporary Europe and Latin America." *Government and Opposition* 48(2): 147–74. https://doi.org/10.1017/gov.2012.11

Rabson, Mia. 2019. "Scheer's Conservatives Rake in More than Double the Donations of Trudeau Liberals in Q1." Global News. April 30. https://globalnews.ca/news/5222533/q1-fundraising-totals/

Small, Tamara A. 2014. "The Not-So Social Network: The Use of Twitter by Canada's Party Leaders." In *Political Communication in Canada: Meet the Press and Tweet the Rest*, edited by Alex Marland, Thierry Giasson, and Tamara A. Small, 92–110. Vancouver: UBC Press.

Statistics Canada. 2019. "Canadian Internet Use Survey." https://www150.statcan.gc.ca/n1/daily-quotidien/191029/dq191029a-eng.htm

Thomas, Paul E. J., and Jerald Sabin. 2019. "Candidate Messaging on Religious Issues in the 2016–17 Conservative Party of Canada Leadership Race." *Canadian Journal of Political Science/Revue Canadienne de Science Politique*. September 13: 1–23.

Tóth, Tamás, Dalma Kékesdi-Boldog, Tamás Bokor, and Zoltán Veczán. 2019. "'Protect Our Homeland!' Populist Communication in the 2018 Hungarian Election Campaign on Facebook." *Central European Journal of Communication* 12(2): 169–86.

Trammell, Kaye D., and Andrew Paul Williams. 2004. "Beyond Direct Mail: Evaluating Candidate E-Mail Messages in the 2002 Florida Gubernatorial Campaign." *Journal of E-Government* 1(1): 105–22.

Tubbs, Ed. 2019. "Maxime Bernier Rejects the Expert Consensus on Immigration Rates and the Climate Change Crisis." *Toronto Star*. September 24. https://www.thestar.com/politics/federal/2019/09/24/bernier-warns-against-letting-too-many-immigrants-in-and-says-there-is-no-climate-change-crisis.html

Vaccari, Cristian. 2014. "You've Got (No) Mail: How Parties and Candidates Respond to E-Mail Inquiries in Western Democracies." *Journal of Information Technology & Politics* 11(2): 245–58. https://doi.org/10.1080/19331681.2014.899536

Van Kessel, Stijn, and Remco Castelein. 2016. "Shifting the Blame. Populist Politicians' Use of Twitter as a Tool of Opposition." *Journal of Contemporary European Research* 12(2): 594–614.

Waisbord, Silvio, and Adriana Amado. 2017. "Populist Communication by Digital Means: Presidential Twitter in Latin America." *Information, Communication & Society* 20(9): 1330–46.

White, Patrick. 2019. "Federal Election 2019: People's Party Fails to Gain a Single Seat in Disappointing Night for Maxime Bernier." *Globe and Mail.* October 21. https://www.theglobeandmail.com/canada/article-federal-election-2019-ppc-fail-to-gain-a-single-seat-in-disappointing/

Williams, Andrew Paul. 2004. "Self-Referential and Opponent-Based Framing: Candidate E-Mail Strategies in Campaign 2004." In *The Internet Election: Perspectives on the Web in Campaign,* edited by Andrew Paul Williams and John C. Tedesco, 83–98. Lanham, MD: Rowman & Littlefield.

Williams, Andrew Paul, and Evan Serge. 2010. "Evaluating Candidate E-Mail Messages in the 2008 U.S. Presidential Campaign." In *Techno Politics in Presidential Campaigning: New Voices, New Technologies, and New Voters,* edited by John Allen Hendricks and Lynda Lee Kaid, 44–58. New York: Routledge.

Williams, Andrew Paul, and Kaye D. Trammell. 2005. "Candidate Campaign E-Mail Messages in the Presidential Election 2004." *American Behavioral Scientist* 49(4): 560–74.

Williams, Andrew Paul, and Roxanna Maiorescu. 2014. "Evaluating Textual and Technical Interactivity in Candidate Email Messages during the 2012 U.S. Presidential Campaign." In *Presidential Campaigning and Social Media: An Analysis of the 2012 Campaign,* edited by John Allen Hendricks and Dan Schill, 171–84. New York: Oxford University Press.

CHAPTER 8

Benjamin Netanyahu and Online Campaigning in Israel's 2019 and 2020 Elections

Michael Keren, University of Calgary

Introduction

Before the advent of online media in Israeli elections, the election campaigns were often heated but the candidates had to settle for straightforward political messages because of the nature of the electoral system. In Israel, the Knesset (Israel's 120-member parliament) is elected in general, national, direct, equal, secret, and proportional elections. Voters are presented by party lists and the lists that pass a qualifying electoral threshold (which is currently 3.25 percent) are represented in the Knesset by a number of members proportional to the lists' electoral strength. The distribution is done by the division of valid votes by 120, in order to determine how many votes entitle a list to a single seat. Contrary to majoritarian electoral systems in which candidates appeal to a political center, the proportional system in Israel requires the parties to adapt to the needs and wishes of given groups, even marginal ones. Thus, from the first elections held in 1949 on, workers have mostly been courted by workers' parties, the middle classes by middle-class parties, religious Jews by religious parties, Arabs by Arab parties, communists by communist parties, and so on (Galoor and Blander 2018).

However, the increasing use of online media has altered this state of affairs. The first elections in which a majority of parties used the Internet in Israel was in 2003, when websites served mainly as sources of top-down information. In elections held in 2006, the online arena played a greater role, but it was only in 2009, after the success of Barack Obama's 2008 U.S. presidential

163

campaign, that numerous Internet channels were used simultaneously and that candidate-centered politics have taken hold (Haleva-Amir 2011). In the elections of 2013 and 2015 online media use grew exponentially. New online platforms came into play, Facebook accounts of individual leaders popped up, and unofficial websites with anonymous operators were run to rally against political rivals (Haleva-Amir and Nahon 2015; Orkibi 2015; Katz 2018).

All over the world, the introduction of online media has changed the nature of political campaigns, which have become more consumer-oriented and more influenced by media consultants (Karlsen 2010). In Israel these processes were exacerbated as a result of the intense use of the Internet by the population and the widespread use of social media in political campaigns (Steinfeld 2016). This had a major impact on the political system. The proportional representation system demanded of Israelis to continue voting for party lists, but the image of certain individuals on those lists received greater weight, and messages catering to the interests of given social groups were replaced by an appeal to a mass audience. So much so that in 2015 a public commission headed by former chief justice Dorit Beinisch has been appointed out of fear for the deterioration of Israel's party system.

In 2018, the Israel Democracy Institute published a report expressing concern over the impact of digital media on the electoral process in Israel. The report stated:

> All agree that the digital space makes an immense contribution to improvement of the political process by multiplying the sources of information, increasing the options for civic participation, empowering individuals, maintaining connections and involvement between elections, crowdfunding, and so on. At the same time, however, we also see the manipulation of voters' thoughts and of the voting process, infringements of privacy, and a lack of transparency. Sometimes these take the form of disinformation or fake news, which are amplified by the use of techniques of planned marketing or targeting based on the processing of personal data. In recent years it has become increasingly evident that data analysis, automation, opaque algorithms, and computational advertising based on analysis of big data can be exploited for unprecedented manipulation of public opinion and undermine the viability of a public sphere based on individual choice and autonomy. (Schwartz and Lurie 2018)

The greatest concern was raised over the use of digital media as a tool of incitement. In 2015, the Berl Katzanelson Foundation, associated with the

Labor Party, launched "Israel's National Index on Hate and Incitement," a technological platform that monitors hatred in Israel's online and social media. The index tracks millions of conversations on an hourly basis (statuses, reactions, talkbacks, tweets, etc.) and aggregates the information to indicate levels of tolerance and incitement in the public and media discourse (Katznelson Foundation 2018).

Reports released by the foundation reveal a rise over time in Internet incitement and calls for violence against government institutions including the cabinet, the IDF (Israel Defense Forces), the Israeli Police, and others. It also reveals an increase in verbal violence aimed at judges, the judiciary, and the country's president. In 2015, for example, an election year, a 20 percent increase over the previous year has been reported in the number of inciting and racist statements on social media in Israel. An even bigger increase of 40 percent has been found in the number of calls for physical violence on social media. The breakdown was as follows:

> In first place is Arabs, with 263,000 hateful comments directed to them in 2015, followed by LGBTs with 76,500. Leftists were in third place with 73,000, followed by ultra-Orthodox (73,000), refugees (68,700), right-wingers (28,000), Mizrahim [Jews of Middle Eastern origin] (18,500), Ethiopians (8,000), Ashkenazim [Jews of Western origin] (7,900) and Russians (5,100). (Cohen, 2015)

In what follows, I focus on the group that has made the top of the list—Israeli Arabs—who in four subsequent election campaigns have become the target of incitement by Prime Minister Benjamin Netanyahu. I begin by explaining the political background that led to Netanyahu's decision to exploit anti-Arab sentiments for political gain; I then describe the way in which his so called "online media empire" has been mobilized as a tool of incitement; and I conclude by some thoughts on the political implications of that endeavor.

Background

After the establishment of the State of Israel in 1948, about half a million Palestinian Arabs found themselves within the state's boundaries. They were granted Israeli citizenship but their position in the Jewish state was difficult because of the ongoing Arab-Israeli conflict. For close to two decades they were subjected to martial law. After martial law was lifted in 1966, Israel's

Arab population continued to suffer from inequality in the distribution of state resources. Over the years, Arab citizens integrated into the life of the state but there were serious setbacks, as when in October 2000 Israeli police killed thirteen Arab citizens who demonstrated in support of their brethren in the Palestinian occupied territories (Smooha 2002).

In Knesset elections, lists formed by Arab political leaders have covered the whole range of communist, nationalist, Islamist, and other ideologies held within the Arab population. However, as a result of the raising of the electoral threshold from 2 percent to 3.25 percent in 2014, the Joint List has been formed, composed of four Arab parties: Hadahsh (The Democratic Front for Peace and Equality), headed by lawyer Ayman Odeh, an offshoot of the Arab-Jewish Communist Party believing in coexistence and in a two-state solution to the Israeli-Palestinian conflict; Ta'al (Arab Movement for Renewal), headed by medical doctor Ahmad Tibi, promoting both citizen rights and recognition of Palestinian nationalism in Israel; Ra'am (United Arab List), founded by the Southern Islamic Movement; and Balad (National Democratic Alliance), a party calling for the transformation of Israel from a Jewish state with an Arab minority to a "state of all its citizens." Despite great ideological differences within this alliance, Ayman Odeh who headed the Joint List managed to keep it together most of the time and under his leadership it won 10.61 percent of the general vote in 2015 (thirteen seats in Israel's 120-seat Knesset) and 12.67 percent in 2020 (fifteen seats).

The formation of the Joint List, and its electoral successes, came at a time of significant progress in the integration of Arabs into Israeli society. Arabs have increasingly occupied prominent positions in medicine, business, literature, the arts, sports, and other fields. A strategic survey published by the Institute for National Security Studies in January 2020 has noted "the clear aspiration among Arabs in Israel, especially among the younger generation, for civil and even political integration—despite the low starting point and significant social, economic, and cultural barriers—along with their desire to maintain a separate national identity" (INSS Report 2020).

In politics, the voter turnout among Arabs has increased and the Joint List has gained support by Jewish voters as well. Although many Jews have been dubious toward Arab politicians, such as Ahmad Tibi who served in the past as advisor to Palestinian leader Yasser Arafat, the Joint List achieved a degree of legitimacy in spite of the Balad component whose members called for the dismantling of Israel as a Jewish state.

With the Joint List becoming a significant political force in electoral politics, Benjamin Netanyahu, head of the right-wing Likud (a political party taking a hard line in Israel's never-ending conflict with the Palestinians), had to make sure the List does not form an alliance with Likud's political rivals, as happened once in the past. In elections held in June 1992, Yitzhak Rabin, head of the Labor Party, won forty-four seats against Likud's thirty-two and formed a coalition government consisting of Labor and two smaller parties (Meretz and Shas) that supported Labor's program to advance peace with the Palestinians. This gave Rabin a tiny majority of sixty-two seats out of the Knesset's 120, but he was able to pursue the peace process (the Oslo process) because his coalition was supported from outside by the five members of the two Arab parties at the time: The Democratic Front for Peace and Equality and The Democratic Arab Party. Netanyahu has learnt the lesson.

In November 1995, a vast incitement campaign against Rabin, in which then opposition head Netanyahu took major part, led to his assassination, and in the elections that followed in May 1996 Netanyahu became prime minister. In the next elections held in 1999 he lost to Labor. When Likud gained power a year and a half later, he served in several ministerial posts until he regained the headship of Likud and in 2009 became prime minister again.

The term of Israel's Knesset is four years but can be shortened by a resolution passed by the majority of its members. Netanyahu's government of 2009 held on until 2013, but elections were called again in March 2015 as a result of a coalition crisis. Then three additional elections were held in April 2019, September 2019, and March 2020. This unprecedented frequency was related to Netanyahu's legal ordeal. In 2017 the police began investigating serious suspicions that resulted in the attorney general's decision to file charges against him for bribery, fraud, and breach of trust, which carry a long prison sentence. The attorney general's announcement was made on February 28, 2019, and the bill of indictment was filed on November 21, 2019, following a hearing. All that time, Netanyahu was determined to gain a Knesset majority that would get him off the hook by legislation, which made him call new elections when that majority was not achieved. In all three elections, Likud tied with a party named "Blue and White," headed by former chief of staff Benny Gantz, which ran on an anticorruption ticket.

This background explains why frequent elections were called by the prime minister in 2019 and 2020. It also explains the nature of the election campaigns. Netanyahu's desperate need to avoid a coalition between Blue and White and the Joint Arab List made him engage in fierce incitement. A major case of incitement occurred on the afternoon of election day, March 17, 2015, when Netanyahu, finding out that voter turnout was still low, posted a twenty-eight-second video on his Facebook page urging his supporters to go out and vote by saying: "The right-wing government is in danger. Arab voters are heading to the polling stations in droves. Left-wing NGOs are bringing them in buses" (The Guardian, March 17, 2015).

It is significant that Netanyahu chose to convey this message on Facebook and also spread it via text messages and other online channels. Election law in Israel does not allow press conferences or other appearances by candidates on election day. Netanyahu was specifically reminded of it by Supreme Court Judge Salim Joubran, chairman of the Central Elections Committee. He thus sidestepped the conventional media, as he often did as a result of his perception, reminiscent of American president Donald Trump, that the media are part of a leftist conspiracy trying to get him, and took to the online arena in which he excelled. Much of his success in holding on to power and surpassing legal and normative barriers, such as the ban on media appearances on election day, has been attributed to his online presence and his mastery of an online media empire described as follows:

> This is what Netanyahu's social media empire looks like. Every day Netanyahu broadcasts messages to millions of followers on Facebook, Twitter, Instagram, YouTube and Telegram via dozens of accounts, some of them run with state funding, and some via private funding from less-than-transparent sources. His posts have thousands of shares, tens of thousands of likes and responses, and one of the highest user response rates for any politician—certainly in Israel, but also internationally (Goichman 2019).

In 2019, *The Times of Israel* estimated that by the time Netanyahu prepared for the April campaign, his online empire had about six million online followers. It included a private Facebook page, an official prime minister Facebook page, an official Likud page, many Facebook fan pages, an online TV channel, an official Twitter account, a personal Twitter page, and an Instagram account (Surkes 2019). This online network, unrivaled by any other Israeli politician, was put to use in full force.

The Proxy

During his years in office, Netanyahu earmarked unprecedented budgets to Arab communities and never refrained from political deals with Arab Knesset members. But as a campaigner, he made every effort to weaken the Joint List by delegitimizing Israel's entire Arab population. In 2019, he repeatedly claimed that Blue and White intended to form a "blocking majority" with the Arab parties to prevent him from heading the next government, as if this would be a crime, and accused the elected representatives of the Arab community as supporters of terror.

Since it is inappropriate for a prime minister in a democracy to engage in hate speech against 20 percent of the citizenry, however politically useful, the most notorious statements were left to his elder son, Yair Netanyahu. Yair, a person in his late twenties living with his parents and known to spend most of his waking hours on Twitter, practically ran the online media empire and served as the prime minister's proxy in the campaigns. For example, in December 2018 he was banned from Facebook for twenty-four hours following a series of anti-Palestinian and anti-Muslim posts defined as hate speech. One such post read: "Do you know where there are no terror attacks? In Iceland and Japan. Coincidentally there's also no Muslim population there." Yair attributed the ban to "the thought police of the radical progressives at Facebook" (The Guardian, December 17, 2018).

This was one of many incidents in which Yair's extreme social media messages stirred controversy. At times, the controversy became uncomfortable for the prime minister, as when the son posted a cartoon inspired by anti-Semitic images featuring Jewish philanthropist George Soros, a supporter of liberal causes, as a lizard creature. The prime minister expressed his disapproval of the cartoon, after it was shared by the Ku Klux Clan and hailed by Neo-Nazi websites. Yet, even when such disapproval was occasionally announced, the consistency between the son's tweets and his father's political interests could not be overlooked.

As the *Los Angeles Times* put it, the son was "Benjamin Netanyahu's Not-So-Secret Weapon," citing such examples as Yair's lashing out at Israel's president Reuven Rivlin for defending the civil rights of Arab citizens after the senior Netanyahu said that Israel was "not a state of all its citizens" (Los Angeles Times, June 7, 2019). While the prime minister was obliged to certain norms of international diplomacy, the nightly tweets by his son expressed positive feelings toward Hungarian prime minister Viktor Orbán, Brexit Party leader Nigel Farage, and Matteo Salvini, leader of Italy's League Party, which led critics to describe Netanyahu Jr. as "cheering on fascists" (Jewish Chronicle, May 22, 2019).

Many observers have described Yair as the prime minister's "alter ego," a concept denoting a second side of one's own self, as in Robert Louis Stevenson's 1886 novel *The Strange Case of Dr. Jekyll and Mr. Hyde*. In that novel, two persons—a humanitarian and a murderer—reside in the same human body (Berta and Saiz 1999). The father and son's online communications in the present saga may indeed be described as two sides of the same political figure. As Netanyahu's biographer Ben Caspit noted on the *Al-Monitor* media site,

> Prime Minister Benjamin Netanyahu's son Yair expresses openly the far-right and Arab-hating positions expressed a bit more discreetly by his father and his official entourage. . . . According to many sources who are knowledgeable about what goes on in the Prime Minister's home, Yair does not merely listen to the dialogue between his parents and translate it in the external world. Instead, they say . . . Yair is the engine behind his father's right-wing radicalization. (Caspit 2017)

Incitement

As stated before, the elections held in April 2019 and September 2019 ended in deadlock. None of the contending political blocs, the one led by Netanyahu's Likud and the other by Gantz's Blue and White, were able to form a coalition, so a third round was called. The campaign leading to the third election held in March 2020 took place after the attorney general's release of the bill of indictment, which turned the elections into a "pro Bibi-anti-Bibi" competition ("Bibi" is Netanyahu's nickname). In his attempt to achieve a majority that would use its legislative power to handicap the legal system, Netanyahu was accused of using "Mafia-style tactics" (Reis 2020). These tactics included, for example, contracting a business intelligence firm to gather damaging information about Gantz; forming fifteen Facebook profiles spreading rumors about rival politicians' personal lives; and blackmail of a Blue and White Knesset Member, threatening to leak sensitive personal information about her unless she joined the opposite camp.

As part of the effort to prevent Benny Gantz from forming a coalition supported by the Joint List, the incitement against Arabs breached any normative barrier (Fuchs 2020). In previous elections Netanyahu was careful not to be associated with hate speech. For example, when in September 2019 Ayman Odeh complained to Facebook about an inciting post on Natanyahu's official Facebook page suggesting that Arab Israeli politicians "want to annihilate us all" (Times of Israel, September 12, 2019), the prime minister's office issued a statement that it was put up by a campaign worker by mistake. But in the 2020 campaign, the gloves were taken off and the digital team, overseen by son Yair, went to work.

In November 2020, the prime minister called an "emergency rally" of his Likud Party where, surrounded by stern-faced government ministers, he declared that the rival party was "conducting negotiations with MKs [members of the Knesset] who support terror organizations and want to destroy the country." Establishing a minority government supported by the Joint List, he said, would be "a breaking point in the country's history." He then added, "If a minority government like this is formed, they will celebrate in Tehran, Ramallah and Gaza, the way they celebrate after every terror attack. This would be a historic national attack on the State of Israel" (Israel Ha'yom, November 18, 2019).

The Arab political leadership became concerned. Odeh and Tibi approached the Knesset's ethics committee complaining about Netanyahu's incitement campaign, after which, they said, they were flooded with threats. "Bibi has crossed all redlines," Tibi said, "He won't stop targeting us for assassination until one of us is harmed by an extremist. Netanyahu already incited against a prime minister, and we saw what happened to him. Netanyahu is an expert at incitement and lies against minorities" (Jerusalem Post, November 18, 2019). At this point, however, Netanyahu no longer dissociated himself from incitement.

In order to extricate the narrative created in the prime minister's online media empire, it is useful to follow his Hebrew Twitter feed (https://twitter.com/netanyahu). Although, for security reasons, Netanyahu did not possess a smartphone or computer, and did not personally operate his five Twitter accounts in Hebrew, English, Arabic, Russian and Farsi, the Twitter feed includes the campaign messages he chose to present under his own name. It is also where one can find links to the prime minister's Facebook pages, YouTube channels, and other social media platforms.

On January 28, 2020, after Netanyahu had to give up his parliamentary immunity, the attorney general officially filed the corruption charges against him. The prime minister called the charges on Twitter "a circus" and "a dirty game" and retweeted right away a Likud YouTube video that, according to "simple math," showed that Benny Gantz has no chance to form a government without the Joint List. Many tweets from now on were devoted to that point. In most tweets, however, it was not the Joint List that was named but Ahmad Tibi.

The choice of Tibi as target was not obvious. Although Tibi was one of the most vocal critics of government policy in the Palestinian territories, the medical doctor who served in the Knesset for two decades and speaks perfect Hebrew has been acclaimed as an excellent parliamentarian. In 2010, for example, while serving as the Knesset's deputy speaker, he gave a speech denouncing Holocaust denial, which then-speaker Reuven Rivlin called the finest speech ever given in the history of the Knesset. Yet his name came up in Netanyahu's personal Twitter feed almost every day until the elections.

When in former campaigns Netanyahu came out with the slogan "Bibi or Tibi," Tibi responded with humor: "I didn't know that against my will I was a leading candidate for prime minister." Tibi was worried, however, about the effort to delegitimize the Arab parties, Arab lawmakers, and the Arab public in general. Netanyahu, he said in an interview, "is trying to transmit that it is either me, the supposed patriotic Jewish leader, or the Arabs will take over the country and decide who will be the prime minister. And he portrays this as a nightmare" (Ynet, October 3, 2019).

The prospect of a Gantz coalition supported by the Joint List has indeed been framed as a nightmare. On January 28, President Trump announced the "deal of the century," a Middle East peace proposal that included the option of transferring an area inhabited by Israeli Arab citizens to a future Palestinian state, an idea that has previously only been proposed by supremacists and bigots. When Tibi demanded of Gantz to clarify his party's position regarding population exchanges, Netanyahu tweeted: "Tibi decides, Blue and White executes." And when on February 4 Gantz declared that he would support Trump's plan if it receives international endorsement, Netanyahu mocked the declaration, asking whether Gantz expects endorsement from the UN, the European Union, and Ahmad Tibi. This tweet was accompanied by a YouTube video in which Gantz is seen seated in a meeting with Tibi and Odeh and a caption reads: "Gantz has almost succeeded in forming a coalition government with the Joint List. It should not be allowed to happen in Israel." This video appeared frequently on Netanyahu's online media until election day.

Netanyahu's Twitter is filled with videos showing the many rallies he held in Israeli cities, sometimes several a day. The footage of these rallies always contains the same images. Surrounded by local Likud leaders and cheered by enthusiastic crowds, the prime minister makes election speeches in which he never fails to bring up Tibi's name in a way that would trigger boos from the crowd.

On February 5, an urgent message on Netanyahu's Twitter proclaimed that a deal between Gantz and the Joint List has been closed and it is essential to prevent a leftist government dependent on "Balad and Tibi." In a rally on that day, Netanyahu stated once again that Gantz had no chance to form a coalition without Tibi. Occasionally the name of Odeh, who declared his willingness to support Gantz under certain conditions, came up, but "Tibi" always remained at the forefront. Even when Gantz was shown seated between the two Arab leaders, Tibi's image has been emphasized.

On February 9, another name was added. On that day, Israel's Supreme

Court reversed by a vote of five to four a decision by the Central Election Committee two weeks earlier to bar Heba Yazbak of Balad to run for the Knesset. In a 2015 Facebook post, Yazbak praised Lebanese terrorist Samir Kuntar, who in 1979 shot an Israeli civilian and killed his four-year-old daughter by smashing her skull against a rock. "Benny Gantz depends on Yazbak who praises terrorists," Netanyahu tweeted that day, and a few days later added that Gantz waits for approval for the Trump peace plan by Tibi and Yazbak.

During the month of February, southern Israel was under rocket attacks from Gaza and the question came up whether Netanyahu would risk a military campaign against the territory shortly before the elections. When Tibi announced he would not support a government that launches such a campaign, a video shown on Netanyahu's Twitter accused former chief of staff Gantz for his apparent willingness to castrate the Israel Defense Force at a time of war for the sake of forming a coalition. In a flood of tweets, Netanyahu accused Gantz of yielding to every dictate by the Joint List and for relying on Ahmad Tibi, who would do anything Palestinian leader Mahmoud Abbas instructs him to do.

On February 15, a former General Security Service officer, angered by the Blue and White Party not placing his name high on its candidate list, tweeted that this was the result of the party yielding to the Joint List, even though he was not disqualified before, when he was chasing "Palestinian terrorism, including Arab Israeli public figures and traitors." This incredible statement, associating Israeli-Arab public figures with treason, has been retweeted by the prime minister, who added that he was concerned over a government supported by the Joint List whose members, "every one of them," seek the liquidation of the State of Israel. These words, associating by innuendo Israel's Arab population with treason, have never been removed from the prime minister's Twitter account.

Conclusion

In the 2020 elections, Likud ended up with thirty-six seats, Blue and White with thirty-three, and the Joint List with fifteen. Since sixty-one Knesset members, including the fifteen members of the Joint List, endorsed Gantz, the former general was given the task of forming a coalition. The political events that followed are beyond the scope of this article but the use of digital media as a tool of incitement warrants some discussion.

In recent years, observers all over the world have noted the rise of populist authoritarianism associated mainly with American president Donald Trump, Hungarian prime minister Viktor Orbán, and Brazilian president Jair Bolsonaro (Krepec and Wise 2020). "Authoritarian populism" refers to "the pitting of 'the people' against 'elites' in order to have the power to drive out, wipe out, or otherwise dominate Others who are not 'the people'" (Miller 2018, xiv). It has also been argued that Netanyahu has joined this unrespectable club of leaders who replace traditional pragmatic politics with "new populist-driven politics that prioritize absolutist positions, which resonate loud and clear with relevant constituency groups" (Shany 2019).

However, as much as Netanyahu has endorsed Trump, Orbán, and Bolsonaro, and however contemptuous he was of academics, journalists, legal professionals, and other incumbents of the traditional Israeli elites, Netanyahu has always been aware of the difficulty to override the elites by a direct appeal to the "people." His populist rhetoric during election campaigns never made him forget that once the elections are over, the coalition-building process in Israel requires a return to "politics as usual," as when he negotiated a national unity government with Gantz after the 2020 elections. Moreover, the Israeli public has not been an easy target for authoritarian populism reminiscent of the fascist regimes in Hitler's Germany and Mussolini's Italy. Israel's democracy, formed in the aftermath of the Second World War, has traditionally had little tolerance toward fascist parties, as evidenced by the failure of the ultra-nationalist party *Otzma-Yehudit* (Jewish Power) to pass the votes threshold in Israeli elections, and the electorate has traditionally not tolerated racism, a sentiment associated with the rise of fascism (Adorno 1950; Billig 1977; Rokeach 1960). In surveys conducted before the September 2019 elections, for example, 75 percent of Israeli Jews supported adding an equality clause to all the country's basic laws (Yemini 2019).

How, then, has racist incitement become a campaign strategy? This is where digital media come into play. Although digital media in themselves can obviously not be seen as the cause of political change, I would like to argue in conclusion that the Internet has coarsened the political discourse in Israel to such an extent that Israeli politics has never been the same again.

In the past, election campaigns were always heated but, for the reasons I discussed above, the parties' propaganda had to be addressed at given groups and cater to their interests. For example, in the 1949 elections the Communist Party sought the vote of those objecting to what it called "the Anglo-American warmongers" in the Cold War, in 1959 the Orthodox parties sought the vote of believers objecting to the conscription of women to the military, and in 1977 Labor sought the vote of supporters of the peace process. In such a system, racism has no place in election campaigns and may even turn out to be dysfunctional.

However, the Israeli electorate, like any electorate, is not immune to racism, defined as "Prejudice, discrimination, or antagonism directed against a person or people on the basis of their membership of a particular racial or ethnic group, typically one that is a minority or marginalized" (Oxford Dictionary). And the immediacy and anonymity of Internet discourse have inflamed racist sentiments and brought them to the surface in Israel as elsewhere (Keren 2010). Again, this is not to say that digital media have generated racism in Israel. As a newspaper article titled "Does Racism Now Define Jewish Identity in Israel?" rightly states, "We are inundated by surveys and statistics that tell us that racism is on the rise, but none of those who collate these figures can tell us how bad things were before every nasty word was broadcast in real-time on social media and before each act of racial violence was recorded on smartphones and uploaded to the web" (Pffefer 2019).

Digital media have made it easier for political campaigners to openly engage in propaganda associated with European fascism of the past. This is not because Twitter, Facebook, and other online media allow incitement more than the loudspeaker or radio have allowed in the past but because of the cheapening of the written and spoken word in the digital age.

In 1930, Spanish writer José Ortega y Gasset wrote *The Revolt of the Masses* in which he related the emergence of European fascism to the abandonment of the norms and standards that, he believed, define civilized discourse. "Whoever wants to have ideas," he wrote, "must be disposed to want truth and to accept the rules of the game which truth imposes. There is no use speaking of ideas or opinions if there is no acceptance of a process which authorizes and regulates them, a series of norms and standards to which appeal can be made. These norms are the principles of culture, whatever form they take" (Ortega 1985, 60).

The digital age has freed us from many of these norms and standards. The rules of political discourse have been loosened and the value of truth diminished. As Anne Mintz puts it, "Bending the truth or telling outright lies is not new. It's just the messenger who has changed, and this messenger spreads the word lightning fast and to far-flung places" (Mintz 2012, 9). Political campaigning, concerned with winning elections rather than with the value of truth, is therefore a main beneficiary of online media (Lee 2015). Moreover, Internet communication turns easily into propaganda, and fake news have become commonplace in a world in which information is spread swiftly, widely, and irresponsibly in social media. As Jamie Barlett writes: "Racists on Twitter will come and go: but social media is making all of us—even those who detest the ideology—adopt that fascist style of politics" (Barlett 2018).

There are, of course, major differences between today's political scene in

Israel and that of German or Italian fascism in the twentieth century, but the resemblance between the vicious, violent language of the fascist movements of the past and much of the online political discourse held in Israel in the last election campaigns has led scholars to question the common assumption that fascism would never take hold in Israel. For example, Zeev Sternhell, Israel's foremost expert on European fascism, made the following observation in 2018:

> I frequently ask myself how a historian in 50 or 100 years will interpret our period. When, he will ask, did people in Israel start to realize that the state that was established in the War of Independence, on the ruins of European Jewry and at the cost of the blood of combatants some of whom were Holocaust survivors, had devolved into a true monstrosity for its non-Jewish inhabitants. (Sternhell 2018)

And in 2019, after the two election rounds ending in deadlock, Daniel Blatman, head of the Research Institute of Contemporary Jewry at the Hebrew University of Jerusalem, wrote:

> The end of the Weimar Republic in Germany, which occurred officially on January 30, 1933, with the appointment of Hitler as chancellor, was preceded by three Reichstag elections within two years: in September 1930, July 1932 and November 1932. The situation in Germany in that era recalls that of Israel today: political instability, inability to form a stable government either of the left or of the center-right, intrigues and infighting among politicians, and a violent and sophisticated fascist force whose intention was to wrest control of the government and bury German democracy. (Blatman 2019)

One need not endorse these analogies to realize that Israeli democracy has suffered severe setbacks in recent years as a result of the changing political discourse in the country. The experience discussed in this article thus carries a lesson for Israel and other democracies in the digital age: the need to maintain and encourage civilized public discourse if democracy is to survive.

Bibliography

Adorno, Theodor W., et al. 1950. *The Authoritarian Personality*. New York: Harper.
Altshuler, Tehilla Schwartz, and Guy Lurie. 2018. "The Municipal Elections 2018: Digital Resilience." Israel Democracy Institute, October 29.

Barlett, Jamie. 2018. "How Social Media Makes Fascists of Us All." *UnHerd* (blog), August 28. https://unherd.com/2018/08/social-media-makes-fascists-us/

Berta, Mario, and Mario Saiz. 1999. "The Alter Ego in Psychiatry." *The Lancet* 354. https://www.thelancet.com/journals/lancet/article/PIIS0140-6736(99)90398-7/fulltext

Billig, Michael. 1977. "The New Social Psychology and Fascism." *European Journal of Social Psychology* 7(4) (December): 393–432.

Blatman, Daniel. 2019. "A Lesson from Weimar 1932: A Third Election Could Save Israel." *Haaretz*, October 13.

Caspit, Ben. 2017. "Is Netanyahu's Son Pulling Him to the Far-Right?" *Al Monitor*, August 21. https://www.al-monitor.com/pulse/fa/originals/2017/08/israel-us-donald-trump-benjamin-netanyahu-steve-bannon-yair.html

Cohen, Gili, and Barak Ravid. 2016. "IDF Deputy Chief Likens 'Revolting Trends' in Israeli Society to pre-Holocaust Germany." *Haaretz*, May 4.

Cohen, Sagi. 2015. "Loving to Hate: Social Media Incitement on the Rise." YNET, December 16. https://www.ynetnews.com/articles/0,7340,L-4740313,00.html

Fuchs, Amir. 2020. "Hollow Democracy." Israel Democracy Institute, March 9. https://www.idi.org.il/articles/30945 (in Hebrew).

Galnoor, Yitzhak, and Dana Blander. 2018. *The Handbook of Israel's Political System*. New York: Cambridge University Press.

Goichman, Rafaella. 2019. "Netanyahu Presides Over a Social Media Empire. Here's How He Runs It." *Haaretz*, January 17.

Haleva-Amir, Sharon. 2011. "New Media, Politics and Society in Israel." *Israel Affairs* 17(3): 467–85.

Haleva-Amir, Sharon and Karine Nahon. 2015. "Electoral Politics on Social Media: The Israeli Case." In *Routledge Companion to Social Media and Politics*, edited by Axel Bruns et al. New York: Routledge.

INSS Report. 2020. "Strategic Survey for Israel 2019–2020." The Institute for National Security Studies. https://www.inss.org.il/publication/israeli-society-challenges-to-societal-resilience/

Karlsen, Rune. 2010. "Does New Media Technology Drive Election Campaign Change?" *Information Polity* 15: 215–25.

Katz, Yaron. 2018. "Israel's Social Media Elections." *Open Journal of Political Science* 8(4) (October). https://www.scirp.org/journal/paperinformation.aspx?paperid=88221

Katznelson Foundation. 2018. "The Hate Report." April 29. http://hasata.berl.org.il/

Keren, Michael. 2010. "Blogging and Mass Politics." *Biography* 33(1) (Winter): 110–26.

Krepec, Oldřich, and Carol Wise. 2020. "Transnational Lineages of Authoritarianism: Hungary and Beyond." *Global Dynamics of Authoritarianism* 13(2) (May 12). https://www.21global.ucsb.edu/global-e/may-2020/transnational-lineages-authoritarianism-hungary-and-beyond

Lee, Sihyung. 2015. "Detection of Political Manipulation in Online Communities through Measures of Effort and Collaboration." *ACM Transactions on the Web* 9(3) (June): 1–24. https://doi.org/10.1145/2767134

Miller, Jeffrey C. 2004. *The Transcendent Function: Jung's Model of Psychological Growth through Dialogue with the Unconscious*. Albany: SUNY Press.

Mintz, Anne P., ed. 2012. *Web of Deception: Misinformation and Manipulation in the Age of Social Media*. Medford, NJ: CyberAge Books.

Morelock, Jeremaiah. 2018. "The Frankfurt School and Authoritarian Populism—A Historical Outline." In *Critical Theory and Authoritarian Populism*, edited by Jeremaiah Morelock. London: University of Westminster Press.

Orkibi, Eitan. 2015. "'New Politics,' New Media—New Political Language? A Rhetorical Perspective on Candidates' Self-Presentation in Electronic Campaigns in the 2013 Israeli Elections." *Israel Affairs* 21(2): 277–92.

Ortega y Gasset, José. 1985. *The Revolt of the Masses*. Notre Dame: University of Notre Dame Press.

Pfeffer, Anshel. 2019. "Does Racism Now Define Jewish Identity in Israel?" *Haaretz*, February 9.

Reis, Harry. 2020. "What to Watch in Israeli Democracy: Special Post-Election Edition." *New Israel Fund Blog*, March 5. https://www.nif.org/blog/what-to-watch-in-israeli-democracy-special-post-election-edition/

Rokeach, Milton. 1960. *The Open and Closed Mind: Investigations into the Nature of Belief Systems and Personality Systems*. New York: Basic Books.

Shany, Yuval. 2019. "Israel's Political Crisis and the Challenge of Populism." *Israel Democracy institute*, December 9. https://en.idi.org.il/articles/29093

Smooha, Sammy. 2002. "The Model of Ethnic Democracy: Israel as a Jewish and Democratic State." *Nations and Nationalism* 8(4): 475–503.

Steinfeld, Nili. 2016. "The F-campaign: A Discourse Network Analysis of Party Leaders' Campaign Statements on Facebook." *Israel Affairs* 22(3–4): 743–59.

Sternhell, Zeev. 2018. "In Israel, Growing Fascism and a Racism Akin to Early Nazism." *Haaretz*, January 19.

Surkes, Sue. 2019. "With Over 6 Million Online Followers, PM's Internet Empire Prepares for Election." *Times of Israel*, March 28.

Yemini, Ben-Dror. 2019. "Israel's Identity Politics is Failing Voters." *Ynet*, August 4. https://www.ynetnews.com/articles/0,7340,L-5491168,00.html

CHAPTER 9

Stabbed Democracy

How Social Media and Home Videos Made a Populist President in Brazil

Francisco Brandao, University of Brasilia

1. Introduction

Latin America has a long lineage of populist leaders (Conniff et al. 2012; Laclau 1978; Mudde and Kaltwasser 2013) and, since democratization in the 1980s and 1990s, strong media effects on presidential elections (Schneider 1992; Waisbord 2003; Weyland 2001). Nevertheless, the 2018 election in Brazil would be the first time a populist candidate won with a campaign based on homemade videos, streamed live on social media.

One of the most remarkable aspects of the election of right-wing leader Jair Bolsonaro is that the candidate lacked any of the resources conventionally assumed as the main determinant in a campaign. He seemed doomed to lose both in the ground war and the air war. First, Bolsonaro was affiliated with a very small party, the Social-Liberal (PSL), which elected only one deputy among the 594 congressional representatives in the previous election, in 2014. Second, he had much less TV time than other candidates. Finally, there was scarce public or private funding, and Bolsonaro spent only a fraction of what was destined to other candidates.

Considering these factors, how to explain the election of Jair Bolsonaro? What was the role of social media in his campaign? This chapter provides a descriptive account of digital media use in the 2018 Brazilian presidential election, analyzing how negative messages and personalized communication provided Bolsonaro's campaign with some of the characteristics of a social movement. I demonstrate how the context of the crisis in the party system offered the political opportunity and framing for an underdog populist, based on the ideology that separates "the pure people" from "the corrupt elite" (Mudde 2004). The polarized political environment reached its climax when Bolsonaro was stabbed in a campaign rally, almost one month before the first round. If the stab hurt his possibilities of campaigning on the streets, it also increased public attention to his homemade Facebook videos and exclusive interviews on TV.

Bolsonaro took advantage of that and ran a very contentious campaign, attacking not only the Worker's Party (PT) but the party system and corporate media as well. Conversely, he was also the target of an intensive negative campaign and media scrutiny. Following, I ask:

> **Research Question 1.** To what extent the politics of conflict and political polarization fueled Jair Bolsonaro's campaign on social media with negative sentiments and mobilized voters?

The fact that Bolsonaro effectively bypassed the traditional media raises questions about accountability and deliberation on campaigns in the digital era. Though Bolsonaro was able to communicate directly with his voters through social media, without the press mediation there was little informed and substantive debate about his program, which could have enhanced the quality of voters' decisions and opinions. Inhaling the spirit of the personalized proimpeachment protests against the PT, Bolsonaro's campaign relied on digital networks to mobilize voters, using a low-budget communication style. Considering these factors, I intend to answer:

> **Research Question 2.** How personalized was Bolsonaro's campaign on social media?

I discuss the role of social media with a content analysis of Facebook videos from presidential candidates and sentiment analysis of Twitter posts from their networks. The dataset comprises thirty-three million posts on Twitter about the three main candidates—Jair Bolsonaro (21.8 million tweets); Fernando Haddad (9.2 million); and Ciro Gomes (2 million). Facebook data summed up to 1,912 posts from the official pages of Bolsonaro (439 posts), Haddad (911), and Gomes (562). Together these posts had more than 102.2 million interactions. I focus my analysis on videos because 53 percent of those interactions came from them. Together the three candidates posted 943 videos that received more than 415.7 million views. Yet the 329 live videos from that sample got 141.9 million views.

These numbers are impressive, even considering the advanced stage of social media campaigning in Brazil. Based on a survey of Brazilian households and the age distribution of voters, I estimate that 100.7 million voters had Internet access, about 68 percent of the total registered to vote (Brazilian Internet Steering Committee 2018; Brazil Superior Electoral Court 2020). Among Internet users, 75.5 million (51 percent of voters) were on social media, and 7 million (5 percent) used Twitter. The Latinobarómetro Survey (2018) found that 58.8 percent of the population used Facebook, 37 percent watched videos on YouTube, and 65.9 percent exchanged messages on Whatsapp.

In this chapter, I first evaluate how Latin American populist politicians, who were historically benefited by strong media effects, might get a new boost with social media. Then I analyze the context of crisis in the Brazilian political system and its effects on the 2018 election. After describing data collection and methods used in this chapter, I use content analysis of Facebook videos and sentiment analysis of Twitter posts.

2. Populism and Media

The context of developing democracies, marked by a weak civil society, high levels of poverty, weak political parties, and clientelism, makes voters behave differently than in advanced democracies (Lupu et al. 2019). In Latin America, weak party identities and unstable party systems result in a more volatile electoral behavior (Baker, Ames, and Rennó 2006). Limited partisanship and campaign swings are the norms. Many voters shift from an initial vote intention to support one of the candidates before the campaigns go to a final vote choice for another candidate (Greene 2019). Electoral volatility is perceived not only within elections but also across consecutive elections. Therefore the supply of political information, without shortcuts provided by stable parties, behave differently, with consequences to voting decisions.

Also Latin American voters are not exposed to a pluralistic media system that could provide more divergent political views, since the media system is structured in monopolies or oligopolies with little competition and strong political bias (Skidmore 1993). That is why the literature on the region points out stronger media effects on elections (Castañeda and Ibarra 2013; Lima 1988; Lawson and McCann 2004; Pérez-Liñan 2002). If voters have no meaningful choice among TV networks—because of the near-monopoly of viewers by one broadcast channel or because different stations are biased toward the same candidate—than television can change the intended vote of the viewers. The influence of media effects can be perceived in the emergence of outsider neopopulist politicians in the 1980s and 1990s, who are not connected to traditional parties and target the atomized poor electorate in their campaigns. Television exposure played an important causal role in the presidential elections of Brazil in 1989 and Peru in 1990 (Boas 2005; Castells 1997).

Media effects on Latin America might change together with the transformations on broadcasting and new media. Prior (2007) observes that broadcast television increased political knowledge among less educated people, narrowing the knowledge gap between those with more education and those with less. As new media offers new ways and options of communication, the regular evening news has lost part of its audience. As a result, cable television and the Internet increased the knowledge gap between people with a preference for news and people with a preference for other media content. With the changes in the media environment, one can expect changes in voter behavior, as an increased political polarization. Valenzuela, Arriagada, and Scherman (2012) demonstrate that social media use was significantly associated with protest activity in Chile.

To Latin America, new media represents the opportunity of more pluralistic channels and views that would not be available in a corporate media intrinsically connected to the political system. This could bring not only new ways of political organization but also new ways of collective action that does not require substantial cost or organization (Bimber 2003). According to Bennett and Segerberg (2013), large-scale "connective action" is possible when coordinated by personalized digital networks, with access to communication centered on personal action frames and personal expression.

In Latin America, that would be not only the case of social movements but also of populists challenging the party system. Since 2007, populists in Latin America incorporated Twitter as a platform to lash out at critics and get media attention (Waisbord and Amado 2017). Right-wing populist leaders use Internet platforms in order to represent the relationship between them and "the people," justify the exclusion of out-groups, elaborate populist ideology, develop a populist identity, and circumvent the traditional media (Krämer 2017). Populism is particularly well-suited to be communicated through the Internet in three ways: (1) populist antielitism ideology is more convincing when directly addressing the people, in a media that favors nonelite actors; (2) populist style of simplification, emotionalization, and negativity is in line with the Internet's attention economy; and (3) the Internet provides populist leaders with personalized communication that allows them to exert their charisma (Engesser et al. 2017). In other chapters in this book, politicians also use populist messages to mobilize voters. In chapter 7, Budd and Small reveal how the populist People's Party of Canada used emails with antielitist discourse to appeal to supporters and call for action. In chapter 11, Doroshenko shows that Ukrainian candidate Voldymyr Zelensky used Facebook to promote citizen engagement and more open communication with supporters.

A comparison of populist communication strategies on Twitter and Facebook shows that populism manifests mostly by political extremists, by opposition parties, and on Facebook (Ernst et al. 2017). Parties are generally more inclined to use populism-related communication on Facebook and Twitter than in talk shows (Ernst et al. 2019). Voters also tend to evaluate politicians as more honest on social media, compared to talk shows and news (Enli and Rosenberg 2018). Messages on social media blaming the elites tend to bolst citizens' populist attitudes, but only for those who support the source of the message (Hameleers and Schmuck 2017). This is true for both those citizens who identify themselves with the populist politician or those who highly identify with other citizens transmitting the message. These findings show the importance of social identification and give support to a media strategy based on personalized messages. Social media polarization can also have an impact on news organizations, as a polarized readership will further polarize publishers (Aruguete et al. 2021). In the context of the crisis in the Brazilian party system, Bolsonaro used social media to engage directly with voters and mobilize his partisans unlike any of the conventional practices of communication seen so far.

3. Crisis and Context

The party system crisis in Brazil offered the political opportunity, connective action structure, and framing for an underdog populist candidate. The investigation of the corruption scandal by Operation Car Wash (Moro 2018) led to a new electoral regulation, which affected funding and the campaign timeline. The protests that resulted in the impeachment of President Dilma Rousseff in 2016 were largely organized and mobilized through Facebook and other social networking services, which would provide the platform to launch a challenger candidate. The politics of conflict and polarization offered the proper framing and fueled a populist campaign against "the corrupt elite."

The Worker's Party did not show a proper response to the scandal and the economic crisis that followed, insisting on the candidacy of former president Luiz Inacio Lula da Silva, who was under investigation by the so-called Operation Car Wash anticorruption unit and was later arrested on April 7, 2018. It was six months before the election, which was divided into two rounds: the first on October 7 and, if none of the candidates reached 50 percent of the valid votes, a runoff election on October 28. Even after Lula's arrest, his party chose no alternative name to fill in the ballot. The PT started a long and unsuccessful campaign to free Lula, still presented as a candidate behind bars. Surrogate candidate Fernando Haddad, former minister of Education during Lula's term, was formally introduced to voters as the PT candidate only on September 11, less than four weeks before the first round.

The election of the union leader Lula, in 2002, marked the beginning of a thirteen-year rule of the left-wing Worker's Party, but it came with a price. To build a large coalition majority in Congress, the PT introduced a system of payments to representatives affiliated to smaller parties who were willing to vote with the government in return (Balán 2014; Pereira, Power, and Raile 2008; Power and Taylor 2013). The corruption web later evolved to a scandal of 14.3 billion reais in illegal payments to politicians and company executives of private and state-owned companies (Brazil Ministério Público Federal 2020). That is the equivalent of 6 billion dollars in the average US Dollar to Brazilian Real exchange rate of 2014, when the Federal Police started investigating the scheme, with the task force Operation Car Wash.

Hunter and Power (2019) observe that the economic and political crises in Brazil hurt establishment parties, while Bolsonaro spread an anticorruption message that strongly resonated with the public. In addition to resentment against the PT, moral issues and strict views on law and order influenced Bolsonaro voters. Before the crisis in the left-wing government, Bolsonaro was a not very well known right-wing representative in the Chamber of Deputies. A former army captain, he started his career as a politician in 1988, during the first civilian government after two decades of military dictatorship. In a certain way, his origins resemble those of the union leader Lula, who also got into politics during the democratic transition. Lula organized metalworkers' strikes, whereas Bolsonaro was discharged from the army because he led a protest against low wages in the armed forces (Bolsonaro 2017). As the first investigations about corruption in the PT government started, in 2005, he gained national recognition after the head investigative judge concluded that Bolsonaro was the only representative who did not receive a bribe in his party.

Bolsonaro also indulged public attention on late-night television shows in which he attacked the policies of the Worker's Party. While the PT government implemented a policy of gun control in 2003, violence continued to reach new records in Brazil, with 64,000 killings in 2017 (Human Rights Watch 2019). Propositions to legalize abortion or same-sex marriage were blocked in Congress, where Bolsonaro denounced the introduction of LGBT issues in sex education textbooks. Resisting investigations about human rights violations during the military regime, Bolsonaro also made statements endorsing torture.

There was continued popular support for Lula and his successor, Rousseff, in the face of multiple corruption allegations throughout their presidencies (Balán 2014) while there was economic growth and decreasing economic inequality. However, that changed after 2014, with the Car Wash investigations and an unprecedented economic crisis (Melo 2016). Corruption accusations spilled over all the main political parties and politicians, including the opposition leader and senator Aécio Neves, from the Brazilian Social-Democratic Party (PSDB), who lost the 2014 presidential election by a narrow margin of 3.4 million votes (3.2 percent of valid votes).

Bolsonaro was among the first and few politicians who joined the street protests against Rousseff, starting in March 2015, which later contributed to her impeachment in 2016 (Avritzer 2017; Nunes and Melo 2017). The wave of proimpeachment protests gathered millions of people and is considered the largest political event in Brazilian history, even surpassing the numbers assembled at the end of the military dictatorship (Fuentes and Hilderbrand 2016). Unlike the mobilization on democratic transition, proimpeachment protests were largely organized through social media, especially Facebook, without the support of political parties or other formal groups, like unions, churches, and established movement organizations. In 2018, Bolsonaro relied on the individualized publics that participated in the impeachment protests, not inclined to join formal political organizations. Bolsonaro built his campaign like a connective action social movement—digitally networked and with personalized action frames.

To run for president, Bolsonaro left the Progressive Party for the Social-Christian (PSC) in 2016 and finally joined the Social-Liberal (PSL) in 2018. This was not uncommon in the Brazilian party system, where both voters and politicians have weak party identities. In the transition from authoritarian to democratic rule, the two-party system of the time increasingly fragmented. There were twelve parties in the National Constituent Assembly in 1986—an Effective Number of Parties of 2.8. Yet the Chamber of Deputies elected in 2014 had twenty-eight parties (ENP = 13.3).

Party fragmentation is partially explained by electoral laws, especially by coalitions (Calvo, Guarnieri, and Limongi 2015; Figueiredo and Limongi 2000). Small parties have the incentive to join a larger coalition to get more votes on the proportional election for the Chamber of Deputies. On the other hand, larger parties that are competitive in the presidential election have the incentive to form coalitions to get more TV advertisement time, even if they might lose votes on the proportional election. TV and radio campaigns are publicly funded, and the time and number of ads are distributed according to the number of representatives each party or coalition has.

Among the multitude of political acronyms represented in Congress, Bolsonaro's PSL was one of the smallest. With only one deputy elected in 2014, and not sufficiently appealing to form a larger coalition, Social-Liberals got only nine seconds of daily TV time, or eleven ads of thirty seconds, distributed along thirty-five days before the first round. This represented only a 1 percent share of TV ads among the thirteen candidates. In contrast, the Worker's Party had 189 ads, or a 19 percent share. Demonstrating that TV advertisements were not a significant factor, other candidates privileged with airtime performed poorly. The governor of São Paulo, the most populous Brazilian state, Geraldo Alckmin (PSDB) had 44 percent of TV ads share but ended up in fourth place, with only 4.8 percent of valid votes.

If Bolsonaro did not count on a strong party or resources, the institutional change after Operation Car Wash helped to level down the costs of campaigning and give more balance among the candidates, though still against his odds. As public contractors were involved in the scandal, new regulations banned corporate donations. There were also limits on the amount an individual donor can contribute, and limits on the amount a candidate can spend. Before, candidates could spend freely, as much as they could raise. To make campaigns cheaper, even the timeline of the election was reduced, from ninety to forty-five days. The campaign on TV was shortened from forty-five to thirty-five days.

In return, parties and candidates got more public funding, also distributed according to the number of representatives. Bolsonaro's campaign was funded by only US$465,000, in the U.S. Dollar-Brazilian Real exchange rate of the time. Yes, this is not a typo. Some candidates to the Chamber of Deputies spent more than Bolsonaro, up to the limit of US$675,000. The PT candidate, Haddad, who came in second place, spent US$9 million, or twenty times more than his PSL opponent did. Though the Worker's Party outspent the Social-Liberal, this was short compared to the previous PT electoral machine. While Haddad spent R$39.2 million in 2018, Rousseff's reelection had cost her R$318 million in 2014 (US$135.1 million at the time).

4. Data and Measures

Data collection comprises both the first round, from September 1 to October 7, on election day, and the second round, from October 8 to October 31, with a total of sixty-one days. I collected posts from the three main candidates' networks on Twitter and their official pages on Facebook: Jair Bolsonaro (PSL), Fernando Haddad (PT), and Ciro Gomes (PDT). As Gomes did not participate in the runoff election, his posts were not collected in the second round.

Though thirteen candidates were running for president in 2018, I decided to analyze the main three based on the Effective Number of Candidates, which was equal to 3.16. This measure is based on Laakso and Taagepera (1979) to indicate the adjusted number of political parties in a country.

Posts from a candidate's network were downloaded daily from the Twitter REST Application Programming Interface (API), which returns a collection of the most recent tweets based on indicated keywords. To define the keywords, I followed the advice of Kim et al. (2013), compiling the list of search terms in an iterative process, using campaign-generated messages as a starting point. The method follows three steps:

1. Collect all the data from a candidate Twitter handle.
2. Using data collected in step 1, identify hashtags, political slogans, frames, and Twitter handles that are constantly cited by the candidate. Terms or hashtags that are used by more than one candidate, or are also used for nonpolitical purposes, were excluded.
3. Using the candidate Twitter handle and other keywords identified in step 2, collect data from the candidate's network.

In the end, I collected 21,810,270 posts from Bolsonaro's network; 9,189,058 posts from Haddad's; and 2,080,263 posts from Gomes's—a total sum of 33,079,591 posts.

Facebook data was collected weekly and summed up to 1,912 posts from the official pages of Bolsonaro (439), Haddad (911), and Gomes (562). The analysis focuses on campaign videos, which stand out as having more than 52 percent of all types of interactions (Comments, Shares, Likes, and other Facebook buttons Love, Wow, Haha, Sad, and Angry). Personalization is measured by the images of actors present on Facebook videos: candidate alone, candidate with family, candidate with partisans, partisans without the candidate, crowd, press conferences, and exclusive interviews.

To classify tweets by sentiment analysis, I use the National Research Council Canada (NRC) Word-Emotion Association Lexicon (Mohammad and Turney 2013), which has the advantage of supporting classification on Portuguese, spoken in Brazil. To build the lexicon, 14,182 unigrams (words) were manually associated with positive and negative emotions by crowd-sourcing on Amazon Mechanical Turk. Using this lexicon to classify a tweet, each word in a post receives a polarity of −1 (if negative) or +1 (if positive). If the sum of all the classified words in a tweet is greater than 0, the post is categorized as positive; if lower than 0, negative; if sum equals 0, or there are no words associated with the lexicon, the tweet is neutral.

Net Sentiment is calculated by the positive posts about a candidate minus the negative posts, divided by the sum of positive and negative posts, as follows:

Net Sentiment = (Positive—Negative) / (Positive + Negative)

Neutral tweets are not used, as they do not express rejection or preference.

5. Findings

5. 1. Twitter Posts and Negative Campaign

Twitter data was used to answer RQ1: To what extent the politics of conflict and political polarization fueled Jair Bolsonaro's campaign on social media with negative sentiments and mobilized voters? In Figure 9.1, it is possible to see that Bolsonaro's networks on Twitter were more negative as compared to the other candidates. However, sentiments were shaped by Facebook Live videos and campaign events, with the knife attack against Bolsonaro among the turning points. Gomes's network is the most positive, with an average Net Sentiment of 0.362. Next, Haddad's has 0.221 on average. Yet Bolsonaro's network has the lowest Net Sentiment, with an average of 0.034.

On twenty-five of the sixty-one days of the campaign, there were more negative than positive posts on Bolsonaro's network, with a Net Sentiment between −0.012 and −0.265. Haddad's got more negative on only five days. Bolsonaro has his highest Net Sentiment on October 29, the day after he won the election, and October 4, the day he broadcasted a live video at the same moment of the Globo TV debate, which the Social-Liberal declined to join. Those were among the few days in which Bolsonaro's Net Sentiment was higher than Haddad's.

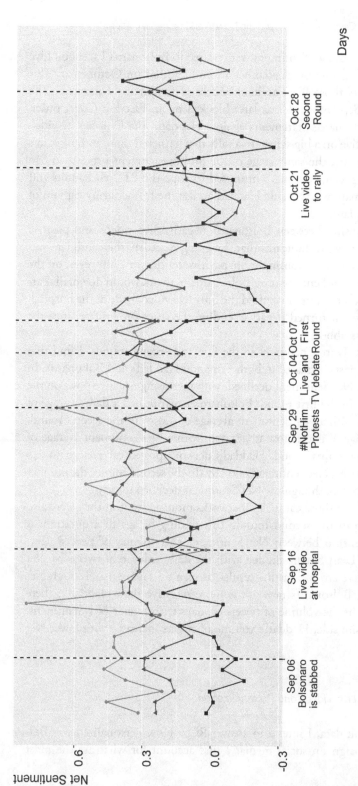

Figure 9.1. Net Sentiment in candidate's networks on Twitter, by day

Note: Net Sentiment = (positive tweets−negative tweets)/(positive tweets + negative tweets).

N of Bolsonaro's Network = 21,810,270 tweets; N of Haddad's network = 9,189,058 tweets; N of Gomes's network = 2,080,263 tweets.

Other spikes of Net Sentiment were related to Bolsonaro's Facebook Live videos, including one on September 16 and another on October 21. This is intriguing, as those live Facebook videos were extremely negative. The recording on September 16 was later blocked by an Election Court order, because of Bolsonaro's statements against Haddad. The October 21 video was projected live on a big screen to a rally that gathered thousands of voters at Paulista Avenue, the same stage of the proimpeachment protests in São Paulo. In his speech, Bolsonaro promised to wipe the PT "red bandits" off the Brazilian map, which made Haddad accuse the former army captain of authoritarian plans.

The relationship between Bolsonaro's negative live videos and positive tweets on his network indicates that, by going negative, the candidate was pleasing his voters and arousing more positive sentiments. However, on the following days, Net Sentiment on Bolsonaro's network would downfall. Particularly on the week after he posted the only live video made at the hospital, the Net Sentiment turned negative, ending the truce on Twitter since the candidate was stabbed.

Comparing Twitter networks in the first and second rounds, I find that the volume of posts increased to both Fernando Haddad's and Bolsonaro's. In the meantime, Net Sentiment declined, with increasing negative posts on the two networks. In the first round, Bolsonaro's network had a daily average of 276,950 posts, with a Net Sentiment average of 0.050. In the second round, the daily average of tweets rose to 481,796, with a Net Sentiment average of 0.008. Yet on the first round, Haddad's network posted on average 59,747 posts by day, with a Net Sentiment of 0.267. In the second round, the number climbed to 290,766, though the Net Sentiment declined to 0.151.

Not only were those campaign networks more active, but they were also more negative in the second round. This finding brings to a question: is there a relationship between Net Sentiment and volume of tweets? Testing Ordinary Least Square models with the daily volume of tweets by Net Sentiment, there are contrasting results, as seen on Figure 9.2. Though Net Sentiment on Bolsonaro's network is more negative than Haddad's, there is an increase in the volume of tweets on days with higher Net Sentiment. On the opposite side, Haddad's volume of tweets increases with lower Net Sentiment.

5.2. Facebook Live Videos and Personalization

With Facebook data, I intend to answer RQ2: How personalized was Bolsonaro's campaign on social media? I first account for what are the most

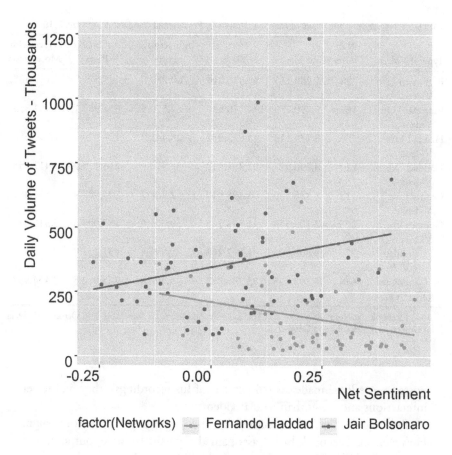

Figure 9.2. Daily volume of tweets on candidate's networks by Net Sentiment
Note: N of Bolsonaro's network = 21,810,270 tweets; N of Haddad's network = 9,189,058 tweets.
y = Bolsonaro Twitter Daily Volume = 346,432 + 330,698*Net Sentiment. Residual standard error = 215,200 on 59 degrees of freedom. Multiple R-Squared = 0.056. N of days = 61.
y = Haddad Twitter Daily Volume = 211,543−275,046*Net Sentiment; Residual standard error = 136,000 on 59 degrees of freedom. Multiple R-Squared = 0.072. N of days = 61.

popular videos. Among the one hundred Facebook campaign videos with more views, sixty are from Bolsonaro, thirty-one from Haddad, and only nine from Gomes. Not only did Bolsonaro's videos get more views than the other candidates but some of the most successful ones aired live (see table 9.1). Bolsonaro produced twenty-eight live videos, and twenty-four of them reached more than one million views. The top ten videos ranged between four million and eight million views. In contrast, Haddad posted 286 live videos, but only one crossed the mark of one million views. Though Haddad

192 Electoral Campaigns, Media, and the New World of Digital Politics

TABLE 9.1. Interactions and Views of Facebook Videos by Presidential Candidates in Brazil, 2018

Type of Video	N of Posts	Interactions	Views	Interactions/ Posts	Views/ Posts	Video with Most Views
Bolsonaro Live Videos	28	21,288,115	95,356,014	760,289.8	3,405,571.9	8,138,488
Bolsonaro Other Videos	167	13,790,770	140,110,507	82,579.5	838,985.1	8,454,933
Haddad Live Videos	286	8,134,114	45,022,332	28,441.0	157,420.7	1,796,656
Haddad Other Videos	222	8,296,577	92,391,047	37,372.0	416,175.9	3,412,155
Gomes Live Videos	15	186,580	1,498,919	12,438.7	99,927.9	558,469
Gomes Other Videos	225	2,106,358	41,288,703	9,361.6	183,505.3	3,316,878
All Candidates Live Videos	329	29,608,809	141,877,265	89,996.4	431,237.9	8,138,488
All Candidates Other Videos	614	24,193,705	273,790,257	39,403.4	445,912.5	8,454,933

Note: Facebook data from Bolsonaro and Haddad was collected from September 1 to October 31. Data from Gomes was collected up to October 7.

posted more live broadcasts (56 percent of his recordings), they had fewer interactions and views than regular videos.

Bolsonaro's live videos started at the beginning of the campaign. However, his Facebook broadcasts gained a particular style, purpose, and dynamic with the turning point events that followed. In his first live videos, Bolsonaro was commonly seen walking through the crowd at rallies on the campaign trail. In those videos, sometimes the main character is the crowd and the candidate's image is lost among faces and arms of voters. There is no speech to hear, nor discussion about public policies, just the present roar of the people trying to get closer to their populist leader.

Those images faded when Bolsonaro was stabbed in a street rally, on September 6. The candidate lost 40 percent of his blood and was rushed to a hospital, where he stayed until September 29. The campaign did not use the graphic images of the attack, which were already all over TV and social media. From now on, his Facebook page would only show Bolsonaro in closed spaces, at the hospital or his home. Bolsonaro did not post any live videos on the weeks after the attack. There was only one broadcast from the hospital, on September 16, which was later blocked under court order because of his statements against Haddad.

On the same day when Bolsonaro was leaving the hospital, protesters were marching in the streets. Inflamed by the congressman's misogynistic statements in the past, groups of women organized protests against what was then a real possibility of Bolsonaro winning in the first round. The frame spreading on social media was simple: #NotHim. On the same weekend, Bolsonaro's voters also took to the streets in rallies and marches in a counterprotest.

From his home, on the following Monday, October 1, Bolsonaro started to produce videos to air live on Facebook. Claiming he had not properly recovered from the attack, the candidate refused to participate in two debates after he left the hospital, one on Record TV, on September 30, and the other on Globo TV, on October 4. However, he scheduled a Facebook Live video at the same time as the debate among other candidates on Globo—a leading open TV network with whom he had a long-running feud. Despite recurring calls from Haddad, there would be no more debates. That did not mean Bolsonaro was off the air. Captivating the media after being attacked and almost winning in the first round, the candidate agreed to participate in exclusive interviews, hosting different news crews in his living room. That was a much friendlier terrain to fight the air war. Conveniently, those interviews were later posted on Bolsonaro's Facebook page.

In the meantime, Bolsonaro's live home videos got most of the interactions and views in the second round. On those videos, the candidate directly answered questions from voters. Frequently, Bolsonaro was at the dinner table, sitting beside partisans, future cabinet members, his wife, and his sons, who were also representatives. One of them, Eduardo Bolsonaro, was seeking to be reelected to the Chamber of Deputies. Flavio Bolsonaro, a state deputy, was running for the Federal Senate. A third one, Carlos Bolsonaro, worked as a council member from Rio de Janeiro and at the same time coordinated the candidate's pages on social media.

Those live videos were the ones that most reflected a personalized communication style. It is hard to say how much those low-cost productions were authentically improvised or carefully crafted to connect with voters. One aspect is clear: the format and style of the videos are as important as what is being said in them. The images and context are an expression of the identity the candidate intends to project as a conservative and simple family man, an underdog challenging the "corrupt elite" and the mainstream media with homemade videos.

In one of those scenes, Bolsonaro has a Brazilian flag hanging on the wall with duct tape. Before the video ends, the flag falls. Carlos Bolsonaro shows up and attaches the flag to the wall with more duct tape, while his father

194   Electoral Campaigns, Media, and the New World of Digital Politics

TABLE 9.2. Personalization and Views of Live Facebook Videos of Candidates in Brazil, 2018

Who is on video	Bolsonaro—PSL	Haddad—PT	Gomes—PDT	All Candidates
Candidate and family	41,936,655(11)	728,116(1)	-	42,664,771(12)
Candidate and partisans	37,449,760(10)	7,622,745(42)	237,479(4)	45,309,984(56)
Candidate alone	4,951,472(2)	633,295(3)	-	5,584,767(5)
Crowd and candidate	2,879,639(4)	16,780,274(147)	1,147,548(10)	20,807,461(161)
Press conference	-	10,977,441(65)	-	10,977,441(65)
Exclusive interview	-	7,791,488(24)	113,892(1)	7,905,380(25)
Partisans (no candidate)	-	488,973(4)	-	488,973(4)
Blocked by Electoral Court	8,138,488(1)	-	-	8,138,488(1)
Total	95,356,014(28)	45,022,332(286)	1,498,919(15)	141,877,265(329)

Note: Cell entries are views with number of videos within parentheses.

keeps talking as if nothing had happened. During one of the most important campaign events, Bolsonaro gave a live speech to voters gathered in a rally in São Paulo, on the weekend before the runoff election. He was standing in his backyard, and the video showed the clotheslines full of bedsheets hanging in the background. Most of the comments on Facebook are about this scene. If Bolsonaro basked in this historic moment in the backyard, his first press conference as president would be in the garage. There was no bully pulpit: journalists and camera operators had to place their microphones on a surfboard.

While Bolsonaro has more videos and views inside the house, with his family, Haddad spends most of the time and gets more views on the streets, with the crowd. Both candidates rarely appear alone (see table 9.2). The timeline on Haddad's page resembles much more a hybrid media system (Chadwick 2017). Press conferences account for 23 percent of the videos and got almost eleven million views. There were also twenty-four exclusive interviews posted live, with 7.8 million views. Together, interactions with the press have almost 42 percent of the total views on Haddad's live videos.

6. Conclusions

Jair Bolsonaro is a byproduct of the crisis in the Brazilian party system. Changes in electoral regulation offered the political opportunity for an underdog challenger. Protests against corruption in the PT government provided the framing for a populist campaign. Personalized digitally networked politics bloomed during proimpeachment protests and substituted the party organization Bolsonaro did not have. Political polarization and the stabbing that almost cost Bolsonaro's life only attracted more public and media attention, even if the candidate was not able to return to the streets and was forced to resume his campaign using home videos on Facebook and exclusive interviews on TV channels.

Despite his radical positions, Bolsonaro was brought to the center of the public sphere. The volume of posts on his Twitter network spiked, and the Net Sentiment of tweets turned from negative to mostly positive. Able to avoid debates with other candidates, due to his medical condition, he could also get media and public attention with exclusive interviews and live home-made videos, one of which aired at the same time as a TV debate.

A mediated debate between the two main candidates could have increased the legitimacy of the election and promoted mutual respect between parties through inclusion and civility. Bolsonaro's negative campaign not only targeted the Worker's Party but also manifested hostility against the news media. It is troubling when key political actors use their bully pulpit to make negative comments about the media, especially because of the asymmetry of power between politicians and journalists and the harmful consequences for democracy.

Though hostility against the media is an old strategy in the populist's playbook, a digital media campaign facilitates the conflict because the candidate communicates directly with voters and does not depend on the press. This does not mean that the news media are not relevant anymore in Brazilian elections, but the candidate can select channels more aligned with his positions or even negotiate better terms in exclusive interviews. Nevertheless, this impairs the communicative processes of opinion formation before voting and the accountability of public policies.

With their personalized style, Bolsonaro's live videos mobilized voters on Facebook, with more views and interactions. On Twitter, those recordings not only stimulated a higher volume of posts but also more positive sentiments—even when the speech was largely negative in its barrage against Haddad, Lula, and the PT. Bolsonaro's network on Twitter was more negative than the other candidates' networks. Though running a successful digital campaign, Bolsonaro did not count on a large staff of collaborators, as one might assume. The headquarters of his online campaign resumed to a closed circle of partisans who could fit in the living room.

On the runoff election night, after the Electoral Court formally declared Jair Bolsonaro the next president of Brazil, the populist leader started a live

196   Electoral Campaigns, Media, and the New World of Digital Politics

video on Facebook to thank his voters. Only after that, he came to his front door to make a speech to the journalists who were anxiously waiting. This enraged news anchors who were live on TV. It was a clear statement for whom Bolsonaro owed his election and which media channel he valued the most.

Since inauguration, President Bolsonaro continued to antagonize the news media and broadcast live Facebook videos every week. However, the ability to mobilize voters through a personalized social media campaign did not coincide with the capacity to run an effective government. Thanks to a coattail effect, the PSL elected fifty-two representatives—a considerable gain compared to the previous election, but still only 10 percent of the seats in the Chamber of Deputies. Unable to build a large coalition in Congress, the Social-Liberals were also divided into different factions in less than a year into Bolsonaro's presidency.

References

Aruguete, Natalia, Ernesto Calvo, and Tiago Ventura. 2021. "News Sharing, Gatekeeping, and Polarization: A Study of the #Bolsonaro Election." *Digital Journalism* 9(1): 1–23.

Avritzer, Leonardo. 2017. "The Rousseff impeachment and the crisis of democracy in Brazil." *Critical Policy Studies* 11(3): 352–57.

Baker, Andy, Barry Ames, and Lucio R. Rennó. 2006. "Social Context and Campaign Volatility in New Democracies: Networks and Neighborhoods in Brazil's 2002 Elections." *American Journal of Political Science* 50(2): 382–99.

Bennett, Lance, and Alexandra Segerberg. 2013. *The logic of connective action: Digital media and the personalization of contentious politics.* New York: Cambridge University Press.

Bimber, Bruce. 2003. *Information and American Democracy: Technology in the evolution of political power.* Cambridge: Cambridge University Press.

Boas, Taylor C. 2005. "Television and neopopulism in Latin America: Media effects in Brazil and Peru." *Latin American research review* 40(2): 27–49.

Bolsonaro, Flavio. 2017. *Mito ou verdade: Jair Messias Bolsonaro.* Rio de Janeiro: Altadena.

Brazil Ministerio Publico Federal. n.d. "Caso Lava Jato: Resultados." http://www.mpf.mp.br/grandes-casos/lava-jato/resultados

Brazil Superior Electoral Court. n.d. "Estatísticas do eleitorado—Por sexo e faixa etária." http://www.tse.jus.br/eleitor/estatisticas-de-eleitorado/estatistica-do-eleito rado-por-sexo-e-faixa-etaria

Brazilian Internet Steering Committee. 2019. *2018 ICT Households: Survey on the Use of Information and Communication Technologies in Brazilian Households.* São Paulo: Comitê Gestor da Internet no Brasil.

Calvo, Ernesto, Fernando Guarnieri, and Fernando Limongi. 2015. "Why coalitions?

Party system fragmentation, small party bias, and preferential vote in Brazil." *Electoral Studies* 39: 219–29.

Castañeda, Gonzalo, and Ignacio Ibarra. 2013. "Las preferencias de los electores y la importancia de las campañas en las elecciones mexicanas de 2006." *Estudios Sociológicos* 31(93): 793–822.

Castells, Manuel. 1997. *The Power of Identity*. Malden, MA: Blackwell.

Chadwick, Andrew. 2017. *The hybrid media system: Politics and power*. Oxford: Oxford University Press.

Corporación Latinobarómetro. n.d. "Banco de Datos." http://www.latinobarometro.org/latContents.jsp

Engesser, Sven, Nayla Fawzi, and Anders Olof Larsson. 2017. "Populist online communication: Introduction to the special issue." *Information, Communication & Society* 20(9): 1279–92.

Enli, Gunn, and Linda Therese Rosenberg. 2019. "Trust in the Age of Social Media: Populist Politicians Seem More Authentic." *Social Media + Society* 4(1). https://doi.org/10.1177/2056305118764430

Ernst, Nicole, Sina Blassnig, Sven Engesser, Florin Büchel, and Frank Esser. 2019 "Populists prefer social media over talk shows: An analysis of populist messages and stylistic elements across six countries." *Social Media + Society* 5(1). http://doi.org/10.1177/2056305118823358

Ernst, Nicole, Sven Engesser, Florin Büchel, Sina Blassnig, and Frank Esser. 2017. "Extreme parties and populism: An analysis of Facebook and Twitter across six countries." *Information, Communication & Society* 20(9): 1347–64.

Figueiredo, Argelina Cheibub, and Fernando Limongi. 2000. "Presidential power, legislative organization, and party behavior in Brazil." *Comparative Politics* 32(2): 151–70.

Fuentes, Esther, and Rachael Hilderbrand. 2016. "The Role of Pro-Impeachment Protests in Brazil's Uncertain Future." *Council on Hemispheric Affairs*, March 15.

Greene, Kenneth. 2019. "Dealigning Campaign Effects in Argentina in Comparative Perspective." In *Campaigns and Voters in Developing Democracies: Argentina in Comparative Perspective*, edited by Noam Lupu, Virginia Oliveros, and Luis Schiumerini, 162–86. Ann Arbor: University of Michigan Press.

Hameleers, Michael, and Desirée Schmuck. 2017. "It's us against them: A comparative experiment on the effects of populist messages communicated via social media." *Information, Communication & Society* 20(9): 1425–44.

Human Rights Watch. 2019. *World Report 2019. Events of 2018*. New York: Human Rights Watch.

Hunter, Wendy, and Timothy Power. 2019. "Bolsonaro and Brazil's illiberal backlash." *Journal of Democracy* 30(1): 68–82.

Kim, Annice, Heather Hansen, Joe Murphy, Ashley Richards, Jennifer Duke, and Jane Allen. 2013. "Methodological Considerations in Analyzing Twitter Data." *Journal of the National Cancer Institute Monographs* 47: 140–46.

Krämer, Benjamin. 2017. "Populist online practices: the function of the Internet in right-wing populism." *Information, Communication & Society* 20(9): 1293–1309.

Laclau, Ernesto. 1978. *Política e ideología en la teoría marxista. Capitalismo, fascismo, populismo*. México: Siglo XXI.

Lawson, Chappell, and Jamesa McCann. 2005. "Television News, Mexico's 2000 Elections and Media Effects in Emerging Democracies" *British Journal of Political Science* 35(1): 1–30.

Lima, Venício. 1988. "The State, Television and Political Power in Brazil." *Critical Studies in Mass Communication* 5(2): 108–28.

Lupu, Noam, Virginia Oliveros, and Luis Schiumerini. 2019. "Toward a theory of campaigns and voters in developing democracies." In *Campaigns and voters in developing democracies: Argentina in comparative perspective*, edited by Noam Lupu, Virginia Oliveros, and Luis Schiumerini, 1–27. Ann Arbor: University of Michigan Press.

Melo, Marcus André. 2016. "Latin America's New Turbulence: Crisis and Integrity in Brazil." *Journal of Democracy* 27(2): 50–65.

Michael, Kenneth Roberts, Jorge Basurto, Michael Conniff, Paul Drake, and Steve Ellner. 2012. *Populism in Latin America*: Tuscaloosa: University of Alabama Press.

Mohammad, Saif M., and Peter D. Turney. 2013. "Crowdsourcing a word–emotion association lexicon." *Computational Intelligence* 29(3): 436–65.

Moro, Sérgio. 2018. "Preventing systemic corruption in Brazil." *Daedalus* 147(3): 157–68.

Mudde, Cas. 2004. "The Populist Zeitgeist." *Government and Opposition* 39(4): 541–63.

Mudde, Cas, and Cristóbal Rovira Kaltwasser. 2013. "Exclusionary vs. Inclusionary Populism: Comparing Contemporary Europe and Latin America." *Government and Opposition* 48(2): 147–74.

Nunes, Felipe, and Carlos Ranulfo Melo. 2019. "Impeachment, crisis política y democracia en Brasil." *Revista de Ciencia Política* 37(2): 281–304.

Pereira, Carlos, Timothy Power, and Eric Raile. 2008. *Coalitional Presidentialism and Side Payments: Explaining the Mensalão Scandal in Brazil*. Oxford: University of Oxford, Latin American Centre, Brazilian Studies Programme.

Pérez-Liñan, Aníbal. 2002. "Television News and Political Partisanship in Latin America." *Political Research Quarterly* 55(3): 571–88.

Power, Timothy, and Taylor Matthew. 2013. *Corruption and Democracy in Brazil. The Struggle for Accountability*. Notre Dame: University of Notre Dame Press.

Prior, Markus. 2007. *Post-broadcast democracy: How media choice increases inequality in political involvement and polarizes elections*. Cambridge: Cambridge University Press.

Schneider, Ben. 1991. "Brazil under Collor: Anatomy of a Crisis." *World Policy Journal* 8(2): 321–47.

Skidmore, Thomas. 1993. *Television, Politics, and the Transition to Democracy in Latin America*. Baltimore: Johns Hopkins University Press.

Valenzuela, Sebastián, Arturo Arriagada, and Andrés Scherman. 2012. "The Social Media Basis of Youth Protest Behavior: The Case of Chile." *Journal of Communication* 62(2): 299–314.

Waisbord, Silvio. 2003. "Media populism: Neo-populism in Latin America." In *The media and neo-populism: A contemporary comparative analysis*, edited by Gianpietro Mazzoleni, Julianne Stewart, and Bruce Horsfield, 198–216. Westport: Praeger.

Waisbord, Silvio, and Adriana Amado. 2017. "Populist communication by digital means: Presidential Twitter in Latin America." *Information, Communication & Society* 20(9): 1330–46.

Weyland, Kurt. 2001. "Clarifying a contested concept: Populism in the study of Latin American politics." *Comparative politics* 34(1): 1–22.

CHAPTER 10

Memes; a New Emerging Logic

Evidence from the 2019 British General Election

Rosalynd Southern, The University of Liverpool

Introduction

After every major political announcement or event there is likely to be a plethora of jokey online reaction and the sharing of memes on the subject. Even the most mundane political announcements or outcomes can elicit such a reaction. Several Internet scholars have observed this, with Milner stating, "it is hard to imagine a major pop cultural or political moment that doesn't inspire its own constellation of mediated remix, play, and commentary" (Milner 2016, i).

There has been much debate over the definition of memes and what constitutes them but one useful definition for this work is the following, also by Milner: "Internet memes are 'multimodal artefacts remixed by countless participants, employing popular culture for public commentary" (Milner 2013, 2357). Expanding on this, memes as public commentary or debate can vary in type and have variously been referred to as "memeing," "shitposting," and "clapbacks." Memeing can cover a range of actions but can take the form of adding text to a picture to change the meaning, Photoshopping a picture for comedy effect, or using an existing meme template (see knowyourmeme. com) and adding words or other content to make a comment on the event. Shitposting can cover all of the above but also encompasses obviously fake stories or purposefully or ironically low-quality content or retorts for effect (Manavis 2019). Clapbacks are more specific and are usually when someone has been directly attacked and responds either by replying or, in the context of Twitter, quote tweeting them, or in a political context, where someone's party or "side" is attacked and they respond. There is often overlap between each type, and some of this sits outside the strict definition of memes (which I will expand upon below). Due to this, here I will largely refer to all these activities as "online reaction." These reactions are popular, to the extent that there are now thousands of dedicated political meme pages and accounts that exist to gain online clout from such reactions, to the extent that this has been referred to as the "meme industrial complex" (Miltner 2017, 422). Even meme pages that are not dedicated to politics but are focused on more general "social news" often incorporate or appropriate political memes into their content offering, suggesting that there is an audience for political memes outside of those with an active interest in politics (McLoughlin and Southern 2020).

Memes were once a near-incomprehensible form of communication on niche message boards. Indeed, in these early online fora, oftentimes the very point of the memes was to be incomprehensible to outsiders, to draw in-group/out-group lines based around in-jokes (Nissenbaum and Shifman 2017). This is certainly still a feature of online reactions in certain instances; however, the rise of social media has meant that this culture has now become at least somewhat mainstream. Many people who spend even a little time on social media will likely be familiar with the most common meme formats, to the extent that they could be "in on" the joke (Miltner 2018). Now rather than going out of one's way to make sure as few people as possible understand your niche in-joke, online commentators will often rely on the fact that many people understand the messages communicated in memes to leverage this into "numbers," that is, a high level of engagement in the form of likes and shares. Furthermore, as social media has become more central to political communication, a portion of political commentary online is now conducted via humorous online reaction and memes. As Highfield (2016) points out, memes are now simply part of how politics are discussed by the politically interested and social media savvy. Despite this, most of the research on memes and political communication focuses on the use of them by citizens, with little to date examining formal elite-level campaigning output. This is something this work seeks to address.

It is important to state here that with regard to elections and the media, in the United Kingdom at least, the mainstream press still dominates the conversation (Fletcher et al. 2020). Despite some development in the area of online campaigning, U.K. parties do still somewhat lag behind their North American counterparts when it comes to developing and integrating online elements into their broader campaign strategy (Gibson 2020). However, it is still important to study new political communication phenomena, especially one that is seemingly so popular. At the last U.K. election in 2017, political memes were viewed forty-five million times and shared almost 750,000 times across just eighteen Facebook memes pages (McLoughlin and Southern 2020), and they show no sign of becoming less popular. Furthermore, the mainstream press themselves have lately begun to pay attention to memes, within particular "digitally-born" outlets (that is, media outlets that were launched entirely online with no print version), often running pieces that consolidate the best online reactions to certain political events (e.g., Parkinson 2017). As will be discussed below, during the 2019 election there was discussion in the mainstream press of the memetic content being produced by the main parties, and one politician was forced to issue a rebuttal to a shitpost about themselves, showing that political memes are gaining some mainstream currency.

Work has been done outlining what has been termed "memetic logics" (Milner 2016). This refers to the fact that much of our media engagement and social activity now is governed by memes, whether this be with social movements like #blacklivesmatter and #metoo or responses to crises and disasters such as #prayforparis after the Paris terrorist attacks or the current #clapforourcarers in the United Kingdom, in support of health-care workers assisting COVID-19 patients. This is informative for this work but overall too specific to fully encompass the range of activity I am attempting to examine here. The literature on memes is largely in agreement that memes are when something can be altered, remixed, or incorporated into new content (Shifman 2013). The range of activities assessed here would not all fall under this definition. For example, the reaction to a politician for an errant comment may involve memes but may just involve humorous or even serious criticism that would not fall under the strict definition of memetic reaction, but is still online reaction. For this reason, I will use the broader "social media logic" here as the underlying framework to analyze these activities in this context as it encompasses the full range of activities that may be shaping current online campaigning. It will be used here to provide a framework for examining whether this wide range of potential online reactions to political campaigning content may be shaping the thought processes behind what now appears in online campaign content.

With all of this this in mind, then, this chapter seeks to shed light on whether, and to what extent, candidates and their campaign teams a) are aware of memes, online reactions, and the communication cultures and practices that surrounds this activity, and b) whether they have sought to change or amend campaign content or behavior in response to this. It does so by conducting in-depth, semistructured interviews with campaign staff to assess these questions in detail.

Politicians Noticing Memes?

Despite this now widespread form of political communication, and despite the fact that in the United States as early as 2012 the presidential election was dubbed "the meme election" due to the myriad memes that arose from it (Melber 2012), until recently there was little evidence that politicians themselves were aware of this. Some incidences of late, however, suggest politicians may be starting to not only notice memes about themselves but also incorporate them into their campaigns and online presences. During the 2016 presidential primaries, a meme emerged joking that Ted Cruz was the "Zodiac Killer." This riffed on the fact that he bore a passing resemblance to a police drawing of the suspected murderer and perhaps also the fact that some of his opponents believe him to have an odd personality. Whilst running for the U.S. Senate in 2018, Ted Cruz acknowledged and played upon the "Zodiac Killer" meme about himself, to mixed reception (Santus 2018). Some praised that he was able to laugh at himself while others felt it was a strange thing to highlight considering how condemnatory the joke at the heart of the meme is.

Democratic representative Alexandria Ocasio-Cortez has also responded to memes about herself posted by her detractors with a series of "clap-backs" on her Twitter feed. For example, when Donald Trump Jr. tagged her in a meme suggesting that socialists eat dogs (see figures 10.1a and 1b), she responded with, "Please, keep it coming Jr—it's definitely a 'very, very large brain' idea to troll a member of a body that will have subpoena power in a month. Have fun!." This appeared to be received with amusement by her supporters, although others thought it unwise to threaten to use her position against an opponent for making a joke, however tasteless. It is also interesting to note that politicians largely appear to clap-back only at other elite actors rather than ordinary citizens who send them abuse. It is likely that this would be seen as "punching down" or, for politicians with a large and ardent following, like Alexandria Ocasio-Cortez, as potentially setting a Twitter mob onto them. It is likely therefore that this is seen as a poor strategy image-wise and is therefore avoided.

Politicians in the United States have also started to employ their own

Figure 10.1a and b. A meme posted by Donald Trump Jr. about Alexandria Ocasio-Cortez, and her "clap-back" response

memes to criticize opponents. A very high-level example of this would be President Trump using a version of the "look at this photograph" meme.[1] This is a meme based on a widely mocked music video by the Canadian band Nickleback, where the lead singer implores the audience to "look at the photograph" before holding up a picture the camera. This has led to people replacing the picture in a still of the video with all manner of different images, many of them nonsensical or simply based on recent or current events. Donald Trump posted his own version to criticize his likely rival in the 2020 presidential election. In it was a picture of Joe Biden and his son Hunter Biden meeting a Ukrainian gas executive in a clear reference to a brewing scandal where it appeared Biden may have used his position to help his son's business interests in the country (Ivonova et al. 2019). He captioned the picture "LOOK AT THIS PHOTOGRAPH!" (figure 10.2). It is unclear whether he was fully aware of the background of the meme or whether he found the picture and merely thought it would be politically

---

[1]. https://knowyourmeme.com/memes/nickelbacks-photograph

Memes; a New Emerging Logic   205

Figure 10.2. President Trump deploying a popular meme against Joe Biden

expedient. However, the use of the exact line from the original song suggests at least a passing awareness of it.

This trend also appears to have made its way into the U.K. context. As early as 2010, there was evidence of memeing during election campaigns. MyDavidCameron.com appears to be the first instance of memes directly based on U.K. general election materials. This was a website that had an adaptable template of the Conservative Party's flagship campaign poster. On it, there is a picture of an earnest David Cameron, leader of the Conservatives at the time, who went on to eventually become prime minister in a coalition government. Besides his face there was a series of campaign pledges. People could come to the site and add their own slogans for instance changing "Vote Conservative, I'll protect the NHS" (National Health Service) with "Vote Conservative, or I'll kill this kitten." This developed further in the 2015 election with memes such as Milifandom, an online fandom for then-Labour leader Ed Miliband (Jewell 2015). However, these were largely fringe stories in this campaign mainly played out among digital subgroups. At the 2017 election, however, memes as political commentary by citizens and commentators became mainstream. The "Maybot" meme, where Primer Minister Theresa May was mocked as being robotic for her staid demeaner and near-constant repetition of her "Strong and Stable" soundbite, was a stalwart feature of the campaign (Smith 2017). Furthermore, one prominent event during the campaign was when May was interviewed and asked what the naughtiest thing she had ever done was. Clearly uncomfortable, she replied "when me and my friend, sort of, used to run through the fields of wheat, the farmers weren't too pleased about that" (ITV 2017). This sparked an outpouring of memes and only added to her image as someone who was not particularly relatable. All of this led certain journalists to ask "was it the . . . memes wot won it?" (Parkinson 2017) in relation May's poor performance on election night. However, despite memes becoming a mainstream form of communication among certain citizens and online commentators in the United Kingdom, there was little evidence that politicians in the country even acknowledged this extensive online discourse let alone let it shape their campaign activities.

In late 2018, however, then-prime minister Theresa May entered the stage to give her flagship Conservative Party Conference speech. As she approached the lectern, the song "Dancing Queen" by ABBA started to play and instead of walking normally she made some half-hearted attempts at dancing. This was almost certainly in response to memes and online reactions that had circulated when a clip of her awkward dance movements on a South African state visit went viral (figure 10.3) (Cole 2018). In the wake of this entrance, headlines of her speech largely focused on the dancing rather than any substantive content in the speech (Belham 2018). In the political context at the time, this was likely a good thing, as talks over the Brexit withdrawal agreement had stalled. This provided a good distraction from her political woes. It was also a good antidote to her disastrous speech the previous year. In this speech, she lost her voice and struggled through much of it barely audible. As she recovered somewhat, a comedian approached the stage and handed her a P45 (a notice workers are given when they are made redundant from their jobs). The reports following this were mocking and harsh (Belham 2017). The contrast in reporting between the two speeches could not have been more stark. Some even suggested the dancing had helped soften her image, showing that she was aware of online culture, not as out of touch as some thought, and that she was able to laugh at herself (Scott 2018). This shows that awareness of memes and clever incorporation of them into campaigning could have political benefits. This also leads to the proposition that not only are politicians at all levels now aware of memetic culture but that they may be incorporating it into their own campaigns and attempting to benefit from it.

Wider Implications—A Fourth Era of Political Campaigning?

Most broadly, the question of whether social media logic is shaping campaign content sits within the debate about whether campaigns are moving into a fourth era (Roemmele and Gibson 2020). There is a general consensus in the campaign evolution literature that there are three stages of campaigning (Farrell and Webb 2000; Blumler and Kavanagh 1999). These stages have had various labels placed on them but one of the most widely used is Norris's (2000) typology of the premodern, modern, and postmodern. The premodern phase describes the era before the end of the World War II. This era was defined by localized, grassroots organization of campaigns and face-to-face communication. In the United Kingdom, the pivotal 1945 election is generally identified as the last election of this era, taking place as hundreds of local campaigns, with only minimal steering from the central party or leadership. It was shaped almost exclusively by party or political logic in that policies were largely the focus of the campaign. The modern era describes the period from around the 1950s to the 1990s. One of the key drivers of the move into this second era of campaigning was the rise of television (Farrell 2006). This advanced a large shift in political communications, moving it from one of direct linkages between voters and local party organizations toward more centralized and mediated linkages. It also meant that the prevailing logic of campaigning moved from political logic to media logic (Strömbäck and Kiousis 2014), outlining a clear link between the shift in communication technologies and patterns and the way political campaigns are run.

The postmodern era encompasses several different hallmarks and features and started from about the 1990s. In terms of changes in media, this era is defined by a fragmentation of messaging as television itself fragmented and audiences moved away from one or two channels, as well as the Internet competing for attention. Campaigns adopted new communication technologies, including mailshots, phone-banking, text messaging, and email. Overall, however, the central feature is a move toward a more professionalized model of campaigning, based on market or marketing logic. This led to the introduction of professional campaign consultants and methods such as focus-grouping to develop policy, basing it on voter preference rather than ideology, and with policies being marketed as products (Butler and Collins 1994).

Recently, however, scholars have started to posit that campaigns are now entering a fourth era (Magin et al. 2017). Work is still ongoing around what exactly the hallmarks of this fourth phase are (or whether we have even reached this stage yet), but one suggestion is that in this phase there is an awareness of a new "hybrid" media environment (Chadwick 2013). This echoes one key driver of the move between earlier eras that were also driven by shifts in communication and media technology. The environment in this posited fourth era requires parties and candidates to work within an environment where traditional outlets are still important but who also have an awareness of the rise of social media platforms, the different patterns of communication on each, and their potential impacts. Furthermore, this new media environment opens up space for campaigns to become, as Rommele and Gibson put it, "both more and less professionalised at the same time" (2020, 600), with a new role for citizen-initiated campaigns or a greater scope for input from nonprofessional, ordinary citizens. This is significant for this work because research to date on political memes suggests they are largely produced by ordinary citizens (McLoughlin and Southern 2020). Incorporating or attempting to harness these less professional elements into formal campaigns provides more evidence for the move into this fourth phase. This chapter is also an attempt to flesh out the "look" and "feel" of this phase by proposing a logic for it. In the earlier three phases these were, respectively to eras, political logic, media logic, and marketing logic (Strömbäck and Kiousis 2014). Here I ask the question of whether there may now be elements of "social media logic" shaping campaigns, and if so propose this is more evidence that there has been a move into the fourth phase of political campaigning.

Methodology

Most current studies of memes as an online political culture or form of political communication tend to either assess the metadata that can be derived from memes in terms of reach and patterns of use (Davis et al. 2016) or select a case study and analyze either the content of the memes related to it or online discourse that surrounds them (Seiffert-Brockmann et al. 2017; Rentschler and Thrift 2015). Here however a different approach was needed. This chapter seeks to establish whether memes and other online reactions are directly shaping formal campaign content. Elements of this might be observed directly from candidates' social media feeds and inferences might be made about the decisions for this; but to really assess whether a new logic around online campaigning is emerging, a qualitative approach was needed to reveal the thinking of the people behind the campaigns. Here it was decided that talking to either politicians themselves or their communication and campaign staff was the only way to establish this clearly.

The data here, then, is comprised of five semistructured face-to-face interviews. The initial list of MPs approached was purposive in that I had identified Members of Parliament (MPs) who had used elements of online reaction in their social media already. Initially it was hoped that I would be able to speak to candidates and MPs directly, but I was almost always referred to speak to the communications officer or equivalent. Due to this, all five interviews are with communications and campaigns staff of MPs. From initial information drawn from the participants, four of them oversaw the social media as well as other aspects of the local media campaign, while one of them was solely in charge of digital media for the campaign. This perhaps points to the fact that, in the United Kingdom, social media campaigns are still seen as somewhat marginal, at least at the local level. Three were the staff of Labour Party MPs and one each respectively were the staff of a Conservative Party MP and Liberal Democrat MP. Three interviews were conducted prior to the 2019 election being called (but when it was almost certain one was imminent and when most parties had already moved onto an election footing) and two were conducted during the campaign itself. The average length of the interviews was around an hour and ten minutes. The interviews were all recorded and sent to the interviewee postinterview for approval. None requested any material was removed, and so the analysis here is based on the complete data. The interviews were then transcribed and themes were identified in relation to the central questions considered in this work. The project was approved by the appropriate University Ethics Board at the University of Liverpool.

Findings—Evidence from the 2019 U.K. General Election.

As stated above, the 2017 U.K. general election was where memes became a central part of the conversation surrounding the election, even leading some to claim memes had an impact on the outcome (Parkinson 2017). However, as already pointed out, in 2017 there was very little to no evidence in the actual formal content of the campaign that memes or other forms of online reaction had entered into the formal online campaigning outputs of any party or candidate. This changed in the 2019 U.K. general election.

In the run-up to the 2019 election, the Conservatives' main Twitter feed posted a picture of a man in a chicken suit with then-Labour leader Jeremy Corbyn's head Photoshopped onto it. This was accompanied by the text "Hey @KFC_UKI (the U.K. account for Kentucky Fried Chicken) we found an even bigger chicken than you." This was in reference to the fact that at the time the Conservatives were attempting to call an election that the Labour leader said he would not support until various conditions surrounding Brexit were fulfilled. The post itself, however, incorporated many elements straight out of the shitposter playbook, with a nonsensical caption, poor quality image, and pointless tagging of KFC. It prompted a great deal of online comment, many simply laughing at how ludicrous the post was but others stating there may have been a more serious strategy at play. Although distraction in political communication and strategy is nothing new, the means of this distraction, incorporating as it did these elements of meme and shitposting culture, was new.

Similarly, during the campaign itself The Conservatives were accused of producing and sharing deliberately bad "boomer memes." "Boomer" has become shorthand for the generation known as "baby boomers," born after World War II. Boomer memes refers to a certain style of meme typically shared by older users on social media. They tend to be poor in design and occasionally confusing in their intent. The first of these posted was a picture with a plain white background with "MPs MUST COME TOGETHER TO GET BREXIT DONE" (figure 10.4), in the much-maligned Comic Sans font. This led to much online reaction and a host of memes, partly because many people found the incumbent party tweeting something of such poor quality baffling, but also because it was so easy to replicate with one's own slogan. They repeated this almost exactly on election day itself with "Today's the day. Vote Conservative. Get Brexit done" but in the (again much-maligned) Papyrus font. Throughout the campaign they posted poor quality and incongruous content, much of which did not match party branding, made use of garish, clashing colors, and in one meme even seemed to be purposefully poorly cropped, in that only half of Leader of the Opposition Jeremy Corbyn's head was visible. They also posted a picture of "Corbyn's Christmas Advent Calendar" where two of the "doors" were erroneously numbered with a seven. This led many Labour supporters online to implore others to stop reacting to the memes as they seemed to be a clear strategy to gain reach or purposefully distract. Some journalistic commentary came to a similar conclusion, positing that this was a deliberate tactic (Stokel-Walker 2019; Urwin and Silver 2019).

This type of communication did not only come from the Conservatives, however. Although there was not that much evidence of this from the Labour Party official accounts, Labour leader Jeremy Corbyn's official Twitter feed posted several tweets based on common memes. He posted a tweet based on the "open for a surprise" meme[2] where the image that appears in one's feed obscures some element of the full picture, which is revealed when the picture is clicked on. Here they posted an ordinary picture of Jeremy Corbyn, but when it was expanded there was a picture of Corbyn celebrating and a "Vote Labour" slogan. Labour also posted a variation of the "zoom in on"

---

2. https://knowyourmeme.com/memes/open-for-a-surprise

Figure 10.3. The "boomer memes" deployed by the Conservatives in the 2019 U.K. general election

meme[3] where someone posts a picture with a tiny caption that followers are instructed to find, which can often be incongruous to the image. There was also evidence of this trickling down to campaigns at the individual candidate level. Rosena Allin-Khan, a Labour candidate, used a much-memed scene from the movie *Love, Actually* where she held up signs at someone's door echoing the scene but also canvassing. There were many other examples. Indeed, in one rather surreal moment during the campaign, Jo Swinson, the leader of the Liberal Democrats, was forced to deny during a television appearance that she enjoys killing squirrels. This was after a shitpost about her, which mocked up old Facebook comments of hers where she referred to squirrels as "pleb bunnies" and talked about how much she enjoyed shooting them, went viral (Southern 2019). The post made its way onto Facebook and was seemingly believed by many people before being picked up by some journalists. So it can be seen that some elements of memeing were making their way into campaigns, but it is impossible to tell from these examples whether there is a new pattern of thinking emerging or whether incorporating these elements was a deliberate strategy. This is where interview data from campaign staff will be particularly revealing.

Findings from the Interview Data

The interview data produced here suggest that there may well be an emerging "social media logic" in the way certain elements of campaigns and candidate communications are run, particularly online via social media, but

---

3. https://knowyourmeme.com/memes/zoom-in

also perhaps beginning to emerge in offline aspects of campaigns too. This was identified as happening in three ways. One, some campaigns are aiming to generate and furthermore harness online reaction and discussion to their advantage, even if it might be satirical, unserious, or even critical. Two, online reaction is directly shaping the content of online campaigns in terms of attempting to avoid unintentional ridicule or criticism (referred to as "Twitter Proofing" by one respondent), but also by incorporating memes into the content of posts themselves to avoid looking "boring" or to increase positive engagement.

Finally, some of the respondents that I spoke to suggested that offline elements of the campaign are now incorporating elements to appeal to social media shares and reaction. This latter element was particularly surprising and potentially more broadly significant, suggesting that online reaction may be shaping elements of political communication beyond the online sphere.

Seeking to Provoke and Harness Online Reaction

One of the interviewees expressly stated that prompting online reaction was a central tenet of their online campaign.

"In a way that was one of the strategies [of our campaign]. We wanted to generate online buzz and commentary, even if it was silly, funny, maybe a bit sarcastic. . . . You can't totally avoid negativity on social media nowadays so you might as well go for it. It's all good exposure and shows you are open to different types of debate, different views. I think that worked for us."

This shows that some campaigns are now harnessing online reaction for extra exposure, and in some ways they seem unconcerned about whether the reaction is necessarily positive. This indicates a shift from early research in this area that suggested campaigns would shy away heavily from negative online reaction (Stromer-Galley 2000).

A second respondent went beyond this, suggesting that campaigns will have to think about online reaction and the hosts of nonprofessional activists and incorporate the likelihood of this happening into their online strategy when planning it, if they don't want to accidently give their opponents an advantage.

It [just buying online ads without thinking about the potential reaction] won't be an option this election I'd say. Last time [the 2017 U.K. general election] we thought just buying ads on social media was enough and we did spend there. But we failed to understand that's not really how it works anymore. You need to generate organic stuff. [The opposition party] probably spent a fraction of what we did on online ads but they didn't have to because they seemed to have an army of keyboard warriors pumping out memes, replying to every tweet or post by us refuting something. I saw a promoted tweet from [our] main account with scores of replies, all negative. We were paying for people to see one message pro-us and 50 anti-us. We'll need to think of our own ways of accounting for that.

This suggests that marketing logic may be being eroded as the dominant logic in online campaigns. Online reactions are disrupting this, with "an army" of activist nonprofessionals, essentially hijacking posts paid for by opponent parties and neutralizing or even undermining the message. This is not to say marketing logic is completely sidelined. There is much evidence that the "data driven campaign" based very much on marketing logic is present in online campaigns that use audience data to micro-target and shape messages accordingly (Dommett 2019). However, it could be that parties might seek to shape their messages with organic shares in mind, perhaps moving toward a hybrid of marketing and social media logic.

One way this may have been approached in the 2019 general election was suggested by another respondent. They followed on from the quote above by stating that they needed their "own ways of accounting for that." This respondent suggested that rather than trying to avoid negative comments, they were instead embracing them and utilizing this to their advantage. They suggested that sparking online reaction could be deployed as a distraction technique if a campaign was struggling. In one of the interviews conducted during the election, the respondent said:

I'm not well enough connected to the top team to know, but if you look at some of the stuff coming from the main accounts, I'd say that (purposefully provoking online reaction even if negative) is something that's at least part of the plan. Nothing seems to be sticking but one narrative that was taking hold online—with the fridge and Andrew Neil—is that Boris is a bit of a coward. Some of this is almost certainly trying to distract from that.

"The fridge" here refers to an incident during the campaign where Johnson appeared to duck into an industrial refrigeration unit rather than answer questions from waiting reporters (Stewart and Mohdin 2019). "Andrew Neil" refers to the fact that despite promising to be interviewed by Andrew

214 Electoral Campaigns, Media, and the New World of Digital Politics

Neil, a veteran BBC journalist known and feared for his tough interviews, Johnson never did despite all other leaders having done so. This respondent confirms that some of the seemingly poor-quality output on social media from the Conservatives may have been being deployed to harness online reaction and serve as a distraction technique.

"Twitter Proofing" but Not "Playing It Safe"

From the above evidence it seems that some campaigns were trying to harness online reactions to their favor even if those reactions were not necessarily positive. In tension with this, there emerged evidence that campaigns were also becoming aware of the negative side of online reactions and are moving to a place where "Twitter proofing" of all content posted might be occurring, or where they were deploying memes in their content to attempt to ensure positive engagement. This tension with the finding that some campaigns are actually seeking to provoke online reaction can be reconciled in that unintentional ridicule is different from purposefully manufactured reaction that may be deftly deployed at certain opportune moments, with a good idea of what the reaction will be in advance.

One responded spoke of an incident where they posted a series of pictures that could have suggested the candidate was discriminatory toward a certain group. This was seized upon by many online.

"Yes. That was a learning curve actually. The internet is merciless in picking up these things and although it was all fairly lighthearted, the broader implication was serious. It's a lesson learnt. I'll certainly Twitter proof all future posts with that in mind really because it probably does shape certain things and we'd worked hard to get away from that old image and look modern. It can be undone with a thoughtless tweet."

Another suggested the same, joking that all online content might be run by a "meme consultant" to ensure their candidate was not leaving themselves open to ridicule from Internet wags.

"Maybe we need a millennial to run everything by before posting? A meme consultant! (laughter) Yes maybe all MPs will have them in future."

A third spoke of a specific incident informing their own approach.

"You don't want what happened to Andrew Bridgen happening to your boss. I've urged [them] to avoid holding white signs up! Too easily Photoshopped, you don't want them to look daft."

Andrew Bridgen is a Conservative MP largely known for his ardent antagonism toward the European Union. In the lead-up to a pivotal parliamentary vote on Brexit, he tweeted the picture in figure 10.5a that contained a poster behind him baring the legend "Freedom is in peril. Defend it with all your might." This instigated a slew of memes as people added their own caption, for example "I'm naked from the waist down" to the poster behind him, the example in figure 10.5b.

However, this awareness of not wanting to post something that will be ridiculed seemed to be furthermore balanced with not wanting to look "boring" and therefore incorporating memes into their own output in order to do so.

"You don't want to look stupid, but maybe looking boring is even worse? There's a balance and I really feel that uploading the same old doorstep pictures won't cut it anymore. One of our most successful posts was a meme of the [opponent party]'s use of polls (to make them seem as though they are the main opposition in the seat when they aren't). We could have got a backlash, but got tonnes of quote tweets, replies, discussion on Facebook, largely supportive. That's what you want, I guess. You do need to be aware of how this stuff works nowadays. It's a fine line."

This was supported by another respondent:

> Before I came on board, we got no engagement on our feeds during campaigns. Just the activists liking posts, so really what's the point? So we started to incorporate more fun stuff and, yes, memes. People like them, it's fun. You can get points across easily and I feel people are less afraid to share something if it's light-hearted rather than too serious.

Overall this shows that an understanding of the way engagement works on social media both in terms of potentially being ridiculed but also in terms of using this new culture to provoke positive engagement is now forming part of the logic behind campaigns. This is thematically different from the first category where the strategy there is seemingly about provoking any reaction, and then harnessing that attention. This second theme suggests campaigns now anticipate reaction and then shape content to ensure mostly positive reaction, or at least avoid unintentional ridicule.

This suggests that this emerging logic is a complicated one, and one deployed differently in different contexts. Some campaigns are seemingly embracing the fact that negative comments will happen and seeking to turn this to their advantage. Others seek to avoid this and use the awareness of the online reaction and memes to tread a fine line in their content, of avoiding ridicule or criticism and deploying elements of social media culture in their content to attempt to elicit only positive engagement.

An Incorporation of Online Reaction into More Traditional Political Communications?

Finally, one of the most surprising aspects was something that I had not even anticipated asking at the start of the research but that emerged during discussions. This was that offline, traditional aspects of campaigns and other political communications are potentially being influenced by online reaction.

> Having spoken with some of the speechwriters in LOTO (Leader of the Opposition Office), there has been a shift. It used to be about the 10-second soundbite at the start of the 10 o'clock news. So (during the 2015 election campaign) you had those absurd videos of (George) Osbourne (the Chancellor at the time) repeating "long-term economic plan" over and over in interviews . . . but it didn't matter because the soundbite was on the news and not enough people were seeing it on social media to matter. May tried it with "strong and stable" but the reaction online last time means that's now seen as a risk. So there hasn't been a slogan (for the 2019 election campaign) at least yet. On our side, I know lines are prepared for PMQs (Prime Ministers' Questions) with online shares in mind. I'd say there will be half an eye on that with lines prepared for the debates, lines in the speech at the manifesto launch, because we know the first reaction is on Twitter.

This quote directly suggests that offline campaign activities, even traditional ones like manifesto launches, but also more modern ones such as selection and repetition of soundbites, are being influenced by the potential social media reactions. This is evidence that social media, and the reaction to it, are now shaping the logic of offline campaigning, if even to a small degree. This also backs up the inference drawn from Theresa May's "Dancing Queen" Conservative Party Conference entrance, that offline campaigning activities may now be drawing on memes and social media logics.

Another respondent confirmed this to an extent:

> A colleague told me they knew [their boss] was very "GIF—able" and that this was something they might use to their advantage if [they] run for leader. Getting a few funny lines in that can be used online as memes etcetera. It's not a bad thing, it's good for [their] image and

not a bad thing to get something in in a TV debate that then gets shared all over Twitter, Instagram [or] whatever.

This again points to offline campaign activities being shaped by potential online reaction and furthermore to the idea of using an army of nonprofessionals to boost a candidate's coverage organically. This last quote is additionally interesting in that in part it echoes debates that occurred when TV first emerged as a dominant campaign medium. Politicians who performed well on TV suddenly had an advantage they might not have had before (Brody 1991). This is not to suggest that being "GIF—able" will be anywhere near as impactful, but it is interesting that politicians who are so are now seen by some as having certain advantages in campaigns over those who aren't.

Conclusion

Overall, then, the interview data here reveal that there may well be a new social media logic shaping campaign output to an extent, both online, which is expected, but also more surprisingly possibly offline too. Firstly, this takes the form of harnessing what is now seen as inevitable online reaction into campaign strategy in terms of attempting to "boost" paid content with organic shares, even if they are sarcastic or potentially negative, as a distraction technique but also to extend reach. Secondly, memes and online reaction seem to shape the content of online campaign output in terms of incorporating memes and other online reactions into posts to avoid looking "boring" and to increase positive engagement, or to avoid ridicule (which sits somewhat in tension with the first theme). As stated above, these findings may seem to be in opposition, but purposefully and deftly anticipating and harnessing online reaction, even if negative, is very different to unintentional ridicule or censure. Finally, there is some suggestion that certain offline elements of campaigns are now shaped to some degree by anticipation of what the online reaction might be. This is perhaps the strongest evidence here that campaigns are entering a fourth phase with the potential for a "social media logic" to have an impact beyond just online campaigning.

However, it is important to contextualize this in the broader media ecology of campaigns. As stated at the start of the chapter, the traditional media still dominates campaigns in the United Kingdom (Fletcher et al. 2020). It may well be that the reason the Conservatives here felt so confident in running such a perplexing online campaign is because the traditional press coverage of the election was so hostile to their main opponent (Deacon 2019). Nonetheless, small changes to campaigning are still important to document and it is interesting to note the rapid evolution of the use of memes in general election campaigns in the United Kingdom. From being a fringe element that caused largely bafflement in 2015, to being something widely adopted by voters but largely ignored by parties and candidates in 2017, to something adopted and deployed at the highest levels of campaigns in 2019.

References

Belham, M. 2017. "The cough, the P45, the falling F: Theresa May's Speech Calamity." *The Guardian*, October 4. https://www.theguardian.com/politics/2017/oct/04/the-cough-the-p45-the-falling-f-theresa-mays-speech-calamity

Belham, M. 2018. "The Dancing Queen Steps Out Again." *The Guardian*, May 3. https://www.theguardian.com/politics/2018/oct/03/dancing-queen-theresa-may-steps-out-again

Blumler, Jay G., and Dennis Kavanagh. 1999. "The third age of political communication: Influences and features." *Political communication* 16(3): 209–30.

Brody, Richard. 1991. *Assessing the president: The media, elite opinion, and public support.* Stanford: Stanford University Press.

Butler, P., and N. Collins. 1994. "Political marketing: Structure and process." *European Journal of Marketing* 28(1): 19–34.

Chadwick, A. 2013. *The Hybrid Media System: Politics and Power.* New York: Oxford University Press.

Cole, H. 2018. "Theresa May does another hilariously awkward dance as she wraps up trip to Africa." *The Sun*, August. https://www.thesun.co.uk/news/7137473/theresa-may-does-another-hilariously-awkward-dance-as-she-wraps-up-trip-to-africa/

Davis, C. A., et al. 2016. "OSoMe: The IUNI observatory on social media." *PeerJ Computer Science* 2(e87): doi:10.7717/peerj-cs.87.

Deacon, D. 2019. "Press hostility to Labour reaches new levels in the 2019 election campaign." Centre for Research in Communication and Culture. December 19. https://www.lboro.ac.uk/media-centre/press-releases/2019/december/press-hostility-to-labour-reaches-new-levels/

Dommett, Katharine. 2019. "Data-driven political campaigns in practice: Understanding and regulating diverse data-driven campaigns." *Internet Policy Review* 8(4): 20–48.

Farrell, David M. 2006. "Political parties in a changing campaign environment." In Katz, R. S., & Crotty, W. J. (Eds.). (2005). *Handbook of Party Politics.* Sage: 122–33.

Farrell, David M., and Paul Webb. 2000. "Political parties as campaign organizations." In *Parties without partisans: Political change in advanced industrial democracies,* edited by Russell J. Dalton and Martin P. Wattenberg, 102–28. Oxford: Oxford University Press.

Fletcher, Richard, Nic Newman, and Anne Schulz. 2020. "A Mile Wide, an Inch Deep: Online News and Media Use in the 2019 UK General Election." Reuters Institute, February 5. https://reutersinstitute.politics.ox.ac.uk/mile-wide-inch-deep-online-news-and-media-use-2019-uk-general-election

ITV. 2017. https://www.itv.com/news/2017-06-06/theresa-may-defends-temporary-exclusion-orders-and-her-record-on-security/

Ivonova, P., M. Tsvetcova, I. Zhegulev, and L. Baker. 2019. "What Hunter Biden did on the board of Ukrainian energy company Burisma." October 18. https://www.reuters.com/article/us-hunter-biden-ukraine/what-hunter-biden-did-on-the-board-of-ukrainian-energy-company-burisma-idUSKBN1WX1P7

Jewell, H. 2015. "Ed Miliband has developed a small but growing fandom of teen girls." *Buzzfeed*, April 21. https://www.buzzfeed.com/hannahjewell/the-milifandom

Magin M., N. Podschuweit, J. Haßler, et al. 2017. "Campaigning in the fourth age of political communication: A multi-method study on the use of Facebook by German and Austrian parties in the 2013 national election campaigns." *Information, Communication & Society* 20(11): 1698–1719.

Manavis, S. 2019. "What is shitposting? And why does it matter that the BBC got it wrong?" *New Statesman*, November 8. https://www.newstatesman.com/politics/media/2019/11/what-is-shitposting-and-why-does-it-matter-bbc-brexitcast-laura-kuenssberg-got-it-wrong

Melber, A. 2012. "Why Romney is losing the meme election." *The Nation*, October 17. www.thenation.com/article/why-romney-losing-meme-election/

Milner, R. 2016. *The world made meme*. Cambridge, MA: MIT Press.

Milner, R. M. 2013. "Media lingua franca: Fixity, novelty, and vernacular creativity in Internet memes." *Selected Papers of Internet Research* 3: 1–5.

Miltner, Kate M. 2017. "Internet memes." In *The SAGE Handbook of Social Media*, edited by J. Burgess, A. Marwick, and T. Poell, 412–28. London: Sage.

Nissenbaum, Asaf, and Limor Shifman. 2017. "Internet memes as contested cultural capital: The case of 4chan's/b/board." *New Media & Society* 19(4): 483–501.

Norris, Pippa. 2000. *A virtuous circle: Political communications in postindustrial societies*. Cambridge: Cambridge University Press.

Parkinson, H. 2017. "Was it the Corbyn memes wot won it?" *The Guardian*, June 9. https://www.theguardian.com/politics/2017/jun/09/corbyn-memes-wot-won-it-some-of-the-best

Rentschler, C. A., and S. C. Thrift. 2015. "Doing Feminism in the Network: Networked laughter and the 'binders full of women' meme." *Feminist Theory* 16(3): 329–59. https://doi.org/10.1177/1464700115604136

Röemmele, Andrea, and Rachel Gibson. 2020. "Scientific and subversive: The two faces of the fourth era of political campaigning." *New Media & Society* 22(4): 595–610.

Santus, R. 2018. "Ted Cruz joked that he's a serial killer so please like him now." *Vice News*. https://news.vice.com/en_us/article/vbk533/ted-cruz-jokes-that-hes-a-serial-killer-so-please-like-him-now

Scott, J. 2018. "Why was Theresa May Dancing? And did it work?" BBC News, October 3. https://www.bbc.co.uk/news/uk-politics-45733370

Seiffert-Brockmann, J., T. Diehl, and L. Dobusch. 2017. "Memes as games: The evolution of a digital discourse online." *New Media & Society*, 20(8): 2062–79. https://doi.org/10.1177/1461444817735334

Shifman, L. 2013. *Memes in digital culture*. Cambridge, MA: MIT Press.

Smith, P. 2017. "The 57 Times Theresa May has said 'Strong and Stable' since she called the election." *Buzzfeed*, April 28. https://www.buzzfeed.com/patricksmith/here-are-57-times-theresa-may-has-said-strong-and-stable

Stewart, H., and A. Mohdin. 2019. "Boris Johnson 'hides in fridge' to avoid Piers Morgan Interview." *The Guardian*, December 11. https://www.theguardian.com/politics/2019/dec/11/boris-johnson-hides-in-fridge-to-avoid-piers-morgan-interview

Stokel, Walker C. 2019. "They're doing this badly on purpose. Why the Tories latest ads look so ugly." *New Statesman*, October 23. https://www.newstatesman.com/politics/media/2019/10/they-re-doing-badly-purpose-why-tories-latest-online-ads-look-so-ugly

Strömbäck, Jesper, and Spiro Kiousis. 2014. "Strategic political communication in election campaigns." *Political communication* 18: 109–28.

Stromer-Galley, Jennifer. "On-line interaction and why candidates avoid it." *Journal of Communication* 50(4): 111–32.

Urwin, R., and L. Silver. 2019. "Tory Digital Gurus' Latest Wheeze: deliberately terrible tweets." *The Times*, November 3. https://www.thetimes.co.uk/article/tory-digital-gurus-wheeze-deliberately-terrible-tweets-pn22qpfvr

CHAPTER 11

Populists and Social Media Campaigning in Ukraine

The Election of Volodymyr Zelensky

Larissa Doroshenko, Northeastern University

Populism and its spread across the world have received mostly negative assessment. Research has explored the circulation of far-right xenophobic messages and populist views through traditional media outlets and social media (e.g., Ernst et al. 2017; Brandão 2021). Previous studies have also produced important insights into the negative effects of populist messages on people's attitudes and behavior (e.g., Sheets et al. 2015; Reinemann et al. 2019). Naturally, this development poses the question whether a liberal democracy can coexist with populism and have any positive effect on citizens' democratic engagement.

This chapter seeks to explore uniting and mobilizing effects of populism during the most recent presidential race in Ukraine. To this end, this research addresses the following questions: Can digital populism have positive consequences for democratic development? How do people respond to populist messages on social media? This project is guided by the theory of connective action logic (Bennett and Segerberg 2013), research on the use of the digital media by populist parties (Essen et al. 2017), and studies on demand-supply approach to parties' social media campaigning (Xenos et al. 2017).

The Ukrainian presidential campaign of 2019 attracted international attention because of a leading populist candidate, Volodymyr Zelensky, who almost doubled the result of the incumbent president Petro Poroshenko in the first round of elections and won the second round with a landslide victory

221

of 73 percent of the popular vote. While Zelensky is a famous comedian and a film actor, his campaign became popular, especially among younger citizens, largely because of its reliance on multiple social media platforms. The previous election cycle was characterized by the rise of nationalism (Doroshenko et al. 2019), polarizing the country and exacerbating ongoing military conflict in Donbass. However, Zelensky's team through its inclusive, albeit populist messages, was able to unite the country, demonstrating voters' support in both western and southeastern Ukraine, as well as gaining supporters among Ukrainian and Russian speakers. Moreover, this campaign through various interactive affordances was able to mobilize Ukrainians for various participatory activities, ranging from taking a selfie at a polling station to signing up for being an election observer. Thus, while Zelensky's presidency seems problematic from a technocratic perspective, his presidential bid presents a unique opportunity to examine how such a nontraditional candidate can leverage digital technology to promote citizen engagement and more open communication between a campaign and its supporters.

Connective Action Logic and Election Campaigns

With the development of digital technologies, election campaigns have undergone substantial changes in mobilization strategies. Scholars more often talk about shifts in parties' online engagement and the people's role in electoral campaigns. The use of interactive technologies by social movements forced parties to give in and incorporate more interactivity in their campaigns (McAdam and Tarrow 2010), even if these features are closely controlled and monitored by the campaign staff (Stromer-Galley 2019). Recent research has documented shifts from institutional collective action engagement to personalized entrepreneurial activities through social media during presidential campaigns (Bimber et al. 2012).

Reflecting upon these changes, scholars have started talking about a "party-as-movement" mentality (Chadwick and Stromer-Galley 2016) and the "cyber party" model (Margetts 2006). These developments in party membership reflect more negotiable and personalized membership opportunities through citizen-initiated campaigning (Gibson 2015) and more flexible and less demanding engagement options. Previous scholarship has aptly distinguished between *institutional* and *entrepreneurial* modes of organizational engagement (Bimber et al. 2012). The former mode and style aligns with the traditional approach to mobilization for collective action, where an individual's access to the organizational process is strictly bound within a system that defines and controls opportunities, and where the motivation to participate stems from civic duty. By contrast, the latter mode and style places emphasis on the individual and their ability to engage with an action on their own terms and to develop activities not officially sanctioned by the organization, which are motivated by a desire to share personal values and style of life.

Building upon these theoretical developments in understanding collective action and engagement in an era of technological change, Bennett and Segerberg (2013) proposed a theoretical framework for the study of mobilization in the digital age that places communication and connection at the center of mobilization efforts and is applicable to both social movements and organizations. One of the theory's main tenets says that mobilization relies upon *personalized communication*, which is comprised of symbolic inclusiveness and technological openness.

Symbolic inclusiveness refers to the type of action frames used by an organization or a movement. Collective action narratives describe a single shared identity, which requires bridging differences among individuals and groups that have different goals and ways of understanding issues. In contrast, connective action narratives eschew one-size-fits-all phrases in favor of personalized ideas, which are "inclusive of different personal reasons for contesting a situation that has to be changed" (Bennett and Segerberg 2013, 37). *Technological openness* describes interactive digital affordances that enable individuals to determine the degree of their participation and to permit interaction and networking among individuals and organizational actors, or directly between individuals. Thanks to technological openness, citizens can more quickly and easily get involved in campaigns in accordance with their interests, abilities, and amount of free time.

At first sight, it may seem that personalized participation can create tensions between a party's desire to maintain control over its agenda while offering its supporters various ways of communication and engagement. Nevertheless, more political actors employ personalization and various levels of interactivity in their campaigns, especially among smaller and newly created parties. Chadwick and Stromer-Galley (2016) invoke the examples of Grassroots for Sanders, started from a discussion thread on Reddit, and the People for Bernie collective, initiated by two Occupy movement organizers. These movements helped to organize supporters for rallies and coined the hashtag #FeelTheBern, which was employed by social media users to share their reasons for wanting political change. The far-right political movement Pegida also actively used social media and personalized action frames when discussing pressing political issues in Germany (Stier et al. 2017), while Ukrainian far-right parties used various interactive technologies on their web pages to boost online and offline engagement during and after the Euromaidan revolution (Doroshenko et al. 2019).

This research shows that personalized communication strategies can be adopted not only by social movements but also increasingly by traditional and radical political parties. The next part zooms in on populist communicative strategies to understand whether these strategies are compatible with personalized campaigning and whether we can expect populist leaders to embrace an entrepreneurial mode of campaign engagement.

Populist Communication and Social Media

As populist politicians have gained in appeal and prominence internationally, particularly in Europe but also South America and other regions (Aalberg et al. 2018; Brandão 2021; Budd and Small 2021; Keren 2021), scholars have sought to identify the core elements of their appeal. Invariably, some conceptual ambiguity has arisen. Populism is considered both an ideology (Mudde 2007) and a style of performing politics (Taggart 2004). The former approach describes populism as a worldview, which attempts to achieve political advantage by exacerbating divisions between urban centers and the rural heartland, between "the people" and ostracized "others" (i.e., immigrants), and between corrupted elites and ordinary citizens (Jagers and Walgrave 2007). In this vein, populism has been defined as a "thin" ideology (Mudde 2007) with a chameleonic nature (Taggart 2004) that may latch onto more substantive ideologies, such as liberalism, nationalism, and socialism, allowing it to be assimilated by both left- and right-wing politicians alike.

This chapter treats populism as a style and its operationalization combines approaches from political science and communication research. The latter has been driven by the surge of far-right populism in Europe and the United States, while the former also takes into account rising left-wing populists in Latin America. All scholars agree that populist style focuses on the people and its antagonism with the elite and out-groups; however, they measure these dimensions along different criteria. In this chapter I adopt operationalization of populist style developed by Cassell (2020), which strikes the middle ground among the most influential research on populism from both disciplines. Populism is described through three communicative strategies: pro-people, anti-elite, and dispositional blame attribution, which correspond to the three necessary and sufficient elements of populism (Hawkins and Rovira Kaltwasser 2018).

The first communicative strategy puts emphasis on the people, their virtues and achievements, where a politician is a "true representative" of the people, speaking in their name and putting their problems at the center of the political agenda (Cranmer 2011; Engesser et al. 2017; Casero-Ripolles et al. 2017). The anti-elite strategy juxtaposes a populist politician to "business as usual" and criticizes existing political establishments, such as the current government, established politicians, or the media (Cranmer 2011). Lastly, unlike the antielite strategy that does not necessary call out a specific perpetrator, the dispositional blame attribution allows politicians to place the responsibility for a particular failure on concrete institutions or groups, emphasizing their intentions to exploit interests of the people (Hawkins and Rovira Kaltwasser 2018). For instance, as Brian Budd and Tamara Small write in this volume (chapter 7), such antielitist populist discourse and attacks on partisan elites were widely used by the People's Party of Canada (PPC) in their appeals to supporters. Similarly, Brazilian populist leader Jair Bolsonaro challenged the "corrupt elite" and the mainstream media with his homemade Facebook streams (Brandão 2021).

Personalized communication strategies, described by the connective action theory, align well with communicative strategies employed by populist political actors. People-centrism and anti-elitism can be coupled with symbolic inclusivity, where the people and their concerns are captured by personalized slogans, which can be adopted to express various concerns (e.g., #FeelTheBern to share people's desire and need for change, "We are the 99%" to unite the people and create a contrast to the 1 percent). Similarly, technological openness and the opportunity to personalize participation accommodate citizens' constraints, such as lack of time or financial resources, offering various low-stake ways to get engaged. At the same time, antielitist position of populist politicians and opposition to the business as usual can compel them to relax supervision over engagement options, giving citizens opportunities to create their own ways of political participation.

Summarizing this discussion about the shifts in mobilizing strategies of political parties toward more entrepreneurial engagement and alignment between personalized participation and populist communicative strategies, this chapter seeks to answer the following research question:

RQ1: Do we observe personalized communication strategies following the logic of connective action in populist election campaigns?

In addition to other digital platforms, social media provides populists with a direct link to the people, allowing for uncontested message dissemination and a megaphone for criticism and attack. These platforms also provide opportunities for personalization, including but not limited to displays of the private and personal life of the populist actors and by offering an insider look into the election campaign (Jacobs and Spierings 2016). As Francisco Brandão describes in this volume (chapter 9), Brazilian candidate and now President Bolsonaro directly addressed questions of voters during his live streams, as well as offered them a glimpse into his personal life, making his personality closer to regular people, gaining positive feedback from his supporters, and ultimately mobilizing them to cast their ballots in his favor. While previous research has explored what parties employ populist communicative strategies on their social media platforms or how people perceive populist communication, there have been very few studies investigating what response these strategies receive from social media users (for an exception, see Brandão in this volume). To fill in this research gap, this paper seeks to address the following research question:

RQ2: How do variations in the populist communicative strategies of a candidate's posts on social media correspond to variations in user response?

As this chapter analyzes effects of populist social media messages on users' engagement, it is important to consider other content features that are commonly used by political campaigns to mobilize supporters. The most common strategy is a call for mobilization, which is defined as posts that provide information where or how citizens can take political action (Heiss et al. 2019), which may range from calls to change one's profile picture or follow a politician's profile on social media to volunteer for elections or participate in political protests. Previous research has shown that such mobilizing appeals increase collective efficacy in users (Heiss and Matthes 2016), but these engagement calls did not result in more likes or comments on social media (Heiss et al. 2018; Xenos et al. 2017). At the same time, scholars have found that posts about endorsement of politicians on social media increase the number of likes, while messages of gratitude and posting a photo decrease the number of comments (Xenos et al. 2017).

In order to account for these content features when exploring the effect of populist communication strategies on social users' engagement, this chapter proposes the last research question:

RQ3: How do variations in the content of a candidate's posts on social media correspond to variations in user response?

Clown President: Volodymyr Zelensky's Presidential Campaign as a Case Study

Prior to delving into the 2019 presidential campaign in Ukraine, it is important to understand political and societal processes that preceded it. Previous elections in 2014 to both legislative and executive branches of power happened after the Euromaidan revolution, which solidified geopolitical orientation for this post-Soviet country but also exacerbated divisions between eastern and western Ukraine, leading to an ongoing military conflict in Donbass. Petro Poroshenko, the so-called chocolate oligarch and a prominent political figure since the Orange Revolution in 2004, became president largely due to the support of voters in central and western Ukraine. He promised to not only bring Ukraine closer to the EU but also to fight corruption. He pledged to step out of his confectionary business to set an example of the change to come. Five years later, corruption in Ukraine was still flourishing, while Poroshenko continued combining his government and business roles. Lack of tangible changes since pre-Euromaidan times and the absence of his pledged sweeping reforms ultimately decreased his popularity.

In this context, the candidacy of stand-up comedian Volodymyr Zelensky, who gained popularity criticizing the government, offered a fresh antielite alternative to Ukrainian voters. His campaign was characterized as populist from its early stages, with political experts and journalists drawing parallels with campaigns of Beppe Grillo in Italy and Donald Trump in the United States. Indeed, Zelensky had no experience or training in politics except for his role as a newly elected Ukrainian president in the popular sitcom *Servant of the People*. According to the plot, an ordinary schoolteacher serendipitously becomes a president against his will and starts fighting a corrupt government, following the pro-people and anti-elite tenets of populist style. Striving to make the sitcom a reality, Zelensky launched his presidential bid on New Year's Eve, minutes before the traditional address of the country's leader to the nation.

While many attribute success of the campaign to the sitcom, especially since its last season went on air during the election campaign, Zelensky shied away from traditional press conferences and put a lot of emphasis on social media mobilization, making it one of the main pillars of his campaign. He started recruitment of his team with an online questionnaire that people could complete on the campaign's website and by maintaining active profiles across several social media platforms, ranging from traditional Twitter,

Facebook, and Instagram accounts to news channels on Viber and Telegram. There were also regional Facebook groups to help organizing local efforts, as well as volunteers who interacted with social media users in the comments section on behalf of the campaign. His campaign's YouTube vlog featured special videos devoted to various election issues, debunking misinformation about voting procedure and raising awareness about election fraud. All these platforms were interconnected with each other, posting links to similar content, but reaching various segments of the audience with distinct social media preferences.

As a result, the campaign gained widespread popularity, especially among the younger generation. It successfully mobilized supporters to volunteer for the campaign. More than sixteen thousand people served as observers at polling stations and more than 325,000 citizens changed their registration so they could vote at a polling station different from their official residency. Zelensky paid special attention to the issues concerning younger demographics, such as education, job opportunities, and army recruitment, as well as the IT-sector and e-government. According to the Democratic Initiatives Fund (2019), voter turnout among younger people increased by 1.4 times compared to 2014. His support among the younger generation (people below thirty) was 57 percent (versus 14 percent for the incumbent president), and 42 percent of students (versus 17 percent for the incumbent president) supported Zelensky. He was also the only Ukrainian president who received a majority of votes across the country with the exception of just two regions in western Ukraine. Such popularity was achieved at a relatively low cost: Zelensky spent 148 million HRN (around 5.5 million USD at that time), while Poroshenko's budget was more than three times larger with 516 million HRN (just over 19 million USD) (Central Election Committee of Ukraine 2019). The head of Zelensky's digital campaign said in an interview that online campaigning took just 5 percent of the overall budget (Gordon 2019).

Thus this election campaign presents an intriguing case of populist strategies combined with a personalized social media mobilization campaign that resulted in civic mobilization and a unification of the country, outcomes generally considered beneficial for democratic development. The following analysis uses this case study to better understand populist mobilizing strategies online, bridging theoretical insights from the theory of connective action logic, populism as a style and a thin ideology, and supply-demand approach to users' engagement with politicians' posts on social media.

Methods

To address research questions, I conducted a quantitative content analysis, focused on the main campaign website and Facebook posts published by the campaign on its official account during the presidential campaign. There were twenty-one million Internet users in Ukraine in 2019, which constituted 64 percent of the population (Ukrainian Internet Association 2019). Of these users, almost 70 percent, or 14 million people, were also registered on Facebook (PlusOne 2019), making it the most popular social media platform in the country. The platform is popular across all regions, with the highest penetration of about 55 percent in the capital city Kyiv and its metro area. The majority of Ukrainian Facebook users are quite young with the largest group ranging from eighteen to thirty-five years old (PlusOne 2019). Ukrainian Facebook audience is also very active, compared with the rest of the world, and is eager to interact with ads and sponsored posts, as well as like, share, and write posts (PlusOne 2019). All of this makes the platform particularly attractive for politicians and marketing managers alike.

Zelensky's presidential campaign, running from January 1st to April 24, 2019, yielded 632 Facebook messages posted by his team (I excluded from the content analysis thirty-nine live videos that did not have any message attached to them). The first part of the content analysis evaluated narratives on the campaign website. Following previous research exploring presence of connective action logic on the websites of movements and nongovernmental organizations, I analyzed two ways in which the electoral campaign could personalize communication on the website: appeals to action and digital affordances for interactive communication (Bennett et al. 2011; Bennett and Segerberg 2013).

Symbolic inclusiveness was qualitatively assessed based upon the visual and verbal information presented on the website. In particular, I evaluated slogans and photos used by Zelensky's campaign. Exclusive political slogans, as described in previous research, would have a notable degree of drama and crisis, offering drastic solutions and narrowly defining concerns. More inclusive slogans would emphasize the priority of people and unity while downplaying any specifics of the problem or solution (Bennett and Segerberg 2013). When evaluating photos posted on the website, I characterized pictures with supporters or with national colors and symbols as inclusive, whereas pictures of a political leader alone or among other elites were described as exclusive. *Technological affordances* were coded as features or functionalities that enable people to do things pertaining to engagement with the action beyond the basic features of reading web pages or navigating the sites (Bennett and Segerberg 2013). Overall, the more interactive affordances were included on the websites during the campaign, the more opportunities supporters had to negotiate participation on their own terms. These affordances were then sorted in terms of features that belong together, such as branded social media platforms (Twitter, Facebook, Instagram), generically named technologies (e.g., RSS feeds, email lists, Telegram chats), and other, similar types of technology (photo posting, calendars). The many custom, one-of-a-kind affordances were left as unique items. Technological affordances were coded by two coders independently, results were compared, and any discrepancies were resolved by going over the website archive again and reaching consensus.

The second part of the content analysis evaluated Facebook posts that were scraped from the official account of Zelensky's campaign using Crowd-Tangle. I coded content features of these posts for presence or absence of several features. First, campaign messages were evaluated for the presence of populist communication strategies, which were operationalized along the three dimensions: pro-people, anti-elite, and dispositional blame attribution. One of these dimensions was considered present if at least one of its components was present in the post (for the definitions and examples, see the appendix). Second, I determined whether posts had mobilization appeal, which included posts with information on how or where citizens could take online and offline political actions, ranging from watching a vlog about an upcoming election to volunteering to become an observer. Third, I coded for the content features, such as mentions of endorsements (from other politicians and/or foreign leaders), media mentions, messages of thanks, presence of hashtags, and inclusion of media content—photos, links, and videos. To verify accuracy of the coding schema, a native speaker of Ukrainian coded 10 percent of the posts independently, reaching a high level of agreement from 86.9 percent for dispositional blame attribution to 93.3 percent for media mentions and endorsements.

The principle dependent measures captured forms of user engagement with each Facebook post in forms of "likes" (thumbs up), "love" (hearts), "haha" (laughing face), "wow" (surprised face), "sad" (crying face), and "angry" (red face), as well as the number of shares and comments. The distributions of these variables were predictably and markedly skewed (likes: $M = 3942$, $SD = 6518$; love: $M = 285$, $SD = 729$; haha: $M = 47$, $SD = 116$; wow: $M = 17$, $SD = 70$; sad: $M = 11$, $SD = 73$; angry: $M = 50$, $SD = 260$; comments: $M = 519$, $SD = 2136$; shares: $M = 1232$, $SD = 3883$). Because my dependent variables are counts, and the variance of each one of them surpasses its mean,

I used negative binomial regression. Negative binomial regression models are designed to control for highly skewed distributions of dependent variables using maximum likelihood procedures and so do not make assumptions about the equality of the conditional mean and variance, making them particularly well-suited for overdispersion in the data, when the variance is greater than the conditional mean.

Results

Website Content Analysis

The first research question is asking whether personalized communication strategies, as they are described in the theory of connective action logic, are present in election campaigns. If the theory explains the logic of mobilization in the digital age, we should observe similar strategies employed not only by social movements but also political parties. As for the *symbolic inclusiveness of images* that animated the campaign website of Volodymyr Zelensky, they were very leader-centric, featuring the candidate in various settings, but never with regular supporters or with national symbols, which would make the portrayal more relatable to regular citizens. The only instance where Zelensky was surrounded by other people was one photo featuring him in the middle of a group of journalists. Thus the overall imagery framing of the campaign message was very self-centric and did not put regular citizens or the country in the center of the campaign, making it hard to personalize or relate this visual appeal to regular website visitors. At the same time, this focus on a personality of one politician is in line with populist communication strategies that emphasize the charisma of a party leader.

On the other hand, *campaign slogans*, used in hashtag form and popularized through website and social media platforms, were *symbolically inclusive* and allowed citizens to personalize their messages by including many reasons to support Zelensky. The main hashtag/slogan of the campaign #зробимоцеразом ("let's do it together") avoided clearly defining what "it" means. Social media users could use this hashtag when telling their own stories of campaign contributions or personal achievements, be it as simple as sharing a post or making a selfie after voting and as time-consuming as being an election observer. This hashtag also emphasized commonality of people's effort, making every small deed count and aligning this slogan with a people-centric strategy of populist style. Likewise, two other hashtags #зробимоїхразом ("let's do them together") and #зробимойогоразом ("let's do him together") were targeted against other candidates in the first round and the incumbent president in the second round of elections. However, these slogans did not specify exactly who "them" or "him" are or how beating them should be achieved, leaving room for customization and interpretation. Such juxtaposition between "us" and "them" in the campaign slogans also corresponds to anti-elite populist strategy.

Other slogans/hashtags relied on a wordplay between the first two letters of Zelensky's last name and an English definite article "the." Supporters were encouraged to add "ze" to all other campaign-related hashtags, such as #зекоманда (ze-team), #зелюди (ze-people), #зевибори (ze-elections), #зестатистика (ze-statistics), #зеситуація (ze-situation), #зефейк (ze-fake), #зепрезидент (ze-president), #зепроголосувати (ze-voting), and so on. The campaign also created several hashtag campaigns. One started when the incumbent president at that time called Zelensky "a clown," which triggered development of a Facebook messenger selfie mask with a clown's red nose and appeal to supporters to film their stories using this mask, sharing why they might be clowns too, using the hashtag #яклоун ("I'm a clown"). The reasons for being a clown that were given to people as starting points ranged from low salaries to fighting corruption in their everyday lives. One more hashtag campaign, #наблюдательчеллендж ("observer challenge"), invited supporters to register as election observers to prevent electoral fraud, while another hashtag #зеповернусь ("ze-return") asked Ukrainians living abroad to share what changes in the country might bring them back. All these hashtags were highly customizable, enabling supporters to personalize their stories of supporting Zelensky, while loosely maintaining the campaign's overall message.

In addition to inclusive campaign slogans, Zelensky's campaign website also featured *technological openness* manifested through many personalized ways to support his candidacy. Figure 1 summarizes the technological affordances featured on the campaign website. The three largest groups of these affordances included regional Facebook groups, Telegram chats, and Instagram blogs, which allowed participants to tune into and contribute to local campaign efforts, as well as connect and interact with each other. In addition to downloadable logo templates for several clothes items and accessories, the campaign team also offered twenty-one unique affordances to support the Zelensky candidacy. Some of the easiest options included spreading customizable posts and video messages through social networks, posting a selfie from a polling station on the election day, or downloading and using sticker packages with Zelensky's image in Telegram messenger. Other more time-consuming options included volunteering as a social media representative, responding to users' comments on behalf of the campaign, or becoming a "fake-hunter" by spotting and reporting misinformation campaigns

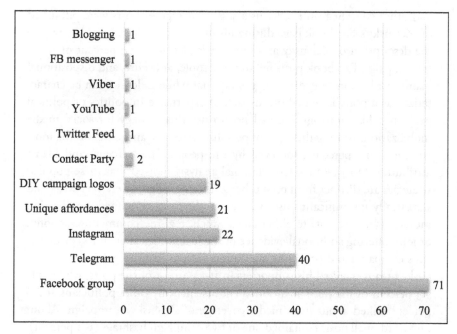

Figure 11.1. Technological affordances presented on Volodymyr Zelensky's campaign website

against Zelensky. The most motivated and politically active citizens could also become part of the team or an election observer. Zelensky started his election campaign with an open appeal to all interested citizens to fill out an online questionnaire and join his team, emphasizing that it does not matter where a person lives and what language they speak, using both Russian and Ukrainian interchangeably, which made an important symbolically inclusive move in the country where language issues have become so divisive after the Euromaidan revolution (Kulyk 2016).

Overall, while the campaign website only featured its charismatic leader visually, it nevertheless offered personalized participation opportunities to its visitors in terms of several symbolically inclusive customizable slogans/hashtags and multiple creative ways to participate in Zelensky's presidential bid.

Facebook User Engagement

The second part of the campaign's content analysis focused on Facebook posts and users' engagement with them. Before addressing research questions about variations in user response to populist communicative strategies and other content features, let us assess what type of posts were published on Zelensky's Facebook page during his presidential campaign. Contrary to the description of Zelensky as a populist leader, just 17.9 percent or 113 of his campaign Facebook posts fell in pro-people, anti-elite, and dispositional blame attribution categories, suggesting that while Zelensky can be characterized as a populist based on his lack of experience in politics or political programs, his campaign decided not to use this strategy for social media mobilization. Among the types of populist strategies, anti-elite was the most common (9.3 percent), followed by pro-people (4.4 percent) and blame attribution (4.1 percent). Correlational analysis showed that these populist strategies are distinct from each other as the coefficients were very weak and statistically insignificant. Just over half of the posts contained mobilization message (52.5 percent) to either click, watch, register, comment, cast votes, or join, offering additional evidence of the technological openness of Zelensky's campaign and providing supporters various ways to get engaged. Zelensky's team thanked his supporters in 11.2 percent of the posts, while only 7.3 percent of the posts mentioned endorsement by other politicians and 6 percent talked about mass media coverage of Zelensky's campaign. About one-third of all posts contained one or two campaign hashtags (35.1 percent), and visual content was split almost evenly between photos (51.6 percent) and videos (45.7 percent) with only 2.7 percent of the posts containing links.

The second research question seeks to find how variations in the populist communicative strategies of a candidate's posts correspond to variations in user response. To address this question, I conducted a series of negative binomial regression models. Link category is excluded from this analysis because statistical tests across all the models indicated that this parameter is redundant. The results of this analysis are presented in table 11.1. Although posts containing at least one of the populist strategies comprised less than 20 percent of the total, they consistently predicted higher user engagement with these posts. The positive strategy of putting people at the center of the message elicited more likes, comments, and shares from Facebook users. Two other negative strategies of opposing current political elites and blaming specific political actors for the status quo produced more complex reactions: sadness, anger, surprise, and, of course, laughter, as Zelensky's campaign built upon his previous experience as a comedian. Antielitist posts also featured fewer comments, while dispositional blame attribution in posts motivated people to share this information in their social networks. Overall, populist communication strategies featured in Zelensky's campaign posts increased users' engagement with posts, but these reactions are more complex than what can be captured by a simple "like" button and tend to elicit an array of emotional responses.

TABLE 11.1. Negative Binomial Regression Analysis Predicting Facebook Users' Engagement by Populist Communicative Strategies and Content Features

	Likes B (SE)	Love B (SE)	Haha B (SE)	Wow B (SE)	Sad B (SE)	Angry B (SE)	Comments B (SE)	Shares B (SE)
Pro-people	.39 (.2)*	.39 (.20)*	.02 (.20)	-.19 (.21)	.24 (.21)	.35 (.21)	.89 (.20)***	.65 (.20)***
Anti-elite	.03 (.14)	−.19 (.14)	.54 (.14)***	.17 (.15)	1.14 (.16)***	.71 (.14)***	−.41 (.14)***	.20 (.14)
Blame	.19 (.21)	−.37 (.21)	1.28 (.21)***	1.82 (.21)***	1.76 (.24)***	2.73 (.21)***	.16 (.21)	1.03 (.21)***
Mobilization	−.38 (.08)***	−.93 (.09)***	−.56 (.09)***	−.64 (.09)***	−.80 (.10)***	−.49 (.09)***	−.45 (.09)***	−.21 (.08)**
Endorsement	−.09 (.17)	−.09 (.17)	.18 (.17)	−.04 (.18)	−.30 (.22)	−.86 (.19)***	−.24 (.17)	.10 (.17)
Media mention	.07 (.18)	.08 (.18)	.08 (.19)	−.42 (.20)*	−.13 (.26)	−.35 (.21)	−.40 (.19)*	−.03 (.19)
Thanks	.17 (.13)	.17 (.13)	−.71 (.13)***	−.50 (.14)***	−.75 (.15)***	−.42 (.13)**	−.35 (.13)**	.16 (.13)
Hashtag	−.07 (.09)	−.28 (.09)**	−.16 (.09)	−.57 (.09)***	−.10 (.10)	−.42 (.09)***	−.59(.09)***	−.43 (.09)***
Photo	.26 (.26)	.49 (.26)*	.35 (.26)	.98 (.27)***	−9.18 (6.67)	2.19 (.28)***	1.06 (.25)***	.30 (.26)
Video	.21 (.13)	.50 (.13)***	.51 (.13)***	.46 (.14)***	−4.41 (3.33)	1.17 (.14)***	.77 (.12)***	.69 (.13)***
Intercept	8.10 (.24)	5.33 (.25)	3.37 (.25)	2.18 (.27)	11.37 (6.67)	1.58 (.28)	5.36 (.25)	6.3 (.25)
*p < .05	LRχ² = 40.04	LRχ² = 241	LRχ² = 187	LRχ² = 296	LRχ² = 318	LRχ = 585	LRχ² = 191	LRχ² = 227
**p < .01	BIC = 11760	BIC = 8241	BIC = 6041	BIC = 4642	BIC = 4092	BIC = 5702	BIC = 9047	BIC = 10103
***p < .001	p = 0.00	p = 0.00	p = 0.00	p = 0.00	p = 0.00	p = 0.00	p = 0.00	p = 0.00

236   Electoral Campaigns, Media, and the New World of Digital Politics

My third research question focused on other more traditional features of campaign messages, which along with populist strategies can also explain user engagement with social media posts. Contrary to popular wisdom, mobilization appeals reduced all activities, suggesting that users did not want to engage with such posts. While this conclusion may sound counterintuitive, this finding is actually in line with the previous research (Heiss et al. 2018; Xenos et al. 2017). Similarly, messages of gratitude, which are important for recognition of supporters, demotivated them to further engage with these messages, as seen in fewer comments and less emotional reactions (laugh, surprise, sad, and angry). This surprising trend was previously documented in the context of congressional elections in the United States (Xenos et al. 2017). Posts that discussed how Zelensky was featured in mass media also reduced the number of comments, as well as surprised and sad reactions, while posts about endorsement of Zelensky received fewer angry reactions. Since endorsement and media mentions are positive attributes of the candidate, it is not surprising that they receive fewer negative reactions from social media users. At the same time, neither of these content features motivated Facebook users to engage with posts, unlike the populist strategies discussed earlier.

Lastly, inclusion of hashtag messages was associated with decreased user engagement in terms of interacting with posts (comments and shares) and emotional reactions (love, surprise, anger). However, featuring multimedia content such as pictures and videos boosted engagement with the campaign's Facebook posts. Pictures increased the number of comments and emotional reactions of love, surprise, and anger, while videos received more comments, shares, and emotional reactions of love, laugher, surprise, and anger.

To summarize the impact of populist communicative strategies and content features, my final analysis in this chapter tests these factors against outperforming score computed by CrowdTangle, which measures how many interactions a post received beyond its expected value (table 11.2). In line with previous findings, pro-people and blame attribution in Facebook posts increased engagement of users, along with posting a photo content. Mobilization appeals, on the other hand, decreased engagement, confirming the overall trend observed before.

Discussion

This chapter started with a provocative question of whether digital populism can have positive consequences for democratic development. After studying the case of Zelensky's presidential bid, the answer is positive: this candidate was able to mobilize a lot of (young) people, unite most of the country

Populists and Social Media Campaigning in Ukraine 237

TABLE 11.2. Hierarchical Multiple Regression Analysis Predicting Outperforming Score by Populist Communicative Strategies and Content Features

Populism	Model 1 β	Model 2 β	Model 3 β
Propeople	.123**	.120**	.109**
Antielite	.053	.053	.042
Blame	.145***	.140***	.077*
Incremental R^2	**.036***		
Content features—I			
Mobilization		−.113**	−.116**
Endorsement		.056	−.003
Media mention		.032	.038
Thanks		.051	.043
Incremental R^2		**.027**	
Content features—II			
Hashtag			−.035
Photo			.272*
Video			−.061
Incremental R^2			**.103***

Notes: R^2 = .165 (p < .001).
N = 632
*p < .05. **p < .01. ***p < .001

divided after the Euromaidan revolution, oust the incumbent president with a landslide victory, and achieve it all with a much smaller campaign budget than his main rivals. Along with other factors, the digital campaign of this candidate was undoubtedly an effective tool for citizen engagement and one of the major pillars of his presidential bid. As a political outsider, Zelensky employed a more open campaign strategy than other established politicians, engaging in two-way communication flow with his supporters, listening and incorporating their feedback, and offering various ways to contribute toward the electoral victory. Zelensky's digital campaigning closely resembled the logic of connective action, which has been described previously only in relation to social movements and nonprofit organizations (Bennett and Segerberg 2013), suggesting that the "party-as-a-movement" mentality has been successfully adopted in Eastern Europe and can be used to increase citizen engagement and participation by more established political actors. As such, this chapter demonstrated that connective action logic provides a promising framework to understand modern digital campaigning.

Findings of this research also draw a connection between populism and the entrepreneurial mode of citizen engagement. Placing people at the center of the campaign, going against established political elites and "business as usual," make populist leaders more likely to abandon tight control over forms of engagement and encourage citizens' creativity. While many political analysts dismissed Zelensky's expertise and skillset for being a president, this chapter shows that connective action logic favors simplistic populist rhetoric over clearly defined policies and solutions, which require more bridging capital. Zelensky's team offered customizable hashtag/slogans, which helped his supporters tell their own story of the presidential campaign, as well as provided ample unique technological affordances for political participation, so people could choose the appropriate level of engagement based on their availability of resources. A high level of engagement, especially among younger citizens, as well as widespread coverage of Zelensky's campaign in national and world news, confirmed its worthiness.

This chapter also explored the effectiveness of populist communicative strategies in social media, demonstrating that even though populist appeals might constitute a small fraction of social media presence, they are very effective for generating user engagement compared to traditional mobilization appeals or endorsement from politicians and news media. When citizens engage with posts, they help to amplify these messages on social media and in their respective networks, attracting more attention from other users and further promoting a politician's agenda. Populist strategies made posts more appealing, while mobilization cues used by campaign managers might have been used only to simulate candidate's support, rather than to provide meaningful channels for participation (Heiss and Matthes 2016). On the other hand, those mobilizing messages might have directed attention elsewhere (e.g., website, vlog), so lack of likes or other engagement with these posts does not necessarily mean they were ineffective. Including a hashtag also did not increase users' interaction with the post; however, the use of this content feature might have helped to increase overall popularity and visibility of these hashtag campaigns on social media, ultimately bringing new followers and increasing exposure.

This research is not without limitations. Foremost, this is a single case study based on one presidential campaign and one social media platform. While this campaign is noteworthy and Facebook is one of the most popular social media networks in Ukraine, future research should look at other populist campaigns, preferably across candidates and countries, as well as across various platforms. Nevertheless, this chapter offers the first step in the direction of applying connective action logic to formal election campaigns, understanding positive effects of digital populism, as well as how populist strategies resonate with and promote online engagement.

References

Aalberg, Toril, Frank Esser, Carsten Reinemann, Jesper Strömbäck, and Claes de Vreese. 2018. *Populist Political Communication in Europe*. New York: Routledge.

Bennett, Lance, and Alexandra Segerberg. 2013. *The Logic of Connective Action: Digital Media and the Personalization of Contentious Politics*. New York: Cambridge University Press.

Bimber, Bruce, Andrew Flanagin, and Cynthia Stohl. 2012. *Collective Action in Organizations: Interaction and Engagement in an Era of Technological Change*. New York: Cambridge University Press.

Brandão, Francisco. 2021. "Stabbed Democracy: How Social Media and Home Views Made a Populist President in Brazil." In *The New Digital Battlefield: Social Media and Elections in Comparative Perspective*, edited by David Taras and Richard Davis. Ann Arbor: University of Michigan Press.

Budd, Brian, and Tamara Small. 2021. "'Many Thanks for Your Support': Email and the People's Party of Canada." In Electoral Campaigns, Media, and the New World of Digital Politics, edited by David Taras and Richard Davis. Ann Arbor: University of Michigan Press.

Casero-Ripollés, Andreu, Marcal Sintes-Olivella, and Pere Franch. 2017. "The Populist Political Communication Style in Action: Podemos's Issues and Functions on Twitter During the 2016 Spanish General Election." *American Behavioral Scientist* 61(9): 986–1001.

Cassell, Kaitlen. 2020. "When 'Following' the Leader Inspires Action: Individuals' Receptivity to Discursive Frame Elements on Social Media." *Political Communication*. https://doi.org/10.1080/10584609.2020.1829761

Chadwick, Andrew, and Jennifer Stromer-Galley. 2016. "Digital Media, Power, and Democracy in Parties and Election Campaigns: Party Decline or Party Renewal?" *The International Journal of Press/Politics* 21(3): 283–93.

Cranmer, Mirjam. 2011. "Populist Communication and Publicity: An Empirical Study of Contextual Differences in Switzerland." *Swiss Political Science Review* 17(3): 286–307.

Democratic Initiatives Fund. 2019. https://dif.org.ua/article/khto-za-kogo-progolosuv av-demografiya-natsionalnogo-ekzit-polu

Doroshenko, Larissa, Tetyana Schneider, Dmitrii Kofanov, Michael Xenos, Dietram Scheufele, and Dominique Brossard. 2019. "Ukrainian Nationalist Parties and Connective Action: An Analysis of Electoral Campaigning and Social Media Sentiments." *Information, Communication & Society* 22(10): 1376–95.

Engesser, Sven, Nayla Fawzi, and Anders Larsson. 2017. "Populist Online Communication: Introduction to the Special Issue." *Information, Communication & Society* 20(9): 1279–92.

Ernst, Nicole, et al. 2017. "Extreme Parties and Populism: An Analysis of Facebook and Twitter across Six Countries." *Information, Communication & Society* 20(9): 1347–64.

Esser, Frank, Agnieszka Stępińska, and David Hopmann. 2017. "Populism and the Media: Cross-National Findings and Perspectives." In *Populist Political Communi-*

cation in Europe, edited by Toril Aalberg, Frank Esser, Carsten Reinemann, Jesper Strömbäck, and Claes de Vreese, 299–311. New York: Routledge.

Gibson, Rachel. 2015. "Party Change, Social Media and the Rise of 'Citizen-Initiated' Campaigning." *Party Politics* 21(2): 183–97.

Gordon.ua. 2019. https://gordonua.com/news/money/na-predvybornuyu-kampaniyu-zelenskogo-v-internete-potratili-okolo-200-tys-predstavitel-shtaba-913672.html

Hawkins, Kirk, and Cristóbal Rovira Kaltwasser. 2018. "Introduction: The Ideational Approach." In *The Ideational Approach to Populism: Concept, Theory, and Analysis*, edited by Kirk Hawkins, Ryan Carlin, Levente Littvay, and Cristóbal Rovira Kaltwasser, 1–24. New York: Routledge.

Hawkins, Kirk, Ryan Carlin, Levente Littvay, and Cristóbal Rovira Kaltwasser, eds. 2018. *The Ideational Approach to Populism: Concept, Theory, and Method*. New York: Routledge.

Heiss, Raffael, and Jörg Matthes. 2016. "Mobilizing for Some." *Journal of Media Psychology* 28: 123–35.

Heiss, Raffael, Desiree Schmuck, and Jörg Matthes. 2019. "What drives interaction in political actors' Facebook posts? Profile and content predictors of user engagement and political actors' reactions." *Information, Communication & Society* 22(10): 1497–1513.

Jacobs, Kristof, and Niels Spierings. 2016. *Social Media, Parties, and Political Inequalities*. Basingstoke: Palgrave Macmillan.

Jagers, Jan, and Stefaan Walgrave. 2007. "Populism as Political Communication Style: An Empirical Study of Political Parties' Discourse in Belgium." *European Journal of Political Research* 46(3): 319–45.

Keren, Michael. 2021. "Benjamin Netanyahu and Online Campaigning in Israel's 2019 and 2020 Elections" In Electoral Campaigns, Media, and the New World of Digital Politics, edited by David Taras and Richard Davis. Ann Arbor: University of Michigan Press.

Kulyk, Volodymyr. 2016. "Language and Identity in Ukraine after Euromaidan." *Thesis Eleven* 136(1): 90–106.

Margetts, Helen. 2006. "The Cyber Party." In *The Handbook of Party Politics*, edited by Richard Katz and William Crotty, 528–35. London: Sage.

McAdam, Doug, and Sidney Tarrow. 2010. "Ballots and Barricades: On the Reciprocal Relationship between Elections and Social Movements." *Perspectives on Politics* 8(2): 529–42.

Mudde, Cass. 2007. *Populist Radical Right Parties in Europe*. Cambridge: Cambridge University Press.

PlusOne. 2019. https://plusone.com.ua/research/

Reinemann, Carsten, James Stanyer, Toril Aalberg, Frank Esser, and Claes H. de Vreese. 2019. *Communicating Populism: Comparing Actor Perceptions, Media Coverage, and Effects on Citizens in Europe*. New York: Routledge.

Sheets, Penelope, Linda Bos, and Hajo Boomgaarden. 2016. "Media Cues and Citizen Support for Right-Wing Populist Parties." *International Journal of Public Opinion Research* 28(3): 307–30.

Stier, Sebastian, Lisa Posch, Arnim Bleier, and Markus Strohmaier. 2017. "When Populists Become Popular: Comparing Facebook Use by the Right-Wing Movement Pegida and German Political Parties." *Information, Communication & Society* 20(9): 1365–88.

Stromer-Galley, Jennifer. 2019. *Presidential Campaigning in the Internet Age.* Oxford: Oxford University Press.

Taggart, Paul. 2004. "Populism and Representative Politics in Contemporary Europe." *Journal of Political Ideologies* 9(3): 269–88.

Ukrainian Internet Association. 2019. https://inau.ua/proekty/doslidzhennya-internet-audytoriyi

Xenos, Michael, Timothy Macafee, and Antoinette Pole. 2015. "Understanding Variations in User Response to Social Media Campaigns: A study of Facebook Posts in the 2010 US Elections." *New Media & Society* 19(6): 826–42.

Appendix

Populist Communication Strategies

People-Centrism

- politician talks "in the name of 'the people," referring primarily to its will
- people's problems at the core of the political agenda
- stating a monolithic people

Examples:

1. "Володимир Зеленський об'єднує країну! ✌ Чому так легко? Бо ми не ділимо людей на лівих та правих. Не ділимо людей на україномовних чи російськомовних, на тих чи інших. Ми просто всі разом: всі думаємо однією мовою—мовою рівності! І знаєте—це кайф! 21 квітня ця карта повністю стане зеленою! #зробимойогоразом"

1. "Volodymyr Zelensky unites the country! Why does he do that so easily? Because we are not dividing people into left- and right-leaning, Ukrainian- or Russian-speaking, or create any other divisions. We are just all together: all think in one language—language of equality"

2. Активісти проїхали понад три тисячі кілометрів, відвідали кожне місто і довели всій Україні, що ми—єдині, що ми тут і зараз творимо історію! Тепер Прапор Єдності з підписами представників усіх областей України майорить у головному Зе!штабі! І показує курс на перемогу! Перемога—у єдності! #зробимойогоразом

2. "Activists went over 3 thousand km, visited every city, and proved to the entire Ukraine that we are one, that here and now we create history! Now Flag of Unity with signatures of all representatives from all Ukrainian regions is hanging at the main Ze! headquarters and shows the path to victory. Victory is in unity!"

3. "Як можна зрозуміти, що відбувається в людей? Просто поїхати, подивитись та поговорити. Тільки так приходить розуміння, що потрібно людям,—через діалог!"

3. "How can one understand what's going on among people? Just go, see, and talk. Only in this way through the dialogue one can understand what people need"

Antielitism

- attacking anything that is business as usual or how things have always been done (political adversaries, the state, or the media)
- discrediting the elite
- detaching the elite from the people

Examples:

1. "Запускаємо #LOPATACHALLENGE! Поки всі наші політики на сніданку в Давосі, ми починаємо чистити країну спільними зусиллями, почнемо зі снігу! 😊 Приєднуйтесь, записуйте відео і ставте тег!"

1. "Starting #LOPATACHALLENGE! While all our politicians are at the breakfast in Davos, we are starting to clean the country together, let's start with snow! 😊 Join us, record the video, and tag it!"

2. "Скоро, у кожній поштовій скриньці України! Оцініть складну багатоходівку влади: 1. 5 років гребти з бюджету. 2. Випустити дешеву газетку. 3. Наступні 5 років знову гребти з бюджету. Шановна системо! У ці папірчики народ буде загортати вам передачки у в'язницю😊 Зробимо це разом!"

2. "Soon in every Ukrainian mailbox! Evaluate complicated multitasking of the government: 1. For 5 years steal from the budget. 2. Print a cheap newspaper. 3. Next 5 years steal from the budget again. Dear system! People will wrap up in this newspaper packages for you when you're in prison. 😊 Let's do that together!"

Populists and Social Media Campaigning in Ukraine 243

3. "Відкриваємо гарно запаковані подарунки від чинної «політичної еліти», а там—фейки, лайно, погрози. Не оригінально! Але ми ж відкриті та чесні люди—подаруємо вам навзаєм законні «подаруночки». Що хочете, відпусточку чи путівку в карцер? Нічого для вас не пожалкуємо!"

3. "Open well-wrapped presents from the ruling 'political elite' and find there fake news, shit, threats. Not surprising! But we are open and honest people and we'll give you in exchange 'the gifts' that you deserve. What would you like: day off or an isolation ward?"

Dispositional Blame Attribution

- blaming some specified group of people for a particular failure
- implies that elites/others knowingly exploited the interests of the people
- identifies political actors with agency

Examples:

1. "Офшори! Офшори! Офшори! Черговий фейк, який розносять ЗМІ. Володимир не коментував цю та подібні публікації. Будь ласка, знайдіть фейкову сторінку і поскаржтеся на неї."

1. "Offshores! Offshores! Offshores! One more fake news, which is spread by mass media. Volodymyr did not comment this or similar articles. Please, find this fake page and report it"

2. "Друзі, зараз влада розносить фейк, що змінилися правила голосування. Це не правда! Ставимо галочку за того, кого підтримуємо!"

2. "Friends, now the government spreads fake news that voting rules have changed. This is not true! Tick the box against who we support!"

3. "Жарт чи не жарт? 'Амстердам+'" та інші корупційні схеми олігархів, які потрібно розкривати та знищувати! Вони крадуть, а затикати діри у бюджеті доводиться народу, у платіжках за "комуналку."

3. "Joke or not? 'Amsterdam+' and other corrupt oligarchs' schemas, which we need to investigate and eliminate! They steal, while people need to repair the budget with utility payments."

CHAPTER 12

The Changing Face of Political Campaigning in Kenya

Martin Ndlela, Inland Norway University of Applied Sciences

Introduction

"When we change the way we communicate, we change society" (Shirky 2008). Shirky aptly captures the intersection of technological innovation and social change. The spread of the Internet, mobile phones, and social media are changing how things are done in the field of political communication, empowering social interaction and political organizing. New media and in particular social media are changing the way people communicate in Kenya. Social platforms like Facebook, Twitter, YouTube, WhatsApp, blogs, and many others, which did not exist some years ago, now form a central part of the Kenyan media ecology, affecting the conduct of politics in the country. They represent an ever-growing number of media spaces being harnessed for public actions and political campaigning purposes. Social media have become ubiquitous communication channels for election campaigns, with platforms like Facebook and Twitter enabling candidates to directly reach out to voters, mobilize supporters, and influence the public agenda (Stier, Bleier, Lietz, and Strohmaier 2018). Social media provides prospects associated with both "*liberating*" and "*disruptive*" technologies, creating new patterns of communication, and transforming the ways in which politicians reach their audiences, vice versa. Politicians can communicate directly to followers and potential voters, bypassing all the traditional media filters. In the Kenyan context, social media is changing well-established forms of oral communication tradition as well as disrupting elite forms of control over

244

modern mass media communications. They are creating new and complex patterns of political interaction, whose ramifications on election campaigning are far from being straightforward. Moreover, social media behaviors are constantly changing, as uses and adaptations vary greatly. What is clear, however, is that political communication in Kenya is journeying through a chaotic transition period characterized by a complex communication ecology. Social media has now become an important part of this communication mix, if not a game changer.

The widespread adoption of social media during the 2017 presidential and gubernatorial elections has led to an increased interest in how social media are transforming political campaigning. Several researchers have examined a number of questions related to the use of social media for political communication purposes (Brinkman 2019; Maweu 2020; Mutahi and Kimari 2020). The main objective of this chapter is to examine, from the perspective of social media managers, how political parties and aspiring candidates operate in the "social media" environment.

Methodologically, this chapter uses a narrative inquiry, presenting and analyzing three narratives by social media managers who participated in the 2017 Kenyan elections. In-depth interviews were conducted by a trained research assistant. The choice of narrative method is influenced by its capacity to provide what Freeman refers to as a "retrospective dimension," that is, "the fact that narratives always and necessarily entail looking backward" (2015, 27). In these narratives, these professionals share their experiences on the use of social media in election campaigning in Kenya. They look backwards and reflect on how they or the parties or individuals they worked for embraced social media during the campaigning period.

The Political Campaign Context

Three fundamental transitions in Kenya, the political and economic liberalization in the 1990s and technological developments, profoundly influenced the political campaigning context in the country. Political liberalization saw the end of the one-party state and the reintroduction of multiparty elections in 1992. Political reforms took place alongside World Bank- and International Monetary Fund (IMF)-sponsored economic structural adjustment programs. Political pluralism triggered profound changes in the socioeconomic structure of society, benefiting certain ethnic groups through political patronage and marginalizing others. As Ogachi (1999) notes, the liberalization of the economy saw an emergence of a financially endowed elite from some regions of the country who appeared to be enjoying the political patronage. Consequently, this heightened ethnic tensions and sometimes led to violence. Much of the literature on Kenyan political and economic changes have attempted to explain the causes of ethnicity and ethnic conflicts that have punctuated the country's electoral history (Lehman 1992; Mueller 2008; Mutua 2009; Ogachi 1999). While ethnicity and ethnic conflicts have been a major trait of Kenyan history, it would suffice to argue that the neoliberal reforms intensified these conflicts. Political election and competition turned into an ethnic struggle over economic resources. The stakes were, and still are, very high. Consequently, economic marginalization and poverty in Kenya tends to follow ethnic and gender lines in both urban and rural areas. As Ogachi argues, state patronage is used to the advantage of some classes and social groups, leading to wide economic polarities based on region, ethnicity, and gender (1999, 88). It is reasonable to conclude that there is a strong interplay between the forces of ethnicity, economics, and politics in Kenya. This perception promotes the role of ethnic-based groups, elites, and political parties who mobilize ethnic emotions in order to gain political power, hence economic power. Elections culminate into a struggle for state patronage between ethnic factions. Looking into the history of elections in Kenya, one notes a predominance of ethnic-based coalitions forming governments or contesting elections as alliances. As Ahluwalia (2017) aptly puts it, Kenyan elections have always been dominated by ethnic consideration and alliances. Political leaders and parties mobilized ethnic voters and entered into coalition pacts with other parties built around certain ethnic groups.

Ethnicity and the mobilization of ethnic voters are undoubtedly major factors in the election campaigning. Political competition has been characterized as a high stakes exercise, with divisive electoral contests marked by ethnic constituencies and violence. As Cheeseman, Kanyinga, Lynch, Ruteere, and Willis (2019) note, the presidency came with a potent bundle of powers, combining formal control and influence over a wide range of resources. They argue that "control over such resources made the president Kenya's apex patron—the point of convergence for all networks of clientelism" (2019, 221). Not surprisingly, within this ethnic economic context, elections in Kenya have witnessed postelection violence. During the 2007 postelection violence, more than one thousand people lost their lives and more than 700,000 were displaced from their homes. The violence had a strong ethnic dimension, reflective of the Kenyan party politics of the time. As Mueller argues, Kenya's descent into a spiral of killing and destruction along ethnic lines was precipitated by many factors, including political parties that were driven by ethnic clientelism, and had a winner-take-all view of political power and its associated economic by-products (2008, 186). She argues that "the nature of Kenya party politics predisposed both leaders and followers to see politics as a do or die zero sum game" (186).

The 2010 constitution radically changed the Kenyan polity by introducing a devolved system of government, creating forty-seven new county governments. Devolution meant that the political elite that operated primarily at the national level now encountered a new competitive political arena with the introduction of county governments (Steeves 2016). Article 174(c) of the 2010 constitution sought "to give powers of self-government to the people and enhance the participation of the people in the exercise of the powers of the State and in making decisions affecting them" (Republic of Kenya 2010). Devolution created a new democratic process closer to the grassroots. The 2017 elections, which form the basis of this chapter, were thus held under a new constitutional framework.

Political Campaigning in a Changing Media Landscape

Political campaigning in Kenya has been mainly through traditional forms of party campaigning such as local political activities like mass rallies, party meetings, door-to-door canvasing, places of worship, traditional spaces, poster advertising, pamphlets, and music, as well as a few news media outlets, which did not reach much of the country. In what Norris (2000), describes as a premodern campaign, the campaign organization was based on direct forms of interpersonal communication between candidates and citizens at the local level. In this model, campaigning is *local-active*, "meaning that most campaigning is concentrated within local communities, conducted through more demanding political activities like rallies, door-step canvassing and party meetings" (2000, 137). This is one of the most predominant forms of campaigning in Kenya.

Nevertheless, the mainstream media act as the core intermediary between parties and the public, who mostly become more distant and disengaged spectators in the process. The bottlenecks induced through state media monopolies and ownership structures made political communication elitist in Kenya. Historically, modern media in Kenya, as in many other African countries, were generally limited to urban areas, where the majority had access to newspapers and television. For many people, limited financial resources and poor infrastructural development constrained access to the modern media. In rural areas where radio services were technically available, access to the medium was affected by lack of electricity and therefore not available to everyone. As Waldahl (2001) noted in the case of Zimbabwe, the media had a less dominant part to play in election campaigns than, for instance, in European countries. However, Waldahl is quick to mention that media's political role should not be underestimated, as the mass media spread their message more quickly and over a wider range than private conversations. Even with limited coverage, the media are a central source of information and a major arena for public debate. This made access to the media an important campaign resource. The media are the most important vehicles through which the politicians can get their messages to a wider audience, and faster than other forms of communication. Control of the media in the preliberalization era was therefore "tantamount to control of the content of the country's political debate" (Waldahl 2001, 3). Monopolies or state ownership of the media gave the incumbent parties advantageous positions in politically controlling the arena and denying access to the opposition. One area of dissention in most African countries has thus been on the issue of unequal access to limited public media resources. The era of limited media coverage is almost over in most African countries, due to aforementioned economic and political reforms of the 1990s and the technological advances that have made media pluralism possible.

The media landscape in Kenya has changed dramatically from the era of few media channels to a plural and diverse landscape, marked by adoption of "new media" and an increase and renewal of "old media." As Gustafsson and Nielsen (2017) note in their research, the media ecologies in rural, peri-urban as well as urban Kenya have undergone dramatic changes in the last two decades, with an increased access to radio and television, mobile phones, and social media use. Liberalization of the news media in the 1990s and digitalization has allowed for the growth of a significant number of broadcasting stations and newspapers in the country. "Deregulation of the media market led to an enormous increase of FM stations, and satellite TV has increased the number of available TV stations" (Gustafsson and Nielsen 2017, 292). While there were less than ten radio stations in 1990, the number has since increased to more than one hundred today. According to Owino[1] "it can be challenging to determine how many radio stations in Kenya are operational in the country since new radio stations crop up every now and then" (Owino 2019). These include a number of national, regional, and vernacular-language stations. Media measuring data show that Kiswahili remains the preferred language of national broadcast stations, and

---

1. https://www.kenyans.co.ke/news/40792-kenya-radio-stations-list-all-radio-frequencies

vernacular stations command the second-highest listenership among older listeners aged thirty-five years and above.[2] As such, radio remains a major tool for political campaigning due to its ability to transcend literacy barriers.

In addition to the radio, television is a focal point for election campaigning, especially at the national level. Viewers have more television channels at their disposal. The electoral campaign on television remains the main principal form of national campaign events. Major political parties and candidates battle to dominate the television slots in major television channels like Nation TV (NTV), Kenya Television Network (KTN), Kenya Broadcasting Corporation (KBC), and Citizen TV. Writing about the 2007 electoral campaign, Brisset-Foucault (2008) describes the significance of the broadcasting media:

> The weeks before the elections experienced exponential growth in political programming on both TV and radio, with the setting up of political analysis editorial meetings, daily reports of the different political meetings on news programmes (almost completely focusing on campaigns) and an impressive mobilization of news features. . . . The season also came with a flurry of political shows interviewing citizens by telephone, text messages (SMS) and also directly in the studios. (Brisset-Foucault 2008, 109)

The main effort of party campaigning remains anchored to the mainstream media. Political parties strategize to get favorable coverage on prime-time television channels and getting journalists to cover their rallies. The mainstream media are central to the communication strategies of major political parties and candidates. These media are indispensable actors in the political campaigns. Besides providing a platform for political campaigning, media align with certain political actors. Some politicians have also capitalized on the corruption of journalists, for example through brown envelope journalism, that is, a practice whereby journalists get monitory inducement to write positive story or suppress negative stories. Politicians take advantage of journalists' low salaries and pay them to cover their issues or to influence the slanting of the coverage in newspapers, talk shows, and so on. In her research, Brisset-Foucault (2008) noted a large number of journalists on the campaign teams, hired as experts and press attachés in political communication just like academics. She also found the practice of hiring certain people to appear on radio talk shows on behalf of political parties. Some activists

---

2. https://www.geopoll.com/blog/kenya-tv-radio-data-2019/

from different political parties were specifically mandated by the secretariat to appear in the audience of the talk shows, so that they would play the role of the party representative. The producers in media houses, through their selection processes, determined who constituted the public. She found that the televised image of the "ordinary citizen" or the "common man" hid a complex selection process of the people seen in the studio. As it will be noted below in the case of social media, hired crowds are strategically deployed in different social media platforms to play the role of party "representatives."

Besides the mainstream media, Kenya has experienced a tremendous growth and uptake of new media. Internet penetration in Kenya stood at 89.3 percent by June 2019, and most of these users access the Internet through their mobile telephones. This has seen an increase in the uptake of social media platforms, with WhatsApp, Facebook, YouTube, and Twitter being the most dominant social media applications used in the country. In a country of fifty-two million, there are 8.20 million active social media users (mostly mobile social media users) representing a penetration rate of 16 percent. Even though a significant digital divide still persists in the country, social media applications like Facebook, Twitter, YouTube, WhatsApp, blogs, and other apps, which did not exist some years ago, now form a crucial part of the Kenyan electoral process. Traditional political parties in Africa have had to adopt new technologies and adapt to the emerging new technological environments where individuals and groups have become producers of information. They have had to embrace social media both as innovation and as a strategy to cope with change. Even though the Internet penetration rates are still comparably lower than in other regions of the world, Africans are using social media in ways that are producing changes to political cultures (Ndlela and Mano 2020). The 2017 elections in Kenya to elect the president, members of parliament, governors, and senators were described as the first social media election (Mohamed 2017). In these elections, more than half of the registered voters were youth, a group that also dominates social media usage in Kenya. As Mohamed aptly puts it in a blog article, "the two main candidates—President Kenyatta and opposition leader Raila Odinga—are going an extra mile to come out on top. Their main target: the youth—those between 18 and 35—who make up more than half of the 19.6 million registered voters" (2017). Social media, especially Facebook, Twitter, and Instagram, are the new ways to reach these young voters.

It is therefore prudent to conclude that the media landscape has changed tremendously in Kenya, especially with the coming of age of social media. The present media ecology in Kenya can be described as "a more complex and incoherent environment of multiple channels, outlets and levels" (Norris 2000, 140). So fragmented is the media, that campaign teams can no longer assume that they can reach their target audiences en masse. The following section looks at how political parties and candidates in Kenya campaign in the context of changing media ecologies, focusing mainly on their strategies for social media use.

Narratives on Social Media Campaigning

Due to the growing influence of social media different strategies have emerged within Kenyan politics. Findings show that social media is increasingly becoming an important platform for political campaigning. Kenya has seen a growth of professions centred on social media such as digital marketers and social media managers. Below are narratives detailing the experience of three social media managers during the 2017 Kenyan elections. In order to preserve anonymity, the names have been changed.

Social Media Managers and Their Roles in Political Campaigns

As the job title prefix suggests, a social media manager is a job description that arises from the social media communication platforms. The social media manager is any individual who has adequate knowledge and skills on social media, can develop content, identify target audiences, and can engage with audiences using the social media platforms. For political campaigning, a social media manager would enable candidates and political parties in goal setting, executing their strategies, and attaining tangible results, be it fundraising, attendance at meetings, or votes. In election campaigns, these goals include enhancing visibility, increasing fan base, advocating for issues, and turning fans into votes. Social media managers handle all content in social media on behalf of their clients or employees. This includes "communicating authentically as" those candidates they represent and "communicating on-behalf" of candidates or political parties. Political organizations and prospective candidates in Kenya recognize that the new social media skills demand and engage individuals who can harness the new social media platforms for the purposes of political campaigning.

The three informants were social media managers for individual political candidates and political parties in the 2017 elections. The first informant, James, is a digital marketer who managed digital communities for political candidates during the 2017 elections. He was involved with not only the elections but also the nominations. James's task was to secure the nomination of his client to stand for the Jubilee Party of Kenya, one of the primary competitors during Kenya's 2017 general elections. The party is home to the incumbent president Uhuru Kenyatta and is an alliance of eleven political parties, each with its own regional foothold. Prior to taking the task, James was a university student developing content for other digital marketers to use for their candidates. He was asked by his lecturer to help a certain politician. As social media manager, he managed everything from passwords, posters, all communication, and communicated on behalf of the candidate, maintaining the tone and trying to be as authentic as possible so that people could actually think that it was the candidate who was speaking to them directly.

The second informant, Peter, is an ICT expert and was part of the social media team at Ford Kenya, a party headed by Bungoma senator Moses Wetangula, who in the 2017 general elections joined hands with the then opposition leader Raila Odinga to challenge the incumbent for the presidential seat. They had a team of around ten people who apart from being just bloggers also helped out in the dissemination of information during the campaign.

The third informant, Doreen, describes herself as an entrepreneur, working in the corporate sector. She has been consulting on social media for private companies for more than six years. During the 2017 elections, she was engaged by two political candidates, one contesting for a Member of County Assembly (MCA) seat and the other campaigning for a Member of Parliament (MP) seat in the Machakos area (eastern Kenya). The MP candidate was representing the ODM (Orange Democratic Movement) party, while the MCA candidate was representing Maendeleo Chap, a popular party in Machakos. (Chap Chap is affiliated with the Jubilee Party.) Doreen got these clients through third-party recommendations.

The Social Media They Used and Why

The main reason for using social media platforms in the campaign is the underlying assumption of their widespread penetration and usage in Kenya. James chose to use mainly Facebook because it was a platform most used in the constituency he was campaigning for. As he argued,

> Facebook is where the majority of the constituents were hanging out.
> We tapped Facebook groups because we already had Facebook groups

The Changing Face of Political Campaigning in Kenya   253

for that constituency. Not for politics but for that constituency, for the local football team, for the people who are neighbours. (James, October 14, 2019)

James said that his campaign team used social media because it reaches more people in his client's constituency and also it is a hustle-free way of reaching people. They used Facebook because one of their target groups, the youth, hang out on the platform. The other reason for using Facebook is that the competitors were also using it. They also had a Twitter account, but they did not get as many followers on the platform as on Facebook. They used social media to complement other forms of marketing. The advantage with social media is that it is more sharable than word of mouth campaigning. It is easy to share screenshots.

For Peter, the use of social media started quite early, mainly as an experiment, to see how it will work. His party started its social media presence in 2012, although many people were not investing in that space at that time. The party management was skeptical of the idea of using social media given the limited penetration, which stood at only 1 percent then. In spite of the low penetration, his team created social media platforms for various counties and the national accounts. They were using these platforms mainly for internal communications. The use of social media generated a lot of interests within the party.

When you start something and it turns out to be good, you start getting many people getting interested. Many people who were running for political seats would come to us and want us to create for them and manage their personal accounts, just because they had seen that the one we had formed was gaining momentum. So, that is how we started off and we managed to gain a lot of followers at that time. I think that is part of the history. (Peter, January 28, 2020)

The third informant, Doreen, cites the widespread use of Facebook in Kenya as the primary reason for choosing that platform. For her, it was natural to use social media given its widespread usage in the country.

Social Media Campaign Strategies

The three social media campaign managers adopted different strategies to guide their use of social media in the campaigning processes. Some of the strategies were spelt out in the form of strategic plans whilst others were ad-hoc. James says that his campaign had a written strategic plan. The first major thing he did was to ensure that members of his campaign team were added to all the Facebook groups in the constituency. When they were added to the Facebooks groups, they solicited the services of group administrators. This involved paying the administrators to allow them to use the platform, and also to prevent other competitors from using the same platform. They used Facebook to send requests to the people who were already in the groups. They filtered through locations to ensure that they were sending friend requests to people who were in that constituency. Invitations were sent to target people who were hyperactive in the groups. The response was positive and when their numbers reached the limit permissible in Facebook, they converted the account into pages. As James puts it: "When I did that, all of a sudden, a page had 5000 followers. That's a trick that few of us know in the marketing spheres. I boosted a little and the page ended up with 10,000 followers. This page is what we were mainly using." James says that his work was to develop content to promote the candidate. The content strategy was informed mainly by the use of images showing the candidate "as a leader." They hired a cameraman to take pictures of the candidate in different situations, in a campaign truck waving at people and meeting people. They shared images of real-time interactions. James also used social media as an organizing tool. His campaign team used Facebook to invite people to events such as rallies, meetings, and other campaign activities. They were using it as a precursor for all events. They also used Facebook for validation, that is, to show support for the candidate.

> The more followers we had, the more likes, the more comments we had. We used it to show that the people were ready for my candidate and were responding well to him. There are times when the actual turn-up for a live event was not as crucial as the number of impressions, we got on social media. (James, October 14, 2019)

James' campaign team also used Facebook to address issues brought to the attention of the candidate. They had a strategy not to respond to negative posts. "I did my best to ensure that we did not respond directly to our competitors or to people who were against us. That was a tactic not to give them attention because the more attention you give them, the more they continue trolling and all that." Instead James and his team countered the negative posts through their own posts.

We don't go to respond to them there where they are, we just note down that this is an issue and then we counter them in our own posts that we create. That one lessens the burden and shows that we were not giving attention to individuals; we were just addressing some issues, not addressing people.

It was part of their strategy not to respond to competitors, because, as James argues,

It was not worthy responding to our competitor. There are people you cannot change their minds. You can only respond to the people who are neutral and undecided. If you see that this person is clearly or has clearly decided to vote for a competitor, then it is not worth chasing after them. (James, October 14, 2019)

Peter's narrative provides an account on how social media was deployed by the Ford Kenya Party, and later by the National Super Alliance (NASA), to which Ford Kenya was affiliated. When Ford Kenya started its social media campaign, the main objective was to promote the party's leader, Senator Moses Wetangula, who had declared his interest to run for presidency. NASA later decided to front Raila Odinga as its main alliance candidate. They used various social media platforms to campaign, and most important for them was to understand the target groups and their use of social media.

You know one thing that you can't run away from is the fact that there are those people you want to speak to but they are not actively on social media. There are those people that you can engage daily because they are always on social media. There are those people who are on WhatsApp and they are not on Facebook so you have to understand (the target group). (Peter, January 28, 2020)

Understanding the target groups was vital for setting up communication platforms. They created platforms for different levels of party leadership, that is, the party management, the Parliamentary Group (PG), and the National Executive Council (NEC). They created platforms for all of them so that if they wanted to communicate to the PG, they would specifically craft a message for them. The choice of social media platform was also determined by the type of user groups. For example, when they wanted to reach young people, they used Facebook because "young people are the ones who have embraced it so much more than the old people, though the old people are coming up." Twitter is regarded as a medium for the elite and "there is a perception that it is for the rich." Hence, if they wanted to address the technocrats, they used Twitter. As Peter puts it:

> The first thing that we did was to understand our target group, then we came down and looked at what kind of information we wanted to disseminate. We were able to reach the target group and have what we wanted to do without mixing up issues. (Peter, January 28, 2020)

The strategy was also influenced by the social media platform's characteristics. These characteristics influenced their communication packages.

> When you talk about packaging, you know . . . let me start with WhatsApp, it is like a house whereby you have to bring people together with a common mind, versus Facebook whereby when you send information, it is going to be accessed by an ODM (Orange Democratic Movement) member, Jubilee member and other parties. When we wanted to give information that is specifically for party members, we would use WhatsApp groups. We would make it internal. You want response and let people know that there will be such and such a meeting that is going to happen and we want them to be present. (Peter, January 28, 2020)

They used Facebook when they had long posts or when they had information for the general public, such as the party's position on national matters. They used Twitter when they wanted to get "straight to the point" or respond to issues raised online.

For the third informant, Doreen, the use of social media was driven by ad hoc approaches, following the flow in social media and trying to gain the audience's attention through bait text messages. For Doreen, content matters and hence her approach was driven by a quest to create content that is most likely to generate traffic to the social media cite. As she puts it, we are in a generation where the only way to capture attention is to use visual material like videos or photos. "If today I posted something like just words, chances of you reading are very low but if I put a photo or image, any image, chances of you looking at it are very high" (Doreen, October 8, 2019).

Doreen recognizes the growing difficulties to gain audience attention on social media. Audiences are continually bombarded with different text messages on social media. Hence one has to be competitive and use those text

The Changing Face of Political Campaigning in Kenya   257

types likely to gain traction. If her target market is the youth or the old, she just has to tailor the content—what is the selling point or the catch? While social media works for certain age groups, it does not help for others. One has to recognize that the audience is fragmented. As she puts it in her account:

> For the youth it wasn't so hard because I can say that at least 60% of the youth even in the rural areas have a phone that they can use to access internet which is good enough. For the old and those that do not have phones, we used to have a schedule at least twice every week whereby the road has to lead to those interior places. We'd go door to door, to shops and also set camp at Machakos Junction. People would see us. It was annoying to some people but there were those that would ask questions that nobody on social media or friends had asked before. (Doreen, October 8, 2019)

Doreen also underlies the importance of local language and face-to-face meetings. The most important thing was to ensure that the politicians are well versed with the local languages and that they met people in their ordinary settings. Her quest was for candidates to get real experience with everyday life, an experience one cannot get through social media. She felt that it was good for them (politicians) to know their constituencies, to know what people went through, so that if they won the seat, they would not forget their people. "You have to sit and drink that tea that the old women have made for you. . . . Some cannot afford tea with milk and sometimes if we were to give them something, we had to buy (groceries) for them" (Doreen, October 8, 2019). Doreen notes that this experience made politicians better people. That one-on-one communication was beneficial for the communities and politicians. Some of the politicians embarked on charity projects in these communities even though they lost the elections.

The Use of Influencers in Political Campaigns

Social media influencers are those individuals who command significant followers on social media platforms. These individuals might also have significant followers in offline settings. There is an extensive category as to who constitutes an influencer in the Kenyan context, ranging from bloggers with a million followers, to celebrities, to local musicians. Some social media managers used different kinds of influencers during the 2017 election campaign. James did not use bloggers mainly because there are no bloggers for a constituency.

> If you go to, for example, our biggest bloggers, people like Robert Alai, he will show you that I have reached a million people, give me let's say 100,000 KSH (approximately US$1000), but you see there is no way to tell that this 1 million people, all of them or some of them are from my constituency. You end up spending a lot of money but you are scattering a seed far and away say Kisumu or Kisii. (James, October 14, 2019)

James made a deliberate attempt not to use bloggers but to use local influencers instead. These influencers were people from local radio station, photographers, bar owners, dancers, local musicians, and the people who had many followers on social media platforms. They also posted photographs of famous local people wearing their campaign T-shirts or caps and asked for their endorsement. They would take photos of them wearing campaign T-shirts or caps and invite them to their rallies and also ask them to share on their social media accounts.

Influencers were also used to respond to negative commentaries on social media. On the social media platforms, they also had influencers who could post on their behalf. Some of the responses to negative commentaries were done by the influencers. "We knew that even if we did not respond, somehow someday these people would be taken care of" (James, October 14, 2019). Some influencers were paid, while others were not, but were emotional about the issues or they just liked the candidate. James is quick to add that most of the interactions with influencers were transactional.

> All our marketing efforts were very transactional because we had other competitors and the way you can make these people loyal is by paying them. So, it was a very capital intensive endeavour. The influencers were not cheap. We had to pay top dollar for them. (James, October 14, 2019)

This transactional relationship is also cited by Peter in his account on the use of influencers by the Ford Kenya Party. Peter divides the influencers into two groups. First, there are influencers who can work for the party for free, because of their loyalty.

> We have the loyalists who are just people who can work for you and you don't pay them anything. Why? Because they own the party. You

take advantage of such people. The only thing that happens to such people is that they always want to be engaged. Someone who is a loyalist does not need money from you but appreciates a call from the party leader telling him that this is what I would want you to do. Just that one call is enough for the person. (Peter, January 28, 2020)

Second, there are those influencers who can work for the party, in return for monetary rewards. The party has a team of bloggers that they use and these are specifically people that the party wants to use in engaging the general world. "They don't do this for free. That is why it is very expensive and you have to go with a number that you know you can manage" (Peter, January 28, 2020). The third informant, Doreen, did not use influencers in her campaign due to a limited budget.

Challenges of Hate Speech and Ethnicity

The narratives also highlight the challenges of ethnicity and hate speech in the Kenyan context. Following the aftermath of the 2007 postelection violence, several laws were enacted to curb the spread of hate speech on social media. Nevertheless, hate speech is still a recurrent issue. As James notes in his narrative, there were challenges with some of their followers and influencers getting carried away and abusing rivals. "Some of our posts were being reported. So, we kept fearing that our accounts could be closed one day maybe because of hacking or maybe because people reported our social media accounts. It was very nerve wrecking" (James, October 14, 2019). Peter also notes the centrality of ethnicity in the Kenyan elections. "Our political setting is tribal. It is so difficult for certain parties to infiltrate certain areas. ODM has a lot of infiltration in Nyanza, Jubilee in Rift Valley and Central then at Ukambani you can find Wiper and these other parties" (Peter, January 28, 2020).

Discussion and Conclusion

The three narratives provide details about how social media has grown to be an important space for political campaigning in Kenya. Social media and changes in the media ecology are fundamentally fragmenting the audiences for political communication. A multitude of communication channels have emerged as political actors can reach some of their audiences through television and radio broadcasting services, print media, and different platforms on social media. These communication channels are still limited in reach, compared to Western countries, where politics is mainly mediated, but they are nevertheless important for politicians wishing to air their ideas on issues and mobilize votes. Each medium has its possibilities and obstacles. While television is the most sought-after medium to contest in national competition, access to it is constrained by the production processes and market imperatives not examined in this chapter. The narratives show that gaining access to television is essential for politicians but difficult to realize. The broadcasting media, especially television, can disseminate messages widely and quickly, but then it might not be accessible to target groups, for example in rural and slum areas. The radio has some added advantages in the Kenyan context, especially when political actors want to reach particular vernacular groups. The newspapers are still important, but their reach is diminished by the migration to the online environment, where most media crystalizes with social media.

It is no surprise that new professional titles encompassing digital and social communication are emerging in the Kenyan context. Social media manager, ICT managers, digital marketers, and public relations services are widely sought after by prospective candidates and parties. Not discussed in this chapter is the growing importance of international PR firms, that are reportedly experimenting with different forms of data-driven campaign strategies. There is a growing influence of social media algorithms, and bots in African elections, impacting on the creation, dissemination, and consumption of political content (Ndlela 2020). The magnitude of the influence of bots in African elections is self-evident, as each election cycle sees a surge in machine-like behavior on social media. International firms like Cambridge Analytica, Aristotle International, and other actors are reported to have been actively involved in Kenyan elections (Ndlela 2020). Political parties with resources are integrating social media in their practice and recruiting professional services that can deliver personalized approaches.

A trend that arises in the narrative is the growing role of influencers and bloggers, who are recruited and paid to front for politicians on the social media networks. Influencers can be local people who command a following in a targeted area and have a social media presence (for example, business owners, musicians, and celebrities) or bloggers who have a million followers nationwide. The use of influencers is often transactional. We also noted how politicians hire cyberactivists who advance their clients' campaigns on various social media platforms. There seem to be a widespread strategy of recruiting "campaigners" to represent political candidates online, on radio or television shows, and also on social media. Candidates also get campaign help from other self-organized social media activists, commentators, critics, and individuals.

Campaigning strategies are sometimes ad hoc, driven mainly by a scramble to "get out there" because everyone is assumed to be there. A bandwagon effect is discernible as most politicians are using social media because everyone else is doing it. Some candidates get into different social media platforms without any clear strategies decided, while some make strategic choices depending on which target group they want to reach out to. It can be concluded that social media is adding a new dimension to contemporary election campaigning in Kenya, associated with both positive and negative outcomes. Social media has been singled out for negatively affecting Kenya's fledgling democracy by promoting hate speech, incitement of violence, and spreading of false news (Mutua 2009; Mäkinen and Wangu Kuira 2008). These issues are not dealt with in detail in this chapter. It is important to stress that social media is not supplanting existing communication channels but is rather complementing them.

References

Ahluwalia, P. 2017. "Will the 2017 Kenyan Elections Challenge Orthodoxy?" *African Identities* 15(3): 229–30. https://doi.org/10.1080/14725843.2017.1354418

Brinkman, I. 2019. "Social diary and news production: Authorship and readership in social media during Kenya's 2007 elections." *Journal of Eastern African Studies* 13(1): 72–89. https://doi.org/10.1080/17531055.2018.1547262

Brisset-Foucault, F. 2008. "The Electoral Campaign on Television: Communication Strategies and Models of Democracy." *The East African Review* 38: 109–49. http://journals.openedition.org/eastafrica/696

Cheeseman, N., K. Kanyinga, G. Lynch, M. Ruteere, and J. Willis. 2019. "Kenya's 2017 elections: Winner-takes-all politics as usual?" *Journal of Eastern African Studies* 13(2): 215–34. https://doi.org/10.1080/17531055.2019.1594072

Freeman, M. 2015. "Narrative as a mode of understanding." In *The Handbook of Narrative Analysis*, edited by A. De Fina and A. Georgakopoulou, 21–37. Chichester, UK: Wiley Blackwell.

Gustafsson, J., and P. E. Nielsen. 2017. "Changing communication ecologies in rural, peri-urban and urban Kenya." *Journal of African Media Studies* 9(2): 291–306.

Lehman, H. P. 1992. "The paradox of state powers in Africa: Debt management and policies in Kenya and Zimbabwe." *African Studies Review* 35(2): 1–34.

Mäkinen, M., and M. Wangu Kuira. 2008. "Social Media and Postelection Crisis in Kenya." *International Journal of Press/Politics* 13(3): 328–35. https://doi.org/10.1177/1940161208319409

Maweu, J. M. 2020. "'Fake Elections'? Cyber Propaganda, Disinformation and the 2017 General Elections in Kenya." *African Journalism Studies*, 1–15. https://doi.org/10.1080/23743670.2020.1719858

Mohamed, H. 2017. "Kenya set for its first social media election." *Al Jazeera*, August 7. https://www.aljazeera.com/blogs/africa/2017/08/kenya-set-social-media-election-170807135747761.html

Mueller, S. D. (2008). The Political Economy of Kenya's Crisis. *Journal of Eastern African Studies, 2*(2), 185–210. https://doi.org/10.1080/17531050802058302

Mutahi, P., and B. Kimari. 2020. "Fake News and the 2017 Kenyan Elections." *Communicatio*, 1–19. https://doi.org/10.1080/02500167.2020.1723662

Mutua, M. 2009. *Kenya's quest for democracy. Taming the Leviathan.* Kampala: Fountain Publishers.

Ndlela, M. 2020. "Social Media Algorithms, Bots and Elections in Africa." In *Social Media and Elections in Africa, Volume 1: Theoretical Perspectives and Election Campaigns*, edited by M. N. Ndlela and W. Mano, 13–37. Cham, Switzerland: Palgrave Macmillan

Ndlela, M., and W. Mano. 2020. "The Changing Face of Election Campaigning in Africa." In *Social Media and Elections in Africa. Vol 1: Theoretical Perspectives and Election Campaigns*, edited by M. N. Ndlela and W. Mano, 1–12. Cham, Switzerland: Palgrave Macmillan.

Norris, P. 2000. *A Virtuous Circle: Political Communication in Postindustrial Societies.* Cambridge: Cambridge University Press.

Ogachi, O. 1999. "Economic Reform, Political Liberalization and Economic Ethnic Conflict in Kenya." *Africa Development / Afrique et Développement* 24(1/2): 83–107.

Republic of Kenya. 2010. *The 2010 Kenya Constitution.* Nairobi: Government Printer.

Shirky, C. 2008. *Here comes everybody: The Power of organizing without organizations.* New York: The Penguin Press.

Steeves, J. 2016. "The 2017 election in Kenya: Reimagining the past or introducing the future?" *Commonwealth & Comparative Politics* 54(4): 478–97. doi: 10.1080/14662043.2016.1223375.

Stier, S., A. Bleier, H. Lietz, and M. Strohmaier. 2018. "Election Campaigning on Social Media: Politicians, Audiences, and the Mediation of Political Communication on Facebook and Twitter." *Political Communication* 35(1): 50–74. doi: 10.1080/10584609.2017.1334728.

CHAPTER 13

Social Media as Strategic Campaign Tool

Austrian Political Parties Use of Social Media over Time

Uta Russmann, University of Innsbruck

Introduction

When in 2008 Barack Obama used the power of social media to connect directly with his supporters and to build his brand (Bimber 2014), Austrian parties were merely adapting websites. In the 2008 Austrian national election, websites were considered the new communication tool, as Austrian parties had not yet integrated social media into their campaigns. It took another five years until the 2013 Austrian national election for all major and minor parties to start using social media, or better put, Facebook, as a campaign tool. Bimber (2014, 131) notes that "the U.S. is an electoral outlier rather than modal case" in the use of digital and social media as a campaign tool, which eventuated due to different structural conditions (Lilleker and Jackson 2011). Considering that most parties in Western democracies were eager to adopt social media to their campaigning toolbox immediately after the successful Obama campaign in 2008 (see, for example, Schweitzer and Albrecht 2011 for the 2009 German federal election and Lilleker and Jackson 2011 for the 2010 U.K. general election; see also chapter 8 by Michael Keren in this book), Austrian parties were very late to jump on the bandwagon.

Social media has since changed the entire landscape of political campaigning and this has been the subject of many studies. However, only a few studies have analyzed how party strategists and campaign professionals perceive, understand, and approach strategic campaign communication and social media (Kalsnes 2016; Klinger and Russmann 2017; Lilleker, Tenscher, and Štětka 2015; Magin, Podschuweit, Haßler, and Russmann 2017; Tenscher et al. 2016 for a European perspective and Bor 2013; Kreiss, Lawrence, and McGregor 2018; Vaccari 2013 for a U.S. perspective)—the majority of them focusing on the early adoption phase. My goal is to investigate the process of adaptation and implementation of social media by parties in Austria and to identify the evolution of social media strategies undertaken by parties in Austrian national election campaigns over time. Hence the article takes a comparative longitudinal perspective by focusing on the 2013,[1] 2017, and 2019 Austrian national elections. I conducted personal semistructured interviews with the heads of (digital) communication or the web strategists of all parties in parliament following each of the three elections (for a similar approach, see chapter 12 by Martin Ndlela in this study). The article asks: How do parties implement and deal with this (new) form of communication (in their organization)? What are the main strategies, practices, and challenges for communication via social media in election campaigns from a party perspective? What effects do parties expect from social media campaigning and how do they monitor their performance? How has the approach changed over time with new evolving social media platforms such as Instagram as well as the increasingly habitual use of social media platforms?

Social Media and Campaigns

Political parties are investing in social media to support the main goal of their campaign: to win the election. Previous studies on campaign professionals' perceptions of the Internet and social media have primarily focused on the early adoption phase, but these give us a first impression of social media campaigning from the campaign side.

Studies on U.S. elections between 2008 and 2012 show that social media mainly functioned for dissemination, opinion reinforcement, and to support mobilization and fundraising (Bor 2013; Vaccari 2013). Social media were used to distribute positive messages and present a more personal side of the candidates. These messages were monitored concerning message effectiveness and reception (Bor 2013). These modes and functions were still

---

1. Data on the 2013 Austrian national election campaign has been published in two comparative studies with a comparison with the 2011 Swiss national election campaign (Klinger and Russmann 2017) and with the 2013 German national election campaign (Magin et al. 2017). To avoid repetition, the main findings of these are not presented in the literature review, and are instead incorporated in the longitudinal analysis in the results section.

highly relevant in the 2016 U.S. presidential election (Kreiss et al. 2018). Moreover, social media were used in such a way as to fit with and convey the "authentic" voice of the candidate. Facebook, the platform with widest audience reach, was used to direct communications at various groups of interest and to collect data on supporters, which was then used to target similar audiences with ads. Parties also used social media platforms to track the performance of other campaigns. Twitter served the function of distributing breaking news and discussions with journalists, political elites, and highly engaged partisans.

For Europe, studies with parties and their campaign staff show that Facebook was perceived as the most important social media platform until the year 2013 (Kaslnes 2016; Lilleker et al. 2015; Tenscher et al. 2016). This was true to a greater extent for newer parties than more established parties, yet no differences were found between oppositional and governmental parties (Lilleker et al. 2015; Tenscher et al. 2016). Parties aimed for greater dialogue with voters and feedback on policy and performance but failed in the implementation (Kaslnes 2016), partly because they lacked the human and financial resources needed to manage the often overwhelming amount of comments on Facebook. The parties also described the lack of control over messages as a disadvantage.

The aim of the current study is to examine the development of social media campaigning in Austria by applying a strategic communication perspective.

Strategic Communication Practices

Strategic political communication is about the purposeful use of informational, persuasive, discursive, and relational communication by a party to fulfill its mission (Hallahan et al. 2007; Kiousis and Strömbäck 2015). It focuses on how the party presents and promotes itself through the intentional activities of its leaders, top candidates, politicians, members, and so on. It is about generating meaning, creating and maintaining trust and reputation, and building relationships with internal and external stakeholders such as party members, party supporters, and the mass media in order to support the party's growth and ensure freedom of action (Hallahan et al. 2007; Kiousis and Strömbäck 2015; Norris 2000). This implies that strategic political communication is "intentional and objectives-driven" (Kiousis and Strömbäck 2015, 384) and this separates it from other types of communication. Hence social media campaigning ideally follows a "coordinated plan

266 Electoral Campaigns, Media, and the New World of Digital Politics

that sets out party objectives, identifies target voters, establishes the battleground issues, orchestrates consistent key themes and images, [and] prioritizes organizational and financial resources" (Norris 2000, 10).

The current study follows a model recognizing four ideal types of campaigning that are differentiated by four specific target audiences (Magin et al. 2017) (see table 13.1). The model incorporates concepts of evolving phases in (strategic) political communication (e.g., Blumler and Kavanagh 1999; Strömbäck and Kiousis 2014) but does not connect certain developments to specific timeframes, because new communication technologies can be implemented at different times in different countries and supplement established campaigning practices rather than replace them (Klinger and Russmann 2017; Magin et al. 2017). The four campaigning approaches for various target audiences are: partisan-centered campaigns, mass-centered campaigns, target group-centered campaigns, and individual-centered campaigns.

As outlined in table 13.1 and described by Magin and colleagues (2017), partisan-centered campaigns address core party members and partisans and

TABLE 13.1. Four Ideal Types of Campaigning

	Partisan-Centered	Mass-Centered	Target Group-Centered	Individual-Centered
Mode of political communication system	Party-dominated	Television-centered	Multiple channels and multimedia	Data based
Dominant style of political communication	Messages along party lines to supporters	Sound bites to mass audience	Tailored messages to target groups	Personalized messages and social media ads to individual voters
Dominant media	Partisan press, newspaper ads, radio broadcasts	Television	Television narrowcasting, direct emails, websites	Social media, voter mining
Campaign coordination	Party leaders and party staff	Party campaign managers, advertising and survey experts	Special party campaign units and consultants	Special party campaign units and data scientists
Dominant campaign paradigm	Party logic	Media logic	Marketing logic	Data logic
Campaign preparation	Short-term, ad hoc	Longer-term campaigning	Permanent campaigning	Permanent campaigning

Klinger and Russmann (2017, p. 300); based on Strömbäck and Kiousis (2014, p. 177) and Magin et al. (2017, pp. 1700–1)

do not use social media as a central campaign tool. One-way communication channels are also dominant in the case of mass-centered campaigns in order for parties to reach dispersed masses. With the increasingly fluid electorate, however, parties have started to address voter segments with similar interests. These target group-centered campaigns are characterized by top-down, centralized communication and, besides traditional communication channels, make increasing use of the Internet. In individual-centered campaigns, social media and micro-targeting play a crucial role. Parties use the different social media platforms to individualize campaign content to small groups of voters or even tailor campaign messages to single voters. The application of these data-based campaigns remains rather restricted in most European countries when compared to the United States. In Austria, data acquisition and the tailoring of party messages to single voters without the prior consent of recipients (opt-in) runs contrary to data protection laws. Certainly, real campaigns are "an amalgamation of all campaign practices available at that time. The exact mixture of approaches will depend on what a campaign targets, who it addresses, and the relative importance it attaches to certain functions" (Magin et al. 2017, 1701).

The Setting

Austria has a multiparty political system structure. The National Council (Nationalrat) has 183 members, who are directly elected by universal suffrage for a five-year term of office unless snap elections are called, as in 2017 and 2019. Elections play a major role in Austria because citizens' involvement in decision-making is basically limited to elections.

For the major part of the Second Republic (i.e., since 1945) Austria has been ruled by coalition governments, and for most of this time the two major parties—the social democratic SPÖ and the conservative ÖVP—have governed as part of a "grand coalition." However, the power of the minor parties has been growing since the mid-1980s (Klinger and Russmann 2017). The populist right-wing Freedom Party of Austria (FPÖ) has been in Parliament throughout all three election campaigns under study, even governing together with the ÖVP from 2017 to 2019. The Greens—The Green Alternative—entered the Austrian Parliament for the first time in 1986, yet in 2017 failed to reach the threshold level of 4 percent to get into Parliament. At this time, a new party—Jetzt–Pilz List—founded by long-time member of The Greens, Peter Pilz, made it into Parliament (4.4 percent), but only for the 2017 legislative period. In 2019, The Greens not only reached the threshold level again but are now governing together with the conservative ÖVP. Two new minor parties entered the political arena and both entered Parliament in the 2013 election campaign: the EU-skeptical party Team Stronach, whose end was announced a few month before the 2017 election, and the New Austria and Liberal Forum (NEOS), who describe themselves as a citizens' movement and have remained in Parliament since 2013.

Among the various social media, Facebook was and still is the most often used platform in Austria. In September 2013, Facebook had 3.2 million users in Austria, meaning that about 51 percent of Internet users (over fourteen years of age) used the platform. This number had increased to 3.8 million Facebook users by 2019 (Statista 2019). In contrast, the number of active Twitter users has decreased over the years, from about 100,000 users in 2013 to about 88,000 active users today. Unlike in the United States, but similar to other European countries, Twitter is mainly used by politicians, journalists, and other opinion leaders. As in other countries, Instagram has seen an enormous increase in users over the past three years. Unfortunately, data for 2013 does not exist, but in early 2016 only about 340,000 people in Austria had an Instagram account and this number increased rapidly to about 1.8 million in autumn 2017, and to about 2.35 million in autumn 2019 (Statista 2019).

Today, social media is part of the daily media diet for many people in Austria, although only very few of these users connect directly to a political actor's social media page. Austria remains a so-called newspaper-centric society (Norris 2000), meaning that newspapers are the main source of information in Austria.

Method and Data

To generate an in-depth understanding of the evolution and development of Austrian parties' social media campaigns, open-ended, semistructured interviews were conducted with the heads of (digital) communication or the web strategists of all parties in Parliament following each of the three elections under study (for a similar approach, see chapter 12 by Martin Ndlela in this book). The interview guide developed by the author asked interviewees to discuss party strategies, goals, and challenges for communication with social media, the perceived effects of social media campaigning, as well as the internal organization of social media over time.

Following the 2013 Austrian national election on September 29, 2013, interviews were conducted from October 9 to October 23, 2013, with the Social Democratic Party of Austria (SPÖ), the Austrian People's Party

(ÖVP), Freedom Party of Austria (FPÖ), The Greens—The Green Alternative, and the New Austria and Liberal Forum (NEOS). Representatives of Team Stronach were not available for an interview, as, according to the party, an external agency was in charge of their digital campaign. For the following Austrian national election on October 15, 2017, interviews were conducted with the ÖVP, FPÖ, SPÖ, NEOS, and Jetzt–Pilz List between October 23, 2017, and July 4, 2018. For the most recent election on September 29, 2019, interviews with ÖVP, The Greens, SPÖ, FPÖ, and NEOS were held between October 14, 2019, and March 9, 2020. The fifteen interviews cover the entire political spectrum represented in the Austrian Parliament after each election.

Interviews lasted between thirty and approximately seventy-five minutes. The interviews were recorded, transcribed in full, and qualitatively analyzed by the researcher. The findings are presented along the revealed (major) categories. The author of this study translated all of the quotes presented in the following sections from German into English.

The Rise of Social Media in Austrian National Election Campaigns

Austrian politics has faced an increase in partisan dealignment over the past decades, and voter turnout in Austrian elections has decreased—reaching an all-time low in the 2013 election. Interviews with party web strategists and heads of communication reveal that parties' primary motives for using social media in the 2013 campaign were to attract citizens' attention and interest, interact with them directly, and increase their engagement to secure votes. Despite these motivations, parties were unsure about the benefits of social media and did not expect much gain from its usage; their focus was on positive mass media coverage. Nevertheless, after the 2008 Obama campaign, social media was perceived as part of "modern" campaigning and parties feared negative media coverage on their campaign without social media—particularly as they jumped on the social media bandwagon very late. The exception was the FPÖ, which recognized the potential of social media for unfiltered communication with supporters early on (see also chapter 9 by Francisco Brandao in this book regarding Bolsonaro's campaign strategy). As expressed by the party's web strategist, social media is an alternative to mass media coverage, which generally does not favor the right-wing populist party.

Table 13.2 depicts the number of followers on parties' and candidates' Facebook pages and reveals the FPÖ's leading role until 2017. The 2013 Austrian national election campaign was the first in which all parties used

TABLE 13.2. Followers on Facebook Pages

Facebook page	Page created	Community size in numbers (rounded) ("people like this")						
		Autumn 2010	Autumn 2013	Autumn 2014	Summer 2018	Summer 2017	Autumn 2017	Autumn 2019
Party's main pages								
ÖVP	May 29, 2008	n/a	16.500	15.500	17.500	42.600	46.900	64.000
Die Grünen	July 27, 2008	n/a	44.000	44.000	46.200	63.750	67.800	80.000
H. C. Strache (for FPÖ)*	About summer 2009	**65.000**	**221.000**	**223.150**	**237.500**	**610.600**	**740.000**	**770.000**
FPÖ	November 15, 2012	-	n/a	n/a	n/a	n/a	n/a	131.000
SPÖ	February 3, 2009	n/a	36.000	36.600	36.600	72.400	94.400	122.000
NEOS	September 9, 2012	-	52.000	53.500	52.600	76.800	79.400	87.000
Team Stronach	Summer 2013	-	48.500	51.200	48.100	55.200	-	-
Liste Jetzt—Liste Pilz	July 22, 2017	-	-	-	-	-	7.700	14.000
Top candidates in 2019								
Sebastian Kurz (ÖVP)	May 24, 2011						**705.000**	810.000
Werner Kogler (Greens)	July 9, 2010							25.500
Peter Pilz (Jetzt—Liste Pilz)	July 19, 2010						27.000	40.000
Beate Meinl-Reisinger (NEOS)	October 28, 2012							66.000
Pamela Rendi-Wagner (SPÖ)	May 4, 2017							105.000
Norbert Hofer (FPÖ)	September 10, 2015							339.000

*In May 2019—after the Ibiza scandal—H. C. Strache stepped down as party leader and the party ousted its former leader in December 2019. H. C. Strache was not part of the 2019 election campaign.

Social Media as Strategic Campaign Tool 271

social media in their campaign, but it took another four years until the 2017 election campaign before social media became an important part of parties' communication mix.

The Platforms and Moving from Textual to Visual Communication

Similar to the United States and other European countries, Facebook has been the preferred social media platform for campaigning in Austria since 2013. It is the platform with the widest audience reach among all platforms and, until today, has been the focus of mass media coverage about parties' social media performance.

In 2013, the interviewed practitioners agreed that less social media is more. According to the parties, an online presence restricted to only a few selected platforms ensured optimum and more effective performance. Face-to-face contact with voters was considered as more important. Over the years, the perception of social media's impact has increased tremendously, but even in 2019 parties noted that the mass media have greater impact on voters than social media.

In 2013, Twitter was treated as a secondary medium but was nevertheless regarded as important to communicate with journalists and opinion leaders. Parties also experimented with YouTube, which was considered an appropriate channel to explain messages in more detail. The party comparison shows that the three minor parties followed the international trend of using social media to a greater extent than the two major parties and integrated it more thoroughly with their offline campaigns. Direct contact with the public was essential for minor parties because the mass media gave them only minimal attention. For instance, Austria's NEOS experimented with Tumblr to address first-time voters. The right-wing populist party FPÖ used Instagram and its campaign posters contained references to the party's Facebook page. (The Instagram account had only about 1,500 followers and was closed after the campaign.) The FPÖ was already "thinking of online and offline as one." A primary challenge for parties when using social media was the loss of control over political messages, and this was particularly true for the two major parties, where older functionaries did not know how to handle social media communication and feared the loss of control.

Four years later in the 2017 Austrian election campaign the picture had turned. All parties agreed that both online and offline communications should be considered as integral elements in the overall communications strategy. The production of offline and online content was coordinated in daily meetings. ÖVP and SPÖ had teams incorporating social media savvy people and the older functionaries within the parties began to realize that social media has its advantages. For example, Austria's ÖVP said that social media is the "heart" of all direct communication, and the FPÖ mentioned that "some of the posters were shot during the shooting of the videos." Across all parties, visual communication on social media played a greater role in 2017 (for the growing importance of visual images in electoral campaigns, see chapter 10 by Rosalynd Southern in this study). Instagram was named as the second most important platform by the NEOS and the FPÖ. The three minor parties, FPÖ, Pilz List, and NEOS, highlighted that it had become "quite easy" to produce high-quality videos. The FPÖ started to expand FPÖ-TV by building its own video studio. The two major parties, on the other hand, said that Twitter was still more important than Instagram and YouTube. In sum, in 2017, parties were using multiple channels and multimedia as characteristic for target group-centered campaigns.

With the 2019 campaign, the use of social media had become "part of the daily business" (ÖVP) of Austrian parties. Social media was used to "reinforce the general campaign" (The Greens). Following Facebook, Instagram had become the second most important platform for all parties in the 2019 campaign, while Twitter was now playing only a minor role. Pictures and videos were considered central to communications with supporters and voters because of their capacity to display authenticity and generate emotions. Parties generally produced videos in-house that featured both politicians and supporters speaking. Parties agreed that self-made videos and selfies often have the most impact in generating views and interactions. While for the two major parties YouTube was rather a platform to "park" videos, the platform is more important for minor parties. The FPÖ had its own camera team that "accompanies everything and everyone." The parties' YouTube channel, FPÖ-TV, had about 33,000 followers and about two million views during the campaign. Live broadcasting had become a substitute for mass media coverage (see also chapter 9 regarding the extensive use of Facebook Live by right-wing populist Jair Bolsonaro).

All parties tried out the new tools offered by Facebook and Instagram such as InstaStories to attract their supporters' and voters' attention. However, just like in the two previous campaigns, minor parties displayed a greater propensity to use newer platforms like TikTok (NEOS), SnapChat (FPÖ), and Telegram Messaging (The Greens).

Internal Organization of Social Media

Over time, the internal organization of social media has become increasingly similar between the parties—an indication of the increasing professionalization of social media campaigning in Austria.

In 2013, parties' organizational habits followed either a centralized or a decentralized organization (Klinger and Russmann 2017). A centralized approach means that a small team of party employees, most often based in the party headquarters, is in charge of social media. This approach limits the loss of control. The two major parties featured centralized organization with small teams of not more than four people, who followed a top-down information strategy while marginalizing the role of bottom-up communication. The SPÖ had also hired an external agency to plan and support the social media campaign. In contrast, a decentralized approach means that media-savvy employees from various parts of the organization are involved in the social media campaign. This reduces costs, which was important to the minor parties, who lacked the financial resources and "manpower" for a dedicated social media team in 2013. The Green Party managed its social media with about 150 people from different parts of the organization posting on social media and online newspaper forums. The NEOS conducted its social media campaign with about forty people from different parts of the party.

Much had changed by 2017, with similarities between the parties becoming more evident than the differences, and these common organizational habits hardly changed between 2017 and 2019. With the exception of the Social Democrats (SPÖ), all parties followed a centralized approach in 2017, with partly decentralized activities across the federal states as well as the outsourcing of specific services such as ad management, performance marketing, graphic design, and the production of films and videos. In charge of the digital campaign of the Social Democrats in 2017 was an external agency working closely with eight people from within the party as well as a consultant for ad management and an advertising agency. In the other parties, the core teams consisted of five to fifteen people from within the parties. These organizational structures remained largely the same from 2017 to 2019, with some team members being engaged in both campaigns. A change in 2019 was that all parties used WhatsApp for their internal communication.

Strategies and Challenges of Social Media

The analysis of parties' strategies reveals that similarities between the parties increased over time. The interviewed experts seem to have exerted a significant personal influence on the parties' social media campaign strategies and practices. The basic social media strategies and practices of the FPÖ and the ÖVP did not really change between 2017 and 2019. The FPÖ had appointed the same person as web strategist since 2013 and he announced the same credo for the parties' social media approach in both 2017 and 2019: "being open, being spontaneous, allowing things to happen." In the ÖVP, the same person has been in charge of the parties' social media activities since 2017.

As a "minor newcomer," the Pilz List had hardly any financial and human resources in the 2017 campaign and, according to the head of communication, the party did not really have a social media strategy: "If at all, the last two weeks of the campaign were somehow strategically planned, but it is not possible to speak of a strategy." Hence the social media campaign of the Pilz List is mentioned only fleetingly in the following presentation of parties' main strategies and the challenges of social media.

From Disseminating "Offline" Content to Producing and Sharing "Good" Content

In 2013, a main strategy was to use the potential of social media to disseminate and strengthen the parties' political messages. Four years later, in the 2017 campaign, it was no longer just about "getting your message across." According to the interviewees, the self-declared goal of the campaigns, and at the same time one of the greatest challenges until the 2019 campaign, was to create "good" (ÖVP 2017), "smart" (Pilz List 2017) and "creative" (FPÖ 2019) content. Important was to "capture the right topics and prepare them quickly" (FPÖ 2017). In the last two campaigns, all parties (with the exception of the SPÖ, who did not mention this aspect in the interviews) indicated that for a successful social media campaign it is important to "have the courage to adjust or stop content, if it does not perform" (NEOS). Until today, orchestrating content and generating meaning on social media is a great challenge for parties. In this process of content production, authenticity and spontaneity play a crucial role (NEOS, FPÖ, ÖVP, SPÖ, for both 2017 and 2019). In 2019, ÖVP, SPÖ, and The Greens also highlighted that they focused on more emotional messaging.

From Dialogue to Interactivity

In 2013, interviewees highlighted social media's function to generate dialogue with citizens, even though a meaningful shift toward more dialogue did not occur (see the analysis of Facebook in Magin et al. 2017).

Four years later, parties no longer talked about dialogue and instead it was all about "interactivity." According to the parties, direct contact with citizens had increased dramatically by 2017 compared to the previous campaign. Parties' aims were to achieve "real interactivity" (NEOS) and "real exchange" (ÖVP) with supporters and potential voters, but they faced a few challenges such as attaining "good organic reach" (FPÖ) on social media as well as tackling questions like "Where are the people we want to reach?" (SPÖ).

From Responding to Community Management

Parties agreed that the use of social media allows a quicker and more flexible response to citizens' questions and comments. However, a great challenge for all parties in all campaigns was dealing with the sheer amount of interactivity, particularly on Facebook. For instance, in the 2017 campaign, due to limited resources, Austria's NEOS could only react to "about 50% of the comments" on their platforms. The SPÖ had the support of their call center team, the ÖVP introduced a ticketing system, and the FPÖ had the support of the party's citizen service team and installed new software for this purpose.

After the 2019 campaign, all interviewees said that managing the sheer amount of interactivity gained in importance (see also the following section on inappropriate comments). The use of the term "community management" by three of the four parties, without prompting by the interviewer, indicates a certain professionalization of social media practices. To manage the communities, parties engaged party officials and supporters (ÖVP), paid students of the party's student organization (FPÖ), and enrolled marginally employed people and full-time staff (SPÖ). The NEOS had only two full-time and one half-time position for operating their community management, which "should have been more." All parties indicated that more resources and/or knowledge was needed. The head of digital communication of the ÖVP put into words the sentiments of the other parties: "Our goal is to build a proper community management system over the next few years. Because our experience is that we are in a very poor state now in terms of response rates and speed, we need a team working on this in the long run and a plan for how to keep users loyal to us over the longer term, rather than just sending out a quick response and considering it done." The Greens had no professional community management in 2019, because they lacked the necessary financial and human resources. The party's web strategist described this as a huge challenge and key aspect that needs to be resolved in the near future.

Inappropriate User Comments

Besides the challenge of responding, parties considered inappropriate user comments to be a problem. Since the 2013 election, parties follow a strict approach of deleting discriminatory and insulting comments such as sexist, homophobic, and anti-Semitic content. Some comments had to be deleted for legal reasons, while others were seen to cross moral boundaries. According to the interviewees, inappropriate user comments are a delicate matter, because how the parties deal with them is a topic that attracts the attention of the mass media.

While in 2013 the number of inappropriate comments was considered manageable, parties agreed about an increase in 2017—with the exception of the FPÖ. "It has become much more emotional and therefore more aggressive," said the web strategist of the NEOS after the 2017 campaign. The ÖVP noted that 2017 was the low point "of our political culture." The party had introduced a ticketing system to handle the "massive occurrence of comments with swear words." However, parties agreed that the tonality was less emotional and less aggressive in the 2019 campaign. This shows that the context of the campaign matters. In 2017, the Silberstein affair was a political issue in the final phase of the campaign. Tal Silberstein, a political advisor to the Social Democrats, had focused on dirty campaigning mainly directed at the top candidate of the ÖVP, which was conducted under false authorship using anonymous Facebook pages that gave the impression of belonging to people around the right-wing populist party FPÖ. For many days during the last weeks of the campaign, the SPÖ received bad coverage for this approach in the mass media.

Over time, the interview data reveal an increasing professionalization in dealing with inappropriate user comments. In 2019, for instance, the ÖVP and the FPÖ highlighted that the use of software makes the removal of inappropriate user comments much easier as these could now be identified at an earlier stage.

Social bots are not a significant issue in Austrian campaigns. In 2017 as well as in 2019, all parties said that they did not use social bots and, in sum, parties recorded only three incidents on their platforms.

From "Humanizing" to Focusing on the Top Candidate

Austria has a party-based electoral system, but the interview data reveal that, today, a successful campaign is about the interplay between the campaign and the top candidate.

In the 2013 campaign, only the three minor parties used social media to personalize their campaigns. Particularly the right-wing populist party FPÖ centered its campaign on its top candidate H. C. Strache. The FPÖ's official Facebook page was that of Strache (see table 13.2). The three minor parties used social media to "humanize" their top candidates in order to build a more personal community, hoping to enhance interaction and dialogue within their Facebook communities. Strache was often shown with his dog or in his swimming trunks.

Since 2017, personalization on social media is a key strategy of all Austrian parties. Top candidates have one person and sometimes an additional photographer following them throughout the campaign to collect "moments" for all of their party's social media platforms. However, top candidates only seldom post during the campaign.

Supporters, Supporters, Supporters

After the 2013 campaign, all parties mentioned that their aim was to reach out to their supporters, but parties did not specifically highlight them. This has changed over time and supporters have become key to party strategies. The conservative ÖVP was the driving force in this change. In the 2017 campaign, "our number one goal was simply supporters, supporters, supporters," said the party's head of digital communication. Strategically, the party made a shift from a *Volkspartei* (people's party) to a movement. According to the party, it is easier to identify oneself with a movement than with a party. Crucial to a movement are its supporters and social media was key to this change. It was all about "what are people willing to do for you" (ÖVP). Supporters were less prominent but still in the focus of the social media strategies of the FPÖ and the NEOS in the 2017 campaign. For the NEOS, similar to the ÖVP, it was about "how do we get people interested in becoming activists?"

Following the very successful ÖVP strategy of the 2017 campaign, attracting and mobilizing supporters played a crucial role for all parties in 2019. It was about building (stronger) relationships. The main strategy of the ÖVP was to activate their many existing supporters and have them reach out to less aware voters. Hence the party made use of the advantages of the "movement" they had created since the last campaign.

Monitoring and Targeting

From Assessing Message Effectiveness to Monitoring

In the 2013 campaign, user comments on social media were used for assessing the effectiveness of parties' campaign messages and eventually to inform the modification of published content. Parties also "checked" their opponent's social media to gain an impression of their activities. However, parties neither systematically assessed their own or their opponents' online performance, nor did they use any specific monitoring tools in 2013.

In 2017, Austrian campaigns were more data driven, with parties seeking to measure reach and interactivity on social media. All parties used the analytical tools provided by the respective platforms, but only two parties, the FPÖ and ÖVP, used specific monitoring tools. Overall, when asked about their first experiences in professionally monitoring users' digital traces in an election campaign, parties agreed that they were lacking knowledge and resources such as a specific monitoring unit.

Surprisingly, parties did not invest significantly more resources in monitoring practices in the 2019 campaign, with the exception of the SPÖ. In the previous campaign, the SPÖ had only used the analytical tools integrated within the platforms, yet in 2019 the party had created a research unit that provided daily reports (up to three times per day) with information on the party's own and opponents' social media activities. Monitoring practices of the FPÖ were similar to those in 2017, although, for the first time, the party also tested some of its YouTube videos with brand lift studies. As discussed above, videos play a crucial role in the FPÖ's social media strategy to make up for missing mass media coverage. The Greens, NEOS, and ÖVP continued only to use the tools provided by the platforms, despite the fact that Facebook and Instagram had limited access to free data. The ÖVP, which together with the FPÖ was one step ahead in terms of monitoring in 2017, stated that they did not have the same monetary capabilities after the permanent campaigning over the past two years.

From Mobilizing to Targeting

In 2013, social media campaigning was about mobilizing and organizing supporters. However, Austrian parties did not have clear target groups and they did not assess whether they actually reached their supporters.

The practices of 2017 represent a leap beyond previous targeting practices. Tailoring the "right messages at the right target groups" was a key aspect in parties' campaigns. Parties were now running target-group centered campaigns but not yet individual-centered campaigns. For example, on Facebook, all parties addressed look-alike audiences. Apart from classically recognized target groups such as party members, first-time voters, and seniors, the NEOS, ÖVP, and SPÖ segmented according to interests and interactivity (rates). It is about "what people are willing to do for you" and "what issues are of interest to them," said the ÖVP. The external agency that was running the social media campaign of the SPÖ had adapted the engagement model of the 2008 Obama campaign and targeted according to "social involvement groups." Moreover, in the 2017 campaign, Austrian parties did not buy user data but had begun to create their own data pools containing data on users' sociodemographics, interests, and contacts.

In 2019, just as in 2017, parties were running target-group centered campaigns, but they invested more in targeted communication and were more specific about their target groups. For instance, The Greens specifically targeted the Fridays-for-future generation. The NEOS worked with the sinus-milieu model that identifies groups of like-minded people based on values and views of life. The SPÖ focused on the "relationship aspect" by differentially targeting people with weak, medium, and strong relations to the party. Just as in 2017, the ÖVP and the NEOS segmented along people's willingness to engage in order to activate their supporters. In contrast to previous campaigns, parties had to invest more in targeted ads to improve their reach, because Facebook had changed its algorithmic filtering such that "political content was no longer privileged" (ÖVP). On Facebook and Instagram, a primary targeting practice was again using look-alike audiences as well as targeting by demographic groups, geographical location, and using retargeting.

New in the 2019 campaign were dark ads on Facebook. FPÖ, NEOS, and ÖVP were testing and using dark ads throughout the campaign. For ethical reasons, The Greens did not use dark posts, because their general campaign strategy was "clean environment, clean politics."

Conclusions

When in 2013 Austrian parties finally took an active approach toward integrating social media in their communications for the national election, they were still hesitant about the use of Facebook and Co. and largely skeptical about the benefits of them. Campaigns largely followed a partisan-centered and mass-centered approach (see table 13.1). However, following international modes of campaigning, social media was now perceived as part of "modern" campaigning and parties feared negative media coverage on their campaigns in the absence of social media. The mass media were still the primary channel to reach out to supporters and voters, for while parties aimed to use social media to send out messages along party lines to their supporters they did not have clear target groups and did not monitor their social media performance or message effectiveness. In sum, the results suggest that social media campaigning was in a trial and error phase in 2013.

Despite the limited role of social media in general, the party comparison shows differences between parties, with minor parties showing the first signs of target-group centered campaigns. They experimented far more often with multiple as well as newer platforms and tools when compared to the two major parties, who feared the loss of control over their messages when using social media to a greater extent. This trend continued over the subsequent years. For the minor parties, and particularly the right-wing populist party FPÖ, social media was seen as a way to compensate for minimal media coverage. As in previous studies (Lilleker, Tenscher, and Štětka 2015; Tenscher et al. 2016), no differences were found between governmental and oppositional parties.

With the 2017 campaign, a drastic transformation saw a change from strategic-oriented to strategic-driven social media campaigning. All parties highlighted that offline and online communications form part of "one" campaign and the interviews reveal that social media campaigning had become more intentional and goal-oriented (Kiousis and Strömbäck 2015). All parties placed more emphasis on the top candidate. Social media was used to support the trend of personalization in political communications. Even in a party-centered political system like Austria, a successful campaign today is about the interplay between the campaign and its top candidate. In 2019, a focus on the top candidate was key to all parties' social media strategies. The importance of image performance is rapidly increasing in campaign communication. In this process, authenticity and spontaneity play a crucial role. Nevertheless, parties agreed that a great challenge is the creation of "good" content, often not knowing in advance what kind of content "is working well." In 2019, some parties highlighted that it is increasingly important to transport emotions. Emotions and authenticity are well displayed through visual communication, on which parties have put more emphasis since the 2017 campaign. Supporting this, Instagram was named as the second most important platform in 2019, following Facebook. Specifically for the right-wing populist party FPÖ, YouTube is seen as an alternative outlet to the mass media to reach out to mass audiences.

Over time, Austrian parties have realized that there is great potential in social media to build relationships with supporters. While the ÖVP campaign in 2017 was already all about supporters to aid the party's change from a *Volkspartei* to a movement, supporters were less relevant for other parties' social media strategies. This changed in 2019. With the more widespread focus on supporters, all parties put even more emphasis on interactivity. While interactivity has been key to parties' social media strategies since 2017, the study reveals an ongoing process of professionalization. In 2019, all but one party started to invest in building and running a professional community management system. Just like in the process of creating content, generating meaning when interacting with the community is one of the great challenges for (campaigning) parties.

Thus, since 2017, target-group centered campaigns have followed a marketing logic that dominates until the present day. Differences between the 2017 and 2019 campaigns are rather small. Austrian parties had more or less been in a state of permanent campaigning, with only two years between the two national elections and an additional European Parliament election in 2019. Social media strategies and practices in 2019 were partly influenced by fewer financial resources, as the majority of parties invested less in data-based communication and monitoring practices than they had in 2017, or than they planned after the 2017 campaign. Despite this, targeted communication has developed over time from having no clear target groups in 2013 to ever more specific target groups and using all possible targeting options offered by the platforms, including dark ads, in 2019. Hence there are signs of emerging individual-centered campaigning—just as in the United States—but it seems that data protection laws and privacy regulations as well as ethical considerations (transparency) will limit the degree to which parties shift to this approach in the future. Still, today, also in Austria, social media campaigning is an integral part of parties' "daily business" (ÖVP).

References

Bimber, Bruce. 2014. "Digital Media in the Obama Campaigns of 2008 and 2012: Adaptation to the Personalized Political Communication Environment." *Journal of Information Technology & Politics* 11(2): 130–50.

Blumler, Jay G., and Dennis Kavanagh. 1999. "The third age of political communication." *Political Communication* 16(3): 209–30.

Bor, Stephanie. 2014. "Using social network sites to improve communication between political campaigns and citizens in the 2012 election." *American Behavioral Scientist* 58(9): 1195–1213.

Hallahan, Kirk, Derina Holtzhausen, Betteke van Ruler, Dejan Verčič, and Krishnamurthy Sriramesh. 2007. "Defining Strategic Communication." *International Journal of Strategic Communication* 1(1): 3–35.

Kalsnes, Bente. 2016. "The social media paradox explained: Comparing political parties' Facebook strategy versus practice." *Social Media & Society* 2(2), 1–11.

Kiousis, Spiro K., and Jesper Strömbäck. 2015. "The strategic context of political communication." In *The Routledge handbook of strategic communication*, edited by Derina Holtzhausen and Ansger Zerfass, 383–95. New York: Routledge.

Klinger, Ulrike, and Uta Russmann. 2017. "'Beer is more efficient than social media'— Political parties and strategic communication in Austrian and Swiss national elections." *Journal of Information Technology & Politics* 14(4): 299–313.

Kreiss, Daniel, Regina G. Lawrence, and Shannon C. McGregor. 2018. "In Their Own Words: Political Practitioner Accounts of Candidates, Audiences, Affordances, Genres, and Timing in Strategic Social Media Use." *Political Communication* 35(1): 8–31.

Lilleker, Darren G., and Nigel A. Jackson. 2011. *Political campaigning, elections and the Internet*. New York: Routledge.

Lilleker, Darren G., Jens Tenscher, and Vaclav Štětka. 2015. "Towards hypermedia campaigning? Perceptions of new media's importance for campaigning by party strategists in comparative perspective." *Information, Communication & Society* 18(7): 747–65.

Magin, Melanie, Nicole Podschuweit, Jörg Haßler, and Uta Russmann. 2017. "Campaigning in the fourth age of political communication: A multi-method study on the use of Facebook by German and Austrian parties in the 2013 national election campaigns." *Information, Communication & Society* 20(11): 1698–1719.

Norris, Pippa. 2000. *A virtuous circle: Political communications in postindustrial societies*. Cambridge: Cambridge University Press.

Schweitzer, Eva, and Steffen Albrecht, eds. 2011. *Das Internet im Wahlkampf* [The Internet in the election campaign]. Wiesbaden: VS Verlag für Sozialwissenschaften.

Statista. *Dossier—Social Media in Österreich* [Dossier—Social Media in Austria]. Statista, 2019.

Tenscher, Jens, Karolina Koc-Michalska, Darren Lilleker, Juri Mykkänen, Annemarie Walter, Andrej Findor, Carlos Jalali, and Jolán Róka. 2016. "The professionals speak: Practitioners' perspectives on professional election campaigning." *European Journal of Communication* 31(2): 95–119.

Vaccari, Christian. 2013. "From echo chamber to persuasive device? Rethinking the role of the Internet in campaigns." *New Media & Society* 15(1): 109–27.

CHAPTER 14

Candidate, News Media, and Social Media Messaging in the Early Stages of the 2020 Democratic Presidential Primary

Chris Wells, Blake Wertz, Li Zhang, and Rebecca Auger, Boston University

American primary elections are distinct from general elections in several ways: by definition they concern candidates from a single party vying for the support of that party's electorate; they can involve a large number of candidates competing for news media and public attention; and the large number of candidates can infuse primary contests with a wide variety of policies, issues, scandals, and other points of discourse. Primaries can thus be useful contexts in which to observe the development and competition of narratives about individual politicians.

In such a context, candidates face two fundamental challenges: to be noticed at all and to be understood in a way that is appealing to voters. We are especially intrigued to explore the process of narrative development and candidate meaning-making in the context of digital media fragmentation, and our growing awareness that multiple conversations about political topics are happening in a variety of spaces: candidates must now communicate themselves to multiple publics arrayed across a myriad of media spaces—and which themselves have the opportunity to make their own sense of the campaigns. News media organizations have historically dominated this space,

This research was supported by a Junior Faculty Fellowship awarded to the lead author by the Rafik B. Hariri Institute for Computing and Computational Sciences & Engineering at Boston University.

of course—and they continue to play a vital role in the American public sphere. But they also are challenged by discussions among publics in social media (Chadwick 2013). We want to know, when candidates, news media, and social media publics all attend to an evolving primary contest, do the meanings they ascribe to the campaign and the principal candidates differ? If so, how? And what does this imply for the functioning of our hybrid system of political communication?

We take the early stages of the 2020 Democratic presidential primary process—through the later months of 2019—as an opportunity to examine these questions. Specifically, we are interested in (1) how the leading candidates depicted themselves, in terms of the topics they chose to emphasize in their Twitter messaging, and (2) how each candidate was characterized, again in terms of association with key topics and issues, across news media, Twitter discussions about the candidates, and Reddit.

Branding Candidates in Primary Campaigns

A primary candidate's foremost challenge is to be perceived to be a credible contender for the nomination at all. As Patterson (2016) pointed out in the context of the primary contests of 2015–2016, this is a thorny, recursive problem. The difficulty for candidates is that performance in the polls and success with fundraising are themselves dependent on news media attention, that critical arbiter of political credibility (Swearingen 2019). Well-established candidates thus have a strong advantage, making it difficult for lower-level candidates to break in (Dowdle et al. 2021; Norrander 2006).

Presuming a sufficient level of news and public attention, candidates face the further problem of *how* they are understood. The field of communication has a variety of conceptual tools for studying how a person or other political entity is portrayed in communication and understood in the mind; in this analysis we work mainly within a framework of branding, with a method derived from second-level agenda setting. This leads us to explore what topics, ideas, and portrayals candidates are *associated* with (Oates and Moe 2016).

The crafting of candidate identity is one of the foremost concerns of political strategic communication, and every campaign strives energetically to strategically select and promote particular portrayals of their candidate—as well as portrayals that will disadvantage opponents. To brand themselves, political candidates make use of many, now hybrid tools: emails to mailing lists of supporters, websites, social media posts, press conferences, candidate debates, and other devices (Stromer-Galley 2014). While candidates may maintain some level of consistency across methods, they may also strategically adjust their content to target what they believe is the audience reached through a given platform (Kang et al. 2018).

But of course, much of the process of branding is outside the control of the candidate being branded; the candidate's own strategic communications occur in interaction with often-critical news media coverage, strategically combative counterbranding by opponents, and the messages of hyperpartisan attention-seekers, bloggers, and ordinary social media users. The impressions citizens actually form of candidates are presumably a complex amalgam of these competing and contradictory narratives.

This was strikingly demonstrated months into the heat of the 2016 presidential election, when Gallup sought to tap citizens' impressions of the candidates by asking them to describe what they "recall hearing or seeing" about Hillary Clinton and Donald Trump. Aggregation of the open-ended responses made clear that what was most prominently associated with Clinton was news about various email-related scandals, with anything resembling a policy position much less important. In contrast, citizens' recollections of what they had heard about Trump made clear that his central campaign policy positions on immigration and other issues had successfully been attached to him. Moreover, the authors noted, whereas "email" was consistently a defining element of the Clinton brand over months of study, impressions of Trump changed and varied as his campaign emphasized different things (Newport et al. 2016).

Attention and Branding in the Hybrid Media System

The diversification of political communication has added complexity to these processes and proliferated the spaces in which they take place. Likely the most consequential change here is the decentering of conventional news organizations, and especially newspapers, from their place as the focal points of political campaigns and primary mediator between candidates and the public. To be sure, news content produced by journalists remains the main material by which citizens become informed and make electoral decisions; this is a hybrid system in which conventional news organizations and the journalism they practice continue to play an enormous role (Chadwick 2013). But three points should be made: First, candidates now present themselves in social media, a route that both circumvents news media and provides material for it. Second, news content has become unbundled and dispersed through social media and other online channels, which now play central roles in informing citizens (Saldaña, McGregor, and Gil de Zúñiga 2015). Third, many other spaces, foremost social media, now offer platforms for public discussion about political campaigns (Hong and Nadler 2012).

Those social media conversations are multimodal, as they combine original citizen expressions with the sharing of content from news media and other social media networks (Thorson et al. 2013), and they potentially serve as important sources of the impressions citizens form of candidates. In an early study, Dimitrova and Bystrom (2013) pointed to the potential of social media to shape candidate impressions, showing some positive effects stemming from exposure to candidates' Facebook pages, but also noting that YouTube appeared to be a venue in which damaging content, for example about scandals, could spread and tarnish voters' impressions of candidates.

Candidates have seized, to interestingly differing degrees, the opportunities afforded by social media to project desirable associations (e.g., Walter and Ophir 2019). Much has been made of the innovations in digital media campaigning by Howard Dean and Barack Obama (e.g., Kreiss 2012); since Obama's pioneering use of the web and a custom campaigning tool in 2008, attention has turned to candidates' uses of social media. The relatively greater role played by social media in Donald Trump's 2016 campaign, and its close integration with major social media companies, has been described (Kreiss and McGregor 2017). Sahly et al. (2019) showed the distinctive uses to which Clinton and Trump put Twitter and Facebook, with Clinton's use being more professionalized and sanitized. They found that while Trump's use of Facebook was generally positive and similar to past campaigns, it was on Twitter that he embraced greater conflict and negativity—features that, indeed, spurred engagement on that platform. Studying the same topic, Lee and Xu (2018) similarly saw evidence of issue ownership in the topics Clinton and Trump chose to tweet about, suggesting that they aimed to strategically craft their (and their opponents') associations in the public mind.

In a complex media system, social media platforms and news media do not stand wholly apart; there are myriad intersections and interactions between these spaces (Vargo and Guo 2016). Within our specific scope here, there are important indications that different candidates may benefit to different degrees from these interactions. In an early study of these phenomena in the context of the 2008 Democratic primaries, Heim (2013) found that news media and one candidate's (Hillary Clinton's) press releases succeeded in setting the agendas of other information outlets, while political blogs tended to be in a follower role.

Most pertinent to the current discussion, social media also played an agenda-setting effect in the 2016 primaries: one piece of the puzzle of the disproportionate news media attention Trump received throughout those primaries was the media's focus—almost obsession—with the candidate's messages on Twitter. In comparison to leading Democratic candidates Hillary Clinton and Bernie Sanders, and his primary Republican challenger, Ted Cruz, only Trump had a consistent agenda-setting effect in which buzz about Trump on Twitter spurred subsequent coverage in a variety of news media. Notably, though both Clinton and Cruz saw substantially less engagement with their posts on Twitter, retweets of Sanders' messages were quantitatively comparable to Trump's, but they resulted in no increase in news media coverage for Sanders (Wells et al. 2020).

By contrast, in their analysis of the issues presented by news media and by candidates on their Twitter feeds during the 2016 primaries, Conway-Silva and colleagues (2017) find a variety of reciprocal relationships, highlighting the strongly interlinked nature of these media and parallel responses to evolving issues in the campaign. When it came to temporal influence, newspapers generally set the agenda of Twitter more than candidates' messages did, but the candidates did hold some sway, and in these cases it was Clinton and Sanders, more so than Trump and Cruz, who succeeded in influencing the news media agenda. This research agenda is further advanced in this volume: Wagner and Gainous (chapter 2) and Bentivegna, Marchetti, and Stanziano (chapter 6) both contribute to our understanding of politicians' ability to set news agendas via social media messages.

Notwithstanding these interactions, different platforms can present quite different discursive cultures, and there is mounting evidence that politicians indeed tailor their messaging to specific social media platforms (Stier et al. 2018). These possibilities spur our interest in how different impressions of candidates developed in different quadrants of the hybrid media system during the Democratic presidential primaries taking place in 2019.

Research Questions

Our interests led us to focus on two main research questions. The first concerns the strategic behavior of candidates' messaging through Twitter:

RQ1: What topics did the candidates themselves promote when they communicated through Twitter? How did the candidates vary in the topics they promoted?

288   Electoral Campaigns, Media, and the New World of Digital Politics

The second concerns the meanings assigned to candidates in terms of the topics their names were associated with:

RQ1: With what topics were the candidates of the primaries associated? How did topical association vary across platforms?

Method

To explore these questions, we gathered data about the major candidates of the 2020 Democratic primaries from four sources: the candidates' own Twitter posts via the Twitter timeline API; news articles from several dozen news media outlets via the news media collection Media Cloud; Twitter posts @-mentioning the candidates from Crimson Hexagon; and Reddit posts from an archive of Reddit postings.

Our timeframe was based in the "preprimary" period: though the precise timespans covered by our media platforms vary based on data availability, all of them begin in early 2019 and end in the fall of that year. This is thus the earliest phase of the primary process—the "invisible" primary during which an often large number of candidates strive to be noticed and to establish a brand identity that resonates with a substantial portion of their party's primary voters and influential leaders (Kenski and Filer 2018). Our sample of candidates was defined based on those who had been active in the summer and early fall of 2019: we consider seven of the candidates performing highest in the polls as of August 2019 in the case of candidates' own Twitter messages, and twelve from the same field in the case of the other datasets.

Twitter Timeline Data

To create an archive of the candidates' own tweets during the timeframe, in October 2019 we accessed Twitter's timeline API to collect the most recent 3,200 tweets from each of the candidates' Twitter handles.

News Media

When it came to news media, we set as our sampling frame the period January 1 to October 1, 2019. We searched MediaCloud, using the python wrapper, for articles that contained the mention of a candidate's name (our query required that both a candidate's full first and last name be present, but we allowed for common alternative forms, such as "Joe" instead of "Joseph" Biden) as well as the word "president," "election," or "candidate." We searched for articles from sixty-five news media outlets from across the political spectrum, all of which had "healthy" RSS feeds according to Media Cloud. In total, we collected 67,665 articles. (The news outlets were distributed across the political spectrum. We began with the top one hundred news sources as identified in Faris et al. 2017; after removing sources with poor coverage in Media Cloud and other quality issues, we ended with sixty-five.)

Twitter

We collected tweets mentioning the most-used Twitter handle of each of the candidates. This was meant to parallel our news media and Reddit collections, and consists of conversations "about" the candidates by any Twitter users who mentioned the candidates.

For the collection of tweets mentioning the candidates, we gathered messages between June 1 and October 16, 2019, from Crimson Hexagon. For each query, Crimson Hexagon allowed us to collect up to 10,000 tweets per day; when more than 10,000 tweets meet the search criteria on a given day, we returned a random sampling of tweets meeting our criteria. Our Twitter collection consisted of some sixty-seven million tweets.

Reddit

To locate conversations about the candidates on Reddit, we searched Reddit for the names of each of the fifteen Democratic presidential candidates active in 2019 and identified active subreddits dedicated to the candidates. Each result featuring the candidate's name was examined to verify that it was a subreddit based on supporting the candidate, leading to the exclusion of two subreddits.

Top-level posts made in each subreddit between January 1 and August 31, 2019, were collected from a repository of posts uploaded to Google's BigQuery service (Hoffa 2016). This included every new thread or top-level post, but not replies made to that post. After removing deleted posts and posts without texts, we worked with a dataset of 21,923 posts.

Topic Modeling

We took a parsimonious approach to operationalizing how candidates were presented across the media. Rooted conceptually in notions of candidate branding (Oates and Moe 2016) and second-level agenda-setting (e.g., Heim 2013), we used topic modeling of messages containing mentions of the candidates in an effort to capture the topics each candidate tended to be associated with.

More specifically, we used an unsupervised learning technique, Correlated Topic Modeling (Blei and Lafferty 2007) from the Structural Topic Modeling (stm) package in the R programming language (Roberts, Stewart, and Tingley 2014) to reveal the topics associated with each candidate in each dataset described above. Correlated Topic Modeling (CTM) builds on Latent Dirichlet allocation topic modeling, which has been widely applied in contexts of political communication. CTM allows topics in the model to correlate with each other, incorporating the underlying assumption that some topics may be more likely to cooccur than others in a sample (Blei and Lafferty 2007). We fit a separate topic model for each of the platforms— for Twitter, we fit the model on the @-mention dataset, then applied the model to the corpus of the candidates' own tweets. Within each, we used the Mimno and Lee (2014) algorithm built into the stm package to determine the appropriate number of topics; the algorithm selected solutions of 62, 63, and 61 topics for our news media, Twitter, and Reddit collections, respectively. For each medium, at least two team members manually assessed and named each topic, removed topics that were irrelevant to our study (e.g., topics characterized by punctuation symbols), and collapsed the topics into broader metatopical categories. (When we created the metatopics, we added together the model scores assigned to individual topics, at the message level.) On all the platforms, we found six key metatopics:

- *Policy* topics contained messages that clearly described one or more policy areas, and the candidates' position on them;
- *Horse race* topics tended to assess candidates' standing in the polls and likelihood of securing the nomination;
- *Action and Passion* topics contained expressions of personal passion for the candidates, often contained emotive and curse words, and exhorted supporters of a candidate to volunteer or otherwise take action;

- *Social Issues and Identity* topics contained references to ongoing issues of social justice, specific groups of people, and aspects of individual candidates' identities;
- *Candidate-specific* topics were groups of messages that shared the quality that they were dedicated to a single candidate; and
- *Meta-discussion* topics contained messages that commented on the broader nature of the political campaign, such as critiques of the media's role in the campaign and discussions about the nature of ideology in American politics.

Two further metatopics appeared in the news media and Twitter data, but not the Reddit data:

- *Impeachment/Ukraine* concerned the just-developing revelations of President Trump's phone call with Ukrainian president Volodymyr Zelensky, which was being investigated by Congress at the end of our data collection period; and
- *Scandals* involved discussions of scandals a candidate was involved in.

The presence of these topics in news media and Twitter, but not Reddit data, occurred likely as a result either of the generally more supportive nature of the Reddit communities, which were created to support their favored candidate, or of the fact that our Reddit data ended several weeks earlier (August 31) than the other collections (October 1/16), which captured a greater part of the period during which the Ukraine issue was gaining momentum.

Finally, two metatopics occurred only in the news media dataset:

- *Events* topics identified groups of stories that were about particular news events, but that did not include significant policy discourse or otherwise fit into a different metatopic (for example, news articles about the mass shooting in El Paso in August 2019); and
- *Pop Culture/SNL* topics concerned articles about the candidates' appearances and portrayals in pop culture venues, mostly Saturday Night Live.

Results

Attention to Candidates across News Media, Twitter, and Reddit

We begin by laying out the descriptive terrain in terms of the relative attention devoted to the candidates in 2019. Figure 14.1 presents the portion of all posts collected, by medium, that mentioned each candidate. (Here we are not yet looking at candidates' own posts but the posts *about* them.) We see comparability in the patterns of attention to candidates in news media and on Twitter. In both cases, candidates leading in the polls (Biden, Warren, and Sanders), as well as Buttigieg and Harris, receive the lion's share of attention, while other candidates trail—illustrating again the chicken-and-the-egg difficulty for lesser-known candidates in drawing coverage.

Reddit, meanwhile, presents an attention profile rather detached from that of news media. Posts on Sanders-related subreddits dominate by a factor of two over its closest follower, Yang, who in turn stands well above all others. It is clearly the case that on the Reddit platform there is a very different candidate agenda from that of the mass media, and that it is dominated by a couple of candidates with loyal, young followings. Strikingly, Biden, the eventual winner of the nomination, is nearly last in Reddit attention, with only 1,499 posts in our data collection. (This pattern changed somewhat after our data collection ended as Biden became the presumptive nominee.)

Topics Promoted by Candidates' Twitter Handles

Figure 14.2 presents the prevalence of topics in each of our data collections. To address our first research question, let us focus for the moment on the set of bars on the far left: the prevalence of topics in tweets produced by the candidates' own handles. It is immediately striking, including in comparison to the topics of our other data collections, that candidates' own posts were overwhelmingly focused on policy issues. This is especially interesting given recent discussions (noted by Taras, this volume) suggesting that attack-style campaigning had become a dominant pattern in American elections. At least at this stage of the primary we see quite the opposite from the candidates.

Consulting the underlying data confirms that the candidates were predominantly using their Twitter platforms to articulate policy positions they thought Democratic voters would respond to. To illustrate, here is Cory Booker on September 30, connecting a specific policy issue to citizens' lives and making a commitment about it: "43 years ago, the House passed the

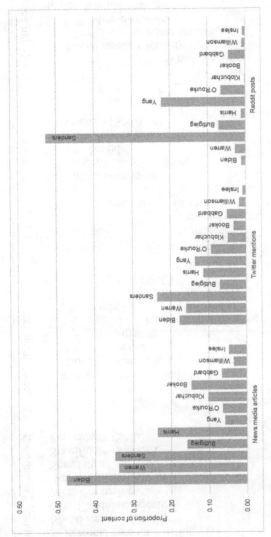

Figure 14.1. Presence of candidates within primary election content of three media platforms
Note: Bars in the news media and Twitter groups sum to more than 1 because of the presence of multiple candidate names in some messages.

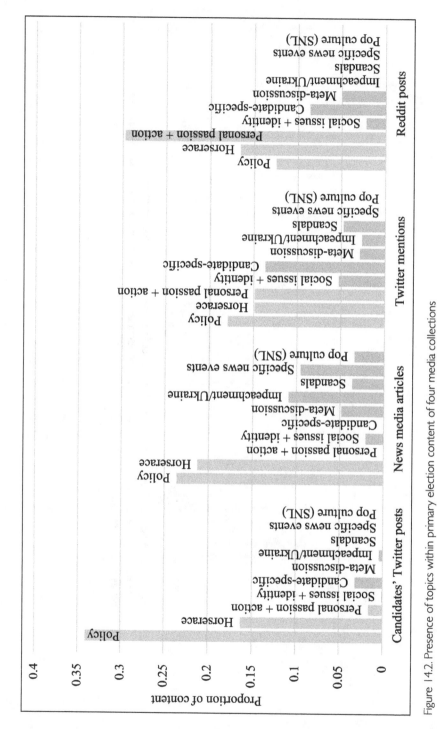

Figure 14.2. Presence of topics within primary election content of four media collections

Note: Bars within each medium do not sum to 1 because of the removal of meaningless topics in the data cleaning process.

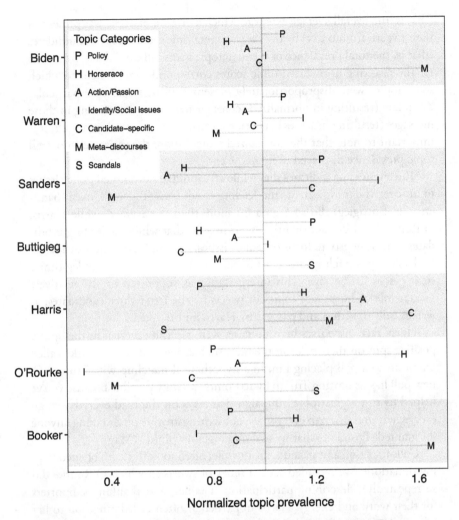

Figure 14.3. Normalized prevalence of topics in tweets from the candidates' Twitter accounts
Note: Topics related to the Ukraine/impeachment issue have been removed.

Hyde Amendment for the first time, denying federal Medicaid coverage of abortion to millions—many of them low-income and people of color. As president, I will fight to end the assault on reproductive health, including the repeal of Hyde [link]"

To further develop our understanding of these patterns, consider figure 14.3. The figure shows a normalized score, for each metatopic for each candidate. This is calculated by dividing each candidates' average topic score (that is, the overall average extent to which a given metatopic was present in their tweets, from 0 to 1) by the average metatopic score across all candidates (that is, the total prevalence of the metatopic across all candidates, from 0 to 1). The resulting normalized topic scores correspond to the extent to which some topics were disproportionately presented in messages by a particular candidate (resulting in normalized scores greater than 1) or missing in those messages (resulting in scores between 0 and 1), with an overall mean of 1. It is important to note that the normalized scores ignore the variation in overall topic prevalence displayed in figure 14.2.

Thus figure 14.3 indicates that while *all* candidates promoted policy issues to an overwhelming extent, the leading candidates (Biden, Warren, Sanders, and Buttigieg) did so even a bit more than the average, while Harris, O'Rourke, and Booker slightly less. It may be that while the leading candidates were at liberty to focus on policy issues, the candidates just outside the leadership group felt greater need to engage in other discourses to legitimize their places in the race. This interpretation is supported by the relatively greater role of horse race topics in tweets by the latter three candidates, as well as calls to action and passion by Harris and Booker.

Horse race discourses by candidates were typically present as they put a positive spin on their place in the race, such as when Beto O'Rourke called attention to a poll placing him in a hypothetical matchup with Trump: "A new poll has us beating Trump by 10 points. It's only possible because you've helped us run a grassroots campaign that stays on the road everyday to go everywhere and listen to everyone—not writing anyone off or taking anyone for granted. Proud of what we're doing together [link]" (May 5).

Calls to action and passion, meanwhile, often took the form of encouraging donations (we recorded several series of tweets in which O'Rourke did so repeatedly), describing participation at rallies, and thanking supporters for their work and energy. Harris in particular often called attention to her rallies and the people attending them, as, for example, on June 10 when she posted, "Grateful to everyone who took time out of their Sunday to attend our town hall in Waterloo last night. No matter your party affiliation, you are welcome in our campaign [link]."

Even when other topic categories did appear, they were regularly paired with mentions either of specific policy or at the least issues that could be traced to a policy area. In a message containing both identity/social issue topics and policy content, on October 8 Buttigieg posted: "All Americans should have the freedom to live and work without discrimination. Today, the Supreme Court will hear three cases that challenge that basic right for LGBTQ+ people. We deserve a Court that sees everyone and rules in favor of equality—for our generation and the next."

Bernie Sanders's account was notable in this respect, scoring the very highest on topics related to identity and social issues. This appears to be a product of his regular reference to named categories of people as he promoted his policy positions, as well as his practice of retweeting supporters who identified themselves as members of a particular group, such as this retweet on October 1: "As an undocumented woman, it's been hard to find a candidate that has truly ever fought for people like me. I'm so proud to say @BernieSanders has never made me doubt we had his support. I trust him and so does the majority of our country regardless of party #UnidosCon-Bernie [link]."

In sum, our evidence strongly suggests a powerful, nearly overwhelming role of policy discourses in the Twitter activity of the candidates. Other topics were present, sometimes to comment on the state of the race, but often to add context to policy positions.

Topics Prevalent in News Media, Twitter Candidate Mentions, and Reddit

But how did candidates' own tweets exist in the wider ecosystem of the campaign? And with what topics were the candidates associated in others' conversations? To address this second research question, let us return to figure 14.2 and consult the other three sets of bars, which reveal the topics present in messages from news media, Twitter mentioners, and Reddit posts about the candidates.

Scholars of political media will not be surprised to see that discussions of policy and the campaign horse race are the modal topics of news media coverage of the candidates—though they may be pleasantly surprised to see that policy discussions slightly edge horse race content. The news media also devoted considerable coverage to the Ukraine/impeachment scandal, which was emerging at the end of our study period—indicative of the powerful draw exerted by Trump even on the Democratic primaries, as well as Biden's indirect involvement in the underlying scandal.

Within our collection of tweets mentioning the candidates, policy and horse race coverage are also important. But in Twitter mentions, those topics are joined by action and personal passion and candidate-specific topics. Topics in the former category contained messages that used a great deal of emotive words related to love and hate; one topic was primarily made of tweets offering profuse thanks to candidates, and another was testimonials about meeting a candidate. Others were negative; a couple stood out for their disproportionate use of curse words. Clearly, this is a space citizens are using (much more so than candidates and journalists) to express emotion, hatred, and bad language (cf. Papacharissi 2014).

The patterns on Reddit display even greater divergence from the elite discourses of candidates and news media. There the personal action and passion frames are the most frequent—on Reddit, these topics often articulate ways to take action to support a candidate, through phone banking or volunteering. Notably, on Reddit we found the greatest prevalence of "meta-discourses," which were often complex and involved discussions of ideology—for example, the role of socialism in the American left coalition.

Candidate-Topic Associations in News Media, Twitter, and Reddit

Finally, we turn to the question of how candidate-topic associations varied across the platforms. Figures 14.4–14.6 present normalized scores, as in figure 14.3, by platform: figure 14.4 shows the associations in news media, figure 14.5 on Twitter, and figure 14.6 on Reddit.

Once again paralleling figures 14.1 and 14.2, the results indicate significant comparability between the discussion of candidates in the press (figure 3) and about the candidates on Twitter (figure 14.4). Note that to facilitate interpretation, in both figures we have removed one group of topics, related to Ukraine and the first impeachment of Donald Trump, that were associated with Biden but not other candidates to a degree that distorted the plots.

Even removing the Ukraine topic, however, we see that topics associated with Biden were disproportionately ones related to scandal, especially in Twitter topic mentions, though the presence of scandals was just slightly more present than average in articles about Biden in news media coverage as well. Thus, in something of an echo of front-runner Hillary Clinton before him, the Ukraine scandal and other scandals (mostly discussions of Biden's treatment of women and his role in the Anita Hill hearings) formed an important part of news media coverage of Biden, and especially Twitter discussion of him. The generally scandal-oriented mentions of Biden on Twitter may also be a reflection of the strength of public support for Sanders and Yang on Twitter, noted above, though here we are not able to test this possibility.

Our results for news media and Twitter indicate rather comparable treatment of Warren and Sanders. Both saw somewhat more than average coverage in terms of policy issues and meta-commentary, with most of the latter consisting of discussions of ideology and socialism in particular. Both were relatively little covered in terms of scandals, and it is notable here that War-

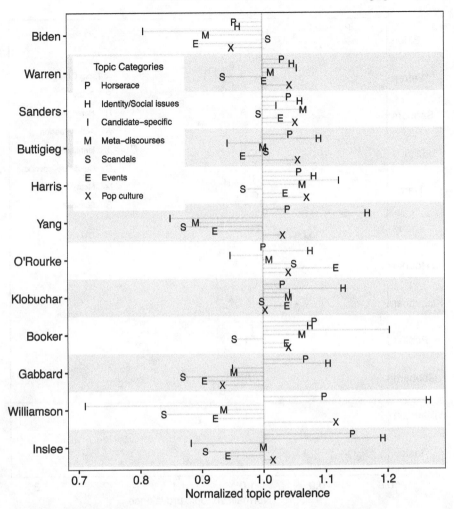

Figure 14.4. Normalized prevalence of topics in news media articles mentioning the candidates
Note: Topics related to the Ukraine/impeachment issue have been removed.

ren's past self-association with Native American ancestry did not emerge as a strong scandal in either platform's discussions of her. Warren's Native American ancestry was mentioned on Twitter, but because much of this discourse did not seem critical or relate to a scandal, we categorized it as related to identity and social issues, which indeed stand out for both Warren and Sanders.

In general, the other candidates in the field saw relatively high levels of coverage in terms of the horse race, in both news media and on Twitter.

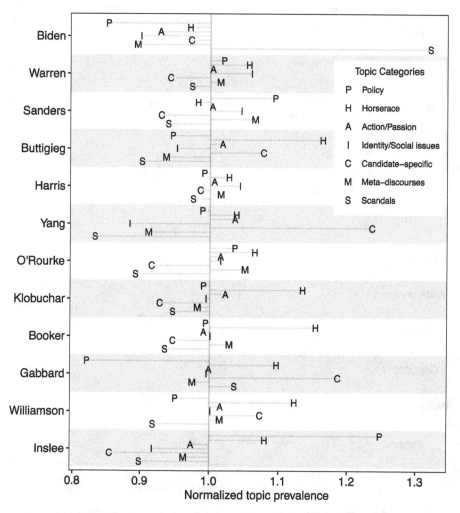

Figure 14.5. Normalized prevalence of topics in tweets mentioning accounts of the candidates

Note: Topics related to the Ukraine/impeachment issue have been removed.

This was a result of their names occurring relatively more often in general discussions of the campaign, who was leading in the polls, and relatively less coverage of other aspects of their candidacies—and presents an interesting comparison with their own communications, which were similarly weighted toward the horse race topic.

A couple of candidates' brands, however, broke through in different ways. Pete Buttigieg seemed able to attract attention unique to his candidacy—

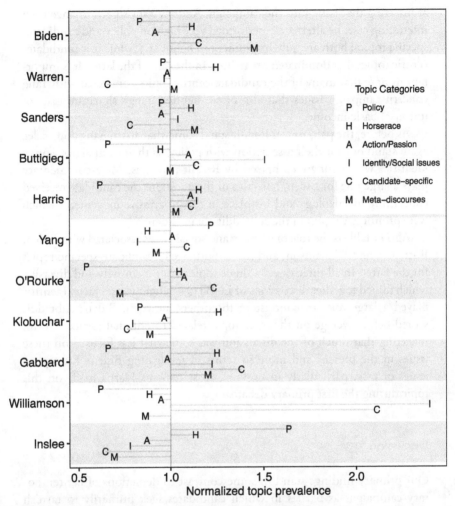

Figure 14.6. Normalized prevalence of topics in subreddits dedicated to the candidates

reflected in quite high levels of candidate-specific discussions in both media. Kamala Harris saw relatively large coverage of her identity and social issues, reflective of her leading role as an African American and woman in the race. We saw similar associations of Cory Booker with identity and social issue topics, for similar reasons. As noted in figure 14.1, however, overall Booker was relatively little mentioned on Twitter.

In a different vein, Jay Inslee's name was strongly associated with policy, a reflection of his campaign's singular focus on climate change—and success at inserting that issue into the campaign. Andrew Yang's performance is an interesting case: he alternately performed very high on policy and candidate-specific topics; both are quite prominent in figure 14.3, while it is candidate-centric topics that dominated on Twitter. In the case of the latter, it is important to note that many of the candidate-centric topics connected with Yang concern campaign issues that also often mention Yang's signature issue of universal basic income.

As before, the patterns on Reddit stand somewhat apart. Yang and Inslee again stand out for their association with policy, as their campaign's wonky identities were strongly embraced by Reddit partisans. Meta-commentary plays a large role for Biden, reflective of the questions the candidate received concerning his ideology and his place in the progressive movement, which were prominent topics in the subreddit about Biden.

Also notable is the role of identity and social issues associated with Biden, Buttigieg, and Williamson, and the importance of candidate-specific topics for the latter. In all three cases, a single topic about inclusivity and diversity, which folded together discussions of LGBTQ+, religious, and racial identity, played a large role. In contrast to the others, however, Biden's subreddit scored below average on the issue topic related to criminal justice reform, reflecting that much of the discussion was somewhat less focused on these issues in the present and more in terms of relitigating Biden's history on issues of race, particularly in response to statements Harris made on this topic during the first primary debate.

Discussion

Our primary findings stand in some contrast to depictions of contemporary campaigns as battles in which candidates seek primarily to tarnish one another's images while invoking divisive identities among potential supporters (Kreiss and McGregor, this volume). At least in their Twitter communications during the first two-thirds of 2019, the candidates for the Democratic presidential nomination messaged, often and repeatedly, about policy issues. Matters of identity, the horse race, personal passion, and scandals were not absent, but they were much less frequently invoked—and often in the context of discussions (or perhaps more aptly, proclamations) of policy positions.

In comparing our work to Kreiss and McGregor's chapter, one of the closest points of contrast in this volume, it is important to note some differences of approach. Our focus was narrowly on candidate communications on Twitter, a highly public medium in which targeting by identity group, such as they describe, is not greatly enabled. Consequently, we might not expect to see the sorts of targeting made possible by targeting niche media or using other social media, such as Facebook, to tailor messages to particular categories of people. Still it was notable that in this very public, and seemingly influential forum, the campaigns were strongly focused on policy messaging.

Further, our study period—the earliest phase of the primaries—may incline candidates toward more substantive, and less combative, communications. Many of the candidates in the early stages may be aware that they are unlikely to win the nomination themselves, and thus calibrate their communications with future opportunities and alliances in mind. At the same time, in line with Kreiss and McGregor, some candidates are likely to embrace attacks on other candidates if they anticipate such attacks will drive coverage and win support from key publics. As American presidential primary processes become ever longer, further study of the evolution of communications during primaries may be fruitful.

Of course, the candidates hardly have control over the overarching narratives of the campaign, or even of their own candidacies. Our broad overview approach allows us to see that news media coverage of the candidates focused only slightly less on policy, as well as the horse race of the campaign. (Though when considering relative coverage of individual candidates, we do see a preference in the news media for scandal coverage over policy.) It was average social media users—on Twitter, and even more on Reddit, who were more inclined toward discussions of topics unrelated to policy; though much of what we saw there was also *substantive*: about the ideological differences between the candidates and how they fit into the American political landscape (our meta-discursive topics, salient on Reddit) and calls to political engagement and the support of favored candidates (the action/passion topics).

Indeed, our results reveal, first, that publics discussing politics on social media do have rather different agendas than candidates and the news media, and second, that the degree of correspondence to those elite agendas varies. In general, we saw that conversations on Twitter more closely resembled the messaging of candidates and news media agendas than those of Reddit—surely no surprise to those familiar with Twitter's important role as both a source and dissemination site for mainstream journalism. Reddit, meanwhile, appeared to foster a space in which rather different kinds of conversations could happen: more meta-discussion about ideology, spaces for online organizing, and so on. Our Reddit data also confirm the presence of

304   Electoral Campaigns, Media, and the New World of Digital Politics

relatively cloistered publics that may be dedicated and very active on the part of certain candidates—in 2019, it was Sanders and Yang that enjoyed this support. However, the history of the campaign, as well as the topics documented here, suggest the limited political impact of even very active communities in these spaces. Future research may want to articulate the conditions under which such publics exert greater influence on the wider polity.

We might describe our results as portraying a diffuse public sphere, but one that is differentially diffuse: at the center of the political discussion, mainstream candidates and the news media articulate a particular profile of topics, which evolves and takes on a different tenor as one moves away from the center of gravity and toward publics on the fringes of discussion (i.e., Reddit). And they point to the need for greater attention to the different kinds of meanings attached to political objects in different communities, and underscores the strategic challenges faced by candidates seeking to project a positive image to a diversity of publics.

For candidates' social media communications, the lesson here may be that the meaning(s) of political campaigns are now developed in multiple places and operate in different ways. While we have emphasized that candidates enjoy far from comprehensive control of narratives about their campaigns, we should also highlight the importance of candidates developing multifaceted social media strategies and embracing the unique qualities of different media—and the unique publics that inhabit them.

References

Blei, David M., and John D. Lafferty. 2007. "A Correlated Topic Model of Science." *Annals of Applied Statistics* 1(1): 17–35. https://doi.org/10.1214/07-AOAS114

Chadwick, Andrew. 2013. *The Hybrid Media System: Politics and Power.* Oxford: Oxford University Press.

Conway-Silva, Bethany A., Christine R. Filer, Kate Kenski, and Eric Tsetsi. 2017. "Reassessing Twitter's Agenda-Building Power: An Analysis of Intermedia Agenda-Setting Effects During the 2016 Presidential Primary Season." *Social Science Computer Review*, July, 0894439317715430. https://doi.org/10.1177/0894439317715430

Dimitrova, Daniela V., and Dianne Bystrom. 2013. "The Effects of Social Media on Political Participation and Candidate Image Evaluations in the 2012 Iowa Caucuses." *American Behavioral Scientist* 57(11): 1568–83. https://doi.org/10.1177/00 02764213489011

Dowdle, Andrew J., Randall E. Adkins, Karen Sebold, and Wayne P. Steger. 2021. "Fundamentals Matter: Forecasting the 2020 Democratic Presidential Nomination." *PS: Political Science & Politics* 54(1): 41–46. https://doi.org/10.1017/ S1049096520001006

Faris, Robert, Hal Roberts, Bruce Etling, Nikki Bourassa, Ethan Zuckerman, and Yochai Benkler. 2017. "Partisanship, Propaganda and Disinformation: Online Media and the 2016 Presidential Election." August 16. Berkman Klein Center for Internet and Society. https://cyber.harvard.edu/publications/2017/08/mediacloud

Heim, Kyle. 2013. "Framing the 2008 Iowa Democratic Caucuses: Political Blogs and Second-Level Intermedia Agenda Setting." *Journalism & Mass Communication Quarterly* 90(3): 500–19. https://doi.org/10.1177/1077699013493785

Hoffa, Felipe. 2016. "1.7 Billion Reddit Comments Loaded on BigQuery." Reddit Post. www.reddit.com/r/bigquery/comments/3cej2b/17_billion_reddit_commen ts_loaded_on_bigquery/

Kang, Taewoo, Erika Franklin Fowler, Michael M. Franz, and Travis N. Ridout. 2018. "Issue Consistency? Comparing Television Advertising, Tweets, and E-mail in the 2014 Senate Campaigns." *Political Communication* 35(1): 32–49.

Kenski, Kate, and Christine R. Filer. 2018. "Themes in Candidate Messaging on Twitter during the 'Invisible' Presidential Primary." In *The Presidency and Social Media: Discourse, Disruption and Digital Democracy in the 2016 Presidential Election*, edited by Dan Schill and John Allen Hendricks, 158–73. New York: Routledge.

Kreiss, Daniel. 2012. *Taking Our Country Back: The Crafting of Networked Politics from Howard Dean to Barack Obama*. New York: Oxford University Press.

Kreiss, Daniel, and Shannon C. McGregor. 2017. "Technology Firms Shape Political Communication: The Work of Microsoft, Facebook, Twitter, and Google with Campaigns during the 2016 U.S. Presidential Cycle." *Political Communication* 35(2): 155–77. https://doi.org/10.1080/10584609.2017.1364814

Lee, Jayeon, and Weiai Xu. 2018. "The More Attacks, the More Retweets: Trump's and Clinton's Agenda Setting on Twitter." *Public Relations Review* 44(2): 201–13. https://doi.org/10.1016/j.pubrev.2017.10.002

Mimno, David, and Moontae Lee. 2014. "Low-Dimensional Embeddings for Interpretable Anchor-Based Topic Inference." In *Proceedings of the 2014 Conference on Empirical Methods in Natural Language Processing (EMNLP)*, 1319–28. Association for Computational Linguistics. https://doi.org/10.3115/v1/D14-1138

Newport, Frank, Lisa Singh, Stuart Soroka, Michael Traugott, and Andrew Dugan. 2016. "'Email' Dominates What Americans Have Heard About Clinton." Gallup.com (blog). September 19. https://news.gallup.com/poll/195596/email-dominates-americans-heard-clinton.aspx

Norrander, Barbara. 2006. "The Attrition Game: Initial Resources, Initial Contests and the Exit of Candidates during the US Presidential Primary Season." *British Journal of Political Science* 36(3): 487–507.

Oates, Sarah, and Wendy W. Moe. 2016. "Donald Trump and the 'Oxygen of Publicity': Branding, Social Media, and Mass Media in the 2016 Presidential Primary Elections." Paper presented at *The American Political Science Association Annual Meeting, Rochester, NY, August 25, 2016*. https://papers.ssrn.com/abstract=2830195

Papacharissi, Zizi. 2014. *Affective Publics: Sentiment, Technology and Politics*. New York: Oxford University Press.

Patterson, Thomas E. 2016. "News Coverage of the 2016 Presidential Primaries: Horse Race Reporting Has Consequences." *Shorenstein Center* (blog). July 11. http://shorensteincenter.org/news-coverage-2016-presidential-primaries/

Perrin, Andrew, and Monica Anderson. 2019. "Share of U.S. Adults Using Social Media, Including Facebook, Is Mostly Unchanged since 2018." Pew Research Center. April 10. https://www.pewresearch.org/fact-tank/2019/04/10/share-of-u-s-adults-using-social-media-including-facebook-is-mostly-unchanged-since-2018/

Roberts, Margaret E., Brandon M. Stewart, and Dustin Tingley. 2014. "STM: R Package for Structural Topic Models." *Journal of Statistical Software* 10(2): 1–40.

Sahly, Abdulsamad, Chun Shao, and K. Hazel Kwon. 2019. "Social Media for Political Campaigns: An Examination of Trump's and Clinton's Frame Building and Its Effect on Audience Engagement." *Social Media + Society* 5(2): 2056305119855141. https://doi.org/10.1177/2056305119855141

Saldaña, Magdalena, Shannon C. McGregor, and Homero Gil de Zúñiga. 2015. "European Public Sphere | Social Media as a Public Space for Politics: Cross-National Comparison of News Consumption and Participatory Behaviors in the United States and the United Kingdom." *International Journal of Communication* 9: 3304–26.

Stier, Sebastian, Arnim Bleier, Haiko Lietz, and Markus Strohmaier. 2018. "Election Campaigning on Social Media: Politicians, Audiences, and the Mediation of Political Communication on Facebook and Twitter." *Political Communication* 35(1): 50–74. https://doi.org/10.1080/10584609.2017.1334728

Stromer-Galley, Jennifer. 2014. *Presidential Campaigning in the Internet Age.* Oxford Studies in Digital Politics. Oxford: Oxford University Press.

Swearingen, C. Douglas. 2019. "Laying the Foundation for a Successful Presidential Campaign: Public Attention and Fundraising in the Preprimary Period." *Social Science Quarterly* 100(4): 1308–21. https://doi.org/10.1111/ssqu.12631

Thorson, Kjerstin, Kevin Driscoll, Brian Ekdale, Stephanie Edgerly, Liana Gamber Thompson, Andrew Schrock, Lana Swartz, Emily K. Vraga, and Chris Wells. 2013. "Youtube, Twitter and the Occupy Movement." *Information, Communication & Society* 16(3): 421–51. https://doi.org/10.1080/1369118X.2012.756051

Vargo, Chris J., and Lei Guo. 2016. "Networks, Big Data, and Intermedia Agenda Setting: An Analysis of Traditional, Partisan, and Emerging Online U.S. News." *Journalism & Mass Communication Quarterly*, December, 1077699016679976. https://doi.org/10.1177/1077699016679976

Walter, Dror, and Yotam Ophir. 2019. "The Elephant and the Bird: Republican Candidates' Use of Strategy and Issue Framing in Twitter During the 2016 Republican Presidential Primaries." *International Journal of Communication* 13: 4960–82.

Wells, Chris, Dhavan Shah, Josephine Lukito, Ayellet Pelled, Jon C. W. Pevehouse, and JungHwan Yang. 2020. "Trump, Twitter, and News Media Responsiveness: A Media Systems Approach." *New Media & Society* 22(4): 659–82. https://doi.org/10.1177/1461444819893987

Conclusion

Richard Davis

Do social media affect electoral campaigns and even democratic systems today? Pundits will offer an answer to that question—usually in hyperbolic terms. Certainly, social media operatives will claim significant effects—to make money. But what is the evidence? Our purpose in compiling this volume was to provide evidence to answer that question. By engaging a group of scholars who were experts in a variety of political/media systems around the world and therefore could tell us what impact social media had on electoral campaigns in the regions they studied, we hoped to provide an answer to questions about what effects these new media forms are having on elections and democracy.

Their response, not surprisingly, was far from uniform. On the one hand, some of our chapter authors discovered significant impacts by social media platforms. For example, Francisco Brandao and Larisa Doroschenko found that populist leaders employed social media to reshape an electoral outcome in recent elections in Brazil and Ukraine, respectively. Presidential candidates Bolsonaro and Zelensky utilized social media to engage voters and ultimately won their respective presidencies. Neither author claims that social media alone caused the election of these respective candidates. But they do demonstrate how social media contributed substantially to that outcome.

On the other hand, Martin Ndlela drew an opposite conclusion about social media in Kenya's electoral process. Social media use only attracts a relatively small segment of the population and plays a similarly minor role in elections at this time. Correspondingly, Sara Bentevigna and Rita Marchetti concluded that traditional media remain dominant in Italian elections. As did Rosalynd Southern in her study of memes in the United Kingdom.

Memes were present in the U.K. campaign, Southern determined, but they played only a minor role in an election that still featured the dominance of traditional media.

Somewhere in the middle between these two extremes are the findings of several chapter authors that social media forums are playing a role in some aspects of campaigning. They concluded that, short of affecting electoral outcomes, social media are causing more subtle effects. Those effects may not seem so dramatic, but they do suggest that social media are becoming integrated into campaign strategies and are altering the way parties and candidates communicate with voters.

One example is social media's role in voter targeting. Microtargeting has become a vital element of many campaigns as candidates and parties seek to identify individual voter concerns based on interest and demography rather than geography. The development of big data and the implications for campaigning have been termed the "fourth era" of political campaigning, following personal contact and party organization role, televised campaigns, and then an era dominated by the Internet.[1] Unlike broadcast media forms (print magazines and newspapers as well as traditional broadcast television and radio), social media drill down to the individual level with media messages. As a consequence, messages can be finely tuned to relatively small groups of voters based on demographics, interests, behavior, and geographical location. As Kreiss and McGregor find, campaigns tailor their usage of social media to identify groups of voters most responsive to their messages. For candidates and parties, a tool that can "slice and dice" voter lists into small bits and appeal directly to voters' narrow interests has the potential to enhance candidate communication with highly disparate voters.

However, there is a potential downside. This capability will enhance identity politics as candidates and parties craft exclusive messages for particular groups of voters. Is this all that different from a century or more ago when candidates would give different versions of a speech as they traveled from one hamlet to another without concern that one group would learn about their distinctive, and perhaps contrasting, appeal to another group? In a sense, it is. The cleavages are not so much over geography today as they are race, ethnicity, gender, sexual orientation, religion, etc. These identity messages reach individuals who live in the same city, neighborhood, and next door to each other. Does a social media forum like Facebook, Instagram, or Pinterest contribute to a further political divide even among those who are physically proximate to each other?

---

1. Andrea Roemmele and Rachel Gibson, "Scientific and Subversive: The Two Faces of the Fourth Era of Political Campaigning," *New Media and Society*, 22 (2020): 595–610.

Another effect is the impact of social media on the general political discourse of a campaign. A recurring charge concerning social media has been its tendency to promote extremist rhetoric.[2] According to Michael Keren, the 2020 Israeli election is another example of the growing strength and agenda-setting power of social media. Wishing to ensure that his main rivals, the Blue and White Party and the Arab Joint List, would not come together to form a coalition government, Likud's Benjamin Netanyahu used social media to attack and delegitimize the leaders of the Joint List by depicting them as traitors and supporters of terror.

Keren concludes that social media messages have coarsened political debate by appealing to a particular base that hungers for extremist rhetoric that legitimizes their darkest fears. Opponents are enemies and scorched earth social media campaigns are employed to mobilize a base to support their party's candidate. Keren worries that the entire well of Israeli politics has been poisoned.

At the same time, Kaitlynn Mendes and Diretman Dikwal-Bot came to a somewhat contrasting conclusion about feminist politicians' use of social media. They discovered that feminist politicians were reluctant to rely on social media to address women's issues. Their analysis of Canadian Prime Minister Justin Trudeau and London Mayor Sadiq Khan during the 2015 and 2019 Canadian federal elections and the 2016 London mayoral race concluded that both politicians used traditional media more than social media to espouse their profeminist credentials and advocacy. They speculate that Trudeau and Khan may have worried that too much profeminist advocacy on social media could have ignited a firestorm of reaction and factchecking, not least by feminists, and it would have detracted from their main campaign messages. They conclude that where the feminist movement has seen opportunity with social media, profeminist political leaders vying in elections have seen danger.

According to Heather Evans, gender may matter in a candidate's approach to social media. Evans found that female congressional candidates did use Twitter to express their positions on women's issues more so than male candidates in the 2016 and 2018 U.S. congressional elections. While Evans does not analyze whether discussing women's issues correlated with winning or gaining votes, 2018 proved to be a bountiful year for electing women to Congress.

---

2. See, for example, Andrew Marantz, *Anti-Social: Online Extremists, Techno-Utopians, and the Hijacking of the American Conversation*, New York: Random House, 2019; and Siva Vaidhyanathan, *Antisocial Media: How Facebook Disconnects Us and Undermines Democracy*, New York: Oxford University Press, 2018.

One question regarding effects is what type of candidate—insider or outsider—is benefited more by social media. As mentioned earlier, Brandao and Doroschenko concluded that social media aided populist outsider candidates. Similarly, Evans found that Twitter was a particularly potent platform for "outsider" Congressional candidates in the United States because of its low cost; its popularity among a younger, more educated, and more affluent audience; and its ability to narrowcast and target messages.

The answer from Brian Budd and Tamara Small was quite different, however. Their examination of Maxime Bernier and his newly formed People's Party of Canada found that the party's extensive email campaign intended to mobilize Canadian voters with messages of populism and nativism flopped ignominiously. They concluded that, although email campaigns can be effective for rallying supporters, fundraising, and voter mobilization, they are not necessarily effective in converting voters.

Context matters as well, including the concerns of the electorate, the candidates in the campaign, or parties competing that particular year, as well as the campaign messages conveyed. For example, despite the frenetic email campaign that appealed to discontent over Canada's immigration policy and with the power of traditional elites, Maxime Bernier proved to be the wrong person, with the wrong message at the wrong time. Canada's two-party system (with two additional minor parties), the media's focus on the main contenders, a political consensus around reducing social inequalities, and Bernier's quirky reputation meant that voters barely paid attention to his new message. By comparison, political instability was high in both Brazil and Ukraine, including widespread dissatisfaction with the status quo. Moreover, both Zelensky and Bolsonaro communicated resonating messages and embodied those messages in a manner that appealed to voters.

Social media integration is occurring at some level in each of the systems discussed in this book. Moreover, that integration is expanding over time. Nevertheless, the process of assimilating social media into traditional campaigns by parties and candidates has initially been quite rocky.

Uta Russmann's study of Austrian political parties' usage of social media found that adaptation by the political parties was not necessarily smooth. Political parties had to hire staff to monitor social media forums to avoid inappropriate messages emanating from the party's platforms. The openness of social media offered challenges for political parties accustomed to unidirectional communication as well as complete control of the campaign message.

Brandao's discussion of the Bolsonaro campaign also illustrates that tension over central message control versus decentralization and more diverse messages from supporters. The Bolsonaro campaign invited users to join the campaign by creating a myriad of hashtags on which they could post. They allowed volunteers to download campaign materials that they could distribute on their own and encouraged people to express their support for the campaign through their own personal stories. As Doroschenko pointed out, the Zelensky campaign similarly offered supporters an opportunity to contribute to the campaign through their social media accounts.

Yet another more subtle effect is the social media relationship with the traditional journalistic community. Several chapters noted the preeminence of traditional media, even in a digital age. Admittedly, we are still early in that digital age, and time will tell whether traditional media can hold their own in the contest for eyeballs. Evidence suggests that some media already are losing. As Bentevigna, Marchetti, and Stanziano found, print media have fallen behind digital news sources in usage by Italians.

But several of our chapter authors found that rather than social media displacing traditional media, the two seem to have achieved some measure of coexistence. In Canada, as Waddell notes, journalists facing massive budget cuts have come to rely on social media as easy news sources about campaigns, although this development presents its own problems for the tone of campaign reporting. Wagner and Gainous find that social media rely extensively on traditional media for content. A symbiosis seems to have developed that leads both traditional and social media to depend on each other as information sources.

Nor is it the case that all social media have played equal roles in campaigning. Uta Russmann's chapter on social media role in Austrian elections found growing use of two social media platforms—Facebook and Instagram. Interestingly, she concluded Twitter has declined in popularity to the point where it has become irrelevant in Austrian elections.

What can we conclude about the extent of social media's role? If this sounds like a "on the one hand, but on the other hand" kind of conclusion, that shouldn't be surprising because it is. Our conclusion is that it all depends.

The political environment in which messages are transmitted matter. That includes the nature of the political system, the role of traditional media, the events of the particular election, as well as the candidates and parties themselves. In a volatile political environment, such as Brazil, social media may be able to break through the traditional media dominance and gain traction as a forum equivalent to the traditional media. As well, as an emerging democracy, Ukraine has not developed lasting traditional political organizations that may mitigate the role of social media. However, a more politically stable campaign environment, such as in the United States, the United Kingdom, and Canada, may make such a development less likely.

Clearly, social media have become a component of electioneering. That applies across a variety of settings where democratic elections occur. Candidates and parties are utilizing various forms of social media to reach voters. In turn, at least some set of voters is paying attention to social media election messages, even in systems where traditional media dominate the communication process.

However, it is important to remember that this book is an essential snapshot in time. Several authors concluded that change is in the wind. Rosalynd Southern forecasts that political campaigners in the United Kingdom are likely to become more "GIF-able," more savvy, and increasingly innovative about the use of social media in the future. Memes will grow in usage and effect. Similarly, Uta Russmann discovered that the Austrian political parties' employment of social media had been magnified over time, predicting that future elections would witness further integration into the campaign landscape. Kreiss and McGregor suggest the growth in usage of social media that will affect identity politics in future U.S. elections.

Yet questions remain about that future. One question concerns the growth of social media's role if political systems become increasingly volatile. Instability may enhance the power of social media forums since traditional political leaders and organizations will lose their respected positions vis-à-vis voters. Populist leaders from Donald Trump in the United States to Boris Johnson in the United Kingdom or Jair Bolsonaro in Brazil use antielite messages disparaging established political figures and organizations to curry popular support.[3] Will this trend spread across democratic societies, thus accelerating reliance on social media?

Yet another question concerns the future relationship between traditional journalism and social media. While the number of users of Facebook, Instagram, Twitter, and so on has exploded in the past decade or so, traditional media sources have faced the opposite phenomenon. That has led to a crisis in the newsroom where journalists are laid off and those remaining cover ever-larger beats. At the same time, the 24 hour news cycle has forced them to produce news stories more often and with less time for their own investigation. Can traditional media last? And if not, what does that mean for social media's reliance on that media?

Even if traditional media continue to exist, albeit in some new form, will the news product look and sound substantially different than today? What

---

3. For a discussion of this phenomenon, see Pippa Norris and Ronald Inglehart, *Cultural Backlash: Trump, Brexit, and Authoritarian Populism*, New York: Cambridge University Press, 2019.

kind of news will be considered reliable when social media are the primary sources? Will social media play a larger role in the shaping of traditional media's agenda? If so, with what consequence to the quality of information traditional news conveys to its readers, listeners, and viewers?

It is time to return to a question we raised at the beginning of this book. Are democratic institutions in danger when social media rhetoric tends toward extremism or populism? Are antidemocratic, authoritarian leaders advantaged in a social media-influenced electoral system? Is democracy in danger?

The obvious answer is that not one of these democratic regimes examined in this book has collapsed into a dictatorship since the rise of social media. Nor is there a danger that any will in the near term. One could even say that social media's electoral role has invigorated democratic politics. The active involvement of so many people in so many systems described in this book suggests that democracy may be healthier because of the presence of social media.

Yet there are worrying trends. The history of populism suggests the potential of the substitution of a democratic system with a dictatorial regime. A classic example is Venezuela's decline under Hugo Chavez.[4] Populist messages flourish on social media. If populists who disparage democracy are able to use social media forums to undermine the very processes by which they took power, then social media have contributed to the demise of democracy. Democracy is a fragile system that carries within it the seeds of its own destruction. Populism and social media, over the long run, may be a lethal combination.

The other worrying trend is political extremism. Certainly, extremist groups—from both the left and the right—have existed for generations. But social media forums help these groups to form and communicate in ways that were not available before. Traditional media forums typically were dominated by establishment elites. Social media, however, are bottom-up platforms that enable extremist group organization and message dissemination. Additionally, the very nature of social media promotes shrillness rather than deliberation. Twitter limits the number of characters, which favors brevity. Brevity, in turn, promotes hyperbolic statements rather than thoughtfulness. Instagram and Pinterest are more visual forms that disadvantage words themselves. Even Facebook posts that lack any real limit are bound by space in the sense that most of a message over a paragraph or two is hidden from

---

4. See Kirk Hawkins, *Venezuela's Chavismo and Populism in Comparative Perspective*, New York: Cambridge University Press, 2014.

view. And a quick scroll through a Facebook feed does not encourage stopping to read lengthy posts.

Democracy may not be in immediate danger. However, time will tell whether that assessment will hold true. Raising the question, however, is a prudent exercise while social media forums are still in their infancy.

With this book, we have intended not only to present a comparative approach to the question of the electoral influence of social media but also to stimulate others to explore the electoral implications of social media in political systems across the globe. As we have listed here, there are yet many questions about social media effects that we have not answered. We invite others to continue to examine how and why social media are impacting the way we elect our leaders and representatives as well as what effect that impact may have on democracy itself.

Contributors

Rebecca Auger is a PhD student at Boston University's Division of Emerging Media Studies from Fort Wayne, Indiana. She is interested in the influence of organizational structures on collective action and collaboration in digital communities.

Sara Bentivegna is Professor of Political Communication at University of Rome—Sapienza. Her main research interests lay in the field of political communication, with specific focus on digital politics. She has published many articles in national and international journals such as *European Journal of Communication, Journalism, Journalism studies,* and *Contemporary Italian Politics.*

Francisco Brandáo is a visiting scholar at the Political Science Department at the University of Brasília (UnB) and a data scientist at the Chamber of Deputies of Brazil. His research interests are Political Communication, Comparative Politics, and Elections.He received his PhD in Political Science at the University of California, Santa Barbara (UCSB).

Brian Budd is a PhD candidate in the Department of Political Science at the University of Guelph. His research explores the contemporary and historical role of right-wing populism in Canadian politics with a focus on leadership, ideology, and discourse. His published work on populism can be found in the *Journal of Canadian Studies, Politics and Governance* and the edited collection, *Populism and World Politics: Exploring Inter- and Transnational Dimensions* (Palgrave Macmillan).

Richard Davis is a Professor Emeritus of political science at Brigham Young University. He is the author of several books and articles on the mass media

316   Contributors

and American politics. He is co-chair of the Civic Engagement Section and a former chair of the Political Communication section of the American Political Science Association.

Diretnan Dikwal-Bot is currently a research fellow in creativity and childhood development in the Directorate of Social Impact and Engagement at De Montfort University. Her research interests and expertise focus broadly on the analysis of media use, social inequality, and cultural change.

Heather Evans is the John Morton Beaty Professor of Political Science at the University of Virginia—College of Wise. She is the author of *Competitive Elections and Democracy in America: The Good, the Bad, and The Ugly* (2014) and is currently writing a book on the role of Twitter in U.S. congressional campaigns.

Larissa Doroshenko (PhD, University of Wisconsin-Madison) is a Postdoctoral Associate in the Communication Studies Department at Northeastern University. Her research interests are centered on the effects of new media on political campaigning, with a particular focus on "the dark side" of the internet: populism, nationalism, and disinformation campaigns.

Jason Gainous is Associate Dean of Duke Kunshan University in China. He is also the Co-Editor in Chief of the *Journal of Information Technology & Politics*. He has coauthored two books (*Tweeting to Power* and *Rebooting American Politics*) and has published many articles and chapters centered on digital communication.

Daniel Kriess is the Edgar Thomas Cato Distinguished Professor at the Hussman School of Journalism and Media and a principal researcher at the Center for Information, Technology, and Public Life at the University of North Carolina. He is Associate Editor of *Political Communication*.

Michael Keren, a political scientist, is a Professor Emeritus at the University of Calgary presently teaching at the Western Galilee Academic College in Israel. He is the author of many books including: *Ben-Gurion and the Intellectuals: Power, Knowledge and Charisma; Professionals against Populism: The Peres Government and Democracy; Blogosphere: The New Political Arena*; and others.

Rita Marchetti is Assistant Professor of Sociology of Digital Media at the Department of Political Science of the University of Perugia. Her main research interests are digital media, political communication, digital religion, and corruption.

Kaitlynn Mendes is Associate Professor of Sociology at the University of Western Ontario. She has written widely around representations of feminism in the media, and feminists' use of social media to challenge rape culture. She has written over fifty publications including *Digital Feminist Activism: Girls and Women Fight Back Against Rape Culture* (2019).

Shannon McGregor is an Assistant Professor at the Hussman School of Journalism and Media and a senior researcher at the Center for Information, Technology, and Public Life at the University of North Carolina. Her work has been published in the *Journal of Communication, Political Communication, New Media & Society*, and *Information, Communication & Society*.

Martin Ndlela is Professor of communication at Inland Norway University of Applied Sciences, and research associate at the Department of Strategic Communication, University of Johannesburg in South Africa. He is also the managing editor of the *Journal of African Media Studies*. He is co-editor of *Social Media and Elections in Africa*, Volume 1 & 2 (Palgrave Macmillan 2020).

Uta Russmann is a Professor at the Media and Communication in the Department of Media, Society, and Communication at the University of Innsbruck, Austria. Her research interests include digital communication, (visual) social media, public relations, strategic communication, political communication, and media and elections.

Rosalynd Southern is a Lecturer in Political Communication at the University of Liverpool, UK. She has conducted studies of online campaigning at the last four UK general elections as well as the Brexit referendum campaign. She has also published on alternative online political communication and gendered incivility online in journals including *Social Science Computer Review*, the *Journal of Information Technology and Politics*, and *Electoral Studies*.

Tamara A. Small is a Professor in the Department of Political Science at the University of Guelph. She is a leading expert on the use of digital technologies by Canadian political elites. In addition to conducting research on digital campaigning in the last seven federal elections, she has published work on political memes and on the regulatory framework for digital technologies in elections in Canada. She is the co-editor of *Digital Politics in Canada: Promises and Realities* (UTP).

Anna Stanziano is a Postdoctoral Researcher at the Department of Political Science of the University of Perugia. Her research interests are political communication, journalistic coverage of corruption, the perception of corruption, and the relationship between media and religion.

David Taras holds the Ralph Klein Chair in Media Studies at Mount Royal University in Calgary, Canada. He is the author most recently of *The End of the CBC?* with Christopher Waddell and *Digital Mosaic; Politics, Media and Identity in Canada*. He and Richard Davis co-edited *Power Shift?: Political Leadership and Social Media*.

Kevin Wagner is an attorney and Professor of Political Science at Florida Atlantic University. He has published research on the effects of technology on politics with studies ranging from American elections to the Arab Spring to East Asia. His work has been published in leading journals including *Political Behavior, Journal of Information, Technology and Politics*, and *The Journal of Legislative Studies* and co-authored, with Jason Gainous, *Tweeting to Power: The Social Media Revolution in American Politics*, was published by Oxford University Press.

Christopher Waddell is a Professor Emeritus and former director of the School of Journalism and Communication at Carleton University in Ottawa. He was parliamentary bureau chief in Ottawa and executive producer of news specials for the network for the CBC and a business reporter, Ottawa bureau chief, associate editor, and national editor of the *Globe and Mail*. With David Taras, he is author of *The End of the CBC?* published in 2020.

Chris Wells is an Associate Professor in the Division of Emerging Media Studies and the Department of Journalism at Boston University, and a founding member of BU's Faculty for Computing & Data Sciences. His current research explores how journalistic media, partisan media and social media intersect to shape the public discussion of political issues.

Blake Wertz is a doctoral candidate in the Division of Emerging Media Studies at Boston University whose research focuses on the intersection of media psychology and political communication in the study of political talk online.

Li Zhang is a doctoral student in the Division of Emerging Media Studies, Boston University. His research interests include political communication, media psychology, and computational methods.

Index

advertising, 27, 29, 37, 53, 89–90, 186, 212–13, 279
algorithims, 27
anger, 2
authenticity, 37–38, 183, 252, 265, 272; effectiveness of, 33–34, 280

bias: effects on elections, 36, 37–38; online, 47, 60; in traditional media, 181. *See also* racism; sexism; xenophobia

campaign phases, 207–8, 245
campaign slogans, 205, 210–11, 225, 231–32, 237–38
candidate biography, 31, 34; effects on appeals, 27, 33
coalition governments, 2
communication, 8, 267, 279, 284; between candidates and voters, 19, 247; from candidates to voters, 36, 52, 128, 130, 244, 259–60. *See also* digital sphere: as political communication
Communications Decency Act, 47
consistency, 34
constituency organizing, 29–31
corruption, 16–17, 74, 135–36, 153–54, 171, 183–85, 227, 249
credibility of traditional media, 20, 54–55, 70, 106–7, 313

debates, 2, 7, 114–15, 193, 195
democracy: development of, 181, 184; future of, 11, 16, 176, 314
devolution of government, 247
Digital Democracy Project, 106–10, 112–13
digital media. *See* social media
digital sphere: as information source, 44, 45, 55–56; as political communication: 44–45, 60–61, 128
diversity, 143; of political experiences, 12
dynamic equilibrium, 4

economic determinism, 3
election campaign strategies, 1–2, 5, 15, 18
election systems between countries, 2–3, 11–12, 14–15, 18
elections as defining events, 3–4, 124
election wars, 1, 124–25
email, 15, 144, 146–47, 150–52, 156–57
ethnicity, 246, 259

Facebook, 16, 18, 48, 183, 190, 191–94, 233–34, 238, 252–56, 265; audiences on, 268
fake news, 48, 116, 164
feminism, 13–14, 60–62, 68–69, 76–77, 83, 95, 309; as identity, 62–63, 67; in male leaders, 64–69, 71–72, 75; scrutiny because of, 73–75, 77

322 Index

field programs, 30
financial constraints: on campaigns, 104, 186; on traditional media, 122
foreign affairs, 108
fundamentals, 3–4

gender differences, 84, 86–88, 90–91, 93–95, 98, 309
gender equality. *See* feminism

hate speech, 169, 170, 259
horse race frameworks, 6, 296–97, 299–300, 302

identities: ownership of, 23–24, 26, 35, 38; performative, 12, 26, 28, 33, 36–37; social construction of, 25, 32–35
identity appeals, 26–27, 32, 36–37
identity construction, 63, 72, 284, 288; through social media, 61, 64–67, 72, 76, 182; through traditional media, 61, 69–72, 76
identity politics, 5, 19, 61, 77, 308, 312
identity representation, 34–35
identity trespassing, 28
ideology, 145, 148
incitement, 166–67, 170–75
influencers, 18, 257–59, 260
interaction between news media and politicians, 134–36
interests of voters: and interests of media, 104, 107–11, 113, 166–18; influence on campaigns, 132
Internet: limitations of, 149
issue ownership, 23, 26, 76, 126, 135–36, 139, 301–2

Joint List, 166, 168, 171–73
journalists: and campaigns, 6–7

liabilities of online publishers, 46–47

mainstream press. *See* traditional media
media: as a battleground, 5, 47, 89; political actors' control of, 55–56, 128, 131, 135, 271, 303–4

memes: impact on elections, 209–10, 212, 214–16, 308; as used by politicians, 203–5, 206, 209–11, 213–15; as used by voters, 205–6, 208
messaging, 6, 8, 264–65
mobilization, 223, 226–27, 230, 232–33, 236, 276, 311
moderation of online content, 47–49, 276
multiculturalism, 143

negativity, 153, 180, 190, 254–55, 258, 286; causes of, 117; effects of, 8, 15, 195; prevalence of, 6, 73, 117, 212, 280

online campaign effectiveness, 12, 17–18
online reaction, 201–2, 208–12, 214, 222, 254
opinion articles, 120
outreach strategies, 29–30, 32

partisanship, 154, 180, 182, 195; effects on voters, 36
passivity, 9
People's Party of Canada, 143–44, 148–50, 152, 157–59
permanent campaign, 3, 9
personalization, 99–100, 180, 183, 193, 224, 229, 231, 233, 264, 277, 280
pink wave, 85
polarization. *See* partisanship
political divisions, 13, 25; created by campaigns, 25, 35; within political parties, 24, 26
politicians as news sources, 55–56
populism, 17, 143–46, 148, 150–51, 153–56, 173–74, 179, 183, 192, 221, 224–25; communication strategies, 221–22, 224–27, 230, 231–34, 236, 238, 241–43, 307; and social media, 144–46, 159, 182, 237, 310
predictions of election outcomes, 3–4
press crisis, 6
privacy, 9
prototypicality, 26, 36
public agenda, 137–39

public commentary, 200
public engagement, 222–24, 238, 287, 303, 311

racial identities, 25, 37
racism, 156, 174–76
radio, 248–50
religion, 31

scrutiny of candidates, 103, 111. *See also* feminism: scrutiny because of
sexism, 83, 86–87
shared agendas among news media, 132–35, 137
social media: accountability on, 69, 78, 180; audiences of, 9, 27, 181, 257, 266, 271, 281; causing change, 164, 207, 216–17, 244–45, 250, 277; and communication, 245, 269, 272, 274, 287; in construction of identity, 37, 49; credibility of, 14; discourses, 75, 175, 309; effectiveness of, 15–17, 49–50, 138, 168, 222, 227; effects of, 8–10, 14–17, 45, 139, 165, 175, 307–8; effects on democracy, 20, 47, 176, 261, 313; as a form of persuasion, 5, 7, 12; as an inciting force, 173–74, 203; interactivity of, 45–46, 223–24, 230, 275–78, 280; managers, 251–57, 264, 273–75,

310; social construction of, 24–25; as a source of information, 126–27, 201; strategies, 252–61, 263–66, 268, 271–76, 279–81; and traditional media, 13–14, 16, 18–20, 50–54, 127, 207, 280, 286, 311–12
strategic political communication, 265–66, 284–85
symbiosis between candidate and media, 53, 54, 259, 311
symbolic inclusiveness, 1, 223, 229, 231, 233

technological openness, 223
traditional media, 129, 201–2, 248, 249, 260; credibility of, 20, 54–55, 121; current issues with, 118–22, 195, 260
Twitter, 44, 63, 70, 87–90, 99–100, 256, 271; audiences on, 9, 14, 18, 268; use by candidates, 14, 50, 52–54, 289, 291–97, 302; use by voters, 298, 301

U.S. primary elections, 28–29

women's issues, 83, 86–91, 93–97, 309

xenophobia, 74, 154–55, 158

YouTube, 9